KU-661-348

ONE DAY AT A TIME

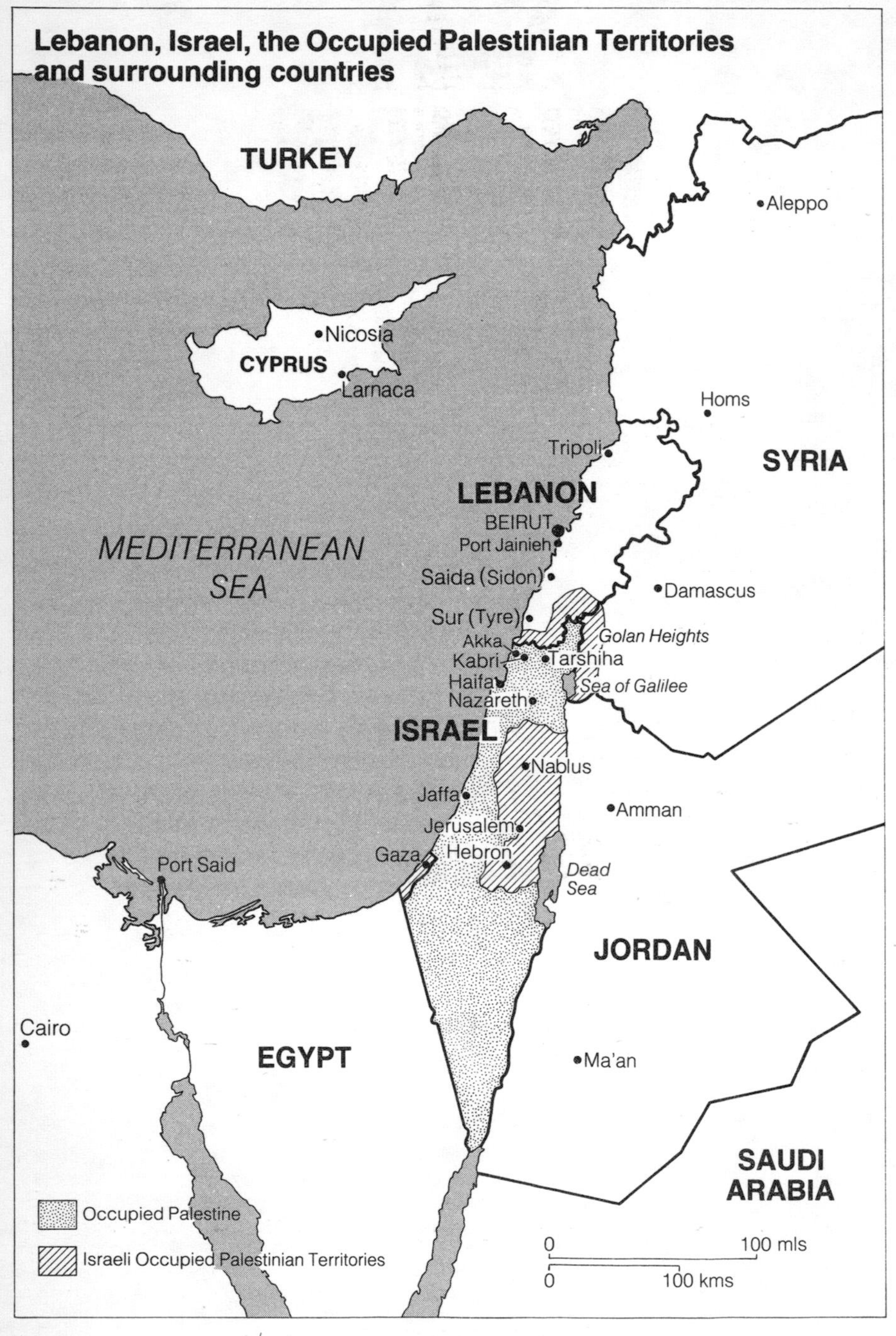
Lebanon, Israel, the Occupied Palestinian Territories and surrounding countries
TURKEY
Aleppo
Nicosia
CYPRUS
Larnaca
Homs
Tripoli
SYRIA
LEBANON
BEIRUT
Port Jainieh
MEDITERRANEAN SEA
Saida (Sidon)
Damascus
Sur (Tyre)
Akka
Golan Heights
Kabri
Tarshiha
Haifa
Sea of Galilee
Nazareth
ISRAEL
Nablus
Jaffa
Amman
Jerusalem
Gaza
Hebron
Port Said
Dead Sea
JORDAN
Cairo
EGYPT
Ma'an
SAUDI ARABIA
Occupied Palestine
Israeli Occupied Palestinian Territories
0
100 mls
0
100 kms

SUZY WIGHTON

ONE DAY AT A TIME

Diaries from a Palestinian Camp

HUTCHINSON
LONDON SYDNEY AUCKLAND JOHANNESBURG

This edition first published in 1990 by
Hutchinson

Century Hutchinson Ltd,
20 Vauxhall Bridge Road, London SW1V 2SA

Century Hutchinson Australia
20 Alfred Street, Milsons Point, Sydney, NSW 2061, Australia

Century Hutchinson New Zealand Limited
PO Box 40–086, Glenfield, Auckland 10, New Zealand

Century Hutchinson South Africa (Pty) Ltd,
PO Box 337, Bergvlei, 2012 South Africa

British Library Cataloguing in Publication Data
Wighton, Suzy
One day at a time: diaries from a Palestinian camp.
1. Lebanon. Beirut. Palestinian Arab refugees. Social conditions, history – Biographies
I. Title
305.8′9275694′05692
ISBN 0–09–174085–1

Set in Baskerville by Speedset Ltd, Ellesmere Port
Printed and bound in Great Britain by
Mackays of Chatham

Contents

Illustration Acknowledgements

The publishers would like to thank the following for their kind permission to reproduce the photographs that appear in this book:

© Frank Spooner Pictures; © Neveu, Gamma; © Eli Reed, Magnum; © Haidak, Gamma; © Roger Mookarzel, Sygma; © Tom Stoddart; © Assem Cheaib, Gamma; © Aziz Taher, Gamma; © M. Attar, Sygma; © R. Haidar, Gamma; © Mehdi Abdo, Gamma; © MAP; © Karim Daher, Gamma; © Ali Mohammed, Associated Press; © Press Association.

Whilst every attempt has been made to trace copyright, this has not been possible in some cases. The publishers would like to apologise in advance for any inconvenience this might cause.

All line drawings in the text are by the author, taken from her original diaries and notebooks.

Acknowledgements

There are too many people whose help and support over the years has sustained me to name everyone individually, but I would particularly like to thank Dr Fathi Arafat, President of the Palestine Red Crescent Society and Hadla Ayoubi, Director of Public Relations, for employing me in the first place; Karma Nabulsi, of the Palestine Liberation Organization; all cadres of the PRCS within and without the Lebanon and all Palestinians within and without Palestine.

Grateful thanks too to Ahmad Aishe, Dr Swee Chai Ang, Dolly Fong, Dr Kirin Gasgesh, Dr Chris Giannou, Tha'ir Mortessen and Looi Pok.

At Century Hutchinson, I would like to thank Kate Mosse for her advice and good humour, as well as the staff whose enthusiasm and energy made this book a possibility. A particular round of applause for the typists – Alison Deery, Jan McCaskill, Lynne Smith and Susan Rae – who slogged on the original typescript, deciphering my appalling handwriting which had been made worse by conditions of siege.

Finally, my love and gratitude to my family and friends, who uncompromisingly have put up with several years of worry and uncertainty.

Suzy Wighton
October 1989

In the geological cliffs of Western Asia vultures thank the sky for the abundance of their food: more dead Arabs than stones on this desert.

Etal Adnan

Author's Foreword

One Day at a Time is based on the diaries that I kept whilst living and working in the besieged Palestinian camp of Bourj al-Brajneh from 1986 to 1988.

While researching the Palestinians after returning from a visit to the Occupied Palestinian Territories in 1985, I had found that there was little literature available on the subject. It appeared as if the Palestinians were being submerged, only to reappear for a moment when a catalyst – usually an event of extreme violence – thrust them back into the limelight. The media archives are filled with the records of the Palestinians' national tragedy, but there is little that shows the reality of their daily existence in exile or under occupation.

It was with this in mind, when I went to work in the Sami al Khatib clinic, inside Bourj al-Brajneh in the southern suburbs of West Beirut, that the diary was started. It was an attempt to record the day-to-day life in the camp, using as often as possible (when my Arabic was up to it) the words of my friends and acquaintances. As soon as the existence of the diaries became known in the camp, it turned into a journal of our collective experience. People began to come to the clinic to tell me to write down this or that event as it happened, with admonitions to make sure that the world outside heard about the life of Palestinians in Beirut and the Lebanon.

In effect, the diary began to act as our witness – to be read, perhaps, in the event of our deaths. The paper it was written on was brought to the clinic after appeals that I was running out of materials on which to write. I used old clinic registers, school books, mathematical jotters, an odd assortment of salvaged papers. Piece by piece it was smuggled out of the camp, past the watchful eyes of the assorted hostile military, by a very brave friend, to whom I am forever indebted as she had already risked her life to bring us food, letters, films, batteries, candles and everything else our besiegers considered forbidden.

I was finally reunited with the first section covering the 6-month war on our evacuation from the camp in April 1987, still in its green bag. The word 'relief' cannot adequately describe how it felt to hold safely in my hands my attempt to document that period – the films, cassettes and diary. We had all made it out safely.

This book is a distillation of those diaries, divided into three parts. Little alteration has been made to the original transcription save for the purposes of clarification and editing out of over-detailed medical and political jargon. It has been considerably cut (almost by half) to relieve the reader of the 'bomb-happy' repetitions that inevitably crept in. Finally, for reasons of personal safety for those concerned and still living in both the Lebanon and the Occupied Palestinian Territories of the West Bank and Gaza, the period from 1987 to 1988 has been omitted.

My spoken Arabic is of the street variety, my written Arabic is worse; so in our transliterations we have tried to use the accurate spelling from the Arabic where it is phonetically possible. Apologies for any inconsistencies that are bound to have slipped in. For ease of reference, names appear in the index – for the most part – under Christian names, to avoid the confusions of Arab family names. The names and context of certain incidents have had to be left undefined for fear they might endanger those still in the area. I hope that this necessary precaution will not make the book too difficult to follow.

Introduction

In September 1986 I arrived in the Palestinian camp of Bourj al-Brajneh, which by this time had already been under partial siege and attack for sixteen months. What has become known as the 'War of the Camps' started in the previous May 1985 with an attack of one month's duration on the Beirut camps (the 1-month war). This, in turn, led to the complete destruction of Sabra camp and with it the Gaza Hospital situated at its edge. Patients and staff were taken from the hospital by the Amal militiamen prior to the looting and subsequent destruction of the hospital, and were tortured and killed.

During this war the populations of Shatila and Bourj al-Brajneh camps suffered heavily. Those surviving the destruction of Sabra camp became displaced, as had many Palestinians living within Beirut. A decision was taken by the Palestine Red Crescent Society (PRCS) to construct field hospitals within the Bourj and Shatila camps that were still partially besieged, and it was to assist with this that Medical Aid for Palestinians (MAP) recruited volunteers to work with the PRCS, sending the first team under Dr Swee Chai Ang in August 1985.

The populations of the camp, already depleted as a result of the Israeli invasion of the Lebanon in 1982 and the subsequent siege of Beirut, were to fluctuate further. People had to try to gauge whether it was safer to live amongst other Palestinians within one of the besieged camps, or to risk persecution from the Amal militiamen controlling large areas of West Beirut by remaining more anonymous outside.

By the time I arrived, the third camp war (known as the 45-day war) had just ended and the population of Bourj al-Brajneh was approximated at 16,000 people, mainly families. By the 6-month war (Part Two of the book) the population had fallen to around 8,500 people as many had fled. Shatila camp, as was to become usual, had borne the brunt of the fighting and was estimated as having 4,000 people inside. This shows the marked difference from the days before the Israeli invasion, when Bourj was estimated at 40,000 inhabitants and Shatila at 15,000.

Housing inside the camps had been considerably damaged by the constant bombardments with heavy artillery (120mm mortars, Grad rockets, heavy calibre automatic weapon fire and dynamite). Around the camp there was now a wasteland or, in time of fighting, a no-man's land, where houses at the camps' peripheries had been blown up by Amal militiamen in the 1-month war in May 1985. In this way Bourj and Shatila were effectively ghetto-ized and most of their entrances were sealed off, leaving only a few passages controlled by Amal militiamen and the Syrian Forces as access into and out of the camps.

Vehicular traffic was prohibited after the 6-month war and everything that entered Bourj had to be brought in on foot. The camp was littered with rubble, the overground sewage and water systems were damaged and the majority of houses had been hit by shells and repaired at least on one occasion. The children's schooling was disrupted as their junior schools (run by the United Nations agency UNRWA) and senior schools were located outside the camp in Beirut's southern suburbs, in territory controlled by the Amal militia.

Medical care was also disrupted as the PRCS, previously functioning with twenty-six medical facilities offering complete health care free of charge to all – Palestinian, Lebanese and other refugees – was now reduced within Beirut to three field hospitals, a couple of clinics and Akka Hospital (now PRCS headquarters), itself only partially functioning as it was located within Amal-held areas. Access to medical facilities was further restricted due to lack of security. Therefore, freedom of movement for Palestinians – particularly males – who were automatically suspected by the militia of being fighters, was also curtailed.

After the deaths of several patients, dragged from their hospital beds outside the camps in Beirut, and the attacking of the wounded who were being evacuated from Bourj and Shatila by the Red Cross, it became all the more urgent to create independent and secure medical facilities within the camps themselves.

In Bourj the PRCS converted the Haifa Rehabilitation Centre into a tertiary care field hospital. It was located at the top of the camp, a two-storey building with an underground shelter and, above that, an operating theatre, X-ray, pharmacy and laboratory. The staff were experienced Palestinian and Lebanese PRCS cadres, many of whom had practised throughout the Israeli invasion, and had survived both that and the sacking of Gaza Hospital. Shatila took the decision to build the field hospital in the centre of the camp, protected from view by a maze of alleyways. Construction began in just one house with a basement operating theatre, but it eventually comprised four houses set around each other and protected by tyred roofing. Again it was staffed by experienced and committed PRCS staff, many of whose families, as at Bourj, lived in the camp. The facilities in Shatila offered the same standards of tertiary care as Bourj al-Brajneh but on a reduced scale. They were run by the Greek-Canadian surgeon Chris Giannou.

The Director of Haifa hospital in Bourj was Dr Rede, who was born and raised in the camp. The planned rotation of staff around the main hospitals was to become increasingly difficult as the sieges of the camps progressed, and increasingly hazardous as Palestinians, who were seen to be contributing to the welfare of the camp populations, immediately became a target for the militia.

By the time the 6-month war commenced the staffing level at Haifa Hospital consisted of seven doctors, six of whom had surgical experience.

Under the direction of Salim, the head nurse, there was a nursing staff of 45, including highly skilled theatre and intensive care registered nurses, practical nurses, nurse-students and volunteers from within the camp.

The foreigners at the time working in Bourj al-Brajneh consisted of Ben Alofs, a Dutch nurse with over ten years experience working with PRCS in Lebanon; Dr Pauline Cutting, an English surgeon who had been working for MAP since November 1985 and had worked throughout the 45-day war; Hannes Fuchslechner, an Austrian physiotherapist; Doctors Dirk Van Duppen and Lieve Sutjens, Belgian physicians who had spent a number of years living and working inside the camp, including the period of the 45-day war; and myself, ostensibly taking over the management of Dirk and Lieve's recently-started primary health care (PHC) programme.

The period spanned by *One Day at a Time* consists of my arrival in Beirut, the 6-month war from October 1986 to April 1987, and then moves, in a sense, to the finale of the three years of continuous attacks and sieges on the Palestinians in Lebanon, the fall of the Beirut camps from the autonomous framework of the Palestine Liberation Organization (PLO) to the pro-Syrian forces. The section of the diary from my return to Beirut in July 1987 until the summer of 1988 is missing. For reasons of security, it was scant, and much of it still cannot be printed.

However, the siege of the camp continued with an intensity which, for many, was often close to unbearable. Even for myself – who had only briefly experienced a semblance of strained normality in the six weeks prior to the 6-month war – the difference in our way of life was very marked. The majority of the men between the ages of 14 and 55 were unable to leave the camp unless they pledged political allegiance to the pro-Syrian Palestinian movements. This also applied to politically active women, and for many perpetuated what had already been an incarceration of two years for a further year. We would idle time away dreaming of freedom of movement, walking to the camp boundaries to look at the sea, watching those sympathetic to Syria's political aspirations passing to and fro with ease, whilst many waited on their mothers, wives and sisters to bring to them the reality of life in the world that continued outside the one-kilometre by half-kilometre boundaries of the camp. For those who desired this dubious proffered freedom there was a price – often consisting of denunciation and passing on information – which was rarely accepted. Some short respite could be gained by the intercession of pro-Syrian political leaders on behalf of those suspected of political activity.

In this period the siege on Shatila intensified too, with regular attacks on the camp and its captive male population. Shooting into the camp by *q'arnass* (snipers) became, as with Bourj, such a regular occurrence that the time of day could be judged by the sound of gunfire associated with it. Likewise the personality of the *q'arnass* could be judged by the way he chose his potential victims. Often Shatila would be 'closed' for days on end, while the besieging forces would mortar and shell the camp with tanks, rockets and grenades. The injured could never be evacuated with safety. All were treated inside the camp.

Shatila became a ghostly place, haunted by tired men. The women and children would enter from 8 am if the road was 'open', bringing fresh food, clothes and other items requested by the menfolk trapped inside. Then, for reasons of concern over the camp's future, they would leave again before 4 pm, the last 'safe' hour before the road would again be closed and the sniping into the camp recommence.

Life inside Shatila continued like this, without electricity, throughout the winter and the rains of 1987 into 1988. The simple term 'misery' is insufficient to describe the privations of living there during that period. Intimidation of the population was the order of the day.

In September that year Mustafa al Khatib and many others were captured by the Syrians whilst escaping the claustrophobia of the camp. He had travelled into Beirut to visit his two little daughters, and was taken by Syrian Intelligence in the early hours of the morning as he slept. Like many others, he has since been languishing in the jails of Damascus which the Syrians reserve exclusively for their Palestinian prisoners. Hissam, Rifat, Haj, Abu Sacker and Mahmud managed to escape to Denmark and have settled there as political refugees. For Hissam things went terribly awry at one point, since he was stopped as his aircraft landed by the airport police, in breech of international regulations governing those seeking political asylum. He spent a harrowing ten days as a 'ping-pong refugee' being held in captivity at various airports, escorted by police on to planes from country to country, and almost being sent back to Beirut from Cyprus where he had ended up via Copenhagen and Vienna.

In December 1988 Maryam was shot dead in front of her house as she stepped outside to fetch water. She collapsed into her sister Samira's arms, sniped by an M-16 bullet through her neck arteries.

This was the life that we describe as: 'Every day the war will end, tomorrow the road will open and the siege will end.'

Who's Who in the Lebanon, 1986 to 1988

A guide to the major political groups, organizations, places and people mentioned in the text.

ABU AMMAR: *nom de guerre* of Yasser Arafat.

ABU FAHDI: leader of Abu Musa dissident forces in Beirut.

ABU IYAD: Second-in-command to Yasser Arafat after Abu Jihad's death in 1988.

ABU JIHAD: Arafat's most senior military commander, until his assassination in Tunis, April 1988, by commando forces assumed to be Israeli.

ABU MUSA: leader of dissident Palestinian group, opposed to Yasser Arafat. Syrian-backed. Also known as the Munshaqine (the Mutineers).

ABU NIDAL: leader of Fatah Revolutionary Council (*see below*).

ABU RIYAD: leader of Fatah military wing inside Bourj al-Brajneh, also known as Sultan.

AIN AL-HELWEH: largest Palestinian camp now remaining in the Lebanon, with a 1989 population of 120,000. On the outskirts of Saida. Frequently attacked by Israeli military.

AMAL: means 'hope'. Shia Muslim militia set up in 1974 by Imam Musa Sadr, an Iranian and friend of Ayatollah Khomeini. Sadr disappeared mysteriously in Libya in 1978. Amal now led by Nabih Berri, currently Lebanese Minister of Justice. Its interest is to promote and protect the Shi'i people in south Lebanon and the Bekaa Valley, who were traditionally the poorest and most oppressed section of Lebanese society. Trained from 1975 by the Palestinians. One of the major West Beirut militias, strong in the southern suburbs; also powerful in southern Lebanon and parts of the Bekaa Valley. Syria's closest ally in the Lebanon, and known to have dealings with the Israelis and their allies in the Lebanon.

AMERICAN UNIVERSITY HOSPITAL (AUH): located in the fashionable West Beirut district of Hamra. Large private hospital with modern facilities and associated with the American University of Beirut (AUB) medical faculty.

YASSER ARAFAT: Chairman of the Palestinian Liberation Organization (PLO). Also known as Abu Ammar (*see also* FATAH, PLO).

HAFEZ AL ASSAD: President of Syria since 1962.

BAR ELIAS: Palestinian camp in the Bekaa Valley, close to the border with Syria/Lebanon.

BARBIR: area of the Gold Market in West Beirut, with the 'Museum' crossing of the Green Line into East Beirut nearby. Also the site of a large junction and flyover with stalls and clothes markets. One of the 'service' taxis' stopping points.

BAYSUR: village east of Saida, taken by the Palestinian forces in an effort to relieve the sieges of the Palestinian camps (*see also* MAGDOUSHE and MAIDOON).

BEDAWI: Palestinian camp at Tripoli, close to Nahr al-Bared camp.

NABIH BERRI: leader of Amal (*see also* AMAL).

BOURJ AL-BRAJNEH: 'stronghold of Brajneh'. Area of the southern suburbs in West Beirut also known as Bourj al-Brajneh. Close to the camp.

BOURJ AL-SHEMALI: small Palestinian camp, near Sur.

DAUD DAUD: was leader of Amal in south Lebanon until his assassination late in 1987.

DEMOCRATIC FRONT FOR THE LIBERATION OF PALESTINE (DFLP): led by Naif Hawatmeh. Soviet-sponsored and with a similar recent history to the PFLP. Known in the camps as Democratia.

DRUZE: part of the Progressive Socialist Party (*see below*).

FATAH REVOLUTIONARY COUNCIL (ABU AMMAR): largest armed faction within the PLO, led by Yasser Arafat. Includes political and military wings. Known within the camps as Fatah.

FATAH REVOLUTIONARY COUNCIL (ABU NIDAL): dissident group outside the PLO, led by Abu Nidal. Known within the camps as the Revolutionary Council.

FATAH UPRISING: led by Syrian-sponsored dissident Abu Musa. Known as Fatah Intifada (Fatah Uprising) or the Munshaqine (the Mutineers). Formed part of the Salvation Front, known as Incas.

FRONT STREET: Gamal Abdul Nasser Street, running along the bottom of Bourj al-Brajneh camp to Haret Hreik. Known as the 'front street', and thus the demarcation line in the siege and wars of the camps with Amal Militia (Shi'i), the 6th Brigade of Lebanese Army and latterly the Syrian forces.

AMIN GEMAYEL: seventh President of independent Lebanon since 1982; a Maronite Christian. Acceded to the presidency after the assassination of his brother Bashir, rumoured to have been carried out by the Israelis who were dissatisfied with his proposed rule of Lebanon. Used as a pretext for the massacre of Palestinians in Sabra and Shatila camps in 1982.

GHAZIYAH: village east of Saida (*see* BAYSUR).

GREEN LINE: the 'Green Line of Peace' dividing Christian East Beirut from Muslim West.

HAMRA: the still fashionable district of West Beirut, containing department stores, banks, offices, hotels and smart residential apartments. One of the 'service' taxi's stopping points.

HARET HREIK: area of the southern suburbs, close to Bourj al-Brajneh camp.

HIZB'ULLAH: known as the 'Party of God' from the Koran – 'Lo, the party of God, they are victorious'. A Shi'ite fundamentalist Muslim militia, directed, armed and paid for by Iran, and originally intended as the vehicle for the expansion of the Iranian Revolution into the Lebanon. First emerged as a significant force in the Lebanon during the 1982 Israeli invasion. Numbers increased by disaffected Shi'ites from Amal. Powerful in southern suburbs, south Lebanon and parts of the Bekaa Valley. Believed to include a number of sub-groups under a variety of *noms de guerre*. No publicly acknowledged head, but its spiritual leader is Sheikh Fadullah.

INCAS: pro-Syrian, anti-PLO groupings. Disbanded in 1987 (*see also* FATAH UPRISING).

ISRAELI DEFENCE FORCE (IDF): has regular troops along the occupied border with south Lebanon, and is ready to support the South Lebanon Army with armour, artillery and air strikes.

WALID JUMBLATT: leader of the Progressive Socialist Party *(see below)*.

KITAEB: the Arab term for the Christian Phalangist party, also known as the Fascists and the Right Wing, which has its strongest base among the Maronite community in East Beirut.

KOLA: Kola Bridge; another 'service' taxi stopping point, located around and under the bridge which is a motorway flyover. All 'service' taxis to the south of Lebanon leave from this point. Commonly known as Kola.

LEBANESE ARMY: official military of Lebanon, divided into bridges along religious lines and drawn from all the different sects; supposedly non-partisan, but increasingly pro-Christian in bias (*see also* SIXTH BRIGADE).

LEBANESE COMMUNIST PARTY: non-sectarian, led by George Hawi.

LEBANESE FORCES: the largest right-wing Christian militia, made up of the Christian brigades of the Lebanese Army after its division during the Lebanese Civil War. The major component is the militia of the Phalange Party (*see also* KITAEB).

MAGDOUSHE: village east of Saida (*see* BAYSUR).

MAIDOON: village east of Saida (*see* BAYSUR).

MAR ELIAS: mainly Christian camp in West Beirut.

MARONITES: one of the Lebanon's major sects (the other major Christian groups being the Orthodox and Catholic Greeks, and the Armenians); a dominant community in the Lebanon since independence in 1943, from whom the President of Lebanon is elected *(see also* KITAEB).

MEDICAL AID FOR PALESTINIANS (MAP): a British-based charity founded in 1984 by medical volunteers who had worked in the Lebanon, including Dr Swee Chai Ang, and by Palestinians in Britain. Non-sectarian, non-political, humanitarian. Sponsors health projects and volunteer medical staff for Palestinian refugee camps in the Lebanon and the Israeli-occupied territories.

MIEH MIEH: Palestinian camp on the outskirts of Saida, next to Ain al-Helweh camp.

MOSSAD: the Israeli Secret Services.

MSF: Médicins sans frontières (Belgium).

MUNSHAQINE: (*see* ABU MUSA).

MURABITOUN: Sunni (Orthodox) militia previously widespread, and now believed almost to have disappeared after the massacres in Tripoli of Murabitoun and their families in December 1986. Once part of the left-wing coalition of interests and groupings before the Israeli invasion, which was known as the Nationalist Movement.

NAHR AL-BARED: Palestinian camp at Tripoli, north Lebanon.

NASSERITES: mainly Sunni Muslims, following Mustafa Sa'ad after the assassination of his father Ma'aruf Sa'ad, and holding the area around Saida. Party arranged on the principles of Pan-Arab nationalism as supported by the late President of Egypt, Gamal Abdel Nasser.

NORWEGIAN AID COMMITTEE (NORWAC): a Norwegian organization sponsoring volunteer medical workers in the Lebanon and the Occupied Territories.

OUZAI: Shi'i area of the southern suburbs of Beirut, close to the airport.

PALESTINE LIBERATION ARMY (PLA): military arm of the PLO, founded in 1964.

PALESTINE LIBERATION ORGANIZATION (PLO): set up in 1964 at the instigation of an Arab Summit Conference in Cairo. Later split into a number of groups, including Yasser Arafat's Fatah. Yasser Arafat is Chairman of the PLO.

PALESTINE NATIONAL LIBERATION MOVEMENT: (*see* FATAH).

PALESTINE RED CRESCENT SOCIETY (PRCS): medical branch of the PLO, equivalent to the British Red Cross. Runs the Palestinian health service in the Lebanon as a national health service, with treatment and medicines available free of charge to anyone regardless of race, nationality or creed. Runs hospitals in Shatila and Bourj al-Brajneh camps in Beirut, and has hospitals and clinics in other parts of the Lebanon and around the world where Palestinians are scattered (eg Egypt, Yemen, Sudan).

PHALANGE PARTY: (*see* KITAEB, LEBANESE FORCES).

POPULAR COMMITTEE: set up to maintain law and order, as the internal government of the camps.

POPULAR FRONT FOR THE LIBERATION OF PALESTINE (PFLP): Marxist organization, headed by George Habash and devolving from the PLO. Part of the Salvation Front grouping until readmitted to the Palestinian National Council in Algiers in 1987.

POPULAR FRONT FOR THE LIBERATION OF PALESTINE-GENERAL COMMAND (PLFP-GC): splinter faction of the Popular Front led by Ahmad Jibril and based in Syria. Part of the Salvation Front. Anti-Arafat Palestinian group.

PRIMARY HEALTH CARE (PHC): the strategy adopted by the World Health Organization (WHO) in 1978 to achieve global health for all by the year 2000. A community health care programme, including mother and child health care, vaccinations, nutrition, hygiene, preventative medicine, environment.

PROGRESSIVE SOCIALIST PARTY (PSP): supposedly non-sectarian, broad-based socialist group, headed by Walid Jumblatt. Includes Druze. Based in Shouf mountains, but controls parts of West Beirut. Strong militia, supplied by Syria and others.

RAOUCHE: restaurant and swimming area in West Beirut.

RASHIDYEH: Palestinian camp in the south of Lebanon, close to Sur and the Israeli border and Occupied 'Security Zone' in the Lebanon.

SABRA: Palestinian camp, destroyed in the camps wars in 1985. Was next to Shatila.

SAIDA: Arabic name for the city of Sidon.

SHATILA: Palestinian camp on the outskirts of Beirut. Next to the Sports City Stadium and near the Kuwaiti Embassy roundabout. Has seen some of the worst fighting, and massacres in 1982.

SHI'ITE MUSLIMS: one of the two major Muslim communities in the Lebanon (*see* AMAL, HIZB'ULLAH).

SIXTH BRIGADE OF LEBANESE ARMY: drawn mainly from Shi'ite Muslims. Closely linked with Amal.

SOUTH LEBANON ARMY (SLA): a right-wing Christian militia which, with Israeli support, controls a sector of Lebanon's southern frontier.

Led by Antoine Lahad, with many forced conscripts from the occupied areas. Sometimes known as Lahad.

SUNNI MUSLIMS: one of the three major Muslim communities in Lebanon. Their militias include: Murabitoun in West Beirut; Taweed in north Lebanon; Nasserites in Saida.

SYRIAN ARMY: in the Bekaa Valley and north Lebanon. Also known as Syrian Armed Forces.

TAL AL-ZATAR: Palestinian camp once in East Beirut, destroyed after a seventeen-month siege and attacks from 1975 to 1976 by the combined forces of the Christian militias led by Bashir Gemayel and Elias Hobeika and the Syrian Armed Forces. The survivors from the capitulated camp were massacred on their march of safe conduct towards the lorries of the Red Cross waiting at the 'Green Line of Peace'.

TAMBOURITE: (*see* BAYSUR).

UNITED NATIONS CHILDREN'S EDUCATIONAL FUND (UNICEF): a UN agency that administers programmes to aid education, and maternal and child health in underdeveloped countries.

UNITED NATIONS INTERIM FORCE IN LEBANON (UNIFIL): a 6,000-man force set up by the UN Security Council to replace Israeli presence in south Lebanon after the Israeli invasion in March 1978. Now patrols the northern borders of the South Lebanon Army's border strip.

UNITED NATIONS RELIEF AND WORKS AGENCY FOR PALESTINE REFUGEES IN THE NEAR EAST (UNRWA): set up in 1949 by the UN as a temporary body to look after the needs of refugee Arab Palestinians who had fled Arab/Zionist fighting in Palestine after British withdrawal in 1948. UNRWA established Palestinian refugee camps in the Lebanon to offer short-term shelter, but many Palestinians stayed on, and their numbers were increased by the Israeli occupation of the rest of Palestine, the Gaza Strip and the West Bank in 1967.

VARDUN: an area of West Beirut, where the Soviet Embassy is located.

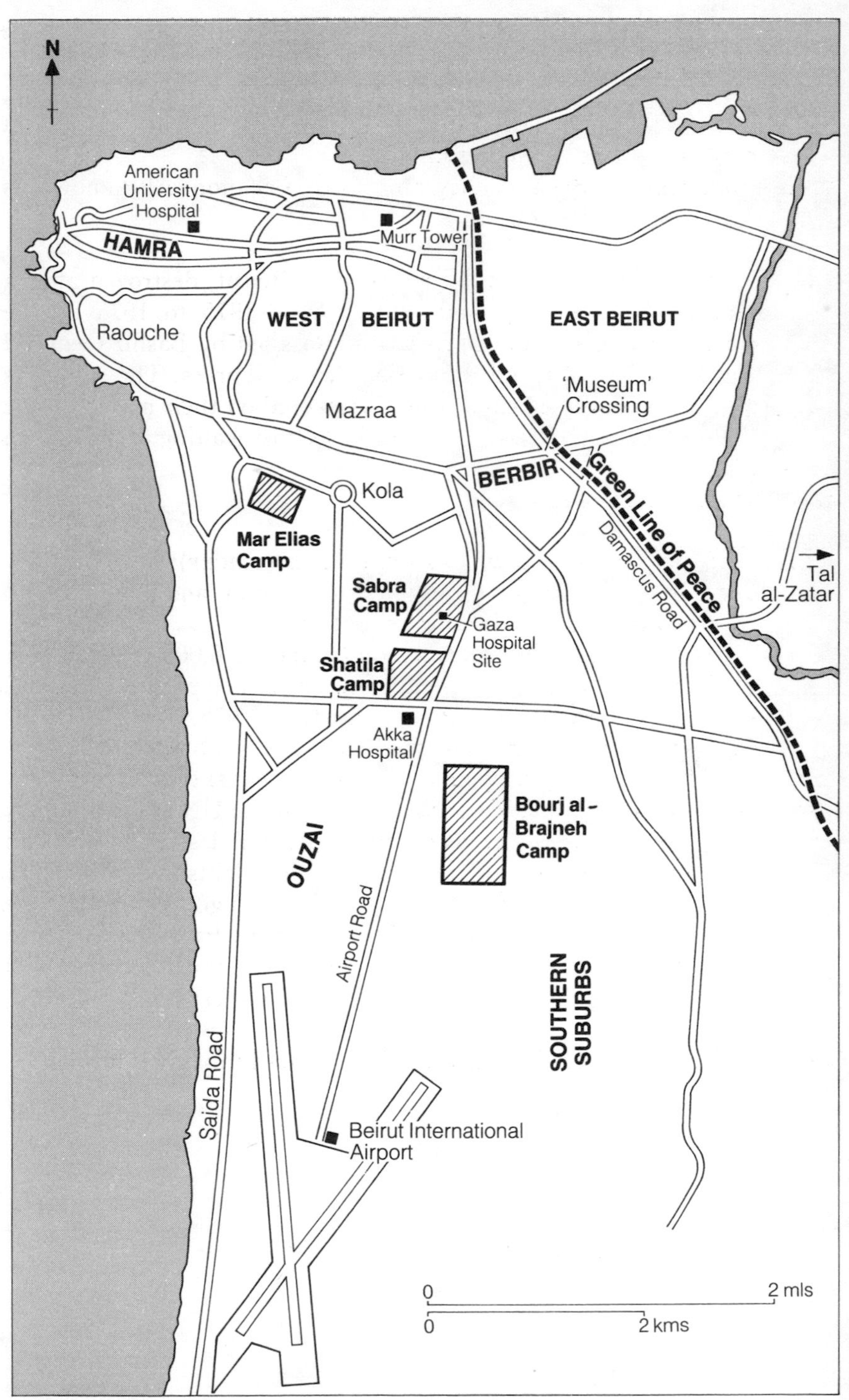

N
American
University
Hospital
HAMRA
Murr Tower
WEST
BEIRUT
EAST BEIRUT
Raouche
Mazraa
'Museum'
Crossing
BERBIR
Green Line of Peace
Kola
Mar Elias
Camp
Damascus Road
Tal
al-Zatar
Sabra
Camp
Gaza
Hospital
Site
Shatila
Camp
Akka
Hospital
Bourj al-
Brajneh
Camp
OUZAI
Airport Road
SOUTHERN
SUBURBS
Saida Road
Beirut International
Airport
0
2 mls
0
2 kms

PART ONE

Settling in at Bourj al-Brajneh

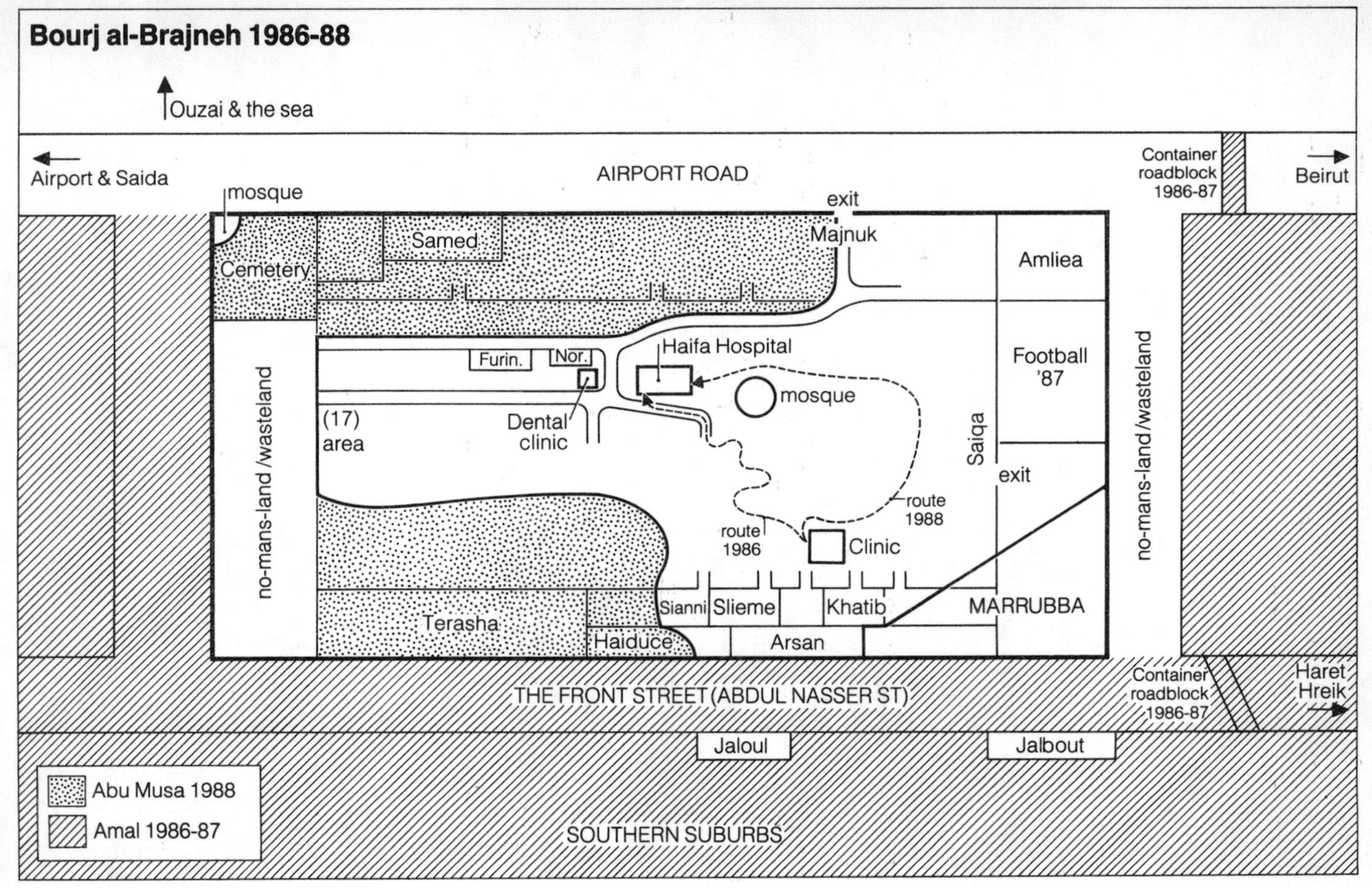
Bourj al-Brajneh 1986-88
Ouzai & the sea
Airport & Saida
AIRPORT ROAD
Container roadblock 1986-87
Beirut
mosque
exit
Majnuk
Samed
Cemetery
Amliea
Football '87
Furin.
Nor.
Haifa Hospital
mosque
Dental clinic
(17) area
no-mans-land /wasteland
no-mans-land /wasteland
Saiqa
exit
route 1988
route 1986
Clinic
Sianni
Slieme
Khatib
MARRUBBA
Terasha
Haiduce
Arsan
THE FRONT STREET (ABDUL NASSER ST)
Container roadblock 1986-87
Haret Hreik
Jaloul
Jalbout
Abu Musa 1988
Amal 1986-87
SOUTHERN SUBURBS

10.9.86 Heathrow Airport, London
The international health worker looks more like an international crumpled disaster – shirt well creased due to copious sweating from lugging twenty-one kilos of baggage on one's back, let alone the 'library' (medical books for the clinic and hospital). One security check of an unattended bag, and the derision of the Middle East Airlines check-in lady: 'Oh, Miss Wighton, why do you have your sleeping bag? [French accent] You won't need it in Beirut; they will give you beds.' I stared foolishly at my un-chic feet muttering about winter and clinics in the south, etc. The rest of the passengers are mega-smart.

23.40 Cockerel crowing. On first impression, Beirut is quite unshocking; more dilapidated and dusty, almost tired-looking. Waited three-quarters of an hour for a visa. Met by Ben after five security checks and shouting soldiers telling me to *stop*! The perfume I had secured in a sock for safe travel was examined in great detail, as were my camera and books at checkpoint. There were only two checkpoints en route to the camp; President Assad on posters at both.

The clinic is small and shell-holed, and I am camping out and around Ben and Pauline. Beirut is apparently the quietest they have ever known: only two sounds of gunshot, probably 'shooting at bats' as Tha'ir (a young Palestinian volunteer who helps out in the clinic) put it. I'm surprisingly unfrightened and unshocked by it all; camp conditions are as I expected. This is the life! – after a year and a half of trying to come here.

11.9.86
Woken by bangs, Amal fighting Hizb'ullah, then by the *Al Fajr* dawn prayer call. The clinic is full of crying children.

Went for a long walk round the camp to the front line street and saw the total damage everywhere; then into buildings with unexploded shells from RPGs (rocket-propelled grenades) or old mortar heads, which Ben throws around carelessly. I scrambled round the camp and across the open sewers with Mirvat, a young girl fighter; then we went into the cemetery. I have never experienced anything like it in my life. I expected an empty graveyard; instead I found a green place, milling with people, mostly mothers, sisters and daughters, tending plants, praying, listening to taped prayers, vigorously cleaning the stone slabs over the graves, or simply staring at the photographs of the disappeared and dead which are displayed above the graves in glass cases; three generations squatting on the stone edges crying, with Syrian observers strolling around the embankment overlooking the whole scene. The dead used to be buried by the sea, but now the Amal militia don't allow people from the camps to cross their territory to visit, so a football field has been bought and the dead are buried there.

I have seen three forms of Palestinian life and I don't think that one is better than the other. All experience the pain of exile, of occupation on their own land, of longing for a Palestinian life while separated from their main community, and of oppression and having to fight for survival in the community they find themselves in and in the camps. As the mother of two brothers killed within days of each other in the last camp war said, 'What can we do?', and Mirvat: 'Now you will see the grave of my love. We were to be married. I don't have the luck.' Her fiancé was 21 (like her), killed on the front line with his younger brother.

Power cut at 18.30.

12.9.86

Lots of children running riot in the clinic after a late start with a huge bronchitic gentleman. Took a service taxi* into Hamra, the main residential and shopping centre in West Beirut, and walked around. Visited the NORWAC flat, which is lovely – green and luxurious – and met the coordinator, Øyvind. Hannes, the Austrian physiotherapist who has been recruited by MAP to work in Haifa Hospital, had arrived from Cairo. Tanks and Syrians visible on the streets.

Shared a makeshift hospital supper at Haifa, where the building of the reinforcement wall is going fast. We had three power cuts, and the emergency generator is a bit of a joke. Khadija showed me a family group photo including her daughter, aged no more than 10, who was shot in the last war. 'She – she is killed!' (A big bang just now – shakes the house.) Climbed to the top of the hospital to look at Beirut in the darkness: beautiful. Walked back in the dark in sandals and saw how easy it is to fall into sewers.

Going south tomorrow: I got pass letters from the Norwegian Embassy.

13.9.86

The Israelis air-raided Saida yesterday and the day before.

The same children came to the clinic: Hamoudi, who starts crying at the far end of the street and sets off a sequence of tears amongst the others until we get him out; Feraz, with his lop-sided head from a birth trauma, running around and peeking through keyholes at children being sutured; little Munzar who is very brave; and Ahmad with the adorable eyes and a birth trauma to his arm which left it wasted, with only partial use in his hand. '*Inta fedai, inta fedai,*' ('You are a fighter, you are a fighter,') said to a small boy crying his head off in the dressing clinic.

A man came in with a flash burn from fiddling with the electricity – right up his arms and singeing the hairs on his chest. He was most worried about his face as he is 25 and getting married. Maybe she would reject him! He

*These are Mercedes cars which take up to five passengers, dropping them off at fixed points along the route to a particular destination.

was lathered in sweat from pain and the heat, and kept grabbing the mirror to check his face while we teased him.

Øyvind visited and was immediately surrounded by children bringing him tea. He gave me a NORWAC pass for the checkpoints on my way south. On the way out of the camp, we pass a small stall, with a man standing next to it dissolved in tears against the wall. As we were next to the Martyrs' Shrine, I thought at first he was grieving for someone from the wars, but his 70-year-old father had just died in hospital. I was invited into the men's reception room in the house to drink bitter coffee; all very solemn.

Travelled south. Checked a couple of times by Amal: Pauline is going to become Scottish – it's better than being English at the moment*! We arrived at Bourj al-Shemali camp in the early evening. It was as though we had walked into a Palestinian village: wide rural roads, women bundled with firewood weaving a difficult route through the narrow alleys; all very calm and overlooking Sur (ancient Tyre) and the sea. After a huge meal at a restaurant in Sur, we were warned off staying at the seafront and to get out quickly because the Shia were celebrating *Ashoura*, the festival marking the succession struggle after the Prophet Mohamad's death, in which the men cut themselves with knives. There was tremendous fervour from the mosque; not so sensible to be foreigners in town. We clambered into the ambulances and left. Visited NORWAC for an interesting meeting on the situation in the south, Saida and Beirut; they have a lovely house on a hill overlooking Sur, very civilized compared to the destruction which surrounds the Bourj camp.

14.9.86

Breakfast of sweet *ignaffi* (a kind of cake) at Bourj; then travelled south into the UNIFIL zone at Tebnine. Stopped on the way for a meal of corn and chicken prepared once a year to celebrate *Ashoura*: lovely house and hospitality. The woman had been pressurized into adopting strict Islamic dress and 'hates Iran' according to her brother, who wears western clothes.

At Tebnine we found the Irish UNIFIL shop stocked with drink and camera equipment from Haifa and Tel Aviv; I quickly put back the film I was thinking of buying and went on to the Norwegian shop, but they refused to open. Climbed up to a very high and beautiful village with a Crusades ruin that looked out over the Israeli-occupied zone, Syria, Jordan and the Golan Heights. There were Amal and Hizb'ullah slogans, posters and graffiti everywhere, even set into stones in the mountainside.

*The climate for British and American nationals had become hostile after the US bombing of Tripoli in Libya in April. Scottish nationality was not immediately identifiable as British (or 'English') at checkpoints between Beirut and the south.

We travelled back to Beirut in a service taxi with a 'heavy'-looking fellow passenger who said 'Shia' at every Amal checkpoint, from Sur to Kola junction (the roundabout at the edge of the southern suburbs of Beirut where people gather to travel south).

We walked back into the camp from the front line street, which was crawling with uniformed Amal militia for *Ashoura* celebrations again.

Met Ali al Masri's family: his son, shy Abu Ali, his daughter and kind wife; there is a huge Gulf-style photograph of Ali over the door.

Some shelling on the Green Line and shooting; Rashidiyeh camp south of Sur is under siege by Amal militia.

15.9.86

More odd gunshots and explosions far away in the Green Line area. Started work with Lieve today, who is explaining her work in the clinic. Went to the Beit Atfal Somud (a Palestinian-funded orphanage for the children of Tal al-Zatar) where I was shown embroidery, and children's drawings, all beautiful and tranquil, of a Palestine they had never known. Trees, sun, houses, orchards, fields, cows, Arabic fairy tales of lions and turtles flying, but also *fedayeen* (fighters), Israeli bombs and planes and soldiers fighting the *fedayeen*, people on stretchers and coming to get others wounded on the streets. The children also learn how to make paper and cloth flowers and to perform *dubké* (traditional dances) in strict classes. Palestinian flags and colours everywhere. We were given coffee and tea wherever we went, from an impoverished house full of fighters idling away the time, to the home of one of the head nurses at the hospital, Salim, who is waiting to move his family safely out to Tripoli in the north as their house is always being destroyed in the fighting. Who can blame him? His 3-year-old son spent the entire 45-day war in the emergency room with his father, even watching leg amputations in the operating theatre.

The problem over the clinic building has been resolved*; the PRCS have bought a house in Martyrs' Square (where I thought it would be nice to live) to be converted into a clinic. We have to completely renovate and paint it – there are wonderful tropical scenes everywhere as it used to be a photographer's studio. The roof garden overlooks Amal; waving at Amal in the morning. . . .

16.9.86

The commemoration of the massacres at Sabra and Shatila camps in 1982. Lots of security on the hill surrounding the cemetery. I had tea at Hussein's and saw videos of *Wahid Wahid*†. Given Abu Nidal calendars

*The current building had originally been used as a nursery school and there was pressure for the school to re-open. It was named after the Palestinian heroine, Dalal Moghrebi.

†The first Fatah military operation on January 1, 1965, and a big celebration in Palestinian life as it symbolizes the foundation of the 'Revolution for the Redemption of Palestine'.

(with Fatah symbols on top to make a statement). Grenades on the table with tea, as well as dynamite and a small pistol. (Even 5- to 6-year-olds have weapons; they learn on a small rifle.) Sisters and brothers who have died were being remembered; the family of Mohamad, whose father and brother were killed. I saw photographs of three badly mutilated children and their mother, all killed by shrapnel, their feet and legs blown off. We visited the graveyard during the Massacre Commemorations.

Mohamad's sister had an arranged marriage; they are twenty per cent of the norm here now. The engagement party was like a funeral and she took an overdose before the wedding, as apparently a lot of women do. Her husband is trying to make her happy.

17.9.86

There was shooting in the streets near the clinic today – two men fighting started with fists and then progressed to guns. This happens frequently. The child next door shot her brother in an accident; a boy in Shatila was given a loaded gun to play with and shot his brother, paralysing him from the neck down. Apparently there is a suicidal fatalism here, which also occurred in Vietnam; as there is no perceivable future, people leave it to 'Allah's will', so they play Russian or Lebanese roulette. A woman asked how her fiancé died and his friend, while demonstrating Russian roulette, shot himself. There were apparently six similar incidents in a week – all shots through the head. Lebanese roulette is known as 'chicken' and is played with snipers in a well-known street: people run across from one sandbagged side to jump over the other, braving the sniper.

I toured the bomb shelters underground located at strategic points in the camp, all in very bad condition: they need cleaning, ventilation, spraying, water, electricity and latrines. Visited a political shelter: Group 79, who are Fatah Marxists, educated in Bulgaria and Russia.

Two Palestinian men and an older woman were beaten up by Amal in the front street today: an escalation of provocation similar to the south, where they have blocked off Rashidiyeh camp and moved the checkpoint closer and closer to the camp boundaries. We were warned off leaving the camp today by three boys.

18.9.86

Went to meet Nabila Brier, a Palestinian who is the UNICEF field officer in Beirut, with our requests for equipment; then on to the American University of Beirut to see the Environmental Health Department. It all seemed as though it was being reorganized after the departure of the foreigners earlier this year*. A very calm, academic atmosphere, even

*After the US attack on Libya, and subsequent kidnappings of British and American nationals.

though Amal came into the campus to kidnap an American a fortnight ago. The Norwegian Embassy is just along the street so we went to pick up newspapers and photocopy the WHO community health agreement (Alma Ata agreement). The Norwegians are debating pulling out as the kidnapping has started again, but Øyvind says they have been talking about this for several months.

Visited Shatila camp; well and truly searched by the Syrians who turned our UNICEF posters inside out. They also nearly destroyed the film in my camera, and I got riled and shouted at them not to. So up we went to their office. 'No cameras allowed.' 'Since when?'

On to the clinic and hospital. Ali al Ma'aruf, the Public Health Officer, trained for four years at the American University in Beirut and in Russia and is well-informed on environmental matters. The main street in Shatila is terribly damaged and destroyed, but the Syrians are refusing to let in building materials for the hospital or anything else. Apparently the camp is filling up with Palestinians from Syria, and the Syrians are again negotiating with the Lebanese government to move all the people from the Beirut camps into the Bekaa Valley (Phalangist territory) so that they will be ghetto-ized as they are in Syria and Jordan. Preparing the way for genocide as well?

Back home and found a stray kitten, very young and starving. Gave it an iodine bath and milk, and it slept wrapped up in a towel in my pink basket. Now I have two, as Lieve found another kitten outside, also a fleabag, and thinking that it was number one who had escaped brought it in. They are now known as Ron and Nancy after the Reagans.

Shooting around the Green Line; fighting and shelling from 17.00, and bullets and shells coming in to the camp. A bullet from the front street wound up at the hospital, and we have to use bullet-safe streets to shop. So much for the Syrians' so-called truce: it was reported on the news that it broke down today and that there is also fighting in the south. The French military attaché was shot in East Beirut.

19.9.86

High news coverage of French attaché's death, and shooting near UNIFIL soldiers in the south; the Israelis are threatening intervention (again) in this area. Reports of 150 bombs over the Green Line last night; some shooting today. A Syrian was killed nearby in clashes with Amal. The camp was put on alert with lots of weapons on show, which I took to be ordinary security.

Prepared a talk on diarrhoea with slides from Shatila. We were going to do breastfeeding but were told that the whole audience would be women who were widows of martyrs, all very young and one pregnant. Two children stole twenty slides and we had to frisk one as she left; in fact she had another ten, which her friend returned to us later.

Quiet evening with Lieve packing ready to leave the camp in a few days. Missed a Sabra and Shatila gathering which turned out to be a pro-Syrian Salvation Front evening, so Pauline and Hannes left abruptly. Last time the three volunteers who attended were photographed and appeared on the front page of the Salvation Front news-sheet: stars and support, so to speak.

20.9.86
The French wish to withdraw from the Lebanon, or have the Israelis withdraw and move to the border as originally planned, with the Israeli-backed militia disarmed and disbanded. The Israelis of course object, especially after they cordoned off three villages two days ago. If UNIFIL have to watch, helpless to act, while the Israelis violate the borders to raid and arrest, then possibly the Lebanese might do the same across their borders in the opposite direction?

Still feeding the kittens who are taking more milk, but the Parakill for their fleas didn't work. Ron is aggressive; Nancy passive and still weak and wobbly.

My instinct last night was right: I had told Lieve that something very fast with a whizz had hit the wall near me; she thought it would be a catapult because of the whizz. So we joked that 'Okay, I've come to die for Palestine, but not to be killed by the Palestinians.' In fact I had been shot at twice from across the rooftops with an air rifle. The culprits were two 15-year-olds, one of whom, Aref al Habet, admitted it during a dressing clinic this morning. MAP may have its first martyr yet – in an unexpected way.

On the way into Beirut, Ben was stopped by Amal and had his Amal card taken away. The NORWAC flat is next to where Brian Keenan, the Irish teacher, was kidnapped in the street on his way to school. Worries in the camp about Syrian Palestinians from Abu Musa's party being moved into the camp with no families to restrain them.

21.9.86
Dr Rafiq Husseini, the Director of MAP, has now been detained in Jordan for thirteen weeks. We don't know why, but this a not uncommon story of Palestinians with Jordanian passports.

Spent last night in an Italian restaurant with incongruous rifles all along the wall; would look ethnically correct in Austria and Italy but out of place here. Hannes and I instantly ill with diarrhoea, nausea and vomiting after eating refundable lasagne. Ill all day.

New doctor arrived from MAP; we went to the airport to meet him and bullets from the Green Line came over among the cars. Øyvind and I ducked, then ran from the open spaces to the safety of the airport walls with everyone else, where we ducked again until we were told to get up by the locals, feeling somewhat foolish. Militia, armed to the teeth, waiting in big American cars for someone – unrecognizable – who got into the car and drove off. Large numbers of Syrians deployed in the city centre with troop carriers and rocket-propelled grenades (wonder why?); car searches, gunfire and the odd explosion.

Two young Palestinians are getting out to Denmark for political asylum, 'travelling' as it is known as here. They speak little English; will fly to West Germany and then travel by train. Poor, poor men, leaving for the unknown, away from their families, friends and homes.

22.9.86
A day of influenza, nausea and frustration: I couldn't find any adequate card record system for the patients, couldn't make the slide projector work, and had to send Sammar and Seeham (the two trainee nurses) home because they were complaining of sore stomachs; then a constant flow of people into the clinic until 19.30.

Quiet outside: only one big explosion about 23.40 and some gunfire. Kittens very active and hungry. The weather is changing already, moving towards autumn and the rains.

23.9.86
Fairly disastrous start in which I showed my slides without a translator to two under-5s, Um Ali our cleaner, who can't read, and eventually Sammar, who speaks only Arabic. Seeham turned up to announce that her mother wants her to work in Haifa rather than here, and that she wants to do emergency room work. But we couldn't find Dr Rede (the director of Haifa Hospital) and Salim the head nurse there wasn't too keen. All *I* really need at the moment is a translator. Had a meal at Seeham's, felt sick, broke into a sweat and offended the family who thought I didn't like the food.

Then went to an engagement party next door on Nasr's roof. The fiancée is 15: a beautiful girl-woman, resplendent in a one-shouldered pink satin and black net dress, with black suede shoes. The future husband is working in the Gulf and is 24. There was much laughter when he gave her the engagement gifts of necklace, bracelets, ring and earrings as he couldn't fasten the earrings on to her ears; everyone fell about laughing at his clumsiness. Both were solemn and shy, sitting on the raised throne with a carpet depicting the Ka'ba at Mecca behind them and flowers in front to match her dress. Then dancing and more music for three hours, give or take the odd power cut. Cookies and juice were brought for the festivities and flower petals thrown: all videoed for posterity. Revolvers were hastily hidden from view before the dancing, shirt-yanking going on all over the place to disguise them, or they were given to friends as they are too clumsy to dance with. The children were regularly thrown out by the adults. Lights were strung up across the roof as darkness came; more dancing until 19.00.

It stopped in the middle for us to watch the Israelis bomb the Shouf mountains twelve miles away. Soundless, too high for anti-aircraft guns to reach, the noise of the latter carrying more than the bombs which were identified by a pall of smoke rising in the clear blue, early autumn sky. The children stopped running around and everyone strained to look, seeing little silver triangles circle again to drop more bombs: the manoeuvres I used to watch on the West Bank all over again. The strain was enormous – everyone wondering if the bombers would come further up into Beirut after the experiences of Saida and Sur. The tension lasted for maybe twenty to thirty minutes with the planes circling and bombing, then dispersed into even more frenzied drinking and dancing, letting off the strain of living here with constant war, either open or subtle. It was strange to see crowds of fighters, young and old, swaying and moving beautifully to the music: carried away.

24.9.86
3.20 Sweating profusely from this wretched cold; explosions on the Green Line woke the kittens. Then furious banging on the door with cries for medicine. I explained in my poor Arabic that there was no medicine here; they still wanted me to come, not a doctor or nurse. I went round the corner to see the sick man, 'Evil' Mahmud, the one with the white trousers who had been dancing perfectly ten hours before. He was showing no clinical signs, but complaining of pain in the kidney region and chest. I told them to take him to Haifa for treatment; meanwhile Hannes woke up, and the cats again. More gunfire.

My cold and flu raging on. Pauline has arrived back safely from her trip to Baalbek with tales of torture of Palestinians by the Syrians. A man whom Ben knew had been ambushed by the Syrians. First someone came in the night to ask him for a list of politically-active Palestinians. He refused, so they ambushed him and took him to a prison in Tripoli in north Lebanon. They asked him to plant car bombs for them; he refused. They offered him money; he still refused. When he said they could do what they liked but he would not do this, they said they would kill him, gave him some paper and let him write a last note to his daughter. Then he was blindfolded and they fired two shots over his head. He was then tortured for a week, suspended from a ceiling for long periods by the hands and beaten senseless with electricity cables and cords. After a week of continuous torture he said he would sign anything they wanted so he gave them any names he could think of. After that he was taken to Syria and held in prison for a year; but at least he wasn't tortured there.

Pauline and Ben brought back a little Hittite figure of a man and some coins, one from the period of Alexander the Great: a concave silver disc.

25.9.86

News at 12.00 that Israeli jets have bombed Ain al-Helweh and Mieh Mieh camps south of Saida. I ask Tha'ir if they will bomb here. He says no; there are rules in war and the Israelis will not bomb purely civilian areas. There were big guns in these camps and the Israelis knew this. News also that three Palestinians were kidnapped from Hamra yesterday; one of them is a cousin of Hussein from the hospital. If they are not released today the Palestinians will capture three Amal from the front street and hold them here until the others are freed. After Ben's recent problems with Amal, Pauline was worried sick when he spent more than thirty minutes in the street today; he returned safely. The 3-year-old daughter of Abu Riyad, the Fatah commander in the camp, also called Sultan, was kidnapped outside her nursery school this morning with a ransom demand for half a million Lebanese lira. She is thought to be held somewhere in the camp.

More banging on the door while I was trying to sleep; a youngish woman who had overdosed on twenty Norgesic tablets was taken on our stretcher to Haifa where her stomach was washed out. The reason given was that her husband wishes to leave and divorce her.

26.9.86

Heavy shelling last night; the BBC World Service sympathetic to Amal and the Israelis.

The three kidnapped boys were found 'dumped' today. They think that they were held in the old Italian consulate on the airport road, and were systematically tortured (including being beaten with electricity cables and given electric shocks), threatened constantly with death and left badly injured. They were found near Shatila camp and initially looked after there before being moved into Haifa Hospital today. I passed their room, but the relatives were all coming in to visit and there was a lot of anger in the air, so we did not intrude. One of them had his face severely beaten and has a ruptured eardrum. Another (a Syrian) had the Amal symbol branded into his back. He is being sent to Syria as he cannot be cared for here.

The 3-year-old was freed by relatives this morning without any shooting; the kidnapper is thought to be in jail inside the camp. No news of Rafiq's release by the Jordanians, nor any likelihood yet. David Hirst of *The Guardian* foils a kidnap attempt in the southern suburbs of Beirut.

Sixteen women, many of them young widows, came to the clinic again today from Atfal Somud: lots of laughing, which is good for them as they are usually alone in their houses and get depressed. Atfal Somud recognizes the strain of single parents, and so organizes activities for the children of the widowed as well as for the orphans.

27.9.86
Woken in the night by an explosion near the clinic, close by as shrapnel fell all around. At first we thought it was a one-off thing, maybe someone fooling about with a grenade, but approximately twenty minutes later a second bigger bang came. We reckoned they were mortars from Amal outside the camp. The whole place was awake and dark and silent except for babies crying, cats meowing, cockerels shrieking.

The fighting that Lieve thought was Israelis bombing the Shouf mountains this morning is in fact the Phalangists fighting heavily with the South Lebanon Army: she was puzzled by the lack of anti-aircraft return fire and I was surprised as the Israelis don't usually fight on *Shabbat* (the Sabbath). We can hear heavy crumping of artillery here at the moment.

Listening to the 'Beirut' song on the radio. How I love this song, from hearing my friends sing it (badly) in Abu Dhabi, then listening to exiled *fedayeen* in Yemen, and now in Beirut, with the sounds of shells and the music drifting over in the wind from the east. Sounds of *Al Fajr* at 4.10 with heavy gunfire mingling with the mosques of West Beirut.

Fighting on the Green Line. Elias Hobeika has surfaced with another excuse, and another rent-a-thug militia has made advances across the Green Line. We were warned not to travel to Hamra today as shells are supposed to be landing in the vicinity, so we took the sea route into central Beirut. Lots of heavy militia equipment moving on the roads and militia seen for the first time since June: this is apparently the heaviest fighting since January. Three people now say we will have another camp war within the month. But where? This is the question.

28.9.86
We ate a quiet dinner last night in Hamra for Lieve and Dirk leaving; we were all a bit dazed by the atmosphere of the city after the fighting. Apparently Hobeika's Syrian, Amal and Christian militia did get through the Green Line into East Beirut, but were driven back with the help of the Lebanese Air Force. A neat piece of patriotism: the Air Force bombs their own people – civil war. Heard them at it again this morning.

Quiet night except for some gunfire. I eventually managed to phone home at 9.30. Radio Free Lebanon (the voice of resistance – ha, ha), in fact Kitaeb Phalangist radio, tells of 100 injured with thirty killed; BBC World Service tells of 200 injured and sixty killed.

Went into Beirut for the NORWAC meeting, then on to the Sports Club to mingle with the bourgeoisie of West Beirut as such. Had a crash course (sic) en route in driving the ambulance; tempers got slightly frayed, especially over third gear and directions. Swam and dived off the rocks at the Club, which is on the seafront at Raouche, a restaurant and swimming area in West Beirut. I was absolutely terrified at first but the sea was gorgeous. I had the whitest and most mosquito-bitten skin there. Great joke over Dirk being asked in the showers where he was from and why he was there. When he said he was with NORWAC, the men said 'Ah, that's why you have your bodyguards with you', meaning Ahmad and Tha'ir. Much joking about the bodyguards having to keep their eyes more off the girls and on us instead. A good ruse for protecting the two boys was to say they were Lebanese not Palestinians, helped by their 'Where's my gun?' walk, which they achieved even in swimming trunks. Offered them both the option of a service taxi home instead of me driving again; they both looked a bit seasick but collapsed into giggles at the thought of better things. Heavy Syrian check on both of them when we returned to camp – ID cards and so on. Someone taken away today at the checkpoint because his name was on a wanted list.

UNRWA send us children's toys instead of tetanus vaccine. Big explosions in the east.

29.9.86

Drove around Beirut with Ben. Only used third gear a couple of times – this, with reverse, is the most problematic.

The SLA retaliated for the death of two militia men by slaughtering the commander of the 5th Brigade in his bed last night with his wife. They used silencers and untraceable bullets – *agents provocateurs.*

Radio Free Lebanon is known as 'Radio of Lebanese resistance to change'.

30.9.86

The siege of Rashidiyeh started.

1.10.86

The rains came today along with a huge, endless, electrical storm. Woke us all up at 4 am with lightning, thunder and rain which continued all day. Power cuts and sewers flooding everywhere. All the children bundled into jerseys, anoraks and wellingtons – and umbrellas. We had fog as well: I watched it blow in again from the sea tonight in half an hour. Massive electricity cut; the clinic is held together by buckets and candles! It's not very easy giving vaccinations by candlelight.

I went to Shatila camp; heard that the Rashidiyeh fighting had stopped, though only temporarily. Apparently Amal had driven into the camp and opened fire, killing a woman and injuring some children. The Palestinians opened fire to drive them out, then Amal started shelling with RPGs (rocket-propelled grenades) and mortars, and there were also rumours of Israeli gunboats in the vicinity. Talked to Chris Giannou, the surgeon in charge of the hospital in Shatila – a very intelligent and dynamic man, who'll let me have milk and instruments when I come in on Saturday for the meeting with Ali, the Public Health Officer.

The Syrians gave us a hard time on the way back into Bourj; they wanted passports which we make a point of not carrying. The camp is still on alert after yesterday's events in the south.

I'm making drawings from Mahmud Darwish's poems, one of the most famous Palestinian poets and highly-respected member of the Palestine National Council.

2.10.86
Pauline called out to see someone who was shot. Fighting stopped again in Rashidiyeh; don't know if *instanfah* (alert) is on or off here now.

Went out to the Najdeh *rauda*, the nursery school. Shelling and more fighting on the Green Line. I finally realized that this *is* the infamous 'southern suburbs' where the Green Line runs parallel three streets along from the front street. At the *rauda*, I examined seventy-odd children for lice. Twenty-five or so have them, so I'm going back on Monday and Tuesday with Parakill for lice, scabies and dandruff. It's a commonly held belief here that if there are only a few nits they are dead! I've got better at spotting the red egg marks at the ears. I'm taking vaccines on Tuesday also.

I had an interesting discussion with the teachers at the school who don't believe that to raise health standards you need first to educate the women. There were protests against this, despite the fact that they themselves are educated. The woman I was speaking with was secondary level and university educated. The others were all literate. The social niceties of nit-finding were excluded today, so I tried my hardest to explain that if one child has lice then all children could get them; not necessarily because they were unwashed or anything like that.

A frustrating work day, so later I worked on a vaccination policy and ideas on PHC (primary health care). Everyone went out, and I cried a little; then a girl with a three-day burn came in. More frustration because the gauze in the sterilizer was not ready, etc. Went to visit Ali al Masri's family and that made up for everything: the house was full of children and laughter and hands poking surreally through the shell-holes in the walls. I met Rifat again, the young man I met with Barbara in Abu Dhabi: he's back in the camp now for good.

The shooting earlier appears to have been because of an argument, leading to a few holes in the colon, a laparotomy which took over two hours by a tired Pauline, and a lot of angry people around.

Fighting has started in Rashidiyeh again since 14.00. Pauline and Ben are talking about going there to help. There is no hospital; just a clinic and a few staff. I offered to go, but I don't know if they'll let me. Amal checkpoints on the roads from the south: more than thirty between Bourj al-Shemali camp and Saida now; all imported militia men from Bekaa.

The little kitten learnt to run today, something I thought she might never do. Ahmad with the withered arm was playing *hakim* (doctor) in the clinic, with the stethoscope and torches. More rain and flooding everywhere again. Power cuts all day, and roof water leaks down the electricity wires. The new doctors are arriving from London tomorrow and going straight down south.

Shooting out over the Green Line – big explosions again.

3.10.86

Heavy fighting around Rashidiyeh. Amal are kidnapping Palestinians, and have also surrounded the camp at Bourj al-Shemali. The lovely meal at Ali al Masri's house is upset by the news from the southern camps; he has relatives at Rashidiyeh. Imad Masri, Ali's half-brother, hit little Hussein three times quite hard before he started to cry. Neither of the children like Imad: he's perhaps a little crazy from too much fighting.

Tha'ir has got his visa to travel to Abu Dhabi. He has waited years for this, and we are all happy and sad at the same time. When we talked about it on Sunday we joked that his fate would be an arranged marriage for certain as his God had only one month to change his life and get him away from the camps. I knew he was too good to be stuck here for ever.

One of the women from Atfal Somud told me how her brother had died during torture by the Israelis in 1982. Poor, poor woman – another who has lost people that she loved.

4.10.86

Dawn in Bourj is beautiful: a lovely clear yellow light, cockerels crowing and kittens meowing, then children waking up and the noises of houses coming alive.

Visited two *raudas* to sort out nits and injections, then on to Shatila where a Lebanese nurse had a small epileptic seizure. True Beirut pandemonium from the other housekeeper. Gave the nurse a lift up the road and got hit by a Mercedes. I had practically slowed to a standstill for the Syrian road block, and the idiot swung in front of me, straight into the right-hand side of the ambulance; it was obvious he had no room. The driver got out and started to shout at me; when he got to 'You can't drive!', I said, 'Why did you pull into my side?' 'You can't drive!' The Syrians moved us on. They had taken the ambulance to bits going into Shatila, even unscrewed the side panels with big knives and asked me if there were any bombs, but they didn't search me on the way out.

Got home to find Ahmad and Tha'ir carrying revolvers. *Instanfah* again? The situation is bad; there is talk of the Palestinians starting some fighting here to divert Amal from shelling Rashidiyeh and Bourj al-Shemali. People in Shatila say that if you are shot in Rashidiyeh you will just die as there are no medical facilities in the camp. Today Arafat appealed to all Arab states to stop the fighting and the massacre of 60,000 Palestinians in the camps. Saudi Arabia has also told them to stop. Amal want all the weapons in the camps to be handed over again, as in 1982. Why? To kill everyone without resistance. All the Amal militia from around here have been redeployed in the south at present. Rafiq Husseini still held in Jordan.

The new Scottish doctor, Iain Henderson, went straight to Saida on arrival yesterday. Apparently he is about 63 and wears a waterproof fishing jacket – quite Scottish. I think it's terrific that he's come to the Lebanon at this time of his life when really he should have a rest from his worries. I'm still thinking of going south after unconfirmed reports that the ICRC are going into Rashidiyeh to evacuate the sixteen wounded.

'Mad' Magda reading the news on Radio Free Lebanon: 'Everything has returned to normal.'

5.10.86

A strange sound of drunken singing in the next door house down below. The two young boys living alone on leave from Saudi Arabia are singing, clapping and shrieking in unison with a very loud cassette recorder. They may end up in jail.

Øyvind returned early from Cairo as reports of war in the south indicate that it seems to be escalating. All camps there are still under fire. 'Evil' Mahmud was in Saida and was warned by a friendly Amal militiaman who used to buy Pepsi from him to get back to Beirut as there was going to be trouble. Everyone is tense and worried. You can see the strain in little signs of craziness in a person who otherwise appears to be quite calm and normal: frenzied foot-tapping or overactive worry beads. Guns being carried around the camp today.

Tha'ir came twice to say goodbye; everyone was kissing him and shaking his hand. Ahmad, seeing I was shy, pushed me forward to say goodbye too. Everyone is happy, sad and apprehensive for him, going to a life we know it would be selfish to deprive him of or begrudge him, so he can save for 'a wedding' . . .

We walked past the new clinic building, where the electricity cable and the outside rocking chair have already been stolen: Ben is mad about this.

I've been joking about wanting to take a look at Coptic or Byzantine art one Sunday: 'the museum' was subsequently shut today because of sniping. Fell into a sewer whilst laughing with Pauline about an attractive man.

6.10.86

The camps are on *instanfah* again. Cancelled all my *rauda* visits then went to Shatila. On the way there in the service taxi, I met some Palestinians and the old gentleman next to me asked where I was working. When I said the clinic he paid my fare and said I should leave the camp. Went to the mosque in Shatila for news of Rashidiyeh which was organized by the Women's Union, who had also printed leaflets giving details: 300 arrested, eighty-five injured, twenty-five killed – very bad. We all want to go there to help. Toured the Martyrs' Shrine at the mosque.

Later I went into Hamra with Ben to change some money. We were stopped at the junction behind Akka Hospital by two men who ordered us out of the Volkswagen. We prevaricated: 'Why? Why?' So they opened the door, pulled Ben's arm, slid off the safety catches on their automatic weapons and repeated the order: '*Out.*' So we showed them our NORWAC cards and asked, 'Why? Why stop nurses, ambulances' and so on?, stalling for time. From them: 'Why do you come out of the Palestinian camps: you work there?' – said with hatred. Fortunately a crowd of cars was gathering. They walked round to my side, as I locked the door and we drove off, my heart in my boots. Maureen, the NORWAC physiotherapist and a fellow Scot, arrived safely from Bourj al-Shemali with Kristine.

7.10.86

Went to Shatila to pick up supplies of tinned milk – thirty-five cartons. The crazy Palestinians had me reversing up Shatila's narrow alleys in a big Volkswagen bus. We now have milk; all we need are vaccines and vitamins.

The Sunni sheikh, Sobhei Salah, was assassinated in West Beirut on the way to the mosque: more provocation by Amal.

8.10.86

Spent today trying to find what's left of the milk. I'm sure we had at least twenty-seven cartons to start with; sixteen have 'been liberated'.

Shooting in the camp this afternoon: differing reports ranging from Amal killing a woman to a jealous fight. One of the men, who was shot in the legs and elsewhere, was sent out of the camp as the operating theatre is awash with dirty water from the sewage which has finally flooded it. The other man was killed instantly: shot in the face and multiple injuries. The camp went on *instanfah* after the shooting: kids were dragged off the street, and uniforms and guns mobilized. Amer, 'the good sniper', came into the clinic with friends and we waited to see if we would need the intravenous infusions we'd put out. (Apparently the Syrian who injured himself the other day has a genital problem and thought he could not marry.)

We went to the hospital to see Dr Rede and, just as we went past the three fridges in the hall, one was opened to show a bloodied white sheet which was then pulled back to reveal a bloodied young head. I had had no idea that we were going to be shown the body of the dead man in the middle of the outpatients' room, but, unceremoniously as death is treated here, this is a common day-to-day occurrence. The fridge has capacity for three bodies. As I stood back from looking at the body the familiar thoughts went through my mind. As of this morning this person got up expecting to go to sleep tonight and get up again tomorrow, and the next day, and to continue to do so for many years. And now he will never get up again – to see Palestine, to fight another camp war, nothing. All this crosses my mind every time I see death again, and has done since I saw my first corpse when I was 17 – late by the standards here. Pauline looked shaken: she knew his family.

I hear that Rashidiyeh has in fact six dead and fourteen injured; the other tales are exaggerated. Amal are forcing the Palestinians in the south into the (ghetto) camps. They post notices on people's houses saying that the occupants should leave within two weeks and move into the camps or else they will be hurt – herding them as every persecuted people is herded into a manipulated position. Terrorizing.

We went out of the camp to jeers that we were leaving because we were scared. Most of the shops in West Beirut were shut in memory of Sheikh Sobhei Salah. We were stared at by some men in a Mercedes who slowed down and pointed at us.

Beirut's big wheel at Raouche beach is lit up after dark with multi-coloured lights against the background of palm trees and the sea: orb-shaped lights against a many-hued sky with a crescent moon hanging in violet pinks and fading sands. The moon (*amar hilal*) then changed also to fading gold in a blue-black sky.

I miss the solitude required for thought: I try to turn inward but still recollect only a third of what I usually remember or think. I'm forgetting names, emotions and reason – lost in the constant distraction of incessantly being with others and of war. Always noise, radio, talk, visits, being an object of attention, never able to make a decision or control my environment, my control relinquished. We are functioning as best we can in this way of life. Pauline is tired.

9.10.86

We came back to tales of fighting. Amal had bombed the camp for around an hour until negotiations concluded between the camp, the PFLP, Abu Musa and Amal. We heard on the news that there is fighting again in Rashidiyeh, and that the tension in Bourj al-Brajneh has developed into Palestinian clashes. The reason given is that groups of men are killing one another over a woman.

We arrange Ben's birthday party.

10.10.86

Ben turned up late for his party at 16.45 – everyone else had arrived early. The children stoned and burst the first set of balloons which we had strung up at the door; the second lot were let loose with biscuits after 'Happy

Birthday' was sung outside. Not much dancing much to my disappointment but 'Evil' Mahmud and Ahmad were on form.

No one showed up for the Beit Atfal Somud talk because of the 'situation' in the camp again.

11.10.86

Rashidiyeh figures: five killed, six severely injured, thirty injured, 300 (approximately) arrested. After an evacuation offer to the ICRC they refused to go into Rashidiyeh at 3 am. The Palestinians had been ordered to hand over their weapons by midnight. We had corroboration of the tales of enforced deportation of the Palestinians yesterday from one of the women from the Beit Atfal Somud: people living in the orchards around the southern camps were given half an hour to leave their houses or be killed; they had orders to move into the non-UNRWA-registered camps in the south, and were not allowed to go to Sur or Saida for safety. They were also threatened that travelling on the roads isn't safe, and people outside on the roads were told to go to the camps. This may validate tales of Amal/Syrian plans to move the whole Palestinian population into one area where they can totally control 100,000 people.

Bourj al-Brajneh is still on *instanfah*; yesterday Abu Musa placed armed guards on the hospital to 'protect' it – from whom? The Syrians are provoking the Salvation Front and Abu Musa to evict Fatah from the camps by force, in the same way as they are using Amal in the south, so we are expecting a war in the camp soon, as the tension is even beginning to be felt in the air. How can we justify this kind of behaviour in every war? There are thugs who will do anything for power, and it looks as if it will happen again here. It is the same situation as the last Abu Musa uprising against the mainline PLO.

12.10.86

When people wear *dishdashas* (long, loose garment worn by men) here, it generally means not that they are holy, hot, or in pyjamas, but that they are hiding the loss of one leg. The *dishdashas* are usually accompanied by crutches. Today men in *dishdashas* are cleaning the Martyrs' Shrine outside the new clinic; lots of little boys encouraging them, and water washing the plants and stone slabs around the house, sweeping the dirt away. I find it strange to see men cleaning for the first time. These men who were once *fedayeen* cannot run, shoot, or defend anyone any more; all their effort is put into moving about in the narrow alleyways.

13.10.86

Rain, thunder and lightning. Hilarious meal at 'Evil' Mahmud's, playing with his daughter Namaat, and served by his wife with cakes from Ahmad. Ben played the accordion and Mahmud an empty water bottle. They danced in the Arab style, and I tried to do Scottish country dancing, solo and then with Hannes, plus the baby on my hips, much to Mahmud and Ahmad's amusement.

Pauline told me later that Ahmad is believed to be in love with a Shia girl who lives outside the camp and, although there are many mixed marriages, after two recent camp wars with Amal it is probably only ('possibly') a '*yumkin*'. Just the day before Ahmad was stopped by an Amal soldier with guns who wanted to see his papers and interrogated him about being a Palestinian. He said he was going to take him 'to the office', but just as Ahmad was thinking that he would be tortured or shot the thug said he was only joking. He described it as his heart 'went into the ground': more terror.

Today Rashidiyeh is supposedly open for the evacuation of the wounded, and 300 women are reported to have fled the camp for neighbouring camps. But there were heavy exchanges again today with no casualties reported. It is possible that the ICRC will be able to enter the camp. There are also reports of heavy shelling in Beirut, but we've not really heard anything. The checkpoint Syrian is kind: this week's irony is that he's a Kurd.

Stripped the walls at the new house. Looked at the moon for a long time.

14.10.86

The wounded from Rashidiyeh were evacuated to hospitals in Saida; contrary to reports there wasn't an Abu Musa surgeon in the camp. *Al hamdo'lillah* (Thanks be to God).

I had a quiet day, working on the new house with a horde of children scraping and painting and brushing and crying. Given bread and jam for free as we are 'here to help the camp when it needs it', so they will help us. We are 'the sons and daughters who are far away in other countries, the brothers and sisters'.

16.10.86

Invaded by people from 8.30 in the morning to 22.30 at night: children everywhere, people wanting dressings, no peace and an incredibly high noise level. I went to the house of the paraplegics and met Hassan, a paraplegic with a dreadful hole in his leg from an infected femoral head removal. He had broken his neck when he was about 16 years old from jumping into a swimming pool. Now a lovely young man of around 26. Also met Mohamad who is a gentle, 'practical nurse' whose new young wife has missed her 'sick time' (menstrual period) by six days. He too looks so young.

The PLO threw three grenades at an Israeli cadet unit in Jerusalem in the car park behind the old city after a swearing-in ceremony at the Wailing Wall bordering Al Aqsa. Of course lots of 'Arabs' were arrested and a cordon was put around the old city. Then Molotov cocktails were thrown at an Israeli bus near Tulkarm. A number of Palestinians were arrested and a curfew was imposed on the area. I heard on the news that fifty Zionist jets bombed Saida at 15.30 in six bombing runs; one of the planes was hit by a shoulder-launched Sam-7 missile and the two pilots parachuted into the hands of Amal who have brought them to West Beirut.

Amal refused to allow bricks to be brought into the camp for re-building work. A young man from the camp has been held by kidnappers since last week.

17.10.86

Working conditions near impossible because of the squabble over the clinic. I went to watch the *dubké* class and saw lots of lovely uncoordinated 6-year-olds counting their way furiously through songs about little cats and the *fedayeen*, and *dubké* about Palestine's towns; older children also counting furiously to the rhythm and steps. I followed this by a catastrophic slide talk with no projector and then a meeting with *rauda* teachers who didn't show up.

Then we heard that Amal had refused the cement for repairs to the hospital – *again.*

18.10.86

The work on the new house is stop-go, and at Pauline's insistence we are supposedly living outside the camp in the NORWAC flat from today. I don't want to leave the camp; we should be able to live and work anywhere, not waste time and energy quarrelling. All this with more suggestions of another war coming with Amal, more cement refused. I have always intended to stay in the camp and 'fight for the Palestinian Revolution' through good, bad or indifferent, ie slog for Palestinian health care while everyone tries to destroy them; so I will go back on Monday morning and stay in the hospital if necessary. I feel it's thoughtless and selfish to be out of the camp, and it's exploiting the people here as we have options and they don't. The fact that the new house isn't ready is really so minor compared to everyday living as a Palestinian. We all have to live with things we don't like.

Dealing with crazy people all day.

19.10.86

Quiet day with the two cats. Went back to camp briefly; the hospital was quiet and dark with more electricity failures. Went for a stroll along the Corniche and bought ridiculous earrings; met quite a few Palestinians out looking at girls. A Sunday afternoon by the sea – all of us taking risks.

20.10.86

Shooting in the camp last night for about fifteen minutes near the clinics, between Abu Musa and Fatah. Poor Hannes was sleeping at the clinic and couldn't go downstairs to safety as all the doors were locked and he had no keys. Apparently some families left the camp yesterday fearing an escalation of the fighting. Ahmad chased away an Amal man who came into the camp with his gun.

I packed up the clinic in preparation for the move to the new premises.

21.10.86

Went to Shatila; questioned on the way out of the camp by Syrians. There have been reports of fighting for three days in Shatila between Abu Musa and Fatah; no injuries. Tight checks again by Syrian plainclothes police for Ben and Hannes, and later for Régine, the French nurse who works in Shatila. I spoke with Ali, the Public Health Officer in Shatila; no clinic from Thursday. No milk to bring back to Bourj al-Brajneh.

The new house is not nearly ready yet; the water supply will either come from the Fatah wells or the Lebanese water company? Went browsing in Hamra, unaware that an American had been kidnapped just before. The British Embassy are moving staff out over Hindawi's trial in London*.

22.10.86

No further news of the PRCS strike in Haifa Hospital or Shatila, although the New Year is too far away for the new pay deals to be implemented.

The PLO submarine chief Abu Ghazil has been assassinated in Athens by Mossad. We live opposite the chief of the Lebanese Army in Hamra: if he goes boom, do we go boom too?

23.10.86

Rafiq still held in Jordan. Shootout in Raouche: PSP and Amal shooting at one another for an hour.

Bad day as the team from Bourj al-Shemali had to be evacuated after Amal raided the house and arrested the neighbours. Maureen, Kristine and Øyvind arrived back safely after being raided and jeered and shot at as they left the camp by militia who had been shooting from the roof of the house. Maureen was very angry and upset by it all. She had *walked* into Rashidiyeh camp as soon as she was allowed to enter. The nurses were carrying in drugs, needles and medical supplies strapped to their bodies. Maureen feels Amal is playing with people until they choose to stop playing and start killing. Everyone is waiting for a massacre to start. Dr Salah is left alone inside Rashidiyeh; his wife was shot, nephew killed,

*Nazar Hindawi persuaded his Irish girlfriend to carry a bomb onto an El Al plane at Heathrow. She was detained, then released when it was proven that she had no knowledge of the device, but he was subsequently caught and jailed.

brother killed – he is exhausted mentally and physically. People are dying there for no reason: there is no equipment, no hospital, nothing but calculated murder to drive the Palestinians out. Last night six or seven Amal were killed in a sea operation – by Palestinians it is said. All of us tired and depressed.

I'm trying to work on a news broadcast on the Rashidiyeh situation for the BBC World Service saying that there is going to be a massacre; we are all waiting for it. 'Do something,' as Dr Salah said in a message he sent out with Maureen. He got caught inside Rashidiyeh when attending his nephew's funeral. The brother of Sami and Ali al Masri was killed yesterday in Rashidiyeh. Many visitors expressed sadness and condolences to their mother today.

Went to Shatila with requests for medical supplies from Chris Giannou. A 6th Brigade Shia soldier who saw us during the Tebnine visit a month ago cornered me at the ambulance, then asked if I could do anything about his brother who was taken in the raid on Tebnine in February this year to the Beit Shams prison in Israel. I felt so helpless – he was very young and upset.

24.10.86

Later in the kitchen in the Hamra flat: wide awake at 4 am exhibiting all the signs that I recognize as anxiety in others. Maureen, who appears to be as intuitive as I am, and who also had a feeling of extreme foreboding before Rashidiyeh, is really very spooked by what is happening here now to the Palestinians. We both think that the biggest war is yet to come: the one that will determine whether Amal, Syria and the Israelis will be allowed to persecute and terrorize the whole Palestinian population for even longer than in 1982, or whether the Palestinians will be able to hold on to the camps and their autonomy and keep them off. We both think this will be longer and bloodier than anything up to now, and will be on the scale of 1982, ie a concentrated full-scale attack on *all* Palestinians living in the Lebanon. The escalation is obvious: shooting, Syrian movement, Amal weaponry, the flying checkpoints, such as outside the camp yesterday. (Gunfire close to us while *Al Fajr* is being sung nearby. Not from the Green Line, I think.) We also discussed if and when Amal will throw the medical volunteers out of the camps. Yesterday there was shooting around the hospital at the same time as front street shooting at the other end of the camp. We were drinking coffee on Haj's roof and couldn't decide whether to leave or not, even when the gunfire got a bit closer. One of us sat on the floor, one wanted to go down, so we compromised and moved to a sheltered part of the roof. It was hit by five mortars in the last camp war.

The dawn *Al Fajr*, my favourite call, has just finished.

25.10.86
Shocked to hear of fighting in Ain al-Helweh and Mieh Mieh camps on waking. Britain breaks ties with Syria. I was not allowed by Øyvind to take a service taxi back into camp as he thought it might be dangerous, but I got in without problems and moved into the new house. We have to stay inside the camp for a while because of the Syrians; that's why we were warned to leave two days ago. Waiting all day for the war to start; grenades being thrown into the camp from all around outside.

Dr Rede is now in the camp. Everyone is inside the camp and waiting for the Amal offensive, even though most of Amal is still hemmed in in Saida by Palestinian forces. They've taken three Amal villages already. All the news reports accuse the Palestinians of amassing troops and trying to control the south, which is why Amal have to defend it. What utter nonsense! Nothing is said about the Amal killings and terror and torture against the Palestinians. Another grenade has just landed. Gunshots outside. Even 'Evil' Mahmud is armed, though still feeling sickly.

We finish moving house tomorrow – *Insh'Allah* (God willing). Oh, gunshots again.

26.10.86
News of Amal (shock, horror) having to fight a Palestinian offensive (whoopee! – cheers of relief), taking the pressure off Rashidiyeh and helping them to fight back. Apparently Palestinian fighters from the Bekaa Valley have gone south and also 125 have come into Rashidiyeh this morning – Abu Musa relief. Amal have now lost forty-four fighters, twenty Palestinians are dead and three villages have been taken by the Palestinians. Dr Rede wants Amal to be besieged for at least ten days, as then they would feel what the Palestinians suffer all the time and have suffered since the 1-month War in 1985.

There is also news that the Amal supply lines have been cut before Saida and they are fighting as well with the PSP both by sea and road, so they are scattering quickly. But they are digging in around Bourj al-Brajneh and Shatila, to attack us also. I hope they have a dose of over-confidence and have bitten off more than they can chew.

Gave away the kittens today: thinking of them.

Very quiet so far, unnaturally so. I'm discovering that I'm now as anxious as everyone else, catching myself tapping my feet, or clicking my fingers, or generally fidgeting as everyone else does here with fingers, knees or feet – what I first called small signs of being crazy, as I have also become now. Borhan's family will protect the new clinic as it is in their military area.

Had a good talk with Maureen about women being suppressed in society here, and how she thinks you can manage for a three-month stint but no longer. We also talked about how you need to be yourself and not suppress it or your natural reactions.

I have this intuition sometimes – like tonight – the camp is *absolutely silent*. Not a sound. There goes the first grenade of the evening just as I wrote that, so I've put on my socks as that seems to take me the longest time to do when I'm panicked.

27.10.86

5.10 The awaited mortars have started, two so far after grenades since 2 am. I'm awake along with everyone else, it seems, and trying to drink tea waiting for the next blast with the Qur'an being broadcast on the radio. The BBC World Service says that a ceasefire has been arranged in the south after 'a weekend of fierce fighting between Palestinians and the Shi'ite militia' and is to be implemented by Syrian Muslim observers. God, their news is so distorted; they were talking recently of Palestinian offensives, and Amal worries of a resurgence of a Palestinian armed presence in Lebanon. It's all such rubbish. They carefully omit the terror, kidnappings, torture, beatings of women and constant threats to Palestinians here; not to mention the siege of Rashidiyeh for the past month, or the fact that the ICRC hasn't been allowed to act as a neutral agency on behalf of all involved. Or the half siege in Beirut camps for a year and a half, restricting food, building materials and freedom of movement.

Sounds of mobilizing outside all night: guns, sandbags being made, guncatches and ammunition swinging around bodies as fighters walk down across the square in the dark; with coughs, and cigarettes being lit. There's also the crackle of walkie-talkies, which are regularly carried now.

The explosions are coming again from the front street area. I suppose with the ceasefire Amal will now be able to travel back up with weapons from the south – damn!

More noises: friends waking up comrades for the change of shift, banging on doors; people filling water carriers at the pumps in the street below; a fighter talking in an office across the square; flip-flops crossing the streets, and general movement from the defence position up the hill at the hospital to down along the front street. None of us is going to get any sleep before the war at this rate.

Despite the ceasefire in the south, fighting is reported again at 6 am. '. . . Acts of self-assertion by Palestinians against attempts by Shia militia to restrict their movements and military strength in the south,' Gerald Butt, BBC World Service. Reports of twenty dead; the PLA (Sunni?) to act as a buffer force. The ceasefire will not hold long. Where does Butt get his ideas from? They're obviously Amal credited.

Later. BBC World Service has been giving biased reports all day.

Øyvind and Maureen came to tell us that Maureen is leaving for Cairo and Iain is leaving Ain al-Helweh for Scotland. The PRCS Volkswagen ambulance (with Hassan driving) was stolen at Akka Hospital by Amal militia at the checkpoint. Ben was stopped in the front street by Amal, fulfilling my awful forebodings about kidnapping when I was in Hamra – a sick gut feeling. But they didn't hold him long.

We're moving the clinic equipment here to the new house tomorrow. More grenades and shooting tonight around the hospital: the camp took twenty grenades last night. Hussein called in today on the way to collect a video, carrying two grenades. Hannes thought one was a torch and nearly pulled it apart. Pauline and I were shouting 'It's a bomb!' but he didn't believe us.

I went to find Dr Rede to offer to drive the ambulance instead of the Palestinian drivers, as so far, *Al hamdo'lillah*, Amal hadn't given me any trouble as I am a woman. He was very upset about the theft of the ambulance; Palestinians must not drive around now, it simply isn't safe at all.

Enthusiastic cleaning up by *fedayeen* who are on duty in the square below and bored. 'Evil' Mahmud going home to sleep to protect his wife as 'it is not safe here alone in the house', even for a Palestinian woman.

Dejected by the news that Maureen and Iain are leaving: I asked her to come here to work, but she is being pressurized by the Norwegians to return home.

28.10.86

So much for the Pope's Day of Peace: a dozen grenades were thrown in here this morning with much shooting. Slept till 9.30 despite the noise of joiners and painters in the house. Drove to Akka Hospital near Shatila; Amal militia at the camp checkpoint instead of the Kurd and Lebanese soldiers. Got hold of some Tegretol* for 'Evil' Mahmud to bribe the Lebanese soldiers who need it. No teachers came for the course meeting today; hardly surprising as even I can hardly write for nervous tension. Brought over emergency supplies from the old clinic: intravenous injections, dressings, gauze, blood pressure stuff, etc. More *fedayeen* clearing the square early today; lots of laughing and joking and fierce *dubké* on a cassette, with clapping and tuneless whistling and cheering.

Arabian dancing lesson at Noora Hammadi's. More sad stories: Juma has been in a Phalange jail, and was in an Israeli prison after the '82 invasion for fourteen months. Banan's† father was also in a Lebanese jail for twelve months. Another boy had lost his brother in the last war and his father before that.

A lighter mood today despite grenades and Amal. Maybe we're all getting used to the idea of the war. A woman asked me why I was here, why

*A drug for the regulation of blood pressure.

†Banan became my best friend in Bourj shortly after my arrival. Her mother Noora had come to see me in the clinic to say that she had an elder daughter who was lonely. She had two young sisters, but both her brothers lived away from here.

I didn't get away as war was coming. Half the nurses at the hospital didn't turn up as they are frightened to get stuck in the camp if fighting starts.

PART TWO

The 6-Month War

October 1986 to April 1987

1986 — ١٩٨٦

SEPTEMBRE أيلول

Poem of Bread (– to Ibrahim Marzouk) p10

"This unique transfer
From the cave of beginnings to guerrilla warfare
To tragedy in Beirut
Who was dying
At exactly fine?"

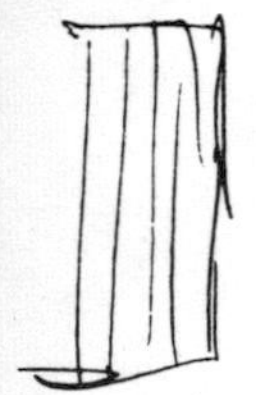

OCTOBRE تشرين الأول

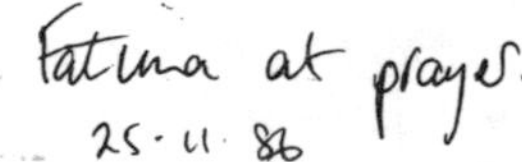

Fatima at prayer.
25.11.86

29.10.86 Day 1 Wednesday

Today was quiet after a peaceful night. We woke, ate breakfast, fetched more emergency equipment; Darwish the plumber appeared to fix the blocked pipe. I made gauze and tried to put it in the sterilizer, but no electricity. Everyone at the hospital was anxious about Pauline, Ben, Hannes and myself going out of the camp to the NORWAC/MAP meeting in Hamra; we decided to return at 16.00 latest. A hurried meeting, then we said goodbye to Maureen, and gave her letters for MAP and a note to phone Mum on her birthday in Glasgow. We returned to the camp in two ambulances after the 15.00 news.

When I got back, I discovered that Hussein had killed the little kitten by drowning it; I'm very angry and upset as he was threatening to kill it all day yesterday, and Ben and I said we would hurt him severely if he touched it. I feel really guilty about having left the poor wee thing with him as it seemed so cheerful and happy running about the new house. I cried a little and will cry more.

Later I met Banan; we were dancing and looking at photos of Austria with Hannes when we heard a *whoosh* accompanied by a flare. I asked, 'What was that?' Banan said it was a B-7. Then suddenly all hell was let loose. We told Banan to go home, and got off the balcony as the chaos got worse with everyone running to the front street, mobilizing.

The war had finally come; it started at 16.30.

We ran to carry all the equipment downstairs to set up an emergency room here. Ben arrived and we got most of the things down, crouching and crawling up the stairs as we were visible to snipers outside the camp. The fighting had started with one of Sultan's (Abu Riyad's) bodyguards being shot; Ben and Pauline had arrived in the nick of time and tried to resuscitate him, but he had drowned in blood and was very dead. Fatah had been inspecting defence positions around the camp when the guard was sniped; we'd noticed that the Syrian post was very well sandbagged today which is unusual. We settled in and lots of friends appeared and took photos of each other left, right and centre, with Kalashnikovs.

I went to the hospital to fetch supplies. Borhan appeared having burnt his arm on the gun. Must save water in case the electricity gets bad later and the pump won't work.

Nothing mentioned about the camp on BBC news; yet this morning the BBC was saying that 'left-wing groups, including Amal and the Shia militia, claim that the fighting in the south was caused by PLO and Yasser Arafat trying to establish a military presence again'. Then Arafat said that Syria is trying to destroy the Palestinian cause. On Voice of the Lebanon radio they got the facts right for once, saying that the sniping of the Fatah chief's (Sultan's) bodyguard near Samed caused the fighting from 16.30. And the airport road is closed. So here it is – my intuition about the war was right. I'm so glad I moved all the emergency equipment over to the new house.

22.45 Seven wounded including crazy Hussein, who turns out to be on Pethidine, so when he had Pethidine for the bullet wound in his arm he (unsurprisingly) didn't respond to it and needed something else. Also someone shot in the back.

Big bombs dropping on us at the top of the camp.

30.10.86 Day 2 Thursday

15.00 The ceasefires in Saida are not holding out as the PSP cannot enforce them. The BBC completely awry with its reports on Lebanon since the new war started. Some say it will be a short war as it began over one person and is not a political war, so there will be a meeting today between pro-Syrian groups. But as there is also fighting in Shatila we think it will last longer so that the Amal strategy of the eviction of the Palestinians from Lebanon can be implemented.

Much rejoicing at 15.30 as a ceasefire with the Syrians had been reported on the front street. I remarked that they were probably there to give Amal their arms. At 16.30 all hell broke loose again as it turned out to be a Syrian trick to clear Palestinian fighters from a key position which they promptly handed over to Amal fighters. Then there was a rush through the square outside our house to re-position *fedayeen* on the front street which had been cleared of Palestinians in preparation for the ceasefire conditions.

The death toll is now three: the guard killed by the sniper; a young man killed by an explosion, whose fiancée had begged him not to leave for Denmark but to stay with her; and a *fedai* killed in the past two hours.

Borhan corroborated that the Syrians had negotiated a handover and had given Marruba buildings to the 6th Brigade Lebanese Army (Shia) who opened fire on the Palestinians in the camp; at the same time Amal tried to retake a strategic position from two wars ago. Luckily the Palestinians were ready, so three members of the 6th Brigade are now prisoners of the *fedayeen* held inside the camp.

23.15 This diary is vetted by everyone here.

More young Fatah with Vietnam T-shirts talking about the 'Arab Revolution'. And soon I will 'see babies shot and blown up', and I will 'run away from the war when the big bombs start' – a five-Lebanese-lira bet has been placed on this – but, being British, where would I run? To the Syrians or Amal? We will see.

At Haifa Hospital Pauline evacuated the young man who had been shot in the head in the front street – the entry hole was in his forehead, the exit below his ear. 'All brains,' as Ben said. He died later in the American University Hospital. Mirvat's young friend was shot through the chest but was DOA (dead on arrival).

Treated about ten people. A *fedai* with shrapnel too near his fifth cranial nerve at the side of his head came in, so rather than paralyse him with inept removal by candlelight, I sent him up to the hospital. 'It is our blood,' he said. There are enough nurses now, but not stores. When the fighting started, the Syrian and Lebanese Army soldiers on the checkpoint ran into the camp and are now stuck with the rest of us as the camp is closed. Amal's stated aim is to keep it shut; they are also intensifying efforts to take Rashidiyeh. Reports of Amal gathering up at the sports stadium.

I'm keeping Mirvat's cat for her as her house is on the front line and is unusable. The ambulance that I carefully parked near Samed has a bullet through the windscreen. 'We are looking after the children and babies,' say the young fighters. (No cohesion whatever to my train of thought. Dead tired and I want to sleep.) More *fedayeen*, Suzy and Kalashnikov pictures by candlelight in the 'safe' emergency room that we have installed in the kitchen area in the new clinic. We now have two rooms set up and ready.

120mm mortars being fired on us today. Listening to the tape Ben made of yesterday's fighting is far more alarming than the actual fighting at the time. Sniping closed the side street next to us today for about three hours; bullets regularly hitting the clinic. Lunch at Banan's house; she was terrified at the start of the 17.00 fighting as it felt as though Amal would be everywhere within a few hours.

31.10.86 Day 3 Friday Hallowe'en

After fighting all night and two fighters coming in at 4.30 am looking for paracetamol for headaches from the guns, I was woken again by 120mm mortars at 8.45. A steady trickle of shrapnel, dressings, bruises and someone sniped at by an M-16 in the 'safe' street – a fractured humerus. Mad panic, blood, we all shouted at each other, and what I had previously thought were lab racks turned out to be splints! Food and lights brought to us by *fedayeen*. I'm surrounded by young boys, all high on adrenalin – Fahdi, Ahmad, Ziad, Jihad and Hussein – and Mirvat's cat.

News that there will be a meeting this afternoon of the people responsible for camp security to try to arrange a ceasefire. Amal are reinforcing around the camp; further south the Palestinians are evacuating positions in Saida but will keep a strategic hill in an effort to break the siege on Rashidiyeh.

The side street behind the clinic is closed again today due to sniping. The situation is getting worse; you can see in everyone's faces that it is not going to finish today or tomorrow or the next day either, for that matter. Now that people are dying, the '*gloire de guerre*' that abounded as a result of being able to shoot back at Amal after three months of harassment is gone. Strain everywhere; no smiles or laughing when jokes are cracked, only very occasionally.

I bought up aspirin and Panadol: eighty tablets of Panadol in all, a shop's whole stock; also sixty child's and eighty adult's aspirin (instructions in Turkish).

One old man, 97 years old, got shrapnel in his chest yesterday and died today; also a well-known old asthmatic was brought in dead to Haifa Hospital. So now the death toll is five and nine wounded (Fatah official figures are three dead and seven wounded). Amal refused to let us evacuate one man with cardiac and renal failure this afternoon; there was also some doubt as to whether Ben (or I for that matter) would be able to return if one of us evacuated him in the ambulance, as intelligence strongly suggested that maybe we wouldn't. Another person was sniped at again during the (temporary) ceasefire; that makes three in three days. In times of peace they shoot someone else to continue the fighting. Every day there is the ritual of dialogue – ceasefire – someone shot – war; then it starts all over again. A 21-year-old Palestinian girl was found dead yesterday, having been taken near Beirut, raped and then killed by Amal militia.

Today saw two shrapnel and two gunshot wounds; people coming in with headaches from the noise of the big guns (another big explosion, shaking the house, and gunfire); and lots of jammed little fingers. Amal apparently using tanks against us as well as the 60 and 120mm mortars. Hoping for sandbags to be built tomorrow. Shatila quiet but everyone wants to fight; Amal digging in around them. A quotation from Abu Ammar (Yasser Arafat): 'The Palestinians have armed themselves with education and the gun.'

Tea with tired Ahmad lying on a plinth and 'Evil' Mahmud slumped in a chair. Ahmad reckons on a two-month war; as he is psychic like me, I believe him. One young man told me all about Scotland, the golf courses which are the oldest in the world, and Edinburgh, and the English occupation of Scotland for many years! Aref al Masri loosed off a round of Mirvat's revolver. I could see it coming and told him to take it outside just in time. So now a *yes* to guns, but *no* to fiddling about with them in the clinic – or pointing them at us – rule is theoretically in force. Both kittens dead now, knifed; very upset by it.

Put up my 'art collection' in the clinic today; it includes postcards of Al Aqsa in Jerusalem, women in El Salvador (poor water and sanitation), Guatemalan women weaving, an ANC salute at the graves of four martyrs in Azania, a Vietnamese soldier having a haircut in a field, Jalal talks with the rose (Indian painting), and a seventeenth-century prayer mat.

Mirvat's elderly father, a septuagenarian, came looking for her tonight, wearing a lovely cute smoking jacket and a Haj hat. Aref appeared again at 22.45 high as a kite through lack of sleep, with a can of pineapple rings. He's really a bit on the wild side with tension; sweet kid though.

1.11.86 Day 4 Saturday All Saints Day

12.20 Bourj being shelled with 120mm mortars and B-7s.

Woken at 2.50 by a poor *fedai* complaining of dizziness and nausea. Now the water is running out: the Fatah well pipes are empty. Yesterday women were disconnecting the water pipes in the middle of the street next to the sewer to collect water from them. I wondered quietly if another Tal al-Zatar* was possible. Today there were people out in the pre-dawn darkness at 4.15 trying to collect water first from the drinking well in the square, then from the stand pipe. I watched the night sky, listening to gunfire and *Al Fajr* again, the beautiful constellations bright white against a deepest deepest blue-black sky. People emerged, first as soft sounds then vague shadows, with water canisters banging together, then, as they were still waterless after the round of two or three water pipes, I got water from the flat above the clinic, sitting on a chair to remind myself to keep my head down from the window and the sniper. They give me cigarettes and nuts in return. Fatah food and water; help from the *fedayeen*.

Woken again by Mohamad al Khatib washing glasses. He and the children cleaned the front of the clinic and the emergency room. Now we are more organized with all our supplies sorted on to shelves, and we have oxygen – God knows what will happen in a blast! We also have newly arrived small Elastoplast, thank goodness.

Sniping on the main street to the clinic; Ziad, one of the fighters, and I walked through practically the whole camp looking for bread. It's like a ghost-camp – no one on the streets, deserted almost. Now people will start to bake their own bread, as none comes in from outside due to the fighting.

Later. The Syrian soldiers who ran into the camp when the war started have been shot. (Total figures are now: 4 dead, 12 injured.) Mohamad al Khatib said it will either stop the war or be a big war. Still being shelled with 120mm mortars; need sandbags – and it's raining. Tired through broken sleep. There's no electricity again. Ben thinks that anyone who is not afraid in this situation is mad. More *fedayeen* changing shift and shooting off bullets in the rain with a pistol – singing and high, too. Rubbish is beginning to accumulate everywhere.

Pouring down with rain. Going to the hospital, I was grabbed by the hood of my jacket in a pitch-dark alley. I squeaked out in surprise – it was Ahmad. At Haifa I squeaked again at the sight of Dr Rede who had once more talked his way into a siege via the Lebanese police. There had been the same story as yesterday for Ben trying to organize the evacuation of a man with heart failure: after two hours he came back; evacuation had been refused again. Later that morning there was a ceasefire: even so Amal

*Palestinian camp once in East Beirut, destroyed after a 17-month siege in 1975–76 by combined Christian militias and Syrian Armed Forces. The people were starved and dehydrated, shelled for 6 months. The survivors from the capitulated camp were massacred on their march of safe conduct towards the Red Cross lorries waiting at the Green Line.

shelled us again, but the sick man eventually went out in the car and Dr Rede came in. What a brave selfless man.

The stories Dr Rede told us about Bourj at about 17.00 on Wednesday are hair-raising. He was in a meeting at Shatila camp when Ali, the Public Health Officer, told him to go back to Bourj as there was fighting. He got in a car, but once he got to the airport road it was swarming with Amal surrounding the camp so he had to go back. He told his driver to take him around the side of the camp and that he wouldn't need him any more as he would try to walk into the camp. But he met Palestinians running away from the area. One boy fleeing past him yelled 'Don't go to the camp – run away!' so he then had two agonizing hours wondering whether there was a surgeon in the camp or not as he had met Dr Wissam outside the camp when he was supposed to be on duty. Eventually he telephoned the Norwegians to find out where Pauline was.

Shatila is quiet, only a few grenades, but Rashidiyeh is under attack and siege still.

Morale is high in the hospital here: lots of families living in*, and there is a rearranged emergency room and confidence in the new concrete protective wall, plus *seven* doctors and lots of nurses. I saw the man who was shot by a sniper yesterday in the area where I had parked the ambulance about seven minutes before; also my neighbour who was shot three times in his left leg. Hassan and all the other paraplegics are in the hospital now. A Fatah notable visited and said they would give us anything that we need.

2.11.86 Day 5 Sunday

Rain kept Amal quiet for the night, so we were able to sleep for about nine hours apart from one explosion at 5.45. But I think the days of finger dressings and plasters are coming to an end: Fatah *jihaz*† has warned us of 120mm shelling imminent and still we have no sandbags. Went to the hospital to collect supplies and visit my shot patient.

20.00. The ridiculous building of the sandbags has taken place. They initially appeared at around 14.30, but two fighters came and took them away. We got a message to Ben that Fatah *jihaz* imminently expect Amal to shell us with 120mm, but as we still had no sandbags, I finally waded through flooded sewers in a rage to see Dr Rede. He promised we would have them within the hour, as we needed the signature of Abu Riyad (Sultan) (who I found out from Noora Hammadi was inspecting positions with the *fedayeen* and was probably unlocatable). However twenty bags duly arrived and we set off at dusk to find the sand to fill them. Down at the

*While we were under total siege, hundreds of people took refuge in the comparative safety of Haifa Hospital, sleeping on the stairs, the entrance hall, under beds, store rooms, wherever they could find space.

†Two-way radio.

front street with Nawoosh and Fatah *fedayeen* we walked in the darkening evening through the deserted shells of houses to face the Amal front line across a wall. But no sand there. So we came back with a spirit lamp to our side street through more shells. In the end we dug up a disused tile floor to get at the sand below. No wire to tie off the sandbags so we had to tear up three bandages. All accompanied by much banging and swearing, overturning of wheelbarrows, going round in circles, talking, giggling and falling over. While we were resting, I was tying up one of the young boy's *keffiyeh* (Arab head covering), when a 107 rocket flashed through the square. I jumped and grabbed the boy's shoulders – it gave us all a fright.

We heard on the radio that Amal are preparing to attack us and are reinforcing all around the camp.

They die so they may not die
        They die overlooked
You Angels,
    Pure Ones,
        Liberators,
            Leaders,
                Wise Men. . . .
At this moment, all I ask of you is a miracle,
Just for you to know how to say Goodbye,
Goodbye,
Just a miracle; a Goodbye.

As distant as our souls,
As distant as a journey into the space of the soul.

3.11.86 Day 6 Monday

A frustrating day of cleaning, putting up a kitchen and setting up the emergency room. Mohamad al Khatib started erecting the most unstable sandbags ever seen, which collapsed after ten minutes: eighteen bags each weighing thirty to forty kilos, ie 540 kilos landing on the floor. After we'd listened to the tale of his phosphorus burn in 1982, for which he had twenty-one operations and was threatened with an amputation, Hissam and Rifat, two of the young fighters, offered to help. For skinny boys, they were both incredibly strong, throwing these big bags around with no problem. Safely installed, I ignore the chauvinism as Hissam tells me that I have a lot of cleaning up to do.

Afterwards we went down to the front line just behind the clinic, and looked across to Amal and the deserted front street through sniping holes, and at the Syrians, and up to the unfinished multi-storey Jaloul building from which on the fifth and sixth floors Amal can see over the whole camp. We listened to Kitaeb radio telling us that fierce fighting had broken out around us for the past ten minutes. Strange, we thought, sitting near Borhan's sniping position in the rain and dusk, underneath what seems at some time to have been a hairdressing salon, with the clouds grey over the blasted-out building. We drank tea and listened to tales of *doshkas* (heavy machine guns) taking down walls, or news of sandbags. Borhan was with his young wife, Lydia, who is pretty and dressed for London not Beirut; and he proudly told us she is pregnant, three months already, and wants to help us in the clinic if the war escalates.

A young Palestinian said that even if they attack Amal outside the camps and could win, they would have to repair the damage of the past, as before 1982 they were 'not so good with the Lebanese people', stealing and behaving like cowboys. So now they would have to be more than good, although the debts had perhaps been more than repaid with the atrocities against the camps since then.

A child was shot in the head – the bullet entry wound in his forehead, the exit blew out the back of his skull – he's now very dead in Haifa emergency room: another accident with safety catches. These happen with people falling asleep over guns, pointing them at each other, getting out of seats with hand grenades stuffed in their back pockets, and so on.

Everyone is wearing articles of dead friends' clothing – hats, beads, guns – all from comrades and good, good friends of the same age, who they saw die beside them, leaving widows and unborn children named after their dead fathers. The boys are complaining of getting cold, 'bored and miserable', sitting on the front street line. A young man described his new sniping hole and testing where the bullets would go, and the one person who didn't scatter – 'But why was he walking? Why was he walking?' – then he shot him.

4.11.86 Day 7 Tuesday

Just getting used to the idea of peace; Kitaeb radio had announced that 500 Amal had gone to fight the Baathis and Hizb'ullah and Nabih Berri, the Amal leader, had declared there was no war with the Palestinians in Bourj al-Brajneh (only those in Rashidiyeh it would appear need to be besieged and starved, and have their water cut off as with Tal al-Zatar). 'Evil' Mahmud had come for coffee and was dancing because of the end of the war, and women were going again to the front street. We were all relaxing in hope of the end, and eating too much. Then Amal launched a mortar into the camp injuring several children and killing one aged 10 – brains everywhere again.

14.20 Now all hell has broken loose again. Mortars are going off everywhere, with shrapnel, and the buildings are shaking. I'm here with a frightened small boy, and now a shouting and excited Um Mohamad al Ashwa arrives to say that Ben has gone to Akka Hospital with the one ambulance not damaged. Damn! I'm here alone now. Borhan's friend ran into the clinic to catch his breath and says that Amal first injured the children with *howens* (mortars), then, when one Amal man went to tell the Palestinians to dismantle the sandbags, they shot him dead. By the amount of Amal artillery going off, they seem to have had no intention of dismantling their own weapons. Um Mohamad is persisting in standing at the front door, watching nothing, but letting in a big blast from stray bullets, or B-7 or 104 rockets. Shrapnel everywhere nearby, and M-16s; *fedayeen* running to Fatah positions. I wish she'd shut the bloody door – she's muttering '*J'arab*' and blocking the entrance to the clinic.

16.20 We need another nurse here as Mirvat also seemed to think that Ben had left the camp. She's still running around in this shelling, which is quite close now as the guns seem to be moving round us. Dust everywhere and the noise is making our eardrums crack a little. I keep waiting for a rocket to land above and throw us all around the room. Shrapnel everywhere and us on the floor nervously waiting for it to drop down a little and for Mirvat to return. She says this is the real war now; I think so too.

16.50 *Nine* children playing in the street were injured by the mortar. All around where we were out collecting sand two days ago has been destroyed; everyone thinks that when Amal came to tell us to dismantle, they were checking the positions for accurate mortar shelling.

24.00 Heavy shelling ended after three hours at 17.00; very close latterly, thank God for the sandbags, as we later discovered the house next door is completely destroyed at the front after being hit by five mortars. The upstairs window is smashed, also windows at the side of the house – dust everywhere nearby. Ben is outside the camp; will he be able to talk his way back in? The *fedayeen* will make an attack to win four buildings on the front street at Nawoosh's trench before dawn; all waiting, anxious and laughing a lot from nerves. Of the nine children hit by the mortar, *five* are dead.

5.11.86 Day 8 Wednesday
The night attack for the four buildings did not take place as the political decision for war has still to be taken. Again complacency rules and everyone at the hospital says the war will stop today – not what I have heard.

13.40 Shelling and gunfire again.

6.11.86 Day 9 Thursday
Did not write much yesterday as I got hit by shrapnel at about 17.30. A

bomb landed on the zinc rubbish roof right across the square from the clinic, and shrapnel flew in through the window which we didn't have enough sandbags to protect. Ahmad saw the flash and ducked, catching some shrapnel in his ear and shoulder. I got it in my right arm. We ran into the next room but another bomb exploded, sending dust and rubble through the window grille, so we ran into the back room for safety. Hysteria reigned as we tried to avoid the bombs, with a lovely trail of blood from my arm. I lay down, feet and arm up, and tried to get Mirvat to treat Ahmad before me. He looked shocked, too: it's bloody sore and gives you a real fright. We cleaned ourselves up and decided it was nothing, and got the giggles out of nerves. But after one and a half hours I was still bleeding a fair bit, so I went up to the hospital promising to return in half an hour, but I was taken by Dr Salim for an X-ray which showed a lovely piece of shrapnel sitting between the bones in my forearm, too deep to fiddle about with, or get out again. Dr Rede made me stay in Haifa to rest.

Hannes called to me to see a woman 'with her brains hanging out'. It was Asmahan, the wife of the plumber Darwish al Masri. Four 120mm *howens* landed next to their house and, although the family were hiding, after the second mortar, she tried to run to a safer place and was blown up. I didn't recognize her at all and had to ask Hannes if she had had red hair before it was shaved off. The rest of the family were also injured: Aref got shrapnel in the leg, the little fat girl in the chest, Mohamad in the ribs, and Darwish trunk and feet. The doctors were trying to get Asmahan out of the camp, but Amal wouldn't let them, so they did a craniotomy last night and she came round from the anaesthetic okay.

Came back, cleaned the clinic, ate breakfast. We all have colds, and I've got ringworm as well. The square looks like a rubble-strewn disaster zone and so does our balcony. Abu Taher's house got hit also; it can only be a matter of time before we take a direct hit too. Trying to get more sandbags as the shelling here is persistent.

Abu Musa is in Saida, and the Salvation Front are threatening to shell from the Bekaa if Amal do not lift the siege of Rashidiyeh within twenty-four hours (forty-eight from yesterday); so this war will either be stopped or be really very big.

Ben came back today in a PRCS car with Hassan, braving sniper fire at the airport road. Brave, brave Hassan: they passed carloads of screaming, wounded Amal militia. Watching the battle from the roof of Akka Hospital (which is very near Bourj), Ben said that the camp looked like an inferno with Amal using tanks and anti-aircraft guns and mortars against us. Twelve *howens* were launched against Nawoosh's *mahwar**. We looked like a dust cloud. Even Ben feels unsafe outside. Have to stop here as my arm is bleeding again. A two-month-old letter (from John Gibson) arrived with Ben.

*Nerve centre of a military operation.

7.11.86 Day 10 Friday
Ceasefire today after Abu Musa, against all popular expectation, did bombard Amal in the southern suburbs from the mountains. The ceasefire was announced immediately after the shelling which left two dead and some injured.

Still nothing has been done about more sandbags; I can't do anything yet as my arm is still bleeding when I use it. Oof – another *howen*, landing near Borhan's position, I think. Ben has run out to see to a 20-year-old fighter who was killed by a mortar explosion which blew his head open as he was being taken to the hospital – very dead and from a very poor family. Darwish came by, limping; Asmahan is a little better and his son Aref also looked a little happier. Perhaps they don't realize how ill Asmahan really is.

Noora Hammadi was brought here screaming with Nigar (who comes to the Atfal Somud gatherings on Fridays). A *howen* landed on their friend's house and they both had very extensive shrapnel wounds to the head, limbs and trunk, but nothing permanent, although Noora is in hospital tonight. Mirvat's kitten is everywhere these days, usually sitting on top of my sling. My fingers are straighter today and not so painful, although rotation and wrist flexing are pretty poor. Got nostalgic about Christmas today, after listening to the BBC World Service. Ahmad and 'Evil' Mahmud came to laugh at me and my sore arm again.

9.11.86 Day 12 Sunday
11.00 Two minutes silence on BBC World Service for Remembrance Sunday. . . . We are waiting for the Palestinian attack to start. Didn't write last night, still wiped out. Very unlike me, especially to doze off during nearby *howens* that are shaking the building. Visited Noora yesterday and today to look at her ten shrapnel holes, which are not doing too badly. She is still in a lot of pain, although better. Nigar also came swathed in bandages. All of us in the immediate vicinity of this street now have injuries: Noora, Fahdi, Fahdi's mother (who lost her son and husband in the last war), his sister; Darwish, whose family were named in Gulf newspaper reports of the situation here, his fat middle daughter, whose breathing problems are better today, and Asmahan, who can now speak after her second craniotomy.

Two Amal tanks were destroyed yesterday by the *fedayeen*. The Lebanese radio continued to report that Palestinians were fleeing the camp, which was in itself truly remarkable as we were being continuously shelled and it was nearly impossible to go outside, let alone flee. The *jihaz* had given orders to clear the streets in this area because shelling was imminently expected. In fact it is the Lebanese people from the suburbs of Bourj al-Brajneh who are fleeing.

A young boy, the last son in his family, was blown up by a tank today –

his face was reportedly blown to bits and unrecognizable. He had gone forward to blow up the tank from the *mahwar* and as he crept up over the sandbags to see where the tank was, it fired and blew him up.

Our neighbour Haj Abu Taher, is alone as his wife is on the outside at his brother's house. She is Lebanese Shia and safe with their new baby. 'I want to see my baby; it's enough – stop this war!' His brother was threatened with death by Amal seven times, so he left for Germany. Haj used to live in the clinic house until he bought his brother's house across the square.

22.15 *Merde!* Those fiends have started shelling again – that's about the fifth explosion. (The kitten keeps going for the pen from all angles.) I'm on the floor, having moved from the wall to the middle of the room, sandwiched between the oxygen cylinder and the gas bottle. Highly unsafe – aagh!

Visited Nawoosh's *mahwar* today, after Ahmad had dragged Hannes there but left me behind because I am a woman. So we climbed between the building and over shutters used as ladders and looked through snipers' holes; they offered me a Kalashnikov, which I declined, so they let off a shot and I jumped in the air from the blast. The sound still frightens me a bit as I remember the blast then the pain of the shrapnel – as though someone was trying to tear my arm apart.

Nabih Berri is in Damascus pleading for more Syrian arms to help Amal, and unable to control Daud Daud in the south to call off the siege of Rashidiyeh and stop the mountain positions shelling the southern suburbs in Beirut. Abu Iyad is claiming that all the Palestinian fighters evacuated in 1982 have returned to Lebanon to protect the camps (thank God) and that now PLO policy is that if one camp is attacked they will open fronts on all camps.

Øyvind has been told about my 'wounding', but we made him swear not to tell anyone at MAP in London. If I still have pain in three months' time from it, they sometimes do explorations to remove the shrapnel.

Our friendly M-16 sniper on the left side, not the one who snipes into the square, is shooting fairly regularly at the walls tonight. Rain and cold weather with snow on the mountains, not that we can go upstairs to look at them. We've had autumn with brown leaves falling and the green ones where the trees have been blown up by mortars lying in the rain. Garbage everywhere, the sewage is flooding, and the camp looks a shambles of litter and rubble.

10.11.86 Day 13 Monday

23.20 Well, the *howens* are later tonight: a little one exploded outside the 'kitchen' door and sent me running into the other room. The flash was nothing compared to the 120s further down the street. Borhan says that his

The two sides of Beirut: as seen from the sea on a summer's day, 1985, and the more familiar sight of shelling over the city.

Syrian troops at their sandbag positions, which have already been hit several times.

Another Beirut car bomb.

Borhan and his brother shooting at Amal, April 1987.

Women leaving Bourj al-Brajneh camp by the 'Death' passage. (Saiqa Passage)

A lone woman looking at the sandhills for tanks, walking towards the deserted airport road.

Women having their possessions searched by a Syrian soldier at the checkpoint into Shatila camp. Often the soldiers ruined food, even dismantled batteries during these militia searches.

mahwar has had over a hundred *howens* since last week as they kill too many Amal from there, and the militia are mad at them. They pound this corner too as they know it is used by all the fighters to reach fronts out in the street.

I've been talking with Hissam, who talks about the necessity of a 'counter' revolution to the old stale revolution that most of the young ones don't know. Why are they fighting? What are they killing, maiming, shooting and dying for? All they understand is that they are protecting the children, women and the camps, he claims. They don't want to fight and live this life, apart from necessity. As we said, the Shia/Amal fighters are used as cannon fodder by the politicians for their own ends, irrespective of the age and life of the fighters; so the young *fedayeen* also feel that they too are being used by the old men who remember Palestine, and tell them they must hate and they must kill. 'Why kill him? He is human – like us!' – echoing the young fighter's cry of 'Why was he walking? Why was he walking?' They feel a need to understand and to change.

'I am 21 years old and very tired,' Hissam says wearily. Why does the world want to kill them, eliminate them, maim them and make life intolerable? But they also speak of having a gun, killing or being killed, and want to leave and get away: Hissam got as far as the airport and a cancelled plane for Denmark; Rifat tried to make a trip to Abu Dhabi on a visitor's visa, but it was not renewed and he was sent back. They look to other countries for escape from this continuous terror, yet are refused and refused and refused; harassment and refusal – the punishment for being a Palestinian from Lebanon.

Haj Abu Taher's house was the victim of that nearby *howen*; it landed upstairs on the second floor and he now has no water, the shower was hit, and he looks pretty shaken. We also have water problems as I think shrapnel has either hit the tank or the pipes – we fill the tank up and then it all runs out after two showers and some washing up. And we are grabbing electricity from wherever possible to sterilize instruments.

The streets look more devastated by the day. No gas cylinders left in the camp. Today, four Shia children were killed on the way home from school by a *howen* from the camp. In Haret Hreik today four Amal militiamen killed a Shia man, tortured (?) and probably raped his daughter who is now in hospital. So the residents demanded that they be executed, and Amal produced four hooded men. The residents wanted to see their faces, but Amal refused and eventually the men were led away. It transpired that the four to be executed were not militiamen but either Lebanese or Palestinian prisoners.

The *Washington Post*, reported by the BBC World Service, had recorded a telephone conversation between Chirac and Kohl, who did not deny it, that there is known evidence of Mossad duping Nazar Hindawi into carrying explosives instead of drugs to blow up the El Al plane from Heathrow. What a jolly surprise.

Noora and Nigar's multiple shrapnels are both looking a lot better. So is Fahdi's. Mine is not bad: rotation and wrist flexion still a bit on the lousy side. Also the fingers are very happy to curl up instead of straightening out, and the cut is oozing. Stuffing myself with vitamins and Ampicillin.

Lost the little cat after she was manhandled by visitors and then there was a big *howen* blast as she went outside. I have been looking for her, but a huge black cat and a very pregnant ginger and white cat appeared. The black one is asleep on my arm.

Nabih Berri is panicking as Beirut Amal has agreed to lift the siege of Rashidiyeh, but Daud Daud's militia have refused to cooperate. They have twenty-four hours to do so before more shelling from the mountains by Abu Musa.

11.11.86 Day 14 Tuesday

Hamoudi came to collect his carefully hidden cigarettes – up high on a shelf in case his father sees him smoking at 15, even though he has been fighting for the 'Palestinian Revolution' since he was 5 years old. Ussama has been fighting since he was 4; he is now 10 and also fights with a Kalashnikov.

One dead from a *howen* last night at 5 am while he was sleeping in the *mahwar*. Three dead from Force 17 from a *howen* in the *mahwar* at approximately 15.45; killed immediately, then taken to Haifa. The dead now total twenty. The fridges are full and if possible temporary burials take place in the camp within the hour if the family permit it. After the war the bodies will be moved to the big cemetery near the airport road.

Mirvat took me on a tour of the *mahwars* apart from Nawoosh's. She forgot the stupid *ajnabiyah* (foreigner) doesn't know about war: when we had to run through a trench in front of an M-16 sniper she ran off saying 'Watch me' but as our guide, Monir, pulled me back against the wall, I didn't see what she was doing. When he pushed me out I just ran as fast as I could – shouted at all the way by those watching and holding my headscarf which was falling off – to discover that one never runs upright in that trench; you either go bent double, slow or fast, or you get shot! So I explained that I am always shouted at, I didn't understand what was being said and I hadn't seen what she did. The way out was better; but the story of the 'upright' foreigner is now the talk – and laugh – of the camp. I told her that really they have to explain everything as simply as to a 5-year-old as I have no idea at all and could endanger them through slowness or naivety. So we climbed across buildings in the rain, on bits of doors and shutters, ran upstairs on the left-hand side to avoid the snipers, jumped on and off sandbags, scrambled over sinks and ran that fucking trench. From the sniper holes every part of the front street looks menacing: it's empty of all ordinary objects, with sandbags at certain parts and barricades erected by Amal on the way into town; devoid of life or any signs of life either. Just a creepy, eerie no-man's land.

People have said that the *mahwar* is strange or subworldly, but inside it is full of life: families near to their brothers, sons and fathers. I found Ali al Ashwa and young Ahmad with the shoulder deformity there today. Women were silently flitting from room to room or doorway, playing with children, nursing babies or preparing food all through the fighting. *Narghilehs* (*hokkahs*) and blazing fires with older men sitting round them in chairs or sofas or any remnants left of what were once lovely houses with beautiful paned windows, the glass and wood still intact. Groups waiting in the rain, in slightly decimated courtyards and under battered trees; holes in ground floors dug for sandbags. And the rain pouring down. Boys waving to friends on the third floor of the next building, waiting and playing about on the balconies, waving and falling over in jest. The street outside is watched by snipers through holes covered by bricks or plastic bags, with warm seats and young kids with Kalashnikovs or Daktiriovs. (An explosion – a *howen* – the third today, next door. Ears pop again and sounds of shattered glass and falling shrapnel.) I saw the famous trench running like a dry red sand river between the buildings.

More bread and coffee were brought to the clinic today, and *manaeesh* (Arab bread with herbs and spices) and *filfil* (chilli peppers) from Ahmad, Bassam and Tariq Aishey, and Borhan's family.

18.50 Jamal, Aref and Sami have just run in from the nearest *mahwar*, cold and frightened after a *howen* exploded near them. They were a little shaken but armed to the teeth, and Jamal has a slight shrapnel cut in his thumb to add to his burn from his gun a few days ago.

My arm seems to be progressing; I take a shower if possible then dress it. Can now snap my fingers and the swelling is down.

Waiting for Abu Ammar's speech at 20.30, and expect Amal to black out the camp and shell us heavily in fury at Arafat's existence. They are apparently negotiating with Israel for a Shia canton in south Lebanon. Still no sign of the kitten although the other cats have been visiting. Mahmud came by, rotten with flu – the damp and cold nights have combined to give everyone the *grippe*. I am waiting out the war day by day, trying to gauge tension by whether or not the streets are empty or fighters are running past the clinic door. If there is shouting, bullet-loading and running, then all hell is about to break loose again. I wonder what the snow on the mountains looks like. I can't see them, even though I crept up the stairs to the roof.

Couldn't find Arafat on the TV – no picture or sound*. Now Amal start

*Yasser Arafat appeared on a Christian television station in East Beirut in an 80-minute interview which had been recorded in Baghdad. The PLO leader accused the Syrians of plotting against the Palestinians in league with the Americans and condemned Amal for besieging the camps in return for a Shia Muslim 'canton' in southern Lebanon.

to shell us after Arafat has spoken; they are early tonight. I feel heart-sorry for all the little ones, 10 years old upwards, sitting in the dark in the *mahwars* with those more and more accurate *howens* falling today, after four deaths in *mahwars* in one day. They must be anxious and scared. Hassan (of electrical engineering fame) has translated *mahwar* as 'axis' as in 'nerve-centre', rather than 'front'.

Fierce fighting is reported around Bourj al-Brajneh today, but to be honest I can't tell the difference any more as myths and fiction seem to abound, and when we are shelled, we are shelled, and when we're not, we're not – yet one day it's reported as quiet, the next day as fierce. And people still die. (More shells.) Poor Hassan seemed surprised that I knew that the camp is surrounded and has been for the past fourteen days. He asked me, 'How did you know?' This came because he said he would read Arafat's speech in the newspaper, and, when I pointed out that he couldn't as we were unable to leave the camp, he asked how did I know this?

Some say our war will end tomorrow – I'm really sick of that statement now. Others guess it will last longer than the 45-day war, perhaps three months? When do supplies run out? How will Rashidiyeh last? Arafat's speech said nothing we didn't know already: about Syrians wanting to rejoin the Lebanon to historical Greater Syria, and Israel trying to make a canton in the south.

Spent the later evening with Rifat, Hissam and Ali, talking about death, souls, life; and drinking coffee, and smoking too many cigarettes. Haj Abu Taher came in and we had a heated discussion on the existence of the Arabs and civilization. I like them all very much indeed. We joke about going disco-dancing. Re-read a bit of John-John's letter to keep in touch with whacky unreality and played disco music too loud and sat alone feeling good with myself. I quite like the frightening solitude these days.

12.11.86 Day 15 Wednesday

Ben and Borhan were just remarking how quiet it is and Ben asked if Borhan thought the war would finish soon as there had been no *howens* today. Borhan in his lovely old/young wise way had just replied that he didn't know, as there had in fact been three *howens* today, when two large ones exploded, near the *mahwars* by the sound of the return fire from here. Now we've had five *howens*.

I was woken at 10.20 by the arrival of the cleaning ladies who again did not clean, just made a lot of noise. Banan, Mirvat and Mustafa arrived, bearing *manaeesh* and *filfil* from *shubarifin* (who knows where), so we all drank Nescafé, with me half-dressed, then I went to do Noora's dressing. All went well until we got to her leg: the second large and filthy *in situ* shrapnel had disintegrated into a pus blister about five centimetres in diameter. I deroofed it, slapped oxygen and iodine on it, and prayed to Allah with a lot of gauze and padding.

Back at the clinic, I went up on the roof to look at the sunset and the trees and sky that I haven't seen for two weeks, and, as it got dark, to watch the M-16 bullets hitting the wall opposite: large bright flashes with a sharp clack as they hit the stones. I still can't fathom why they fire so high unless they want to cause stray bullet injuries, as mostly they land at second-storey level. I would hate to have one go through me: the speed is frightening.

Downstairs again, the stars were still shining in the imagined sky of my scarf, lit by the spirit lamp – and I had a visit from my favourite maniac, sucking a provocative lollipop, crouching in the doorway and asking me if I was alone, then leaving quickly as an honourable married man does here. The Al Khatib family are so kind and lovely in a cute and correct way: Borhan and his young wife; crazy Ahmad, with his obsession about our electricity, his mind preoccupied with worry about his new wife, trapped in al-Bass camp; whacky Taisear who always looks *so* eccentric talking in German, English and Arabic; and Mustafa, with his lovely sad eyes and face, disco-dancing today, or generally sitting about here or below the square.

Ate at Um Mohamad al Ashwa's house: fried eggs, *mujuderra* (lentils, onions, rice), and nice bread, with very precious tomatoes and apples. At first I didn't think twice about the tomato, then I suddenly remembered I hadn't seen one for a week, or a juicy peeled apple either. Um Mohamad buys them green, then lets them ripen in the house. Bliss, even though I threw the food all over the place attempting to eat with my right arm, with my lousy third and fourth fingers and rotten rotation. Then I massaged her slipped disc a little with Tiger Balm. I'm always intrigued to see everyone's undergarments here, and watched Um Akram sugar-and-gum-stripping the hairs off her legs. Very fast and expert – lovely all woman. She married at 15 and has three children. The little boy is 4 and has swollen glands, and cries and throws tantrums a lot; she thinks it is fear. She's also very kind and asked me to stay at her house; I said after the war.

More singing outside by men on the way to the *mahwar*. Last night's singing was derisory to Amal and Nabih Berri, and was causing much mirth to its unknown singers. I rescued the damaged Fatah Unity banner from the mud today and will try to get it rehung soon, bullet holes and all. More solitary singing outside, wishing for a lover. A big *howen* nearby, return gunfire and something explosive going out from here.

13.11.86 Day 16 Thursday

The explosions continue; we've had three so far. Children are running in the street and the sun. There's a ceasefire supposedly in operation, but no agreement. We've had an M-16 sniping into the camp and a 60mm mortar at approximately 16.00 from Amal into a street of houses not far up from the front street. As Ben put it, 'It's meant to kill people.' Sat upstairs sunbathing my arm among the debris.

Later, whilst I sat gazing at the candles lit for the Prophet's Birthday tomorrow and remembering two years ago in Jerusalem, Taisear sat down on the step beside me and had a cigarette, and told me about his brother, taken by the Israelis who held him for ten years in Ashkelon jail, then killed him there. 'But "Jerusalem is lost; Jerusalem is lost"; you know that song by Chris de Burgh? "Jerusalem is beautiful, but Jerusalem is lost".' His brother had been working with Fatah resistance in Palestine. He invited Ben and me for tea in the *mahwar* tomorrow afternoon. (Pauline has run away from the blanket security of the hospital and been on a guided tour of the *mahwar*.)

Mustafa is in the clinic a lot, too; all these delightful men, all married, carrying two or three babies at a time. You could tell there was a ceasefire – fewer weapons around, seeing people without Kalashnikovs for the first time in some cases, and in ordinary clothes instead of fighter greens and browns, boots and weatherproofs. Mustafa with his lovely sad face, who never speaks to me, just sits here, at one point picked up Dina's new baby, Hassan Abdu, named after his newly dead father, and held the poor sleeping soul properly, then like a Kalashnikov. I nearly laughed at the sight of this tiny kohl-eyed baby being slung out from the hip. All the newborn babies have kohl put round their eyes in the belief that it will make their eyes get bigger and bigger. They look absolutely delicious with blacked and smeared black eyes. Nigar's youngest boy never knew his father who was killed by the Israelis in 1982 before his birth.

So a lovely normalish day of sitting upstairs, looking at the sky and the moon through the trees, going up on the roof in the dark and looking across the camp blacked out by a power cut, watching tracer bullets from Amal, also blacked out almost up to the Green Line, I guess. Drinking tea, smoking cigarettes and reading poetry. Watching the sun go down and the man in the moon. Trying to treat my ever-present ringworm by candlelight and inventing a ruler splint for night-time to straighten out my wretched third and fourth fingers which refuse to cooperate. Pauline has a suspected perforation of the eardrum from a *howen* outside her window: she is a bit deaf and has singing in her ear.

I've started the Primary Health Care programme slowly again with the Beit Atfal Somud ladies, taking Parakill for the shelters and supplying milk, weighing babies and giving them weight charts with Ahmad's help to write their names in Arabic.

Steps in the Night
Refashion my time
So I know where to die in vain
– A day passed without martyrs –

And the word became the rose of all of us.
So we withdrew.
Go to a beautiful death –
I went.
Alone I was.
You said: We await the funeral with large
wreaths and drums,
And we'll meet in Jerusalem.
Would that Jerusalem were farther from my
coffins that I might accuse the witnesses.
What is it to you! You have gone to beautiful
death;
And the oil city books a seat in the
Merciful's Paradise. You told me.
And blessed be the financier and the
muezzin and the martyr.*

Young Amer from next door shuffled in today very stiffly from his M-16 wound, and very underweight. He comes from the same village as Mahmud Darwish – Birwa, which no longer exists, but which used to be east of Akka, in the north of Palestine.

14.11.86 Day 17 Friday

Writing in the day of the broken ceasefire again – listening to a *doshka* or something very similar firing loud rounds. I surprised myself again tonight, while cooking with Mustafa's help, by discovering that just as in other cities you become accustomed to and don't hear the noise of cars, buses, planes and general traffic hubbub, here I've grown so used to gunfire that I don't hear it. Later this evening, listening to a tape, I didn't hear explosions at the distant Haret Hreik *mahwar* until I stopped dancing and singing. The same for the *doshka*, and explosive bullets.

There are various stories to account for the end of the ceasefire, which never really held in the first place as there were three or four *howens* this morning and sniper fire all day.

The hospital has no antibiotic dressings so I decide, in true Charles Clements style, to manufacture my own – with no electricity. Boiled the gauze; boiled the cocoa tin, scissors and forceps. Put on sterile gloves.

*'Leaving the Mediterranean Coast', from *The Music of the Human Flesh*, Mahmud Darwish, Heinemann Arab Authors.

Packed and squeezed gauze into a cocoa tin. Heated and put in at intervals two tubes of tetracycline in soft paraffin. Then re-sterilized it all in boiling water for an hour or so.

The ceasefire agreements have now been concluded in a definite manner with the buffer force trying to set itself up and dismantle Amal barricades. Or, as Pauline put it, rather succinctly, I thought, 'The agreements are made, the buffer force comes in; the fighting starts again, the buffer force – some run away, others run into the camp, and some get shot.' It was nice to have the idea of peace again, no more killing or worrying about death – on the same scale, that is, as until the Palestinians re-arm there will always be that terrorization by Amal. For the second time there were fewer weapons, people out on the street relaxing and casually dressed instead of in military clothes. Taisear came by and told me that he had worked for seven years in the Palestinian Research Centre before the Israelis blew it up and robbed it. He used to work in the library for Mahmud Darwish when he was still in Beirut. Everyone came in and read bits of poetry in English or Arabic.

The black scissors, good for cutting off clothes fast, have disappeared as has the little ruler. Shit! I hate thieving and they're the only ones I can use without my hand hurting.

The Rashidiyeh siege is still on with Amal refusing to call it off unless the Palestinians who carried out the reprisal raid are handed over. Do they think that fellow Palestinians would hand them over to be tortured or killed? I'm so glad I worked out my theory of annihilation before I came, as it is not a shock but a confirmation to be here. I don't want to leave; the fear of leaving and not being able to return, as with Jerusalem, grips me.

The big black cat is here; at one point we had four very fat cats, all drinking milk.

Everyone is shocked at Wael being shot today; the 'gang' looked so tired and forlorn, sitting numbed and rooted to their places, and unlikely to smile again; this bloody war making them all so unhappy. Even wee Aref looked miserable, so I rubbed his arthritic leg well and truly with Tiger Balm, which seems to help the pain from his old bullet injury; his burn is healing. And Jamal looked weary and slow, ridden with *grippe*.

Stories of Mahmud's Da'ah's grandfather in the Palestinian uprising of 1936, walking with a barrow selling juices on top and guns underneath: he would give out the juice with instructions on how to use the guns. Ahmad's grandfather knew him; Mahmud's grandfather used to prepare all the maps for the resistance in Palestine against the Zionists and Ahmad's grandfather used to coordinate it, so one of them was wanted by the British and still is, and the other the Israelis came looking for in Saida in 1982, now an old man.

Hissam is reading 'The Wound' by Darwish and points out:

The word is the crosspoint
When the grave reaches
When patience reaches
The tips of our love, our death,
The wound is a sigh.
The wound is in the crossing
For a stone coming from far away,
For a dried-up world, for drought,
For time carried on a stretcher of ice.

Eyes of dust
I hear someone saying,
I am the flourishing world,
Of your small history.

Rain on our deserts,
World charged with a dream and longing.

World charged with a dream and longing,
World falling on my forehead,
And drawn like a wound,
Don't come closer, the wound is nearer than you,
Don't tempt me, the wound is more beautiful than you,
The wound is beyond the fate
Your eyes case
On the lost civilizations,
It's left no sails,
Nor islands.*

15.11.86 Day 18 Saturday

Transferring to a new diary which was an old diary from last year with Samira's writing in it before she was married.

Today we woke with an explosion – Amal started a blanket shelling of the camp at 8.00 and it continued until approximately 10.30. It was obviously designed to hit civilians on the streets when everyone is out collecting bread. We were about to wash when a *howen* landed close – a big blast. Then just as I went out to brush my teeth a second explosion with a bigger blast that shattered the closed window up in the wall. The whole area turned into a dust cloud of explosions, rubble and the screams of people wounded. The cries of fear and pain were the most frightening part. As I said to Ben, it didn't 'sound' like that a week ago with the first shelling as people were expecting it, but today. . . . Men came running for a

**The Music of the Human Flesh*, Heinemann Arab Authors.

stretcher and took Ben off through the shells to a woman wounded in the UNRWA building, into the dust and screams. Then Rifat came in with a large shrapnel wound in his right upper arm. As he had bad scarring from previous injuries it was not easy to fix. In the end it looked quite neat, but he was very shocked and kept refusing to take his T-shirt off. We also dealt with an older lady with a bad shrapnel track through her arm: we gave her a pad-sling and sent her to Haifa Hospital for treatment.

Lebanese News at 20.15: the stock exchange closed today. Political activity is at a standstill. Amal stops contacts with the coordination committee until the killers of the two Amal men are handed over. Two dead and twenty-five wounded.

The girl with the neck wound wandered back into the clinic during the shelling, very badly shocked, dazed and shaking. We really have no facilities for shocked people who have been treated but cannot leave, and when we had a third girl carried in with shrapnel in her leg, we were overcrowded. We need to put mattresses on the floor in the second space as a recovery area. In the middle of it all, a young girl wandered in with a baby for dressing – she must have been about 8 years old or so, walking around with a big baby in the midst of the shelling. And Khadija, the cleaning woman, came to work at 10.00 precisely and went away again at the sight of all the gore and general semi-chaos of us trying to fix people a little before sending them up to the hospital. The shocked girl stayed for an hour or so until led away by Mohamad al Khatib who kept running with Mirvat through the shells to get supplies from the hospital.

The water tank is emptying as there are holes in it and the pipes now; I'm listening to the water trickling away down the wall, and to everyone's glee the *howen* landed on the pump motor, which is now completely out of action; so no water soon. All the sandbags came down because of the explosion, leaving a biggish hole in the wall, so people keep falling over them in the dark at the moment. I put a candle out on the steps, but Ghassan ticked me off saying the light would attract shells, and why did I think there was a sniper barricade up covering the alley? So I put the candle out again.

Borhan came by with his wife Lydia, drank tea and examined the damage. He kindly asked me if I was afraid. I replied that when the bomb landed, 'Yes, I was a little afraid.' He said he thought I would be a good fighter and should come to the *mahwar*. Mohamad Ali al Haj and Hissam called to collect pressure pads and bandages. There is to be an operation behind Amal lines tonight and this time they looked deadly serious, so we asked them to let us know so that we can prepare a little. Now people are talking about a two- to four-month war, as Amal are playing games and demanding that those who shot the armed infiltrators be handed over, and until then they refuse to negotiate any agreements. But as all ceasefires seem to be only to reinforce and rearrange their positions, do we care, we ask ourselves? Rashidiyeh is still under siege. It must be hell there now, with less equipment than here to cope with the camp.

My third finger still refuses to move independently. I can lift one and two (with three), but nothing happens with three and four.

Borhan shot out three tanks today with B-7s, which is good as they are doing a lot of damage here, mostly killing the young. Three people have been killed: one girl aged 9 from the Nasser family, a boy, and a young man after three hours on the operating table. I'd forgotten the awful terror people feel when seeing relations or friends injured and children begging us to stop, '*Ya* Ben, *habibi, la, la, hallus, hallus*,'; 'Suzy , Suzy, *tijani, ijri – tijani, la,* Suzy,'; or numbed and unable to move, '*Ya* Ben, *ya* Ben, *tijani, ya* Ben, *habibi.*' ('Ben, my friend, no, no, stop, stop,'; 'Suzy, Suzy, it hurts, my leg hurts me, no, Suzy,'; 'Ben, Ben, it's hurting me, Ben, my friend.')

In fact it's 0.25 on Sunday. I'm lying on the floor waiting for an offensive from Amal which is slightly different to the earlier plan of a Palestinian attack behind Amal positions. We hear this from a Fatah military commander. He used to be a school teacher in Abu Dhabi and refuses to speak English to us as he thinks we should speak Arabic – quite right. A chauvinist, though, half bragging, half worried, telling Ben that he has sex four times a night but that the fourth time is difficult.

Waiting. Sleeping on the cleaned floor; Ben lying on one of the plinths, trying to sleep as we've been advised to do. Everyone promising us reinforced sandbagging *after this war*?! I pointed out that maybe there won't be any wall to reinforce after this war. The front door is in bits of shattered brick also, after this morning's 120mm mortar. Still finding glass everywhere. Antar, the black cat, is still with us. I'm sleeping in my clothes, waiting. . . .

He came at the end of the night, in the season of old age,
He never slept in a bed of myths,
He didn't live his childhood.

An M-16 bullet hits the wall outside.

16.11.86 Day 19 Sunday

9.55 Waited through the night. Nothing happened until 9.00 when Amal shelled us with 160mm *howens*, shaking the room and door, even though far away by comparison with yesterday. More now, shrapnel hitting the roof. These are the mortars everyone said they had, but had not used. 150mm and 160mm – very loud and quite unnerving – breaking up a serene spell of listening to a Maronite service on Lebanese radio with liturgical singing, very beautiful. Learned that the Maronite religion came with a Syrian monk called Maron, who had fled from the Syrian interior. The ecstasy of praising God, the one God, who is with us and who is the man-made excuse for all this killing – yet still the text seemed undefiled, even though the Maronite church here seems to function in a similar manner to the Roman church at the time of the Medicis in Italy, in the sense of fewer spiritual values and more political power and involvement in the governing of the country.

Little Bassam Aishey (brother of Tariq and Ahmad) and his friend appeared to take the stretcher for the gentleman with long-standing renal colic to hospital: quite a fearless family, yet very calm and kind. The stretcher has just been returned with the same panicked banging at the door that comes when –

Interrupted by one injured child being carried into the clinic by his grandmother, then his other relative carried in bleeding from multiple shrapnel head wounds. The child had multiple shrapnel; another small child was brought in and quickly despatched. The injured woman was quite shocked, but the problem now was of her female relatives' concern for the maintenance of modesty while I was trying to clean her wounds effectively and get it done as quickly as possible to be able to put a less than clean blanket over them. But no; the dress lifting was resisted, and every attempt to do a quick dressing was disrupted so it took far too long and she got very cold and shocked.

One of the stretcher bearers from this morning is dead, shot in the chest four times with an M-16. He was rushed past here to the hospital, face down and bleeding from the chest, although some said he was already dead. They didn't position him correctly or bring him here for resuscitation or haemorrhage pads. Everyone shocked and shouting.

Now three are dead today. The mother of the little boy who we saw with shrapnel in the neck this morning (shrapnel from a 240mm that only the Lebanese Army has): it hit the house and apparently their room was destroyed and covered in blood. The old man who Ben was treating died of heart failure in the night before he could be taken to the hospital. And now that young man. They are all so young; so young. Every day the young are dying. And yet an orthopaedic surgeon refused to come into the camp saying he didn't want to die here. Well, neither do any of us frankly; and he could help so many. So the Lebanese shells are being used against us now – bigger and better – as though they are not already trying hard enough to kill and maim people in the camp. And the radio said Amal had stopped shooting. . . . More feet running past the clinic, and the clanking of guns against belts or bullet packs.

The sad man, Mustafa al Khatib, came in and sat for a while, refusing coffee; he has just come back to tell me the young man is dead, shot through the back into the chest. The problem here is that there is nowhere for us to cry – others can go home, speak to relatives and family, cry in peace, and alone or together. For us there is nowhere. Always people can come in and find us going to pieces; and we can't show this. I went outside to cry; Mirvat was crying too and Mustafa left and went to the *mahwar*. The young man, Mohamad, was 25, his wife of two years is now six months pregnant with their first child, another who will never know his/her father. He was sniped from the side while looking for a tank position; he forgot to look right and left, only looked ahead. He was much loved in the camp.

I'm boiling water for a wash. When will it run out? Got bread and coffee from the hospital and more supplies. Ben and Mohamad got caught

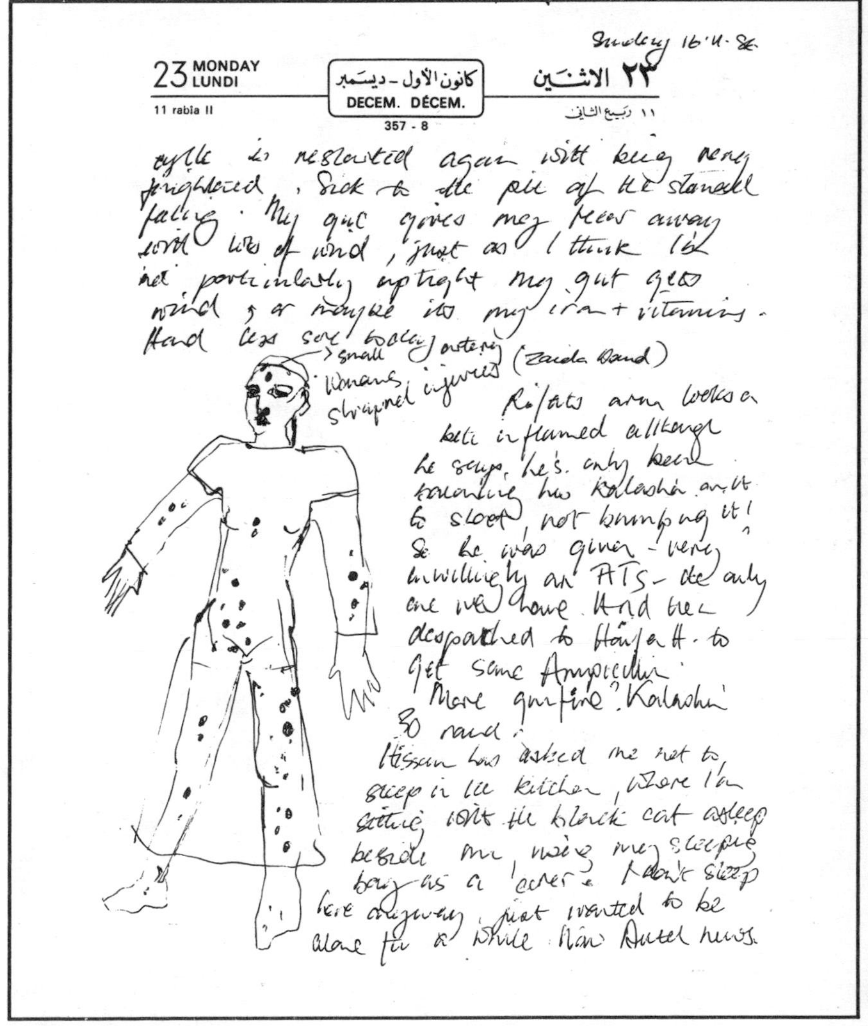

Sunday 16.11.86

23 MONDAY LUNDI | كانون الأول - ديسمبر DECEM. DÉCEM. | ٢٣ الاثنين

11 rabia II | 357 - 8 | ١١ ربيع الثاني

cycle is restarted again with being very frightened, sick to the pit of the stomach falling. My gut gives me heat away with lots of wind, just as I think I'm not particularly uptight my gut gets wind, or maybe its my iron + vitamins. Hand less sore today

> small arteries
Woman's shrapnel injuries (Zaida Daud)

Rifat's arm looks a bit inflamed although he says he's only been polishing his Kalashin and it to sleep, not bumping it! So he was given – very unwillingly an ATS – the only one we have. And then despatched to Haifa H. to get some Ampicillin.
More gunfire? Kalashin so rand.
Hissam has asked me not to sleep in the kitchen, where I'm sitting with the black cat asleep beside me, using my sleeping bag as a cover. I don't sleep here anyway, just wanted to be alone for a while. Now Autel news.

beneath gunfire onto the street and ran into a shop for shelter. They had thought the mortars had started and ran out from the hospital, changed their minds about turning back, then carried on on adrenaline. Mohamad says he doesn't feel his leg pains him when he is running like that.

Everyone is sad and low, too many hurt and dead. The child whose mother died needed a laparotomy today.

Ahmad, Hissam and Mohamad Ali al Haj have just criticized my coffee for being too sweet. I told them that they didn't have to drink it. Hissam called me over to whisper in my ear, 'Why is it that you seem very beautiful today?' I replied, 'Because you need to get out of this camp and live a bit and enjoy yourself – that's why!'

I can hear women on the street in the dark now; they are running and talking, '*Jalla*.' ('Quickly; get going.') More footsteps outside and heavy gunfire. I love being so close to the front line; most people passing are going to Arsan's *mahwar*, although in the morning women and children go down there to fetch water. When a shell landed today, women ran with water pots on their heads.

BBC World Service at 19.00: the Israelis have raided Ain al-Helweh, bombing it for fifteen minutes claiming it to be an Arafat base. One dead and six wounded. In East Jerusalem, after a funeral procession for an Israeli student stabbed to death in the Muslim quarter, Israelis went on the rampage, attacking Palestinians. Al Fatah have claimed no responsibility, but the Israelis for some reason are claiming it was the PFLP.

Another tank shell has hit the *mahwar*. The tanks have been used all day. I was jolted out of my lovely hot wash by two tank shells landing on the front line; it certainly brings reality back – and fear. Some parts of the day are spent being very frightened, other parts in being moderately frightened, and the last part in not particularly caring until something shocks you and then the whole cycle starts again with being very frightened. Sick to the pit of the stomach. My gut gives my fear away with lots of wind; just as I think I'm not particularly uptight, my gut gets wind – or maybe it's the iron and vitamin tablets.

Hissam has asked me not to sleep in the kitchen where I'm sitting with the black cat asleep beside me, using my sleeping bag as a cover. The kitchen's not safe as it isn't reinforced. I don't sleep here anyway, just wanted to be alone for a while. Another big explosion near the *mahwar* by the sounds of all the immediate gunfire that followed.

Ahmad was criticizing the fact that the little kids watch videos all day, but at the moment what else can they do? They can't go out into the streets for fear of *howens* so it takes their minds off the war to watch films and escape a little.

17.11.86 Day 20 Monday

The Fatah leader has just come by, promising me a flower in the morning and telling me I'm beautiful. A woman was sniped through the head by an M-16 today: it blew the back of her head out. A child of 1½ had both its eyes destroyed by shrapnel; Haifa requested evacuation to a specialist hospital but Amal refused – refusing medical treatment to a small baby! A young man being operated on for shrapnel died on the table just as they were closing him up. The relatives forgot to mention that he had previously been treated for a heart complaint. Pauline is very down about this young one in particular. There is no fighting at Shatila camp but the situation there is the same as prior to the Rashidiyeh siege.

Assad was killed by a *howen* at 10.00 as he was stepping into the courtyard to cross over to Nawoosh's *mahwar*. He helped to build the walls here. His friends Hissam al Ashwa and Tha'ir Yunis also came in injured. We had the tea-drinking ritual of death for Assad, listening to the voice of a small boy singing on the radio.

Baashar, one of the fighters, comes running through the deserted streets with his 40-day-old baby to see us about her cold. She is called Maryam. He looked so paradoxical, with his Kalashnikov slung round his back with its shoulder rest out, holding the baby with little pierced ears in a blue blanket and an orange and buff jumpsuit, and his Alpine-style hunting hat on his head, that he waited for three minutes for me to take a photograph using the last of my slide film.

I went to the *mahwar* to see Nawoosh and do his dressing but he wasn't there. One of the fighters asked us for first-aid packs; Mirvat and I took packs to three *mahwars*; we crossed the place where Assad died this morning, the courtyard that Rifat took me across the other day. We went as far as the furthest *mahwar*, running the trench, then further on to run a courtyard with a sniper over it as well; quite a lot of M-16s and Kalashnikovs in action. Sat and had a cigarette, then ran the courtyard and trench again, my head still not low enough, and the staircase too. Up and down, over zinc and sandbags. Then we went to the hospital, oblivious to the fact that the *howens* we had heard earlier were actually falling on or around the hospital itself. The streets were deserted, just as earlier today they were empty or had people only moving by running fast from one building to another. Very spooky. People are obviously psychologically terrorized by the *howens* and sniping now. A week ago we were still quite *ma lesh* (so what) about it, but now we are feeling the effect of all the injuries and deaths, and fear is in our heads. The roads are beginning to look quite destroyed: every few blocks there are rubbish and holes.

We collect splints from the emergency room and then visited Assad in the fridges. I couldn't see him clearly, but saw Mohamad from yesterday – he looked cold and dead in plastic. Soon they will maybe have to burn the dead again as the fridges are full: two bodies to each section and wrapped in plastic. Cremation is against the teachings of Islam.

Later: 22.15 The Palestinians have shelled six Amal positions near the camp on the airport road and up to the the Kuwaiti Embassy using 2m Grad rockets from the mountains. We listened to the whizz of the rockets flying overhead at about 16.00 to 16.30 and at 17.00 Amal asked for a ceasefire.

23.00 Ceasefire (?) is soon to end after only six hours, but it was nice while it lasted. We remarked on how you could tell there was a ceasefire as people were walking about smiling, laughing, relaxing a little, despite the deaths and injuries, slightly secure in the knowledge that perhaps for a few hours there would be no more. We all commented on it. Haj Abu Taher had come in to give us pickled beetroot or turnip or something like that.

The Fatah commander came back to see Ben, although now I suspect that one of the reasons he has problems the fourth time round is that he indulges in too much cocaine! More explosions now and the sound of running feet again. I think they are shelling B-7s on us all along the *mahwar* line. Three little boys come to the clinic after the bang as one of them had cut his tongue: much giggling. He said he was 17½ but I think he was 5 or so. Have just cleaned the floors again after about twenty people visited at pancake hour, and should really clean down the trolleys before I go to bed. It's always busy immediately we get up; there are people before we can brush our teeth and we frequently do dressings in pyjamas, with Ben asleep on the couch and the beds still on the floor. This is the disadvantage of living in your work quarters: people just walk in at all times, regardless of whether you are dressed, undressed, asleep or whatever.

We got a new motor for the pump today thanks to Mohamad al Khatib. Although he is dogmatic and noisy, he's very instantaneous, and harassed the hospital to get us electricity and the new motor for the water pump. It's quick and works away in the large crater left by our 120mm carefully covered with the toppled sandbags. Tonight with the ceasefire I went out with the spade to clear up some of the rubble left from our *howen*. A young fighter, probably appalled at this woman clearing the road with a spade in the dark, immediately offered to help and finished it for me. It's lovely how everyone contributes: a fighter came into the clinic, weaponed up to the eyeballs, sat and had a cigarette and some tea, and promptly started helping to fold the gauze for sterilizing. We have quite a lot of fighters now from Arsan's *mahwar* directly down the road; they come to boil tea and they frequently return with cans of corned beef or cream to give us. Yesterday Nawoosh gave us cigarettes which we already have in abundance from Borhan; Rifat appeared with cakes.

This morning had a dreadfully surreal quality to it: the awful desertion of a normally noisy little square and us all sitting inside a darkened sand-bagged room, examining a new Palestinian baby with Kalashnikovs, listening to Satie and grief for Assad who had just bled to death an hour before in the courtyard. The furthest *mahwar* is so difficult to get to that it would take ten minutes just to get as far as the clinic here even once they got on to the streets.

18.11.86 Day 21 Tuesday

Today started with a *howen* at 7.00 – it woke me up despite not being nearby. I went back to sleep until 8.30 when four to five big *howens* landed nearby, and thinking of the other morning I got up and dressed quickly. The *howens* were less severe during the day although Ahmad Aishey said that one had fallen again on Haiduce at 18.00. No agreement in Damascus and the Israelis are shelling Rashidiyeh from the sea. Some rockets went into Palestine from the south.

Arsan (the commander of the nearest *mahwar*) was shot in the chest and, ignoring his fighters' pleas to go to the clinic first, ran past us to the hospital. As this was the third person in three days we were mad as hell. He had a bleeding chest wound, no pad, pressure or anything, and there was chaos as his fighters ran after him, fearful to disobey their leader. His little brother Aref tried to get him to come here, but to no avail, and needless to say he ended up a little shocked. So we got hold of the leader, second in command to Sultan, and there is now an order out for the injured to come here first for assessment, rather than die on the way to the hospital. The doctors have said that the best-managed patients are those that have come via us at the clinic.

The sad man came, very sleepy having slept in the *mahwar* last night. He fell asleep on one of the plinths, so I gave him a pillow then put a blanket over him. He is still grieving for his wife whom he loved very much: she was shot just before the beginning of the 45-day war. He has two young daughters, one 2½ and one 1½.

Ahmad said the *howens* are now reaching the streets with more accuracy. In the previous wars they bombed the houses, but now they are trying specifically to kill people, which they can do more effectively by killing us outside, and aiming at the ground floor where people are hiding downstairs from the mortars. Apparently Amal have better plans of the camp now, hence the greater accuracy. They also drop a small mortar to cause injury, then the larger one to hit more people as they come to help or look at the injured, similar to the car bomb trick.

19.11.86 Day 22 Wednesday

I had a political discussion of sorts from midnight last night until 2.30 with Rifat, Issam and friends over much-prized coffee. I'm still surrounded by people not doing a lot, but using the clinic as a social centre. The only place to escape from constant fairly trivial demands is into the shower. I'm trying to do some emergency room studying.

20.11.86 Day 23 Thursday

I went with Samira to do her grandmother's dressing: she has a very large radiation burn from treatment at the American University Hospital. They were extremely careless with the dosage and the burn is now infected. I put Flamazine (medication for treating burns) on it and covered it with a large pad and support bandage. She was frighteningly passive about the whole procedure, as though she had no interest in it whatsoever and would prefer not to know or see. She has a lot of pain too so I sent Samira back with some painkillers.

Aref and Jamal have just visited as Aref has fallen yet again on his pretty dreadful legs, so I looked at the damage which was nil, and massaged Tiger Balm into the other leg, giving him a hug beforehand and telling him how much I enjoyed it. Jamal says we both enjoy his leg rub!

Khadija told me today that she is a three-month trained nurse and has worked for three years in nursing. Why didn't she tell me sooner? She can't work in the hospital as a nurse because she doesn't speak English, but neither can a lot of people there either, so I think it is just hierarchical elitism, the plague of nursing.

The bad news today is that Amal are blowing up the buildings that obstruct the shelling of the camp, directly in front of the *mahwars*, or those that they are frightened that the Palestinians will take and use as a front line. The unnerving part is that they detonated a row of six or seven buildings along the street for a period of two hours or so, one after the other at ten- to fifteen-minute intervals. A foretaste of what is yet to come. Already the damage is quite extensive just around this area and as far as the old clinic: rubble and holes in buildings at ground level, where people shelter. Two more *howens* as Mahmud and I ran from fetching cocoa from his shop: we ran into an empty house near the *mahwar*. Then another landed, then a third just after we reached the clinic.

21.11.86 Day 24 Friday

Feeling exhausted and just about to drop into bed when boys from the *mahwar* came visiting, so I sat on my mattress to talk. Then Taisear and the sad man came in to say that maybe there would be a ceasefire, as Saudi radio seemed to think there was an agreement being made. So I crawled under my sleeping bag, forgetting that there was a Kalashnikov lying at the end of it: I wondered why the bedspread was so heavy and I couldn't get my feet to the end of the bed. Anyway, I slept until a young man who had had a close miss with a blast came in thinking maybe he had shrapnel in his eye.

Quite heavy shelling again this morning: three shells dropped while I was in the middle of paying a home visit by candlelight to the old lady who got the chest wound last week. One landed nearby, rattling the windows. Since the buildings were dynamited yesterday, the tanks now have more room to manoeuvre directly opposite the *mahwars* on the front street; fairly regular shelling. The boys said that at night, as well as being in more exposed positions, they now listen to the tanks moving into new sites for bombardment. There is in fact no semblance of an agreement between Amal and the Popular Committees or Jumblatt, so this will continue for a while yet, waiting, waiting. . . .

Iman, Mohamad's lovely wife, and Borhan's wife Lydia brought me some food, so I gave them iron tablets and the remainder of the vitamins as they are both pregnant. Iman wants a little girl this time as she already has the three boys: Ahmad, Mohamad and Ibrahim. The baby should come soon as it looks quite head down and forward.

Tank shells have hit the unprotected first floor of the hospital, into the patients' rooms; Amal were unable to reach this before. Pauline spoke with Øyvind on the *jihaz* yesterday. Iain has reached Britain from Saida, Gerard has also left and is in Britain: just when they are really needed. Kristine had left for Norway. I really miss Maureen; I caught myself joking as I used to do with her, and realized how much I miss her and will miss her when the bloody siege is lifted.

The Israelis have carried out a search raid with the SLA in south Lebanon. There is confusion about the suicide bomb attack on UNIFIL's Fijian contingent yesterday, and about the Israeli raid: as yet no confirmation of claims that an Israeli plane was shot down.

22.11.86 Day 25 Saturday

A quietish morning with the odd mortar until we got a Kalashnikov injury from the Marrubba *mahwar*. The wounded man weighs about fifteen stone (over a hundred kilos), so God knows how they managed to carry him across two sniping fields, up two staircases, over the sink, along the balcony, between two buildings and along the street to the clinic. He was bleeding quite a bit from the exit site but the entry was fine. I later heard that he is lucky to be so overweight as the bullet went in and travelled through all the fat, missing his spine and vital organs, and then went out. No operations needed and he's as well as can be expected after shock and reasonable blood loss.

My lady's radiation burn is spreading, as these wretched things do, from inside, upwards and outwards. So each day more skin is coming off and the dressing is getting bigger. After my home visits, Jihad came running to fetch me to visit her sister who was the lady badly injured in Sunday's shelling. I said I would visit again tomorrow. I had coffee (a luxury) before moving quickly home in the darkening streets at 17.15. Now I have a round of three home visits for tomorrow morning: the old lady with the chest injury, Samira's grandmother and Jihad's sister.

Mustafa, the sad man, visited and gave me a ring that he usually wears on his little finger and fitted my thumb. He put it on my ring finger which is the same for the Arabs, as he showed me. Taisear looked stern and joked that he was now engaged to me.

Visited by Amer the sniper, looking very tired and complaining of ureter pain and *grippe*, and an equally worn-out Ahmad Aishey, who is coughing yellow and black from B-7 flames: I gave him antibiotics.

23.11.86 Day 26 Sunday

The hospital was shelled by tanks again yesterday. No further damage. The blood bank, X-ray, lab and doctors' rooms are all on that side, not to mention the patients. The physio room took a hit two days ago – again.

There is a problem with flies now because of bad sanitation, sewers being hit by *howens* and UNRWA not functioning. I need iron and vitamins for the pregnant ladies. The black cat is still with us – needing protein too.

Sami asked me for a plaster which I thought he needed for a cut finger. No, no, no, plaster for bombs, grenades to be precise. So I duly brought out the right size of plaster for his and Jamal's grenades to be safely strapped.

Then three home visits for dressings that took two hours with an extra thrown in. There are seven children in Zaida's family, four boys and three girls, who are all living in a lovely traditional household with handwoven carpets, and the women knit beautiful jerseys. They asked to make me one, so I offered to buy the wool. Then we ran on, crunching freshly roasted coffee beans, to my irradiated lady who is now quite unwell, with nausea, diarrhoea, shivering, night fever and the large burn site. Then to the little old lady with the chest injury, who is only mobilizing as far as the shower, so it was gently suggested that she should walk to the clinic in two days' time.

Amer al Khatib was shot yesterday in Marrubba *mahwar*. He was taken straight to the hospital with an M-16 injury that is extremely severe: the next ten days will be critical for him.

The news of Rashidiyeh on the radio was very bad, but apparently the camp is stronger than it's made out to be. News of Saida is more encouraging by *jihaz* than by radio. Reports of fighting in Shatila too, so now all the camps in the Lebanon are involved in war.

Hissam and Aref al Masri brought coffee, batteries and a comb for my hair. We decided Hissam was having a love affair with death as he said he could see no future for himself here. I was visited later by Rifat, Mohamad al Haj and some of the other boys. We talked about Scotland and my family and the mountains, and the situation of being under siege: how the camp has been surrounded now for the past one and a half years and movement is limited to one visit out per month. We also talked about how in previous wars they were fighting, but this is a defensive siege war and, they say, the worst so far, as the days are spent watching and waiting for movement. If they see any, they shoot – with guns or a B-7 – but most of the time is just watching and waiting.

The news from Saida is that the Palestinian offensive started at 18.00 to take Shia village positions and besiege them in exchange for Rashidiyeh; it was still going on at 22.00. Good news. Also rockets were being fired from Palestinian positions in the mountains.

The milk has finally run out, and there is also a sustained power cut and perhaps water shortages; so no sterile gauze unless electricity is restored early on tomorrow.

24.11.86 Day 27 Monday

No milk or electricity. A *howen* exploded at the entrance to the hospital: a child standing at the door had her foot blown off with a traumatic amputation and there were about another eight fairly severe casualties. The NORWAC ambulance parked outside is covered with shrapnel and has two deflated tyres: it has no rear windscreen because of snipers' bullets.

Fahdi's mother and sister Lena are fine now, but Samira's grandmother is ill and feverish today with a cold. The burn looks less infected and has not spread today, but is still extremely tender. I'm dosing her with Ampicillin to try to cover a depressed white blood count effect from the radiotherapy; she's finished her other drugs, none of which we have in the camp now. I am doubtful about her resilience to all this.

Monir has promised radishes and green onions tonight from the gardens of houses near the cemetery. The rumours of burning the bodies are unfounded. They have either been buried near the hospital, or ten have been hastily buried in the main cemetery under guard by night, a very dangerous procedure due to its proximity to the airport road.

We have been warned of an impending mortar attack from now until 17.30 and are to stay indoors. There is still fighting around Magdoushe due to the Palestinian offensive and now their capture of the town. This is the best news since the beginning of the war.

22.50 Well, the expected attack has not yet taken place, although there are supposed to be large numbers of Amal amassing on the airport road and front street. The situation in Rashidiyeh is as bad as ever with Amal also trying to gather there. Thank God for the Palestinian offensive. It was Mohamad Ali al Haj who woke us up at 6 am on his way home from the *mahwar* to tell us the news about the taking of the town which is quite large, and once the Palestinians had taken the internal security building they broadcast for the residents to stay indoors to avoid the fighting. He says he woke up most of the camp to tell them: he'd heard the news on the *jihaz*.

I enjoy the home visits very much; if it weren't for the *howens*, they would be a real pleasure. It's good being able to follow a dressing through various stages.

Rifat and Mohamad visited and had coffee. Rifat's arm is still a bit messy; as Dr Rede says, 'don't suture shrapnel', it's done no good. Aref al Masri gave me a Kalashnikov-dismantling lesson; I'm too weak to hold it up front and fire, but I've wanted to learn for a long time. I'm now the big sister to Banan, Mirvat, Aref and Jamal, Rifat, Mohamad and Hissam.

25.11.86 Day 28 Tuesday

15.30 Heard tanks moving outside from half midnight to 1 am last night. Assad has now refused to join negotiations as he is angry about Magdoushe. The 6th Brigade are now amassing around Sabra and Shatila. Jumblatt is still making fairly negative statements. The BBC World Service is omitting names of villages and towns, but broadcasting very biased pro-Amal reports.

At Zaida's house, Fatima and I talked about poetry; she too loves Tawfiq Sayad and Mahmud Darwish. If I go later to the house tomorrow, I can stay to read with her, *Insh'Allah*. She wants to study to become a staff nurse, but her brother thinks she should be a secretary. She is 19 and bright, but before the war there wasn't enough money for her as her brother was in Spain studying, and the problems of Palestinians trying to travel around West Beirut even to Akka Hospital were also a hindrance. I interrupted her prayers today. It's the first time I've seen a woman praying; I usually see only men and in public, not women in the house.

Ben has amoebic dysentery and is on fried *zatar* (thyme), a traditional cure which in theory makes the gut environment so acid that the amoebae can't survive.

Iman, Mohamad's wife, still hasn't had the baby. She married at 15. They all seem to take young wives. Mustafa also married his wife when she was that age. Iman is only 23 now and this is their fourth child; Ahmad, the oldest child, is 7.

We can hear the explosions and gunfire in Shatila now; the sound is travelling across and mixing with the noises of our explosions up at the top of the camp near the airport road. Nearly all the camps are fighting except Mar Elias, as there is gunfire into the camps in the Bekaa Valley now too. But, as one person put it, Amal and Hizb'ullah are movements, not a single people united as the Palestinians are by a common land and need to live in security.

Even candles are getting scarcer. Taisear, who told me off for burning gas unnecessarily a few days ago, has now gently told me that I have two candles burning.

22.45 The *jihaz* is warning everyone to be ready for an expected attack as the outcome of the Damascus meeting will decide when it will begin; maybe at 3 am, or maybe now. But we've to stay indoors and be careful, and be prepared at the *mahwar*. Certainly the range of attack now signifies a long war and, as one of the preconditions for a Palestinian withdrawal into the camps is the lifting of the Rashidiyeh siege, then it will be the long war we are now sitting out.

Zaida has asked her husband to make me a big sweet cake after the war as he is one of the sweetmakers of the camp. (More explosions near Shatila.) And Taisear has promised a good Christmas tree with lights and decorations. I hope we are all still alive after this war. I have dreams, very strong, about being suddenly at home and trying to get back here. I *must* arrange my residence permit in January before leaving the country; I must arrange my return. I think the dreams are paranoia about not being able to come back. I suppose they may know at home about the fighting now, as when Sabra and Shatila are attacked it is usually reported on the BBC news, and they may also mention Bourj now. More sounds of distant explosions carrying on the wind.

26.11.86 Day 29 Wednesday 4 weeks
No milk, electricity, bread, tap water. Visited by a young fighter, Samir, with beautifully spoken French, and his very Phoenician-looking friend, Ghassan, who has a head wound. We just lifted the flap of skin where zinc shrapnel had shoved it up; you could see the hair underneath perfectly. He went off wishing us courage in French. He is with Abu Suhail, the Fatah political commander in the camp, who came to see how he was.

Now we are listening to further manoeuvring of tanks outside and there have been two mortars recently. The whole camp is on *instanfah* for an attack. Each *mahwar* has fifty to eighty people in it at present until 6 am – a spooky and tense feeling as people are always injured eventually, usually through *howens*, and we are all fearful of injury and death to ourselves and those we love, and the children, the innocents.

7.00 We are sitting listening to the BBC World Service news. We have been shelled the shit out of since 6.15 – tanks, *howens* and B-7s. So far most fire seems to be coming from the airport road direction, but already there is lots of shrapnel flying through the air, and bullets, tank projectiles and God only knows what else. When the BBC World Service book review programme recommended *Wanted: Two Guns for a Room*, published by Unwin at £4.50, for anyone in need of a laugh, we simultaneously looked at each other and suggested it with nervous hilarity.

9.50 The fighting reportedly started at 5.30, with sporadic shelling around the periphery of the camp and then united shelling from 6.00. Just shows how adapted we've become, sleeping through explosions. Every shell now brings down bits of masonry and one next door considerable parts of Hassan's house and glass. Most of it is directed around the hospital as the tanks have more manoeuvrability around there. More people running at full tilt around the side of the clinic; more people still going towards Borhan's or Marrubba *mahwar*. Coming down to Arsan they skid to a halt on the corner of the square. The *jihaz* has decoded that attacks will take place here or at the hospital. (More shelling.) The assault at Samed and the cemetery was pushed back early this morning. (The Israelis have just gone through the sound barrier – two planes overhead – came early to have a look.) The news is that there is still fighting around Magdoushe and it has now spread to the camps near Beirut. Funny – I always consider Bourj and Shatila as in Beirut, but news reporters still use the Lebanese pre-civil-war references that exclude the southern suburbs from the city.

Zeinab, the 14-year-old daughter of Omer Salim, has turned up for work with her mother bringing her to the clinic. Ahmad and Mirvat are both running around in the *howens* as usual. If we get a *jihaz* there will be no excuse for their antics and fatalism.

19.06 Amal again attacked down in the front street and up at the airport road in an Iranian-style frontal attack after the heavy tank shelling to soften up the *mahwars* in advance. Aref al Masri and Mohamad al Khatib told us that after the shelling they sat in the *mahwar*, relatively protected, and just mowed them down with machine-gun fire. Ghaleb Abed was shot in the Marrubba *mahwar* with an M-16: hit through the femur, radius and ulna. He is stable in Haifa Hospital. There were 130 Amal killed today at Magdoushe according to *jihaz* reports.

Tea at the Al Khatibs' was a nice break; I played with Ola, who is about 5 months old, the littlest child of their sister Gamili. I fetched her some extra milk and watched Borhan's mother Um Mohamad and wife Lydia sorting out lentils, also for baby food. Mohamad's littlest boy, 2½-year-old Ibrahim, was being taught to pray. The main problem was that the mat was bigger than he was and he couldn't get it straightened on the floor, or fold it up. He is so little, also, that he can't kneel yet, so he stands and bends double, touching his head off the ground. All the kids have skinhead haircuts to protect them against lice.

It was so peaceful to sit in a house and look out of the window at the sky turning blue, then white-gold in the late evening, through a decorated grille, and think how autumn and winter should be. Sifting lentils without bombs.

Later, as I did Hissam's dressing, *howens* exploded further up the road, so on his advice I returned to the clinic instead of going further up to Zaida's house. There was a sniper barricade re-erected on our street; as it got dark there was much swearing as people fell into and over it, with the *shebab* (young men) stepping over and ignoring it.

20.15 The BBC World Service: Jim Muir talks from Cyprus about a 'limited Amal operation against Bourj al-Brajneh camp – the first since

June'!? We are listening in disbelief. This is news to us: after 1000+ shells (a Kitaeb/Amal statement) fell on Bourj al-Brajneh today, we were under the impression it was a full assault – and that there had been a war since four weeks ago. Over 1000 shells and still falling. Borhan's tale of creeping across the front street to put TNT beside the sandbags at the Amal building, then creeping back to the *mahwar* to detonate it, is one of ridiculously high courage. It ranks next to the burials at night and the 'most dangerous chives on earth'.

Good grief! Someone is using the side road, clambering about over the rubbish and rubble from collective *howens*.

Still no electricity and no explanation why as yet either. No bread now as there is no fuel left to bake it. I saw yet another eardrum today, perforated and infected from the blasts. It belonged to small Samir Hallimi: he had blood behind the membrane, and lots of green and yellow pus.

22.00 They've started shelling again with tanks. Apparently all day it was just tanks, mortars and B-10s (from jeep launchers). Alone with the collywobbles and the usual sinking stomach, trying to decide where to stand in the room for safety, with a hastily lit cigarette, wishing fervently for some company. Any company will do. Trying to think the sad man into visiting. I think it is the sight of so much shrapnel from first-floor rooms on the street that scares me. If they weren't shelling the streets it wouldn't be so unnerving. My concentration level is now well gone and shivers are running down my arm from being so unnerved.

23.00 The shelling stopped again after ten minutes and the company arrived in the form of Rifat, Hissam, Mohamad al Haj, Ahmad, the brother of Mohamad Ali, Mahmud and a friend, who came looking for some soluble aspirin, which they are offered instead of a Baralgine injection. Again the same story of headaches commonly caused either by *howens* or by firing B-7s, despite keeping their mouths open – as if smoking a cigarette – to lessen the effects. Another man drops by to talk politics and explains to me that Arafat is good and crazy; crazy because of all the wars. The man's been a *fedai* since '66 when he would be about 14 years old, and remembers 1973 when he was a commander of Palestinian operations inside Palestine, sent by Arafat, via Jordan. He says that now these *fedayeen* are not men but boys; they should not be fighting, but fetching the water and making tea or bringing food – but not fighting. He says the fighting is partly Arafat's fault; he himself is sick of killing, guns and wars, saying why kill Amal? They are all Muslims, and should not kill each other, but follow the one road. The Amal fighters are not a people like the Palestinians, but boys who are again too young to be fighters. His children are outside the camp with their uncle. After the war he wants to leave for Denmark and tear up his Palestinian papers. Like so many here, he is sick and tired of constant fighting and doesn't want his children to live through the life of being a Palestinian here in the Lebanon. He tore a cigarette in two to demonstrate my half-understanding of his detailed explanation in Arabic, far beyond my basic comprehension.

27.11.86 Day 30 Thursday
Haj Abu Taher has just visited (in tears); the wife of the owner of the video shop is dead. She was hit as she went from the kitchen to the bedroom by shrapnel from a *howen* which landed in a house near the one they were in. Haj had gone up to the hospital to stay with her and her husband; when he couldn't find them he asked one of the nurses where they were and was told that she had died after an operation. They have four young children. The video-shop owner had lost his brother in the 45-day war and now his wife. 'Now the family is open.'

My nerves are shot today. More heavy fighting.

18.00 Being shelled again. Sporadic shelling and B-7s with gunfire throughout the day. Six *howens* in succession nearby, shelling the buildings, and I'm listening to the 'Skaters' Waltz' on the BBC World Service, nostalgically thinking of Thanksgiving Day, snow, ice and skating rinks when I was little. The radio is talking about the Christmas rush starting next week; it is December in three days. Today everyone is quite terrified as the Israelis bombed Ain al-Helweh and Mieh Mieh near Saida, claiming as always to be attacking Fatah bases. It is the sixteenth Israeli attack this year. The BBC World Service talks of Palestinian positions; the inaccuracy enrages me as they should come here and see the homes and families the Israelis are blowing up. Not so-called 'positions'. Israel describes them as 'bases belonging to the Fatah faction', 'positions around two Palestinian camps'.

Ran the *q'arnass* (sniper) again today to reach Samira's grandmother. She is better than a few days ago – thank God for Ampicillin – the burn also looks a lot better. I ended up doing six dressings outside.

News of heavy fighting all day at Shatila, like here yesterday. When the fighters took one building, they were warned by *jihaz* to evacuate it in case it had been boobytrapped with dynamite by Amal. The commander sent five men to survey the building; they were spotted by Amal who then detonated the charges laid and the building exploded. Until this evening, the cries of men under rubble could be heard, but no one can go to rescue them until, as Monir put it, 'after the war'.

There was no electricity in the hospital to sterilize the gauze I needed for dressings, so I joined Pauline's round of patients. All done by torchlight; the main job was angling the torch properly to see either the patient, wounds, or notes. We saw one young man with his face swathed in bandages with a naso-gastric tube, very restless and agitated, groaning and quite unresponsive. The story was that a bomb exploded in front of him, blowing sand into his face, which is terribly oedematous, and has blinded him. In fact, Monir told me later that, in the face-to-face fighting with an Amal suicide squad (so called because of their black head ribbons), he was standing too close to his friend's B-7 when it was launched, as he was to give the protective cover fire as it was sent out. The full blast of the rocket's flame came back into his face with a large piece of molten metal hitting his neck. At first, his friends panicked and left him for dead as the entire layer of skin was burnt off his face and he was bleeding profusely. Then Monir rushed to try and carry him under severe shell fire from the area next to Samed and the cemetery to the hospital. He lives near there and had gone to join some friends on a reconnaissance of the area as he knows it very well. They had seen Amal infiltrating and opened fire, only to be met with the tanks swinging up and firing in succession from behind the sandhills and caterpillar dugouts. He was at that dreadful restless just-about-conscious stage, with the cerebral confusion of a neurological patient.

I also saw Amer al Khatib, the M-16 injury of a few days ago, who is doing remarkably well so far, despite a fractured pelvis and malfunctioning colostomy; but he was crying with pain and in need of an analgesic.

Looked in on little Ghaleb twice before I managed to catch him awake on the third visit; he looks worn out and is sleeping with his traction – his leg will need bone-grafting in the future or he will have severe shortening. The X-ray shows a complete mess and, after his friends' awful performance of running him straight to the hospital from Marrubba *mahwar*, too panicked to try to stop the bleeding, he's very lucky.

The hospital took thirty shells yesterday and now the top floor roof has completely collapsed. The joke (sic) of the day is that the most carefully built sniper positions and tunnels of the camp have been completely destroyed – the building could not take the strain any more, gave up and collapsed. It's the same building that I was led across shutters to reach a few weeks ago, at third or fourth floor level. There were about eighteen people in it when they realized there was a strange noise and, thinking that perhaps it was an Amal plan, they came down and left. The others were below in the tunnels when they also noticed a strange sound which they took to be dynamite fuses. Sand started trickling softly into the tunnel and the building was by now obviously vibrating, so they fled too – in the nick of time, as the whole block crumpled down on to its very weakened foundations. It had withstood heavy shelling over the past two years, a severe fire damaging the ground floor, and tunnels being dug underneath it, and all this on sand foundations; the last straw being the TNT a week ago. So Nawoosh is being teased: where is he going to go now? He's stamping around in a black mood, refusing to go home until he finds a new position to fight from. All that loving work which they put into the sniping holes and tunnels has been lost, and luckily the building was not full of ammunition at the time – just one B-7 destroyed.

28.11.86 Day 31 Friday
Gave Samira's grandmother a laugh today as by the time I'd done my five dressings at the clinic and waited for the *howens* to stop it was dusk, so I ran out, praying *Bism'ullah Rahman al Rahim* (in the name of God, the compassionate, the merciful) at the outset, into the dark and got caught with an M-16 sniper hitting the buildings above me. So I stopped, breathed, ran; stopped again, then ran for it, from the old clinic up the street, which was deserted and which spooked me even more. The shops and doors were all closed so I had to knock at Samira's and wait, and just as I got inside a *howen* exploded further up. So they all laughed, and gave me a cigarette and tea to calm me down before doing the dressing. (The ceasefire that never was.) Stopped shaking after the cigarette, then *Bism'ullah Rahman al Rahim*-ed it back across the camp to the clinic, nearly getting lost.

The black cat reappeared for a short while today. Had two *fedayeen* with guns and a 120mm mortar come to visit looking for plaster. Again I refused the precious Elastoplast and they went off into the night with adhesive plaster strapping for their grenades. Luckily I didn't notice the rather large mortar until they were going out of the door, as it was heaved up over the back of one of them like a dead fish, and then they got their heads caught in my bandages that were hanging over the door to dry. Better than my underwear, I suppose.

The explanation for no electricity is that Amal have cut it off by damaging the big power box for this area. There was hope earlier of it being restored, but nothing has come of it. The preventive medicine tape has just been returned somewhat grubby, but it is good to think that prevention has so many meanings and that one of them is preventing tired fighters from blowing themselves up by inadvertently catching their grenades; strapping them with plaster will stop this.

Apparently Amal are taking Palestinians all around West Beirut again, and also killing families and burning housing in the camps near Sur, after looting them first, of course.

14.00 News that a ceasefire agreement is being made in Damascus. We are supposed to be able to leave the camp from Sunday.

If the ceasefire holds, I want to buy onions, lemons, potatoes and green tomatoes, and also make sure we get cans of milk and coffee and eggs to store, plus canned foods and vegetables. We also need to order vitamins, Panadol and aspirin; benzyl benzoate (to counter the extreme outbreak of scabies in the shelters) and Parakill (to fight the outbreak of headlice, also in the shelters).

15.10 The BBC World Service tells us that we have a ceasefire, but in the past ten minutes we have had five mortars nearby and gunfire. Jim Muir, of the BBC World Service, said, 'the Amal blockade at Rashidiyeh should be lifted tomorrow morning for a convoy of supplies to be allowed into the camp. If the ceasefire collapses we may see an attempt by Amal to overrun the camps especially those in the south; it could get very ugly indeed.'

There isn't a ceasefire in Magdoushe after no agreement on the following eight points:

1 Ceasefire from 15.00 on Friday.
2 Palestinians to move from east Saida to camps again.
3 Amal to recover positions at Magdoushe.
4 Internal security forces to supervise the ceasefire.
5 Supplies to Rashidiyeh on Saturday morning.
6 Joint force coastal road – Jumblatt.
7 Sunday: sieges to be lifted at Bourj and Shatila.
8 Monday: enlarged Palestinian/Lebanese meeting in Damascus.

Amal and other forces have been attacking Shatila since 7.00: T-54 tanks and three assaults, the west and cemetery fronts still fighting at 15.40. Since 15.00 twenty-four shells have fallen on the camp nearby. Mustafa and Iman ran in here from the *howens* – Iman is thirty-eight weeks pregnant.

19.45 Kitaeb news: there is no ceasefire. Arafat calls it a 'Syrian trick'. 'Three pm was the start of a new paroxysm of violence at Magdoushe, Bourj al-Brajneh and Sabra and Shatila.' 'Heavy shelling since 15.00 not abating at all. Ceasefire is said to have collapsed.' What will happen in Rashidiyeh? God knows. Nothing if Magdoushe is not handed back. I feel that if Magdoushe were to be handed over, Amal will then intensify, not retreat from Rashidiyeh. Another Syrian trick is right. Another big *howen*.

20.00 BBC World Service: 'Heavy fighting continues despite ceasefire. In this case, though, it would be surprising if the fighting ends without further agreements.' Too right – well, so much for a rest and vegetables.

22.20 We are being shelled again – since about 21.40 – a blanket of mortars and tank shells is falling over the camp. The sight of heavily pregnant women running to avoid the shells is almost incredible to someone educated with the European over-cautious attitude to birth. The BBC World Service has just mentioned that shells from the fierce fighting around two refugee camps in southern Beirut are falling into residential areas. Ben and I looked askance at each other as I commented that I thought we were also living in a residential area. I want to photocopy and distribute our clinic record book after the war. It will show the BBC World Service that the people being injured are not stereotype 'terrorists', but a civilian population trying to live in very poor conditions and being blown to bits by regular wars. It is almost laughable that the refugee camps are excluded as a civilian population.

Rashidiyeh has no food, water or medication left – it's awful. Amal are claiming they are in the process of clearing up small pockets of resistance in Shatila, having taken the DFLP office in Sabra. Mirwan and Hissam looked very tired tonight, and I have a good headache, wind and nausea.

Hissam then came with a small scalp laceration at 2.50. He stayed until Ben returned at 3.30 after watching the M-16 bullet injury repair of small bowel, colon and liver – a nine-hour operation by Dr Atia and Pauline. Unfortunately the guy (Nigar's brother) is an alcohol and drug abuser so his chances aren't rated too well. He was just full of holes. Hissam had told him only five minutes before to move from his position, but he had refused, then got shot.

People running outside – they seem to have been saving the 120mms for the ceasefire. Another *howen*. Another *howen*. The BBC World Service still carries us as its first story and persists in the mythical belief that a densely populated refugee camp is *not* a refugee camp with 10,000 men, women and children being injured, maimed and killed.

29.11.86 Day 32 Saturday

BBC World Service: Abu Iyad has accused Syria of conspiring with Israel to end the Palestinian armed presence in Lebanon, and has said that it pushed Amal into its latest offensive, supplying it with arms to maintain the 70-day siege of the camps.

Today we've had shelling almost every hour for fifteen minutes or so, then random in between. An Amal attack was driven off at 4.30. The street behind is now a heap of rubble, with Ahmad's house completely demolished. It must have taken another two or more shells yesterday. The road all the way to Borhan's *mahwar* was also completely demolished, so today has been spent clearing it again.

Nigar's brother died today at 6 am, and Khadija, Zeinab and I went to pay our respects to her. She was in tears; she is injured, her husband is dead, her brother-in-law is also injured, and now her brother is dead, as are her parents. I don't think her children understood her distress, as they ran about from room to room.

A big mortar has just landed next door – smoke is filling the kitchen, and the smell of explosive is everywhere in the room.

21.40 I'm sitting on the floor behind the table, and the masonry and glass which has come down with the explosion – an 82mm mortar, I think. More explosives now, another and another and another and another and another and another and another, and another.

Today I visited Samira's grandmother who laughed when she saw me after I had been running. The burn is a lot better and new skin is growing. Hissam's leg is all right, but in the dreadful light it is difficult to see. I'm going to force him up to the hospital tomorrow to see Dr Saleh as he keeps making any excuse not to go. I got caught with the 16.00 *howens* today* and had to spend half an hour on the floor waiting for them to end, as they were falling near the clinic and up at Zaida's house. Then we ran for it up the street to Zaida's to do her dressing. Afterwards I learnt why Arab babies are swaddled so tightly: it's to make them into strong young men, from struggling against the swaddling for the first three months of life. They are literally bound by the arms, knees and legs, and cannot move at all.

I picked up a cat with shrapnel injuries today and put him in a big cardboard-box with food and milky *leben* (yoghurt). He's mad as hell as his back legs are paralysed and the children have been tormenting him. He was spitting and lunging out with the front of his body and has a huge shrapnel hole in the region of his spine. I had to use a floor mop to push him into the box. Poor, poor thing.

23.10 The camp is beginning to show signs of the constant shelling everywhere, with debris from mortars in the street, houses with walls blown out, and streets littered with crumpled pieces of metal and stones. Some roads are becoming almost impassable; you have to scramble over stones to get from one side to the other. I am having very strange dreams at night.

Another *howen* with someone limping – running up the street just afterwards – nearby. 120mm. Someone else running up and around the corner with bullets and a gun thumping against his arm as he tries for speed in the dark, thudding footsteps of someone loaded with quite a few extra kilos. Dynamite?

One girl, Fatima, said to me, 'What can Palestinians abroad do for those here?' She doesn't want their money; they have to do something more than that. She especially doesn't want British money. Palestinian money she would almost accept, but 'they give us money but we pay with our blood'. She's right. Everyone talks openly about perhaps dying here. As there is no escape from death in the camps, they have to leave and go somewhere else. But how? And where? Another bullet hitting the wall – *whizz-spat-tinkle.*

The little 1½-year-old girl who was needing to be evacuated, but was refused, has a sympathetic ophthalmia from her traumatic cataract. Two days ago, Salim ran into the doctors' room to say that she could see and was playing with the other children in the corridor. And, today, the news is

*This was a daily routine at 4pm.

that the fighter everyone thought was blinded is able to distinguish light from dark, and asked for the light to be put back on again. It's wonderful news that the two people we thought would never see again have some sight back.

30.11.86 Day 33 Sunday
Cary Grant died after a stroke, aged 82. Heavy shelling of Shatila all through the night. The PLO want an emergency Arab summit 'to halt the liquidation of Palestinian refugee camps' by Amal. The BBC World Service at 19.00 reports that Amal took revenge for the definite Palestinian control of Magdoushe by taking 110 girls in Al-Bass and Bourj al-Shemali, holding them, torturing them and killing them.

Amal are accused of trying to set Bourj al-Brajneh on fire, and there are now several reports of Amal using chemical weapons on Bourj yesterday morning. At first we dismissed them, but now, as many people have told us of this, there may be more than hysteria to it. Palestinians have advanced to Ghaziyeh and Magdoushe. Tonight there will be retaliation for the massacres of Palestinians by Amal a few days ago in which the residents of two small camps near Sur were tortured and murdered, their houses looted and then burned. Some managed to flee into the woods nearby and escape; they were told to leave Lebanon or die on November 27.

A baby girl, Hinnit, for Iman al Khatib, born yesterday. She weighs 3.8 kilos and looks healthy. More 'dangerous' vegetables brought by Monir; I took a photograph of the mint and radishes brought from near Samed and the cemetery under four tank shells.

The ICRC were refused entry to Magdoushe today with relief supplies and to help evacuation. The PLO officially asked for an emergency Arab meeting to stop the destruction and liquidation of the Palestinian camps in the Lebanon.

21.00 We had the tanks shelling us again and, as I ran to Samira's grandmother's, there were shouted warnings of 'Sniper, Suzy' and 'Suzy, *fi q'arnass hon*' (Suzy, there's a sniper here').

I'm writing alone, by spirit lamp; I've got used to no electricity after a week – damn Amal – and no water too. Tried to repair a lacerated eyebrow by torchlight last night, and a punctured lip today the same way – the man had bitten through his lip with his incisor teeth as he was firing the *doshka*, which had swung up hitting his chin.

Weapons and a box of surgical instruments have been bribed through Amal into the camp. I saw four B-10 missiles walking past the clinic, two on each shoulder on the way to the Arsan *mahwar* today.

I'm boiling water for cocoa (without milk) and have just cooked the parsley and eaten a lot of it: raw parsley – nothing spared, lemon (another tank) and half an onion. What luxury. (One explosion every three minutes. Debris falling everywhere.)

Looking at photos of home; I always get homesick at Christmas. I remember how hard Mum and Dad always worked to make it special and how they loaded us with presents. What a spoilt childhood and what ungrateful wee brats we were a lot of the time.

Jesus, a hell of a noise! – maybe from Arsan, although it was in my left ear. More debris nearby – this is hotting up. Wrong – it was a tank or 107 from out towards the hospital; flares now lighting up the camp. 107s or shells from tanks are the *whoosh-crumps* that go over the buildings to the hospital. God – that was scary. At 10.05 Carkar and Ahmad ran in; they had just set out from Carkar's en route to the *mahwar* when the *howens* and the flares started. The flares are the most eerie thing I've ever seen, and have not been used before in this war. The whole camp was lit up with a bright, white light, as though there were thirty full moons directly overhead in the sky. With the sound of *howens* and 107s it was very frightening. Carkar offered me cocoa and a cigarette, which I took, but declined the cocoa, telling him to keep it for the *mahwar* in the cold night. His wife is also outside the camp but in the area of Bourj al-Brajneh.

More *howens*, I think this could be a noisy night, maybe they've moved fire from Shatila back to here. (Bombs from the mountains.) Running and agitation, then silence – absolute eerie silence. . . . More shells on Shatila. It is very unnerving to listen to others being bombed to bits in a similar way to us every third day. The *whoosh* of a rocket overhead to the right. No radio to divert me either as it has gone to the *mahwar* for the news until 24.00, when it has faithfully (sniper fire) been promised to be returned. More shells on Shatila – rain – running and guns banging from side to side as people move fast. The flares can only signify a renewed attack as they try to position their bloody *howens* more accurately.

Resorted to douche with lemon, water and cloves of garlic to relieve a candida infection in a young woman who has been married for only one month. Did a vaginal examination after a description in my poor Arabic to ascertain that it may be thrush, then looked with all the doors closed, a spirit lamp and a torch, on the mattress of the kitchen floor. The husband looked more than askance at my suggestion of inserting a garlic pessary (peeled) up to her cervix and douching with lemon and water.

1.12.86 Day 34 Monday

General strike tomorrow called by General Labour Union against rising prices, exempting hospitals, pharmacies, bakeries. 20.00 BBC World Service: eighth day of fighting (disbelief!) around southern suburbs and in south Lebanon. Negotiations making no headway. A general strike called in Saida in protest at the effect of fighting in the area. Demonstration in Ramallah dispersed with teargas by Israeli troops, the third demonstration in three days. Reports to UNRWA are 'increasingly disturbing' from all Palestinian situations in the Lebanon, says the Director. Lebanese forces welcomed Algerian moves towards the Lebanon in the next twenty-four hours. Algerian delegation coming to Lebanon with Syrian encouragement. The LRC were refused access to Rashidiyeh to evacuate the wounded.

Went to Samira's grandmother, who was taking a shower and looking quite jolly. Her burn looks so much better that after tomorrow she could have bi-daily dressings. Passed more destruction in the rain by the old clinic: bits of trees blown to bits by *howens*, a new hole in Nasser's garden wall and shrapnel damage to the front door of the old clinic. Then we went to visit little Isa al Hoseri and his brother Ibrahim who were injured by shrapnel. Poor Isa was easily embarrassed, and we were descended upon by Ben and several relatives mid-dressing, so we then stayed for cocoa and coffee, and watched fresh bread being baked in a big kerosene stove of intense heat and noise. Poor thing, I hope tomorrow we will have more peace and quiet. Then I went to see Iman al Khatib again; I'm a bit worried about her, so a crash revision course in obstetrics is taking place.

24.00 BBC World Service news: 'The head of UNRWA has appealed for help for Palestinian women and children in refugee camps in the Lebanon.' 'Civilians caught up in fighting' appeal for ceasefire, but negotiations have made no headway. So I guess we won't see the hoped-for ceasefire within two days due to Algerian and Syrian agreements after all.

Mohamad al Masri was sniped at around 16.00 in his home by an M-16. He came in for treatment, and I lost my cool with his friend and shouted at him to get out. I had tried to be fair and ignore him, but when he slapped his hand on the dressing, I yelled 'No!' Part of it is my fault by expecting people to respect my wishes in the clinic, as here it seems to be irrelevant what working conditions we need or what judgement we make about people's condition and treatment. We have to resort to shouting to make any impression, usually, in fact always, only with men. Ben agrees. When he asks people to leave, they don't go; when he resorts to yelling, they *go*! When I ask, they get obstructive and eventually I too resort to stupid, foolish, imitative shouting, but it is the only thing that works. Then I get annoyed with myself afterwards.

The cat was worshipped by the ancient Egyptians and to kill a cat was a dreadful sin, and then they were persecuted as being from the devil. This explains the *haram* (the concept of sinning against God's commandments) of killing a cat in Islam, where the belief must be retained (from *Dogwatching and Catwatching* by Desmond Morris).

Yusuf died from his head injuries; he was another young and unrecognizable head injury from a mortar shrapnel blast. He was lying shaved, bleeding and entubated when I went up to the hospital to collect the hot tin of newly sterilized gauze yesterday. When I went into the emergency room he was being bagged (artificially respirated) by one of the nurses, and when the generator went off she silently stood at his side, pushing the ambubag in the dark, waiting for the light in the screened-off room. He was bagged by hand for five hours but had such severe head injuries that nothing could be done. When they stopped bagging there was no inclination to spontaneous breathing, so the decision was taken to stop resuscitation, but his heartbeat persisted for fifteen minutes after it was withdrawn, which upset us all very much. He was only 22 or 23 years old. So he died from one of the BBC's phrases of 'mortars exploding', in a room sheltering ten people from these very shells in a Palestinian camp. Another statistic of the fighting?

The woman brought in with him, who had a splenectomy, is probably going to die also. She had had no urinary output since the emergency room and is now in acute renal failure. She needs immediate evacuation for haemodialysis, but this now looks highly unlikely. Would these people live with access to intensive care facilities? At least thirty per cent would – proving the murderous aspect of loss of life here.

The paralysed cat is still alive although very weak, and has eaten a little and is capable of lashing out and spitting – it's awful, and I cried for it and every other injury today.

Visited by Ahmad Aishey just as the gas finally ran out, so we joked and drank warm tea. Cold food and no hot water from now on. We were given two flasks of tea by kindhearted mothers until Ben could bring a small camping stove and kerosene heater from the hospital.

Today was 'too quiet' for all of us, as we remarked; a very uneasy quiet, just the odd mortar. Rain and very cold weather; all of us moaning and shivering like an early spring day at home. We could see our breath in the rain and occasional sunshine. I thought again of walking slowly down a street. Only that – it would be enough to walk slowly down a street. Or stand on the roof and look around me – at the change of season, at the trees, or, as the other night, at the lights twinkling on the mountains, in the villages and East Beirut.

It now costs approximately £100 to repair a house – where will people get that amount of money from? Even Iman says she won't have more children now as her husband only has one leg and cannot work.

I think I'll try for a shower in the hospital tomorrow and pick up the gauze at the same time. Then come back, check Iman, *sitti* (grandmother) Samira, and Isa and Ibrahim. I need two cans of milk for a malnourished baby in that house: she's far too small at three months, and being fed only on cereals. I think she's just not getting enough milk. Then force Hissam out to the clinic.

I like the Al Khatib family very much; my 'second family' now. Hossam, the elder son of their sister, was praying with their grandfather today as we ate 'new baby' chocolates. A calm and thoughtful unison of ritual, beautiful to watch. Fatima is teaching me what to say and do for Islam to prevent the devil eating or drinking with me. Khadija also wants to teach me about Islam. Saw the 'ardent suitor' looking very much the 'coke' freak he is reputed to be, with sunglasses – and Ahmad now looking completely stoned for the third day. He was just sitting outside, alone, staring into space, bomb-happy.

2.12.86 Day 35 Tuesday
While examining my lovely newly donated Fatah underwear (and pyjamas, tracksuit, cologne and deodorant), several *howens* exploded all along the *mahwar* line, so I abandoned my explorations of bras and pants – three of each – and took to the floor, after opening the door slightly and placing the cat on my lap. Very exciting to get presents, especially the silver and beige knickers and three versions of lacy front-opening sensible bras. Like Christmas.

22.15 Now listening to a BBC English language programme. 'Counting the Beats' by Robert Graves. We listened to a short Cocteau play the other day, but were interrupted; and to a critique of the new *Lear* which presents another facet of Lear – and now I shall have to listen to see if I can hear and read it, as Edward Bond's play and Kurasawa's *Ran* are both adaptations of the unknown to me, Shakespeare's *King Lear*. How appropriate *Lear* to Lebanon.

Snug as a bug in my Fatah tracksuit and vest – God bless Arafat's socks. The three rather delicious bras are all too big and the pyjamas are fabulously revolutionary from China with a little pattern on them. And (Maureen's) deodorant and 4711 Eau de Cologne – how lovely that someone thought of us and brought us these things. Khadija brought two black training tops, a scarf in baby pink and a lovely white jersey for me. Her sister sells clothes from what I can gather.

I'm listening to Book Choice, *The Art of Stress Survival*: 'There are usually ways of improving the situation.' 'Do I have enough privacy?' (Ha, ha, ha, ha!) 'Taking up regular exercise.' (Ha, ha, ha, ha.) 'The art of stress survival': running the *howens* around the camp to work. 'Accept life's problems as an inevitable part of life.' (Being blown to bits every five minutes.) Now a recital of guitar music from the seventeenth and nineteenth centuries. Then a 'Letter from Scotland' about the effects of the recession on the offshore oil industry and how it has affected the 'region'. I used to believe that Scotland was a country?

My work today was nine people and I was out in the camp from 10.00 until 14.30 – nerve-racking, but I love the visits. I think at last I'm going into primary health care, albeit in a completely different way to that originally envisaged. I saw three new babies, then on to Isa and Ibrahim, and trying to persuade Isa *not* to move his fractured arm while I was changing the dressing and the splint was off. (This was almost as difficult as trying to persuade Khaled Daud to elevate his leg when sitting: it's the nearest thing to a raw steak with holes in it.) Then to *sitti* Samira who is doing as well as can be expected. Then up to Iman's to see her and Borhan's wife Lydia.

Quiet again here, the odd explosion and gunfire; too quiet. I'm pleased with the community direction the work is now taking and I think I will stay on for about a month or so after the war.

Very tired and must get some sleep before going to hospital with gauze again tomorrow and all that work.

3.12.86 Day 36 Wednesday
We were woken early this morning at 4.15 by dynamite, fighting and mortars.

The cat threw up and I feel like throwing up. Haj Abu Taher brought me tea to cure me; I'm feeling ill, so no home visits. Spent today sleeping, burping and feeling generally off-colour.

The Israelis have shelled Ain al-Helweh and Mieh Mieh from the sea – sixty shells, and no real reason given. It seems that Shamir's policy is one of *kill Arabs*. The Israelis are saying that they fired at people's feet, and in the air. In Bir Zeit, a university town in Occupied Palestine, the Israeli army has shot dead three students on the excuse that they were demonstrating, but they also threw teargas canisters into the entrance of Ramallah Hospital where the injured had been taken. They had been harassing students at the university for three days and today staff and students sat down in front of the Israeli roadblocks in protest.

There is a story about 130 Lebanese 1st and 6th Brigade soldiers leaving Shatila in disgust and going to Mar Elias to protect it from Amal incursions. Shatila is again suffering heavy bombardment. It is being razed by 1st and 6th Brigade and Amal tanks; Palestinian sources confirmed that sixty per cent of Shatila has been destroyed by close-range T-54 shelling. There is much hope for a ceasefire tonight; it has been rumoured since yesterday evening, but came to nothing.

Sweet Suhail died today: shrapnel from a *howen* in front of him hit him in his chest mid-morning whilst he was walking out with his fiancée. She had a laparotomy, but he died shortly after arriving in the emergency room. I last saw him yesterday sitting in the sunshine just under the archway next to the Al Khatibs' house. There was the usual pale water-blue sky and some green leaves on the tree behind him. Ahmad is very upset as they were good friends and often went about together. He was a shy quiet-spoken young man with a dreamlike face from another time, poetic more than warlike. Now he is dead. The *khotbi* (an engagement party) that never saw a wedding, another *khotbi* without an end; his fiancée may recover. Just walking, and walking kills you at this moment on a sunny day.

5.12.86 Day 38 Friday
No candles left now.

Woken by the crying and weeping in the street at another death. A young boy of around 14 was sniped in the neck and run straight to the hospital, but is dead. He was called Tha'ir and Khadija tells me that he was always telling her he loved me. I can't place him. He was shot whilst preparing food or getting water; the story isn't clear. People disappear and reappear after weeks on end, so that when you don't see someone for a long time you wonder if they are dead and whether you knew them by a different name to the one everyone gives you.

Then cries of '*Q'arnass, q'arnass hon*' ('Sniper, sniper here'), and the street past the first door to the kitchen was quickly sealed off with hastily erected zinc and wood to prevent people using it. A sandbag was added later as children were ignoring the barricade and running through it.

Apparently there was a ceasefire this morning from 8.00 made in Damascus, but we were shelled again at 9.00, a 'stair drop', from top to bottom of the camp again, and the ceasefire collapsed before it started, as usual. At the moment it is difficult to tell which buildings are safe or not, now that Amal are dynamiting what used to be protection from their sniper positions. Borhan's *mahwar* 'duck-walked' in the street, 'you squat and then start walking', to lay dynamite around an Amal rest-house, then 'duck-walked' back and detonated the charges from the *mahwar*, destroying a two-storey building. Borhan came in to relate the escapade afterwards, his heart pounding, he said; looking completely unmilitary with a bright yellow scarf and a big blue coat.

19.45 Radio Lebanon: 'Iranian initiative has failed' – the Iranian plan to end the camps war; its failure made public by Nabih Berri. The Israelis have killed a 14-year old boy at Nablus today.

Saw pictures of the little Akram (aged 9) when he was younger, being kissed by Abu Ammar in the building that is now Haifa Hospital, and Isa and Ibrahim are both well.

I haven't seen the sad man for a long time apart from yesterday when he translated for the old Haj, while I clutched my head and considered fainting.

The non-aligned countries in the UN have called for an emergency meeting to examine the three shootings of Palestinians in the Occupied West Bank in the past two days. Again the Israelis shot to kill after being stoned. Heard on the news: 'The Mufti of Jerusalem has called for an international UN security force to protect Palestinians in Jerusalem' because of Israeli exactions. Lebanon has not replied to the call by Arafat for an Arab League Summit – fourteen countries are in favour.

Someone has been stealing the cocoa now.

6.12.86 Day 39 Saturday

0.45 Ben has gone to record his article in the hope of getting it out of the camp with the ambulance if this is possible – who knows?

Regardless of the ceasefire, a man with shrapnel has now been brought into the emergency room and needs a craniotomy and evacuation. So many ceasefires, no one even bothered to mention this one; we are all so jaded with the idea of the fighting stopping. God, the prospect of an enduring silence is sweet, though. Everyone now is very wan and pale from a combination of bad diet, tiredness, fear and lack of sunshine.

Wael got an M-16 today from Abu Nidal which delivered three to Haiduce. They also bribed in thirty *howens* from Amal. They say you can buy anything from the Lebanese – this holds true again! I'm told that Syrian soldiers have been seen assisting Amal to launch larger mortars than Amal possess (155mm, 160mm and 240mm) in Saida and its environs.

Wael gave me a candle which I am saving for Christmas (just in case). Even two or three days of peace would be nice. If this ends, Pauline and Ben are going to Cairo, and Hannes also goes home for Christmas, so I will be left here alone. I think I will stick it out and live above the clinic alone until a new team member arrives; there is no other solution despite cultural norms being offended by my being on my own. But Hannes was also talking of extending his stay, and there is no adequate physiotherapy going on at present and a lot is needed post-war – very much needed – so it would be good if he does stay. He could go to Mar Elias for a Palestinian Christian celebration of Christmas.

16.00 Well, the ceasefire lasted until about 13.30 when, just as I stepped into Zaida's house, five *howens* exploded, sending rubble flying through the air.

Listening to the BBC World Service on Prokofiev and the opera sessions.

It was so relaxed in the middle of the camp: people outside with fires in the sunshine, children playing, shops open for basics (such as the last of the matches). Met *sitti* Samira outside and we went to do her dressing. And Juma's new baby, Sara, is now here, four days old and weighing 4.2. kilos. Did Arsan's dressing this morning: it's clean and looking good. Little Aref was with him, wearing Jamal's hat (the red one) and obviously worshipping his big brother quietly.

Mention of Chris Giannou and the underground hospital in Shatila. The clinic is destroyed, but they've all taken to the tunnels and underground camp. Thank God for some foresight somewhere. Ibrahim, the thin Phoenician-looking guard of Sultan (and the hospital), was sniped and killed in the cemetery today whilst burying five of the dead during the ceasefire. The cemetery had been filled with people come to pay respects, heedless of the fact that the word ceasefire here is meaningless. They left their weapons, relaxed, and gentle Ibrahim was shot in the abdomen. He died from internal bleeding almost immediately. He had faced towards the Shia buildings and was shot. He is now the thirty-eighth person to die in thirty-nine days. He was studying, and was graceful and gentle. Now he too is dead. My last recollection is of seeing him sitting on a plinth in the emergency room with his friend, smiling in the thin light of the generator from the gloom of the darkened corridor: shy, quiet Ibrahim, son of the teacher.

19.45 Kitaeb radio: twenty Palestinian students are occupying Arab League offices in Paris, a few days ago the same in the Bonn Arab League office.

20.00 BBC World Service: 'The Israeli army has been out in force today in the West Bank and Gaza Strip. Curfew imposed in Balata and Ramallah. Most shops in the West Bank and Gaza closed in protest at shootings in Ramallah, Hebron, Nablus and Jerusalem.' 'Truckloads of soldiers patrolled the almost deserted streets.' 'Old sector in Jerusalem under heavy Israeli guard.'

7.12.86 Day 40 Sunday

19.00 BBC World Service: 'More violent anti-Israeli demonstrations on the Occupied West Bank and Gaza Strip.' Palestinian demonstrators involved in clashes with the Israeli army – one demonstrator was shot in the knee when troops opened fire. 'Israeli cabinet again rejected criticism' of its soldiers' behaviour. 'Following yesterday's breakdown of the latest ceasefire', fighting in Beirut camps again; 'due to be discussed tomorrow in Tunis, neither Syria nor Lebanon have said they will attend.'

Quiet day of dressings and washing out the clinic. Borhan came in with a TNT inhalation headache, and needing gloves and oxygen for washing after handling dynamite.

8.12.86 Day 41 Monday

From the evening news (BBC and Lebanese Forces): '[Israeli soldiers] appear to reach the stage of using their rifles rather quickly.' The commercial strike continues. 'Berri refuses any recommendation from the meeting in Tunis as he regards the meeting to be illegal as it was called by the PLO.' Questions are being raised as to whether the Arab League will withdraw its 1976 mandate to Syria to establish a stabilizing force in the Lebanon, and replace the Syrians with a multi-Arab peacekeeping force.

Taisear teaches me the Arab word for 'chaos' to describe the clinic today: we saw thirty-three adults and four babies. (Six new babies have been born locally in the war.) One boy gave me a pen, which is lovely. Like the lady who gave me earrings a few weeks ago, and the homemade bread, cookies and potatoes the Al Ashwas keep giving us. Last night Rifat and Al Haj walked up to Rifat's home behind Haifa to prepare chips for us and came back an hour later to give us them with tomato sauce, despite my protests that it was too far and dangerous just to prepare food. Haj had earlier brought me tea, as Ben had taken the gas up to Pauline and Hannes. The boys had guessed the romance long ago from Ben's nightly food visits to Pauline and the fact that they may go to Cairo together for Christmas if the war ends before that – fat chance at the moment.

Hannes gave Ben a really lovely December 5 Santa Claus present of a poem describing all Ben's attributes and a Pancake Cook of Bourj al-Brajneh Diploma: a lot of effort had been put into it. Santa Claus in Holland is a Christian bishop from Turkey who travels to Holland from Spain each year with his black servants on a white horse, and he rides over the rooftops dropping presents down the chimneys for children on December 5.

I've made more decorations and saved a candle from Wael. Aref al Masri brought more pieces of captured chandelier for me to make into little earrings. And tomorrow he can see the big pieces on a Christmas mobile I've made from a cut-up scarf and a coathanger *à la* Blue Peter. Visited by Hisham al Masri who is still not sleeping and looks awful, and is suffering from the ubiquitous cold that even I've got again; we're all so run down. Shehadi and Akram's English lesson was non-existent today due to the rush of people from 10.30 until 18.00, and we didn't get any time like yesterday to sit on the steps and be interrupted by Ringo, Hissam, Rifat *et al.*

I've been told that little Aref al Habet has written 'Aref loves Suzy' on the wall of the *mahwar*. I replied that I love Aref very much and Jamal too, even though Arsan woke me today for his dressing and I didn't get up in time to do it. Tomorrow I must get going early as I've promised to bath little Isa to show him how to do it without wetting his plaster and bending his bones. He deliberately forgets most of the time.

This is the new pen that I'm using. It's very elegant, but I don't think it's working very well – or is it just too dark by spirit lamp?

9.12.86 Day 42 Tuesday

Three corpses of Christians from Magdoushe found in Ghaziyeh, so badly mutilated as to be unrecognizable. Reports of eighteen others slaughtered and pressure on the population to flee, and plunder and kidnappings by Amal. Amal had accused them of having brought in Palestinians. Attempted murder of three Druze leaders for their outspoken opposition to

Amal; they were ambushed near Khalde junction by Amal. Amal then attempted to advance on Shatila just before 18.00, but were repelled.

I got caught by bombs today: I'd been up to collect the stores from the hospital which weren't ready yet so I had to sit around waiting in Mohamad al Ashwa's office. Then I waited on the steps, then inside the storekeeper Abed's office, which turned out to be housing one new 10-day-old baby, plus grandmother, mother, sisters, relatives and two more men, one sleeping in a bed. I had tea and eventually set off carrying an open water bottle containing kerosene and a large black plastic bag of stores, tea and sugar, plaster, etc, and ran. I got as far as 'the corner of great destruction' when a 60mm *howen* exploded behind me. I went deaf for a while, dropped the lot and ran for it, which was to Fatima's house as there were no houses before it. Singing in my ears. Later, after waiting indoors for Mohamad's five-minute post-*howen* rule, during which another four exploded nearby, I ran up with Waf'a, Fatima's sister, to retrieve the bag, which was sitting in the sewer covered in dust and full of holes. We picked it up and I ran on down to the clinic. I had a large lump of brick on my jersey and lots of small pieces in my hair, which I found later, and a small piece in my back which Khadija looked at and washed, much to the surprise of little Mahmud who had come for his dressing.

Then I went to reinforce Isa's gyps and put a 'walker' (plaster cast) on it with an audience of about eight little children, with a spirit lamp and a plastic bag cut up on the floor. Strict instructions were given about walking on it.

Despondent through failure of any sort of agreements at the Arab League Summit and everyone resigned to the inevitable failure of ceasefire for a while to come.

10.12.86 Day 43 Wednesday

I was sitting outside after doing washing and writing out the book when some sort of projectile went overhead and hit farther up the camp. So I moved inside just in time, as the bombing started with a strong smell of gunpowder explosive and dust, the infernal blanket, that gets everywhere, covering everything in a grey film, especially in your chest, and makes everyone cough for half an hour or so afterwards. Ugh! There was glass and rubble everywhere and outside it resembled a London fog on a winter night. The square was layered with dust.

Then, miraculously, Um Mohamad al Khatib appeared out of the dust. She wanted a plastic bag for the broken windows in her home from the *howens*. All the road was hit and is now ankle-breaking rubble. She had negotiated it without a torch, so we clambered up to the house. I played with the children and looked at Lydia's wedding photographs. She and Borhan looked lovely, Borhan happy and solemn. Mustafa the sad man was in a few, looking extra solemn with his two little daughters on his knees, and there were pictures of before the wedding when Mohamad had two legs. Um Mohamad has six sons and two daughters. She is about 55 but looks much older, due to hard work and a heart complaint. She's sweet and again invited me to stay with them. I said I wanted to, but it was not possible until after the war because of work.

Five LRC ambulances evacuated twenty-five people from Rashidiyeh to Saida today, and one truck only of potatoes was allowed in by Amal. Gerald Butt refers to it on the BBC World Service as Rashidiyeh, 'which has been under siege for a few weeks'. I wish I could meet him and tell him it's since September 30 – no end in sight for a while now.

11.12.86 Day 44 Thursday

400 Amal dead at Magdoushe.
45 dead in Shatila: Palestinians and many Amal.
45 dead in Rashidiyeh: Palestinians.
45 dead now in Bourj al-Brajneh.

Last night in a break in the bombing Amal were broadcasting in the street that they would enter the camp and kill everyone, even the children. Today many Amal positions throughout West Beirut have been blown up by a group calling itself Revenge Force 58.

Today little Ahmad Haj was brought in with multiple shrapnel. The poor child has been so obviously frightened for so long, going into a very trance-like shocked state when he heard bombs. This morning he was brought in screaming 'Suzy, Suzy', and it was dreadful trying to struggle his clothes off, as the good scissors are missing and the others are hopeless. He had to be left to Zeinab and Khadija as shortly afterwards a woman was brought in DOA. We tried to resuscitate her but she was drowned in blood, so we had to wrap her in a blanket and send her to Haifa – dead, with a 1½-month-old baby, six children, and her husband in Yemen. Her little daughter stood screaming and crying, watching us trying to resuscitate her mother. I kept asking people to take her out, but no one really bothered.

Found my clothes covered in shrapnel holes.

Had a lovely wash at Khadija's as she made a floor full of bread and heated up the water outside on a wood stove for me, giving me shampoo and soap, closing the *hamman* (washroom) window and feeding me lots of bread afterwards. All that extra work for the *ajnabiyah*, God bless her hands.

The Israelis have bombarded Tripoli camps today in north Lebanon (BBC World Service 19.00). Fifteen people killed and twenty wounded. There are large plumes of black smoke rising over the area. Six planes came in from the sea. 'Today troops lobbed teargas into the grounds of a school', and even the Americans have condemned the over-frequent use of weapons by Israelis in the Occupied West Bank. Funny, as they abstained from censoring Israel in the UN.

Nederlands News at 19.30: Amnesty International has started a campaign for the release of over a hundred Palestinian and Murabitoun prisoners held by Amal, and has protested about the conditions of the Palestinians in the Lebanon at the hands of Amal, the biggest militia in Lebanon, headed in the Lebanese government by Nabih Berri as Minister of Justice!

I saw a photo of Taisear before the war: he has also got thin with the strain, as has Borhan. I'm thinking of all the people who want to leave here now, and if Libya is open are talking of going there – but for passports. Many people have their passports taken away and are then asked for the equivalent of £50 to £100 to get them back. Where can people here on a subsistence income get such amounts? For example, Taisear was asked for £50; it took him four years to get his passport back. Or Rifat, Hissam and Haj who were going to flee to Denmark, but Haj had to find £50 also to get his Moroccan passport back, then the war started. Um and Abu Mohamad al Khatib will go to their sons in Sweden or Denmark when they can move.

12.12.86 Day 45 Friday

There is supposed to be a Soviet-Libyan ceasefire in effect since 17.00 last night. Not that anyone told us until about 1.00 today. Nabih Berri rejects this ceasefire and I am listening to *howens* dropping at the top of the camp. And news is that Amal have just slaughtered four or five armed Palestinians who were in their garden at Rashidiyeh. (Had a very nasty dream about Amal last night.)

There is apparently a plan for the Palestinians to take control of the coastal road and reach Rashidiyeh. Some more villages around Magdoushe will be taken tomorrow, and then they will continue offensives until the siege of Rashidiyeh is lifted and relieved.

13.12.86 Day 46 Saturday

Spent today in a limbo from any routine. Woken at 7.00 by frenzied banging on the door; in rushed Mustafa, Walid and some others from the Binnei Beddi (Borhan's) *mahwar*, carrying Hossam, the lab technician from the hospital. He'd been shot through the foot: reasonable blood loss, no great damage, but silenced by fright and shock. So I cleaned and splinted and sent him up to Haifa. Mustafa had evaporated by the end after telling me to sleep, God love him, so, wide awake, I cleaned the floor, washed the blood out and listened to the shelling at dawn of Shatila. Then it started at the hospital – at a rate of one shell every ten seconds, although Hannes said initially they were almost simultaneously firing shells, constantly hitting around the hospital.

There was a garbled explanation of Hossam's foot injury: one person said he'd been sleeping and shot? We thought someone had accidentally shot him, but then his friend blew it by asking had he shot himself from above. He then told me he'd been running with his safety catch off and shot himself. Taisear confirmed this later.

Kitaeb news at 19.45: the Arab League has postponed the summit until the end of next week. Oh God, another week! The Syrians seem to want an Amal victory at any price to redress Magdoushe. All political mediation is abandoned awaiting the results of military action over the next twenty-four to forty-eight hours. Shatila and Bourj camps are under heavy artillery and mortar battles, killing at least eighteen people. Ten shells a minute. There is a three-sided offensive against Shatila, T-54 at 4.00 for six consecutive hours; the mountain forces intervened to help the camp during the heavy shelling and attack. A radio appeal to stop genocide in Shatila camp; the Palestinians have defeated six attempts so far. The Arab foreign ministers' Tunis meeting postponed indefinitely from its Monday schedule.

BBC World Service at 20.00: 'Concern is now expressed by relief organizations for the Beirut camps.' In Jenin, Israelis shot at Palestinians with rubber bullets, four dead now in the past week. 'Demonstration in Nazareth to oppose Israeli policy in the Occupied Territories.' I wonder whether Jim Muir knows that the other day Amal stole the medical supplies for Rashidiyeh and only let in one truck with rotten onions and potatoes, refusing everything else entry. But at least he's reporting more truth than fantasy now. 'He's learning,' as Ben put it.

Thirteen dead and seventy-five wounded outside in Beirut today; four trucks reported to have entered Rashidiyeh, with four ambulances. Amal refuse ceasefires until the Palestinians cooperate.

One young boy was killed at Marrubba *mahwar* today. I heard the noise outside and ran out, to find him being carried to the hospital, with an argument going on about where to take him. So I yelled to bring him in here – his face was covered and no one said he was dead. They refused, so I screamed for Ben, who they also ignored, so he ran after them and I set up the room again, but he was very dead, shot through the eye and back of his head. He was just a young boy – like all of them – and was the artist of the Grecian *fedai* mural on our outside wall.

I was in the middle of a productive evening making Gentian Violet, far too strong, one per cent instead of a half per cent, and washing out our one stretch bandage, when a man came asking for a male nurse to go on a house visit to a person who was bleeding having been discharged from Haifa today. (There simply is no bed-space left now.) So we went off with a full basket of gauze, plaster, alcohol in the Pepsi bottle, etc, into the moonlit night, and just as we left a *howen* went out from here. This made us both agitated as we then expected one back in reply, so I stumbled and fell on the rubble, climbed through a hole in a wall into a house of sleeping people (it was about 20.30), out through a hall and more rooms of sleeping people in the spirit and candle light, out across a street, 'Quickly, there's a sniper here,' and into another house.

There I saw the man with obvious abdominal difficulties from shrapnel injuries today: a lot of gas in his belly and old blood on his pyjamas, and seepage from a pad over his left thigh. The panic was over as soon as I found a corrugated drain *in situ* on a very large haematoma just over his testes. So I tried to reassure them and asked if anyone had explained that the reason for the corrugated rubber was to bring all the blood and debris up from inside the tissues, and said that the leakage was old blood, fluid and waste from the injury. Then I repadded it and had to stick my ear on his distended tummy to listen for bowel sounds, having no stethoscope with me. His bowel sounded fine and hopefully he will pass a lot of wind soonish. He's to go to Haifa for dressing tomorrow. He turned out to be Um Ali's brother-in-law.

Little Aref, my young *habibi* (darling), came by complaining of *grippe* and a sore chest, so I listened to his chest, which was okay, and he lay down as though to sleep; then perked up and asked me if I wanted to go to the *mahwar*. So we set off to Arsan, through tunnels, past the *doshka*, underground and buildings, up staircases, across ladders, jumping from one window to the next until we reached the remains of houses above the front street. It's still deserted, but with a lot more debris and holes than a few weeks ago. The red corrugated barricade is still in place at the end and sandbags are in evidence everywhere. We then clambered about balcony doors and up beside bathroom windows to look out across the whole of the other side from the third floor. It was amazing to see trees and houses and streets again, clouds and Beirut far off in front of us. We squeezed up onto wooden boxes and clung to each other to squint sideways out of the windows. Aref led me through most of the *mahwar* by hand; he needed to in the tunnels as I couldn't see a thing. Then, on the other side above Haiduce *mahwar*, we stood and overlooked the whole camp up to Haifa Hospital with its demolished roof. Again, exhilarating to see daylight, sky, clouds, and the camp in front of us after an earthbound life for the past six weeks. It was a lovely experience to be out and see most of the *shebab* who come by the clinic: Abed, Jamal, Samir, Tariq, Mohamad, all sitting in sniper holes, and the 'Palestinian guerrillas' that the BBC World Service talked of today, all aged from 14 to 16 years old, sitting waiting and armed to the teeth, around tunnels, dark stairways, ladders and bridges of doors, with fires to keep warm.

Jamal was very put out that I wouldn't fire his Kalashnikov today, or even the revolver or other Kalashnikovs offered by his friends. The price of weapons on the black market was quoted by Kitaeb radio today:

1,000 French francs for a 120mm mortar.
1,500 Lebanese lira for a 155mm mortar.
1,500 American dollars for a Grad rocket.

And now Amal are using 160mm mortars on us again – must be costing Syria. Apart from Russian ammunition, Amal are also using French- and Syrian-made weaponry (confirmed by Ahmad and Monir today).

Saw yet another perforated eardrum; more antibiotics prescribed. Nawoosh at last has a son after four girls; a boy last night, now the ninth new baby in this area. I wonder how many there are now in the camp born during this war. Little Ibrahim's burns are looking good. He got to know the giraffe height chart at the clinic, but wouldn't have his height measured; although he did try to take the 'dog' off the wall and was quite enamoured of it.

What keeps me going through this whole bloody war is the fact that I am getting off on my work and have no time really to mope or get frustrated. Yes, it's frustrating not having vaccines and sufficient medicines, etc, but I usually find other solutions, salt and water being a favourite and garlic being another. Gentian Violet is the all-time hit. I love my daily life here in this society, and especially learning every day from the people here, who know so much more than us about so many things, from flour and bread to lighting wood fires, fetching water, drying herbs and flowers for teas, picking grit out of lentils, and playing with children. For example, Walid and little Jihad aged 2 today: he was effortlessly playing with her, even though he's only about 18 and dressed in fighting clothes with big boots, which he shot off in along the streets today at the sound of someone injured, tearing up the alley over the rubble at very high speed. Yet he sat and taught her, held her, kissed and played with great affection for her, as did Hossam from his bed too.

Every day I see things we 'foreigners' lack. But it's no good standing off at a distance. To learn, you have to humble yourself, to admit you don't know or understand, then try to experience it. Not to play at it – you don't really absorb anything that way, just skim the surface.

How I love it here, despite the moaning. The simplest things I adore, watching and learning all the time. Not the 'clever' *ajnabiyah* who knows a lot, but a stupid *ajnabiyah* who knows only a little, and hopes to trade this little for some of what everyone here knows. I feel overwhelmed at times with affection for everyone here, because of their kindness and generosity. Oh, for us all to come out of this safely – *Insh'Allah.*

14.12.86 Day 47 Sunday
19.45 Kitaeb radio: 'Few observers would place their money on a

ceasefire in the foreseeable future.' 'Fatah have categorically rejected withdrawal from Magdoushe.'

Listening to the BBC World Service version of *Box of Delights* which I think Neil Jordan used for *Company of Wolves*, loosely adapted. It's lovely Christmas music and a fairy tale. I can imagine little Ru listening to it at home along with the endless *Snowman* video. They are excelling themselves on the World Service with the *Messiah*, Italian oratorios; and later *Guys and Dolls* by Damon Runyon, today with the story of Nicely-Nicely and the murderous widow who ended up down the well before he lost all the money on a horse called Apparition.

I will continue the Advent calendar and decorations as I think we will still be in this bloody war for a while yet. Despite this, we took tea at the back of the hospital in a tank-shelled house that I had visited at the beginning with Lieve. We stood on the roof to survey the destruction and sat under one ceiling only, very nervous throughout as the owner declared 'Ceasefire – no ceasefire,' and wanted to take Hannes into the *khander* (tunnels). He declined, saying 'after the war – *Insh'Allah*'.

Today started as yesterday with the sad man breaking the door down just before 7.00 with Isa Dabdoub who had been sniped as he stood up to shoot. A 'sucking' chest wound: the entry hole took some time to find as he had his head turned over it. I padded and pressed it. We got him out of his clothes, all three layers, and ammunition straps – which he implored us not to cut off as they were new – he'll love us after that; and put him onto the stretcher which the sad man set off with to the hospital. Then I discovered my watch was missing. I turned the place over looking for it, and was about to go to the hospital where I hoped to find it, when a sheepish-looking man appeared saying his son had thought it was Isa's. Thank goodness I got it back; it's the only second hand we have here.

BBC World Service 22.00: Hanna Siniora interviewed (the editor of *Al Fajr*), signatory of a Palestinian petition against the violence, who said Palestinian reaction 'shows the extent of anti-Israeli feeling from the past twenty years of occupation'. Felicia Langer: 'they don't know anything more than Israeli soldiers . . . they are born in the Occupation . . . the Occupation is a factor of their very young lives.'*

Borhan destroyed Isa's sniper's position today with a B-7, so that's one less. And Monir says that a sniper was also shot from Samed as he stood on top of a hill to look. Samed has now been levelled to one floor only by the tanks over the last few days. The hospital has now two full floors and the ground floor left, the top two floors are almost completely destroyed, hanging in pieces of concrete on metal twisted beyond belief, suspended in mid-air on the hill overlooking the camp. I saw Isa at the hospital when I

*An Israeli Communist lawyer who defends Palestinians, and author of many harrowing books.

went for supplies and a chat with Pauline and Hannes. Hannes and I both feel that we have found our feet and fulfilment now through our work and our feeling for the people we have got to know and are working for and with. We also discussed never knowing the foreigners as a group, thinking that we never experienced a feeling of community with the other foreign workers and had to feel our own way.

I wrote Pauline a note saying to take Ben to the hospital as really he is so disinterested in the work here that he would be better to move there. There is obviously a lot of work to do here in terms of health care, but Ben is not even remotely interested in the dressing, let alone community follow-up. ('For unto us a child is born', BBC World Service 23.35 *Messiah.*) The question of me staying here alone is unthinkable to Ben and Pauline, yet nightly I am left alone for three to eight hours while Ben goes out, and he even looked askance at me mentioning the cultural inadaptation of having men keep me company (and safe) while he is out, yet he encourages creeps, friends of his like Hisham, to be alone with me, and people I don't know, saying in a war things are different.

Now *The Pearl Fishers* – 'Au fond du temps' – I shall cry at the beauty of it. The injured cat is sleeping on my bed, its injured legs alternatively hobbling or jumping when it wants fish or food. Oh, how I miss some things – affection for one, and the security of someone to care for me for a change. I spend all my time trying to care enough. And Ben's attitude of decreasing care at this end of the camp really angers me beyond description. He has suggested that I shut the clinic down and go and get emergency room experience at the hospital. This is just bloody ridiculous: how can he think that people here don't need care any more than those up there?

Oh dear! The overture to *Tannhäuser* is about to make me cry again. I think my drain man must have farted by now as I haven't heard any more of him today.

Popped in on Ghaleb who is looking thinner but is a bit better, leg still in traction and arm on a slab, poor thing, and he sleeps all the time. Every time I go to see him, he's asleep. Couldn't find little Ahmad to see how he is doing, although he's apparently fine despite a later laparotomy with four holes within one metre of his bowel.

Dr Atia cares a lot about the little kids. He told me the story of one family's father deserting the family and marrying another woman, and not maintaining the children. Then he returned to his first wife just before she died, spending her wages from cleaning work on alcohol. Atia said that when he cried for his wife's death, it was for her wages, not for her.

Saw little 2.3-kilogramme Fatima Warida today. She's looking good so far, with clean eyes and good fontanelles. Her mother was worried about her umbilical cord so we cleaned it with alcohol and gave her some vitamins. Nawoosh appeared beaming carrying his son who is called

Maher (as all the family have names beginning with M). Have to visit my other two tinies tomorrow – Mahmud and Mohamad – both new war babies too, to check weights, milk, vitamins, etc.

We've just made an emergency box so we can grab everything much quicker than this morning, which was a bit slow to put it mildly, not counting running out of plaster. We'll rearrange 'the kitchen' again tomorrow.

15.12.86 Day 48 Monday

14.30 Kitaeb radio: a UNIFIL Ghanaian soldier seriously wounded by three mortars from Hola inside the Israeli zone. An Irish soldier died on December 6 from gunshots fired by an SLA soldier. Yesterday three Palestinians were attacked and burned alive by Amal militiamen, who also attacked and raped Palestinian women. One hundred and twenty-three people have been kidnapped at the airport and airport road in eight months; thirty people have died from these abductions in the same period. The PLO are blamed for holding up the Iranian ceasefire; Abu Jihad says the PLO have agreed to the ceasefire and evacuation of Magdoushe as long as there are guarantees not to use Magdoushe to attack the Palestinian camps in Saida after the fighters leave. Tonight, an explosion at the Amal office in Fakhani in West Beirut by the Beirut Martyrs Organization, whoever they are, who warned Beirut residents not to go close to Amal buildings. Two hundred French UNIFIL from the south have returned to France, twenty-five remaining in Naqura.

Apparently our *howen* collection from nearby is of French origin (you can tell by the curve and the tail; the Russians' are straight-edged triangles). The French *howens* are reportedly the most dangerous as their explosive is also an incendiary. The Amal militiamen were caught and will be imprisoned for selling weapons to Fatah fighters in the camps. The usual practice is a warning and a prison sentence as they are Shia, but if the man has no family he is killed secretly. Amal were also reported to be killing each other today on the front streets in fights over loot from the shops and houses, shooting it out.

Oh, it would be nice just to see people on the streets, to stand on the roof, to sit outside, to sleep at night, to relax, to see friends without worry about coming or going, you or them. People are so brave, constantly carrying in the wounded under shelling in the dawn and going up to the hospital, so slowly, with stretchers. Not like Syrian intelligence and Amal who shot it out in the AUH the other day, over some disagreement amongst themselves.

Zeinab's sister had a 28-week girl who was resuscitated at birth. There are no incubators so I took aluminium cooking foil to the hospital and wrapped her up in it over cottonwool, told them to hold her close, and left the foil for tomorrow.

Expecting a big attack on Shatila all day tomorrow and perhaps shells here too. The mountains are prepared for shelling and Bourj also. Even the BBC World Service used the *Economist*'s Middle East reporter phoning from Nicosia who said that the Syrians are expected to try and save face from the PLO as they've invested too much militarily and financially to accept the Iranian accords immediately, without a last attempt to gain some military ground. So we expect a hot day tomorrow and are praying Shatila won't fall or else we will get it next. Not to mention the massacre that will occur. And we know the Syrians are helping physically, as the other day two officers from the Syrian Army were killed at Shatila as they guided the line of tank fire. They were left on the ground for some time.

16.12.86 Day 49 Tuesday

Hanna's baby died last night.

A 'shaky truce' with PLO, rejecting everything until its points are reached. Berri rejecting many points of the Islamic Forces, Daud Daud refusing to lift the siege of Rashidiyeh until the Palestinians disarm. So we could be here for months yet as the PLO want to settle it well and truly this time.

I went to weigh little Mahmud and Mohamad, who were both very fat, and ended up organizing yoga sessions after the war here, two afternoons a week for exercise, and pre- and post-natal exercises.

Aref came to take me on a home visit to a woman with severe fright. We went underground from Borhan's to Marrubba *mahwar* – very good tunnels and very necessary after seeing Marrubba four weeks ago and now: the destruction from tanks is very obvious, holes and rubble everywhere. Heard also that Zeinab's sister had had a problem two months earlier in the pregnancy just after I saw her and had needed a B-positive blood transfusion. As I left the hospital Abu Salim said, 'Don't run, there is no shelling; don't run.' And I thought, 'There never is any shelling until it starts.' Aref and I gave out milk near the shelters and will do so tomorrow. *Insh'Allah.*

17.12.86 Day 50 Wednesday

Now the fiftieth day. People are being triaged, as to who has the possibility of survival from injuries, as the nitrous oxide and oxygen are in short supply. (In the 45-day war, the *fedayeen* made a raid outside the camp to a pharmacy store and stole some for the operating room.) A man was sniped and fell from three floors in the *mahwar* next to Haiduce (I think these were the floors I visited the other day); he died almost instantly. Then Nigar's nephew died from a *howen* exploding on the *mahwar*. In the first day of the Ramadan war, twenty-six people died; there were no emergency or operating rooms or medicine. There is the same situation now in

Rashidiyeh (where people in the camp are now eating grass: reported on Radio Monte Carlo).

The baby milk is running out; we are on to our last box. So today, Aref, a little boy called Imad, Rifat's sister Wisall who has the twins, and I set off round the shelters with scales, charts and milk. We found three new babies, so the local total is thirteen. There were *howens* and it was all rather nerve-racking doing the most stupid thing of walking around in a procession of four weighed down with equipment, with mortars falling nearby and the two women injured just shortly beforehand. Quite unnerving. Zeinab was similarly foolish: she will not run anywhere, even if there are bombs up at the top of the camp, and today she *walked* me down the wrong side of a road well known for snipers, so that even Omer her father was shouting at her to move and get on to the right side. Then she took the long way by Haiduce to the house of Samira's grandmother – via a sniper. She's another person cultivating a death wish.

Her sister is home after a D and C, and wants the picture of Fatima, her little premature daughter, that Ben took before she died at 5.30. Her husband looked at me and told me he wanted a baby. She had started labour after a *howen* made her run and fall to the ground. They all spoke constantly of the little dead baby.

The night was spent with the quiet sniper Amer who sat for four hours talking, talking, talking. He is living alone in the camp, his father was killed in 1982 and his mother lives in Haret Hreik. We talked of Jerusalem, art, society and love. I put up Christmas decorations and have to make some more. And the news of the day is that *my finger is moving again* – after six weeks.

18.12.86 Day 51 Thursday

Bad news: Nabila Brier was murdered in Mar Elias street today by Amal gunmen who shot at her car while she was driving to work at UNICEF. They killed two others who were in the street at the same time. Ben is upset as he has worked with her for a long time. So now Amal are killing Palestinian women who work for UNICEF, as well as men. She was the Director for Palestinian Affairs in Lebanon, lived in Barbir near Berri, and had been threatened several times before. Now she is dead at 42. I last saw her getting into her car looking chic with Ahmad driving, as she went off to a meeting after I had paid my first call.

Nabila's shooting and that of the others including the headmaster of Mar Elias UNRWA school could have serious repercussions for us. I suppose we'll all have to thrash it out at the end of the war, as we are now clearly vulnerable for working for the Palestinians; the excuse for Nabila's murder, despite working for UNICEF, was that she was thought to be working for the PLO.

Today I treated my first dog. A woman came running into the clinic carrying the little puppy I saw behind the Al Khatib house one day last week; it had been hit by shrapnel causing a bad laceration in one paw and bits of shrapnel in its fur. As it was quite shocked it let me clean it with oxygen and apply an iodine bandage, then refused the blanket and crawled into a corner under stretchers and sat there licking its wounds. Later some children came in to take it home while I was outside the clinic trying to treat my rather overwrought 15-year-old pregnancy, Haweida.

Visited by Rifat, Hissam and Haj, who shot someone from Amal today who was running down the front street and caused the *howens* at 15.00 whilst I was out dealing with the young pregnancy in the house behind Borhan's *mahwar*, which has taken four mortars and now has a sandbag structure on the front wall. Sent young Samir (who winks at me) home with a temperature of 37.9°C. The silly ass went on to the *mahwar*, so I went after him and sent him very much home after he had turned up with a fever for the second day in a row. He's got flu like everyone else here, or a burst eardrum, or a burn. Our most common injuries. Pohsie (my sister) is 25 today – hope she is safe and well.

19.12.86 Day 52 Friday

BBC World Service 22.00: 'Syrian troops backed up by tanks have been involved in clashes with pro-Palestinian Islamic groups in the northern Lebanese port of Tripoli . . . who were forced to accept a peace agreement with Syrian-backed Shia militia after a Syrian siege of the city last year.'

Well, my overwrought girl, Haweida, went to the hospital and promptly fainted and had to be revived by poor Dr Salim. She is now no longer vomiting, just needs some rehydration; she had a litre of vitamins, etc, in Haifa Hospital. She gave me some lovely earrings (as she's now married she has 30,000-Lebanese-lira-worth of gold from Abu Iyad, her 21-year-old husband of a month and a half), and I gave her the purple glass and diamanté which suit her much better than me as she has lovely olive skin and dark hair.

Many people have now said that they are leaving after this war; this is no life and they are sick of it. Of course this is exactly what the Israeli/Syrian/Amal plan always intended: to force people out of the camps, then overrun and empty them completely, wiping them from existence.

All alone tonight. Today was breezy but still warmish, but after more thunder again the rains have come. It's pouring down outside and the sewers had overrun by early afternoon already, let alone after four to five hours of solid rain. My little 20-day-old baby, Fatima, has developed jaundice. It wasn't until I saw her in daylight that I noticed she was bright yellow. It started yesterday and her mother thought that today it was still just localized. But when I stripped her clothes off we saw that it had spread to all of her body. So Shahina (Fatima's sister) and I ran her up to the hospital to see Dr Salim. He also thought it was rhesus incompatibility jaundice, but there is nothing we can do but wait. There is no possibility of an exchange transfusion (which I in my ignorance had been thinking about) and the lab is unable even to do serum bilirubin levels or haematocrit. So we just have to wait and see. It's awful. How can you explain that there are three options for a 20-day-old baby (whose mother may also have problems as she had the small ante-partum bleed a few weeks ago):

1 The jaundice goes away after some time with no ill effects.
2 The jaundice goes after producing cerebral irritation and leaves either permanent brain damage or cerebral palsy due to convulsions.
3 The baby's condition worsens, she fails to thrive and dies.

All because of the war and the inability to transfer her out of the camp to Akka Hospital for blood estimations or phototherapy or exchange transfusion. Just as Zeinab's sister's past history and family history of two babies needing incubators would indicate births in Akka Hospital not Haifa, so also would this wee tot's ante-natal care. So now we wait.

Today I saw Ibrahim and Isa who were carrying on in fine recovered style, and weighed the new Al Khatib baby and Ola who are both fine – 3.5 kilogrammes and 6.5 kilogrammes respectively – and little Fatima who had gained 10 grammes in five days: 2.4 kilogrammes now. Saw Rifat and Haj at little Ahmad's who I finally got to smile, despite being encased in two plaster of Paris casts on arm and leg, and having had a laparotomy.

Shatila is practically demolished now, and again today heavy shelling at ten shells per minute. The gas and petrol situation is now getting tight, including the operating room gas, as the war is in a stalemate and expected to last another three weeks at least. Food has now run out in most houses and, just as we get ours from the hospital, everyone else has to get theirs by going to the political groups for Fatah food, which is stored in shelters underground. The hospital also gets its food this way. So we'll still be here at New Year and into the middle of January as the whole situation is now at a complete standstill. And the Arab League remains as impotent as ever; it will probably delay its meetings again for discussions. Again women have been trying to gather support for a demonstration against Fatah and Arafat policies over the camp wars. I think they were probably as unsuccessful as their previous attempts the other day.

20.12.86 Day 53 Saturday

Tripoli radio 19.45: Bedawi and Nahr al-Bared camps in Tripoli surrounded by pro-Syrian forces. Fighting continues in Tripoli and now is threatening all Palestinian camps in the Lebanon. Fierce shelling of Shatila and Bourj also, after some Amal were taken prisoner; we were shelled for one hour. Daud Daud claims that the Iranian envoy still on hunger strike inside Rashidiyeh's mosque is an agent of Yasser Arafat . . .

I spent most of today from 11.30 outside in the camp. Saw little Ahmad whose injuries are very similar indeed to those of Isa; took ages to dress him as he's terrified of any disturbance of plaster. Went up to see little Fatima who seems (maybe it's my imagination) a little less yellow. Her stools are bright yellow which is not too bad a thing, and she's still eating, had no convulsions and no obvious liver enlargement, thank God. Then saw Zeinab's sister after being told that she had great pain: I ran to the house to find slight vaginal itching, a chest cold and not much else. Then on to the shelter to Fatima's mother's burn and dressed little Suhail's eyes (the child who was blinded in one eye by shrapnel and originally was thought to be totally blind). She was crying and howling as I washed her eyes out and put tetracycline in them.

Haj (Mohamad) came by with Abu Sacker and was talking about Somerset Maughan and psychology. He was also besieged by the multi-named cat, but showed the fatso blacko great affection. After he left, Haj like a gentleman was going to wait for Ben to reappear. Borhan stopped by to hand in sweets.

So the PLO in Baghdad expect a full-scale Syrian onslaught on the camps with Amal soon, and Shatila is being demolished by tanks so as to render it uninhabitable. The PLO expressed concern about a final entering attack on the camp, which Amal deny any intention of. Ha *ha*! Again one shell every ten seconds there, one shell every one or two minutes here. You can really hear the damage now with a wild wind blowing and the noise carrying. The camp sounds as though it will fall down any minute now – bangs, crashes and rubble.

Sakarov was released from Gorky to Moscow today.

21.12.86 Day 54 Sunday

So the war drags on. Luckily for us it was raining heavily all day, turning the sewers into shin-high torrents and stagnant puddles, but making Amal disinclined to stand and be drenched by rain trying to launch mortars. Needless to say, as soon as it stopped, we heard the tanks moving into position on the front street.

Rashidiyeh was shelled again with T-54s and 120mm mortars, and their mosque was also destroyed today, like ours last night, which caused between seven to twelve injured, though not seriously. The World Service again talked of Palestinian guerrillas in the camps. When I get back to London (*Insh'Allah*) I'm going to go to Bush House and show the newscasters some of the pictures of 10- to 15-year-old boys who are fighting, especially Abed, Hamoudi and Aref.

Saw little Fatima who is looking less yellow today, her eyes are less yellow also. Thank God. Pauline and I are puzzled by the sudden appearance of jaundice now. Little Ahmad's stitches have to come out tomorrow.

Got a row from Ghassan for having a candle at the door as the sniper had been shooting into the alley again. They've covered the top of the entrance to Arsan *mahwar* with zinc now to obstruct any view of the street, but all day there was a tall corrugated zinc sniper barricade blocking the alley. Then the stupid foreigner left the door open letting light out into the road again.

Just listened to *The Box of Delights* Part 2, and am now listening to Christmas music from Salisbury Cathedral. Getting homesick at the prospect of a war – working at Christmas, as usual – ugh! Khadija asked me what I wanted for Christmas. I said a ceasefire. Dr Rede said that they are trying to find a tree for us from somewhere.

Amal restated its intention not to enter Shatila, so they just pounded it with tanks and mortars again. There is to be no water for the next forty-eight hours so everyone was scurrying in the dark to fetch water before it was turned off. A frantic knocking at the door to borrow the battery for Arsan *mahwar*. At first we thought that a B-7 had destroyed their battery, but then we understood that it was to launch a 107mm rocket, which needs electricity. It was duly sent out, the battery was returned and I was asked had I not heard the noise.

There is a recording on the radio from Palestine, Nazareth and now Bethlehem, the Church of the Nativity. Funny to think I was there only two years ago. The BBC are even calling it Palestine. The Ottomans rampaged in Palestine, destroying many of Christianity's early churches, but sparing the Nativity as the three kings were depicted in mosaic in Persian dress.

Dreamt last night that I was not cut off from the world and that many letters were given to me from Mum, Dad and Pohsie, and Ghillie and Stewart – missing them all. A lovely old lady, Wafiqa's grandmother, Fatima's great-grandmother, asked me where they all were today and expressed concern at my being alone in a strange place with a war.

I wonder how the Christmas tree looks, with decorations and Christmas cards, and food being made and presents and preparations going on everywhere. I've just given aspirin to a flu-ridden Dabdoub who will go home and sleep after six hours at the *mahwar* with flu, when he needs two days' rest and care, not water and cold and fighting.

That God was man in Palestine
and lives today in bread and wine.

Just heard some sort of rocket go out so I expect some *howens* will come in now. M-16 sniping going on and the little lady I have to visit tomorrow has an M-16 injury on her leg. She ranted at me, blaming the loss of Palestine on the British. She's right. Yesterday I had the same conversation with a young man at Um Bilal's, where we played cards by candlelight while being shelled in the dark. He had been taken by the Israelis to Ansar Jail and held for fifteen months until there was an exchange for a few Israeli soldiers.

22.12.86 Day 55 Monday

Kitaeb radio: reports of atrocities and massacres in Tripoli, similar to operations against Muslim Fundamentalists (20,000 reported dead) in Syria by the Syrian Army, against so-called Sunni Fundamentalists over the past few days*. Apparently men, women and children have been rounded up and killed by Syrians and pro-Syrian sympathizers, and the bodies are being dumped in mass graves near the sports stadium. It's easy to believe. No headway in any negotiations.

Now the fuel is running out and there is supposed to be only enough remaining to fuel one operation of six hours' duration. The internal squabbling and unwillingness to give fuel to the hospital is now leaving the only solution that each organization pays for its fighters' operations in fuel. There was said to be a large tankful inside the remains of Samed, but I don't know whether any is still left. The other alternative is to dig tunnels out to the gas station about 200 metres from one of the front street *mahwars*, so maybe we'll need to dig and dig.

A shootout in the square after Ahmad got into an argument and Hussein shot at him; smoke and dust rising up and a fierce squabble broke out, then a mother started shouting, then Borhan and his father had a shout at each other.

Spent the day running around – from young Ahmad whose six stitches came out, then up to little Fatima who has a bit of a liver today, but is less yellow. Then to Isa and Ibrahim with a promise to visit the hospital tomorrow, and on to the Haji at Hossam Ali's. She'd managed to go up to the hospital for a dressing, as had Hossam. Howeida is still vomiting and had gone back to the hospital.

A lovely evening at the Al Khatibs' watching all the kids being thrown around by Borhan and having intellectual conversations with Ibrahim about 'eating bread and potatoes with *baba* (daddy) today'. Iman came to get some pads as there are no Kotex left in the shops now; we are using half-sterile pads. Spoke with Borhan's father about life in Lebanon before the war. Went with Mohamad on his crutches through the camp to a house behind Zeinab's to see a 1-day-old baby, also called Mohamad, with a very obviously pulled head and a rather large, squishy bruise on the top left-hand side of his head. His cord is fine and he's a healthy 3.6 kilogrammes and feeding. I'll go back in two days on Christmas Eve and see how they

*Known as the Murabitoun massacre.

are doing; in the meantime I gave her vitamins and a weight chart. Saw the sad man pulling Ahmad up the road by the neck.

23.12.86 Day 56 Tuesday
Now 500 are reputed dead in the slaughter in Tripoli by the Syrians, who are trying to blame the Palestinians for the massacre. The bodies are still being secretly buried.

The water is off today, not yesterday as planned, so now we are running out of water. Woken by TNT explosions at 9.15 from around the camp. There are conflicting views on who detonated them – Amal or Syria for a better view of the camp, or Palestinians. Then the occasional *howen*, until at 16.30 a *howen* landed just outside Hassan Abed's house where I had gone to drink coffee, having not managed to go the day before when invited. I had been standing on the spot* just half an hour previously. We went to Sianni *mahwar* where we looked from the third- floor balcony on to an Amal flag a few blocks away, and the next-door roof where mortars and 107s are launched onto Amal positions at Shatila to help them. The house is in a spacious four- or five-storey block with balconies and French windows and chandeliers in the hallways. Part of the balcony was blown away by a *howen* and is now a mass of tangled wires.

Listening to the news detailing suppression by Syria of all reports from Tripoli since Friday, with all news of the Murabitoun massacre also suppressed. The Islamic hospitals were directed by the Syrians to vet the injured as to area and militia, and the hospital is now a massive mortuary. Again Berri accused the Palestinians of violating the ceasefire agreement and the news today is getting bleaker and bleaker. Despite the zinc erected over the *mahwar* entrance, M-16 bullets continue to hit the walls and today a mortar landed nearby without exploding. I'll go up on the roof to look tomorrow if it is quiet.

Had a riotous evening last night with Hissam, Rifat and Haj who are all looking forward to Christmas Eve and Christmas Day. Making the last decorations now, although if the water is off again tomorrow the only thing I'll want for Christmas will be 'a bath'. Throngs of *shebab* looking for water, but we have none either.

I'm tired, a bit fed up and I think I want to go home *now*! for Christmas, not be stuck in this bloody war, waterless, moneyless, foodless and facing the daily prospect of being blown to bits by bloody Amal with a 120mm mortar or rocket.

The fuel situation is solved temporarily by taking fuel from the big Samed tank, which, although it is impure, after speaking to an engineer on the *jihaz* to Mar Elias, they decided can be utilized now. He will come after the war and thoroughly clean the motor of all the dirt and garbage it will accumulate.

*Known with ironic trepidation as the Bermuda Triangle, since so many people were killed there.

One young man, Bilal Shabati, was hit by shrapnel today which fractured a section of his spine. He was initially entubated and then shortly afterwards appeared to breathe spontaneously; but as soon as the tube was removed he started gasping and making tremendous independent efforts to breathe. He was hurriedly re-entubated and taken to X-ray which showed a large piece of shrapnel which had severed his spine. There was complete paralysis and no respiratory capabilities. As he would not be able to be evacuated and, even if he was, he would need a ventilator until he died, the decision was taken to let him die. But, as there was no available morphine, Valium had to be used as the sedation/respiratory depressant. He took a long time to die, as like most young men here he was fit. He had been injured in every war preceding this one, and was a cousin of Mirwan. Everyone is very sad as he was only 18.

24.12.86 Day 57 Wednesday Christmas Eve
What a day for Christmas Eve, absolutely no solution in sight and when I saw Haj Abu Taher who helped me carry the water 'gallon' he told me he was 'very afraid'. I replied I too was very afraid. Later we were just clearing up when Borhan was shot and carried in with great pain. Ben was out and we cut his clothes off to find an entry/exit bullet wound through his clavicle. Thank God it wasn't a few centimetres lower. His blood loss was minimal and we had nothing to support his collar bone and shoulder which I thought were fractured, not even a sling left. So we pressure-padded and sent him off on a stretcher to Haifa. Luckily he had only a single clavicular fracture and is now home with a support bandage. Lydia and his mother were beside themselves, but his dad was very calm and wished him '*Salamtak*' (a greeting to the ill) as he was carried up to the hospital.

BBC World Service: Maidoon in South Lebanon has been attacked by the Israelis with helicopters and the SLA are attacking the villages, buildings and areas around it. They were thought to be trying to attack Hizb'ullah who are based there. A French journalist was released in West Beirut tonight after one year's captivity by the Revolutionary Justice Organization, who are still holding one other Frenchman. They said it was a goodwill gesture as France appeared to be trying to improve its relations with Iran. They released him near the Beau Rivage hotel which serves as the Syrian 'observers' headquarters.

The other story of today was little Imad getting sniped in his arm near his home, from which you can clearly see Shia buildings, and some people make you run it, others dawdle. Anyway, young Imad being swift on his feet, a 12-year-old *fedai*, he clamped his good arm over his shot arm and ran straight away to the hospital where he immediately presented himself to Dr Saleh saying he had been shot. The doctor asked his name; he shouted that he refused to tell him his name, so the doctor shouted back at him, 'What is your name?' 'I refuse to tell you my name – get to work,' shouted back Imad. I can't wait to see him now. The injury is not serious, the bullet went through his muscle and missed the bone, but he's so damn stubborn and brave (and sensible – not many have the brains to stop the bleeding and run to the hospital). Clever wee boy. He gets the prize for the most common sense when injured.

Read *Gatsby* until 3 am.

25.12.86 Day 58 Thursday Christmas Day

Where to start? One of the worst days of this war so far, *al salam*? At the beginning, I suppose. Woken from a nightmarish dream about Taisear being killed, and relieved to be awake and find I was only dreaming. Rockets and *howens* early in the morning, then banging on the door, people letting themselves in and asking for dressings, even though the notice on the door said, 'Closed for dressings. Only emergencies today'. Then Akram and Shehadi al Ashwa, having hammered on the door, let themselves in and shook me awake for a boy with a burn from the *mahwar* – not serious. Now I was awake at 9.40 so I gave the long lie-in I had promised myself for ages a miss, and got up. Then I snarled 'Closed today' at another knock at the door, only to find Ahmad Aishey, Nasser and Hannes.

I went out to do my essential dressings and got waylaid by eight people. Wafiqa al Ashwa, looking wan and ill, took me in for coffee for Christmas (although she is a Muslim she was celebrating Maryam* and Isa† also), and then asked me if I knew any way for Akram to be taken out of the country to be educated as the wars are disrupting all the children's education. I said I would ask Pauline to enquire when she got back to London. I think the visas are based on obtaining an undertaking for a full responsibility, financial and board, etc. Then she told me that I had been mentioned on Radio from Baghdad (PLO information) as 'Suzy working with the Palestine Red Crescent had been injured, a nurse from Belgium'.

Then I visited Ahmad to do his dressing and Um al Abed (Ali al Haj) was making bread, so after Wafiqa's biscuits for Christmas I also got fresh hot *manaeesh filfil*. Then all hell broke loose with two injured men arriving at once, the first with mild shrapnel, the second, Yusuf, with a respiratory arrest. At first I had no idea what was happening as his pulses were still there but thready, so as he had no breathing I got the airway and suction, put it in, no gag reflex, and blew. His lungs inflated and he started coughing, so I suctioned and took out the airway. Then he stopped breathing again, so I put the airway back in, blew again and suctioned until he was coughing well. He was semi-conscious. So we ran him up to

*Maryam is Mary.

†Isa is Jesus, who is considered a prophet in Islam so Muslims can celebrate his birth.

Haifa, me prodding his chest to encourage him every so often. We got there and waited and he recovered fine, and then I decided against intuition to come back, but had to turn back as there were *howens*.

As we waited in the corridor, we heard a shriek and I went back with Ben and Pauline, thinking it was Yusuf, to find Ahmad about to faint and a very blue man being entubated. I held Ahmad's legs up and then another stretcher came in with a boy with blood on his head. Initially I thought it was the little 'camp' boy, Sami, sniped in the head. Whoever it was was dead and had come via the clinic. So Hisham and I made a run for it back down and got in just as another *howen* exploded.

There we found Khaled Daud, and discovered the dead boy was Fahdi al Jarzi's brother Fouad who had been standing in the Al Haj doorway when a *howen* exploded just outside in the Bermuda Triangle (again). He took all the initial shrapnel, and Nada also and Khaled behind him. Somehow he was put on a stretcher and brought as far as the water pump in the square outside the clinic. Khaled hobbled into the clinic to tell Hannes and, as there were *howens* exploding, they had to wait to go out and pull him in, but he was dead. Hannes tried to revive him with suction but he had multiple internal shrapnel, with his arms and legs practically detached from his body. The only thing untouched was his face. We think Fouad must have died outright, so they left him when they realized he was dead and ran Mohamad to the hospital. Poor Dr Salim, who was close to Mohamad and a cousin, came in and started arguing about trying to operate – how awful. But he too died shortly afterwards, from a massive brain haemorrhage, his skull a mush of fragmented bone.

Anyway, Khaled had shrapnel, Nada had two inner aspect thigh wounds and we were all near to tears about Fouad. I used to see him almost daily when I did Zaida and Khaled's dressings. This morning I waved hello to his mother who has now lost her husband and two sons in the last three wars. Poor, poor woman, poor Fahdi and poor Lena, his sister. He was such a lovely boy with a wide open kind smile and a lovely manner. Blown to bits and now he is dead at 17 years old.

Later Haj came for some tablets for the gang of three, so I gave him three Valium, one for each of them, but he took them all as he didn't think they were working. Later, the other two 'gang members' Rifat and Hissam came by so they got five milligrammes of Valium each. Then I had to go to see Ibrahim al Khatib who was flushed, grizzly and listless. He had a rectal temperature of 39.8°C so I led him screaming out to the hall and left him stripped with orders for four-hourly aspirin, Ampicillin and a half-hourly tepid sponge. His ears and tonsils are inflamed, I think. When I went back after the Christmas meal of spaghetti and garlic, he was better and his temperature down, so I had tea and then Borhan's dad walked me back to the clinic. Borhan managed to get some sleep today as last night he had too much pain. So much for Hassan Abed's much-lauded ceasefire today – so much for it.

26.12.86 Day 59 Friday Boxing Day

After a dark day yesterday we are all numbed by Fouad's death. Ahmad's and Nada's dressings were done in Issam Hussein's house which is less exposed than the Al Haj house. Fouad had heard about Yusuf's injury and was about to leave the house to come to the clinic when the mortar killed him. Banan spent all night crying, and looked pale today. Ahmad and Nada talked about Fouad to me while I did their dressings, and the room looked incomplete without him coming in to say hello.

The sheikh of the nearest mosque preached last Friday that if people were behaving badly in the present situation they should be dealt with by Islamic law, starting with his son who had been caught stealing earlier in the week and spent a mere two days in PFLP prison, before a fabulously inventive tale of release – that he had beaten up his two guards and escaped. To where, we ask ourselves? Outside the camp? Pauline expressed the hope that people did not start going around cutting each other's hands off as they had enough work in surgery so far. But the level of crime, mostly stealing, is really beyond imagination. At the moment all empty houses are being plundered and known burglars are seen carrying plastic bags of loot up the road helped by their children.

Pauline spoke to Øyvind on the *jihaz* on Christmas Eve. Because of the code system it's a little difficult to ascertain who is actually celebrating Christmas in Hamra, but we think it was Øyvind, Solbritt, Christa, the Finns and Swedes from Tripoli and some others. At least they are away from the Syrian operations which are still continuing in Tripoli against the Sunni Muslim groups, after one week.

Boxing Day and Dad is 54 now; wonder what kind of a day he, Pohsie and Mum are having. Looking at all the little Al Khatibs lying in a row of four wee sausages, sleeping on the floor last night, reminded me of New Year at home, when we were little and all pushed upstairs to wait for midnight bells. If I come out of this alive, I'll spend next year at home for Christmas and New Year. As Hannes says, all he wants is for me to 'keep breathing' down here – grief and all reactions are submerged in the 'maybe tomorrow I'm next' feelings and staying unmutilated from day to day. As others had told us, we do not grieve now but after the war, when we remember. Today we only hope it won't be us next, as almost every household has one injury now or more, and people are being injured two or three times.

27.12.86 Day 60 Saturday

Amal positions around Beirut are still being attacked, usually with explosives by the Sunni Resistance Forces, which gives us something to smile about when we hear of another attack. Abu Musa and Abu Nidal released a statement today saying that life in the besieged camps was now becoming intolerable with Shatila eighty-five per cent destroyed and Bourj al-Brajneh fifty per cent. The PLO in Baghdad released details of negotiations with Hizb'ullah that obtained the release of the French hostage on Christmas Eve and it is now said to be exerting greater influence at the Arab diplomatic level. Abu Riyad (Sultan) today said he thought the war would continue for about fifteen days; Haj and Abu Sacker gloomily predict another two months, and I think Sultan's initial assessment of three months' duration is fairly accurate.

Had our photographs taken for Abu Suhail, the Fatah political commander in the camp, who is reportedly sending them to the PLO in Baghdad (to Arafat himself, it's rumoured), so I tried to stop laughing and Banan posed in between us for the said photograph. The planned tunnel to the gas station has been dug and Feres who used to work there drew up the plans. First the diesel tank is being emptied for the hospital, then the benzine, then the gas tank. Solves some of the fuel crisis – thank God for tunnels – all twenty-five metres of it.

Visited my yellow Mohamad today, got soaked to the skin in torrential rain and flooding. So had tea after looking at him, and discovered that his mother is Shia from Sur, and married for love two years ago and moved into the camp only three months ago. She says it is safer inside than outside, when there is no war. She's delightful.

During the hail storm, big chunks of hail, swirling and flooding, shifted the carefully laid bricks in the road over the drain holes and everywhere. Rifat and I waded out to the streams of water pouring off the roofs to collect it. We discarded the first lot Ben collected, got absolutely drenched and stood around shivering and laughing our heads off with water pouring over us, around us and under us. We both shivered for the rest of the day, but it was worth it for the sheer letting-off-steam stupidity of it. All the kids were wading in it as it was far too wet for *howens* to be launched at us.

Then Nada Ali al Haj came after seeing Pauline; her shrapnel is okay again, thank goodness, so I went down to her house to do the dressing as she is very shy. Ahmad also visited the hospital and I met him being carried down by Saleh through the flooding in a *dishdasha* with plaster of Paris dangling, as I went up to the hospital to collect instruments from the sterilizer. One nurse tried to show me the new baby born today (dead) with two faces squashed next to each other, but she was in the top fridge and there were far too many children and people standing around to see. Pauline took photographs, though. The rumours are that the child's father's abuse of intravenous drugs and indiscriminate drinking caused her deformities. Poor Dr Salim, after his uterine haemorrhage at Christmas, and Hanna's pre-term dead baby, and now this. Thank goodness for the *jihaz* as the haemorrhage case almost had a hysterectomy at 17 years old, as they couldn't stop the bleeding, but advice was called for from Mar Elias by walkie-talkie, and they managed to stop it.

Had a lovely, very hot wash at Fatima's and saw her mother again who had come up from the shelter. There was flooding inside, so despite her reluctance to be anywhere near her decrepit and ageing husband, who beats all the girls in the family and his wife, she surfaced for a short while.

28.12.86 Day 61 Sunday

Afternoon. Listening on the World Service to fabulously 1960s play about stately homes and American millionaires: 'There is no honour where there is sex – I am happy to say.'

Amal made an attack this morning, and looking out down our rubble-strewn street with a cold wind blowing I can hear tanks and some other sort of machinery moving outside. It's odd to think that this has gone on now for two months. It feels as though we saw Øyvind and Solbritt only a few days ago, so much is the nerve-wearing effect of day-to-day fear and survival. As Pauline said, things that irritated a few weeks ago we no longer notice.

Woke up again with diarrhoea and light-headedness and no water left. The conclusion is that it is amoebiasis on its three-week cycle of faecal diarrhoea and malaise. A disastrous day from an inter-working-relations point of view. With usual intuition I asked Khadija and Zeinab about fetching the water as soon as they arrived. They both ignored it, Khadija being fear-bound and Zeinab thinking it below her. I asked another twice as both were pointedly ignoring me, both flapping around while I did dressings or just standing about. Then the attack began all along the *mahwars* with tanks and the Abu Musa *mahwar* going out on the street. So when I started washing glasses for tea, Khadija took it upon herself to run out in the *howens* and get water from the tap at Abu Abed. I followed her. We heard one explosion far off and she ran into a doorway. I stood in the street a while, then ran in too with Khadija. Once I could make out where I was, I discovered I was in the back of Haj Abu Taher's house. We sat in the dark for a while waiting for more explosions while I looked at what seemed to be a dated picture of the young Abu Taher and a formidable sheikh from many years ago in a heavy frame – a beautiful picture. Then there was a bang and a bright yellow flame. It was outside on the walls of the alley and we could not figure out what it was. It was too small to be a *howen* and too big to be a 500mm bullet. We were mystified and when it seemed quiet Khadija ran out and picked up the little water canister and ran to the clinic. I followed, putting the next canister under the tap and then running headlong up the alley to the clinic doors. Only then did we realize what the explosion had been, as the whole square was covered in a thick white smoke that sent us coughing and choking from room to room. We covered our faces with our jerseys to avoid coughing incessantly. It was a

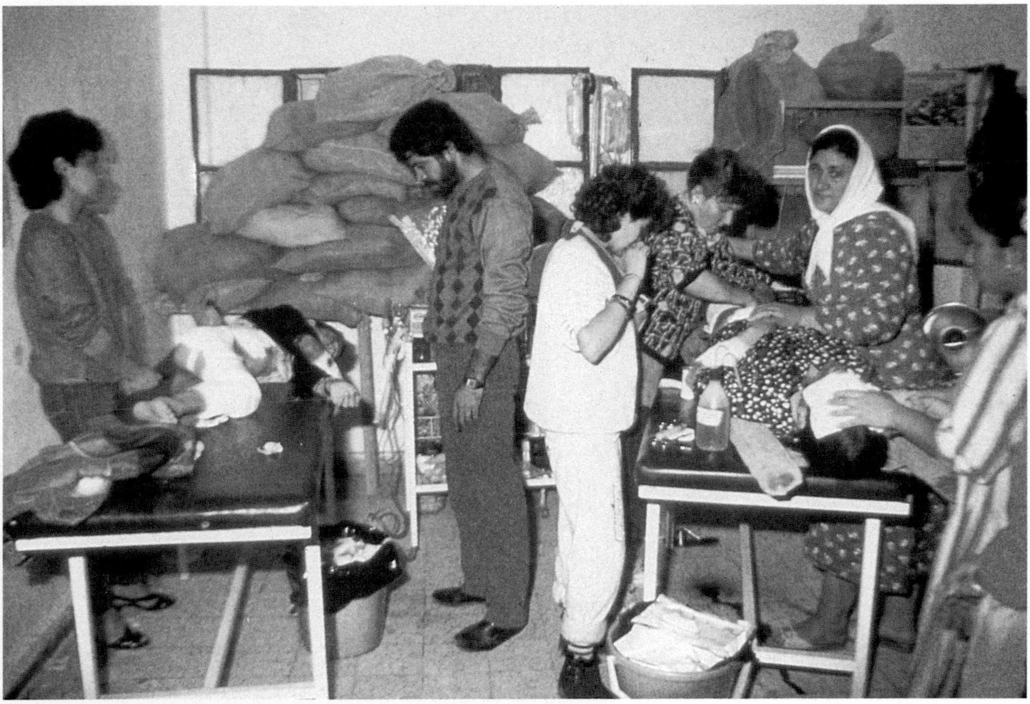

Above: Suzy and Mirvat working on their injured friend, Zaida Daud, in the Bourj al-Brajneh clinic, November 1986.

Left: Bashar and his 40-day old daughter in the clinic kitchen, November 1986.

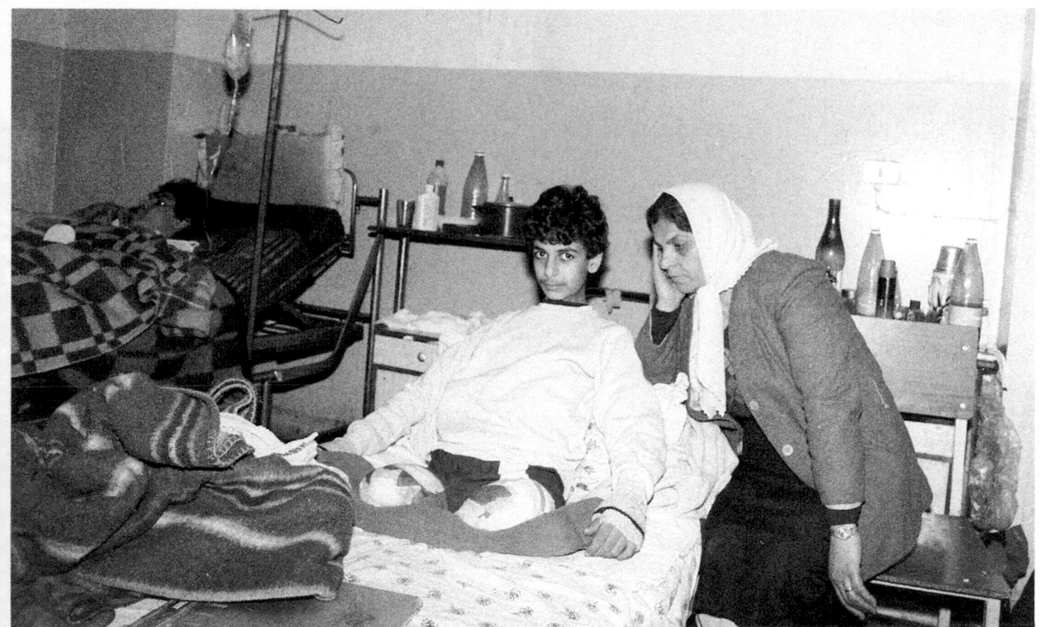

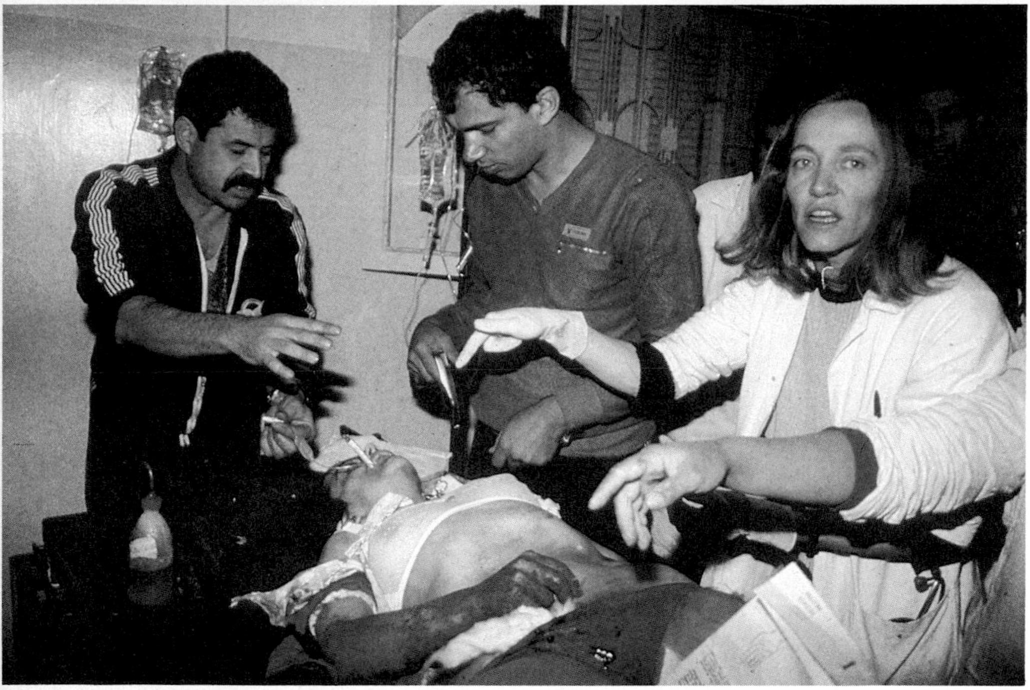

Top: Mohamad Sahnini with his mother at Haifa hospital. Both her sons and her husband lost their legs in the war.

Above: Doctors Atia, Rede and Cutting trying to save a woman who was sniped while trying to leave Bourj al-Brajneh, April 1987.

Opposite: Amal looking at one of the four boys killed in the Flour Ambush at Ouzai, Spring 1987. The body was left as a warning to other Lebanese on the airport road for three days – no one was allowed to collect it for burial.

At 3 am starving women and children come to see the first food trucks arrive, after nearly four months of total siege within Bourj al-Brajneh.

Children receiving food rations from the UNRWA office – their first proper food in months.

phosphorus bomb which, because the wind was coming west, had carried the smoke away from us and up the camp towards the sea and airport road. So we only ran into it as we came back to the clinic. Ben said he had seen the flash which was very big and then the smoke came. We then worried that they might start using the much-talked-about chemical weapons. There were several explosions nearby, so we stayed for an hour or so in the sandbagged room waiting for them to end.

Apparently bad weather is slowing up the Syrian extermination of Sunni resistance groups in the area of Tripoli and the town. We are listening to the planes coming and going. One is about to take off, so obviously Amal have not stolen the fire department's equipment again yet. The airport staff went on strike last week until it was returned. No solutions in sight and Ben too feels the zombie-like effect of our waiting each day to be blown to pieces which is almost monotonous in its daily similarity.

Took back *Gatsby* to Banan and borrowed *Wuthering Heights*.

Akram Haniyeh has been deported from Jerusalem today by the Israeli authorities. He was the editor of the Arabic daily newspaper *Al Sha'b* (*The People*) and they accused him of being pro-PLO and of sending money to them, which is a fairly ridiculous statement to make. No one sends money *to* them. But they have caused international outrage by putting him on a plane to Switzerland. Listened to a fine little BBC World Service report from Jerusalem's Knights of the Order of St John on an eye clinic in the Occupied West Bank, which made the very accurate statement that health care standards for Palestinians are very much lower than those for Israelis and that staffing for Palestinians' health care is difficult to maintain.

Report of between 5,000 and 17,000 litres of gas and diesel being pumped from the gas station, so after three days, *Insh'Allah*, we will have kerosene lamps to work with and hopefully the battery back tomorrow. The little baby girl who had gross deformities had an autopsy done tonight. She's been bottled in formalin now for posterity.

Four dead today: three from Abu Musa from a *howen* on the *mahwar*, and a little boy who died after a craniotomy for head injuries caused by a *howen* exploding on a single-storey house in which the whole family were sitting. He was the brother of little Tariq who had a dreadful foot injury from a *howen* – the initial *howen* that injured nine children at the start of the shelling. Tariq had just gone home two days ago, after almost two months in hospital.

Stuffed vine leaves to eat after Abu Musa fighters went out of the camp, raided a grocery shop and distributed them.

29.12.86 Day 62 Monday

So now two months already, this war, and with all proposals rejected it looks like it will be at least another month. Perhaps the only way to stop it is by Palestinian offensives, as Syria refused to accommodate the Arab League's delegation in Damascus, which does not augur well for the so-called cessation of the war, with admission of supplies by Nabih Berri, by the beginning of the New Year, as there is no will to a potential agreement whatsoever.

Today started at 8.00 with diarrhoea again and then I promised myself an early wash and went back to sleep. Woken by two *howens* just before 10.00 and the sound of screaming coming nearer and nearer. As it persisted Ben and I scrambled out of bed. We still had no battery, as the hospital had kept it and started to use it after recharging it, and we had no gauze either. Abu Nader's house had been hit with seven casualties and two who went straight to the hospital as the younger Al Ashwa said the clinic was closed. The woman screaming was actually screaming for the two children who went straight to the hospital.

Then we waited for gauze and batteries and watched the rain pouring down; after they arrived and we were wading through the dressings that had accumulated, Banan heard a noise and said, 'Injured' and I looked out the door to see a *hamali* (stretcher) coming running up the hill towards us. I went out and yelled, 'In here,' but they were going to ignore me and go up to the hospital. Luckily Sobhei Abu Arab ordered them to come in to the clinic so they redirected and came in. I yelled to Ben that someone was coming who needed everything, complete resuscitation, airway, intravenous infusions, suction, and pressure pads to stop haemorrhage, and looked at a young man covered in a sea of blood from the waist down, looking dead or almost dead. We put an airway in, suctioned him, cut off his clothes as best we could with scalpels and found large clots on his thighs. Eventually after initially looking for shrapnel we found the entry-exit site of a bullet, again through a femoral artery and vein, with a fractured femur. We put traction on the femur and pressed the two wound sites, and then Ben and I both ran with the stretcher to the hospital, Ben putting pressure on as best he could, and me blowing into his airway as far as possible in the pouring rain and narrow alleys, and falling against walls and sewers, getting a breath when possible rather than a regular timing. He looked awful and when all I got was a dreadful rasping sound as I blew into his airway, I thought, 'Oh, not now, not now' as we were so close to the hospital. We got him in, comatose and yellow, and Dr Saleh entubated him. He was then stabilized and taken to theatre.

I ran back here to the clinic in case we had a repeat of Christmas Day with a second set of casualties and no one here. I arrived to four people waiting for dressings. I did one, then changed out of my soaking clothes, having fallen into the sewers to above knee level several times.

Hissam appeared with a sore foot having hurt himself jumping from one storey in the *mahwar*. They had been going to a new building from Slieme to Haiduce and, as they were about to cross one of the adjoining ladders in mid-air, they were spotted by Amal who opened fire on them. Haj then jumped, Hissam jumped and hurt his foot, Rifat jumped, and they saw bullets whizzing over his head. Thank God, he is okay: a very close shave. Then I went to do Nada's and Ahmad's dressings and collect rainwater as the *mahwar* pipes are empty.

So I got soaked after the emergency, soaked mucking around with Hissam, and soaked again collecting water from the streams coming off buildings at certain points in the streets. The initial dirt from all the *howen* dust has now been washed away and the water is clean. I met Salah Ali al Haj who asked me to give an injection to the lady I saw a few weeks ago with chest pain. I waded through the dark and rain to Haiduce, to find the lady had left to go to the clinic an hour before. So we about-turned and went back again to the street. Then I fell again thigh-deep into the sewage which Saleh reassured me was clean. In the darkness I picked up the second water bucket from under a drip and walked sodden back to the clinic.

I changed again, gave up drying my hair and washed it instead, and sat trying to get past the introduction to *Wuthering Heights*.

30.12.86 Day 63 Tuesday
Day of Nabih Berri's much-proclaimed ceasefire!!!

Well, today was a busy one; woke at 10.00 and tried to dry out my socks and underwear. Then I got caught up with many long time-consuming dressings and at 12.30 sat down to eat, then went on home visits until 14.35. Ran up to the hospital for milk to be told there was none, not even in the store. Met a grieving woman and relatives beside the *rauda*, bewailing the death of a young boy called Hamoudi. I thought it was Abu Nader's son, but it turned out to be a boy who was mistakenly shot by his brother, who had been cleaning his gun and as usual forgot that there was a bullet in the chamber and shot the boy at close range. Amal today sniped a 7-year-old child in the chest.

There were many *howens* at 15.30 just as I was due to go up to Fatima's for a cup of coffee. After the bombs stopped I ran to Arsan to get water. I stood at the exposed end of the *mahwar* under one storey only, apprehensively waiting in line while our canisters were filled, and when the men saw me waiting they took first the tank then the gallon canister down to the front position and told me to go back to the clinic. Suhail and Tariq Aishey brought them back to the clinic for me. Ahmad said it was because they have to take care that the foreigners do not get killed or else the world will say the Palestinians killed us and not Amal. So the *ajnabiyah* was privileged again.

Then invaded again by *shebab* so I went up to the roof to look at East Beirut's lights twinkling on the mountains.

Then we had two emergencies. Amal had thrown TNT towards their position and both sustained injuries. Little Hassan came in first, semi-conscious and murmuring '*Ras, ras.*' ('Head, head.') Eventually his racing heartbeat settled and he went off to sleep in Slieme *mahwar* as his house has been destroyed and his family are living in the shelter. Rifat invited him to stay at their house, but I wanted him to stay with someone who could keep an eye on him tonight as Dr Rede had sent a message that if he had a severe headache he was to go to the hospital. Hassan didn't want to go though, so he stayed flat for two and a half hours here.

Another message to go to Haiduce to see Nawoosh, but on investigation it was revealed to be his toe, so I explained again that at 23.00 there was nothing Ben or I could do for an ingrowing toenail apart from giving him some aspirin!

31.12.86 Day 64 Wednesday Hogmanay

'The sound of gunfire off in the distance, getting used to it now,' as *Talking Heads* say.

The bread is reported finished in the camp. The carbon dioxide is very low in the operating room. Hogmanay again. Last year I celebrated in the over-opulent surroundings of food, food, food, wine and comfort. The year before in a bunker on the West Bank looking at the lights of Aqraba on the hill, watching the pine trees sway and thinking about being here eventually. And here I am, transported from suburban nightmares to real nightmares, and considering my three narrow escapes this week. First the *howen* near Hassan's house; then the phosphorus bombs exploding in the alley where I'd been standing collecting water five minutes before, then tonight coming back from the Al Khatibs'. Two *howens* had gone out from us just as we left the clinic to see Lydia who was having severe stomach pain; she's now twenty weeks pregnant. As we left and came to the shattered part of the road we saw the flame of an explosive shoot past us before sending shrapnel everywhere. Luckily we were under the arch of the buildings and were protected. Borhan then grabbed my hand and we ran full pelt down to the clinic. Of course I was wearing floppy sandals as I'd been about to take a wash, and he had one arm still in a sling from his fractured collarbone. We both arrived panting in the clinic. We later found out that it had hit Nawoosh's house, and seriously injured his little daughter.

Today started out with frantic knocking and searching for little Hassan from last night. Neither Ben nor I in our sleepy states could recognize which of at least three Hassans they were looking for. In fact Hassan was fine after his shock and had gone off with his father. I ran the snipers to see my little yellow baby and as we reached the open square, Banan told me that an old man had been shot there this morning. So we ran on to the house and ran all the way back across the camp. Then, after coffee and talking about pregnancy with Fatima and friends, back to the clinic and dressings. Sat and giggled a lot with Banan and then sutured a boy's hand, which he had cut on a stone, and while we sutured it someone stole the otoscope (a medical instrument for examining the external ear), so we are considering strike action until it is returned. The light is vital for our work with tonsils, eardrums and eyes in head injuries.

Later Borhan came to take me to Lydia who was lying in bed crying. It was the fright of Borhan being injured several times in the last few weeks, following his near death from a bullet injury in the 45-day war whilst they were engaged.

New Year Lebanese style, mortars exploding in Shatila as the chimes strike midnight. Borhan said that they had been ready for Amal with their much-vaunted New Year ceasefire, with the release of ten Amal prisoners taken by the Palestinians at Magdoushe and Berri speaking at midnight on Kitaeb radio about his magnanimous plans for peace. So much for all the talk; *howens* and TNT and gunfire exactly at midnight to help us celebrate *Wahid Wahid.**

1.1.87 Day 65 Thursday

Absolute chaos and all our New Year's resolutions broken within about six hours of making them. The first wounded came at 0.20 after the first set of *howen* explosions, then after we'd tidied up and calmed down and gone to bed we were woken by Borhan at 4.00 to tell us that there were two wounded coming. We got up, prepared by candlelight, and Taisear appeared on a stretcher, then another man, both injured with shrapnel. The others had had the foresight to pad and bandage them as they couldn't come up immediately because of *howens*. We treated them and Borhan organized their removal to Haifa. Then after we'd cleared up and calmed down again it was 5.00 and, just as we got to sleep, there was a furious knocking to return the *hamali* at 5.30.

Woken by shaking at 8.40, 9.10, 10.00 and 11.00, and eventually dozed until 13.20 when I got up to total chaos which continued all day. The otoscope has definitely been stolen, so tomorrow we are going to the *mahwars* to look for it and will strike on Saturday.

I visited Taisear in Haifa Hospital. He could not sleep despite Valium, which is hardly surprising with bone pain and inadequate analgesic, as all the good drugs have run out in the pharmacy and they are using everything from Phenergan to Largactil 'cocktails' for pain relief.

Abu Salim, the head of UNRWA, opened his heart to Ben about working in the camps being too dangerous, and how it was impossible in a war, and that he was stopping after the war. I felt like walking him around the camp with me for a day doing dressings.

*The anniversary of the foundation of the PLO on December 31 1964, and the first military Fatah action on January 1 1965.

Too little gauze and plaster now, so only dirty and new dressings will be done from tomorrow. Nawoosh's little girl had to be ventilated for two hours tonight and Dr Rede has told Nawoosh that she's not expected to live. She's in the bed next to the little 7-year-old paraplegic boy, the one who was sniped yesterday. It's ironic that until he had a son Nawoosh didn't visit his home during the war, but this time he goes every hour or two hours, and now after all the fuss about having a boy, one of his daughters may die.

Monir who took me to Marrubba *mahwar* and taught me to run the sniper trench got shot there today in the hand and abdomen. He was running to the *mahwar*, but went over the tunnel not into it, and got shot. He came here, then went on to Haifa, so we had four emergencies on New Year's day, all going to Haifa after coming here.

2.1.87 Day 66 Friday

Nawoosh's little daughter died today at about 16.00 after twenty-four hours ventilation and every drug under the sun. She was 4 years old.

I nearly got Banan and myself shot today as I went to see if Taisear needed a dressing. As I went into the courtyard a bullet bounced off the wall opposite – an M-16 and dust. A little boy came running after me yelling, 'Suzy, Suzy, *Q'arnass, q'arnass*,' and Banan said we shouldn't go there as it was dangerous. I turned round to look at them and the shot was fired. Taisear's wife had walked me down the middle of the road yesterday, not warning me about it, just sauntering along. Went to Noora Hammadi's for lunch and fell asleep until woken by a *howen*. Banan massaged my neck and after she left I tried to get some sleep, dozed for a few hours with constant interruptions, then woke feeling less nauseated and achy. Haj came in and asked if I had any problems with Hissam, and I replied none whatsoever. Apparently for the past two days he's been making arguments with everyone he knows.

They announced from the mosque that our otoscope has been stolen and that we need it back.

3.1.87 Day 67 Saturday

Slept late, until 11.20 as very tired and still feeling unwell. Woke up with a swollen lip that swelled all day, then went away. Still puzzled by the cause of these strange swellings that appear then disappear.

Saw Borhan later who was worried about strange people hanging around the clinic, Fatah and other problems in the area. Apparently there's a nonsense story going around that I'd been raped by one of the junkies. He was concerned about Rifat, Hissam and Haj at the clinic at night. I tried to explain that they were my friends, protecting me, usually two at a time, if they had no duty at the *mahwar*, until Ben comes back. But he was clearly really alarmed and insisted on sending a fighter each night to guard me. My initial reaction is one of dismay at the thought of having to sit with a man I don't know armed with a Kalashnikov until Ben's return each night, although I suppose I do know many of the fighters from Borhan's position. But I can't say I'm wild about the idea of being locked up like their sisters and other women. He also thought that only those working in the clinic should be there. I tried to explain that it is nearly impossible to keep everyone out, even with notices. Pauline says it's just the same in the hospital. Oh well, we'll see how it goes.

Today was quiet, thank God, as I still feel unwell. Apart from a screaming fight between Khadija and Fatima, there were no great problems. Discussed Borhan's ideas with the gang of three who were mildly annoyed by him, as an insult on their characters. Pauline came down and we had spaghetti, homemade wine (made from spirit and canned fruit, fermenting in a bleach bottle), and cake.

Hannes and I went to Hissam's house and spent the evening looking at art postcards and an encyclopaedia of art. It was so relaxing and warm, laughing, lying around in a large, dimly lit room, with curtains, mattresses, pillows and blankets. I explained the meaning of paintings of women in art, and ownership and colour. I could have stayed there the whole war, snug and forgetting, although it is very near Borhan's *mahwar*. Lovely and relaxing – I want to go out again tomorrow. Rifat explained that Abu Sacker and Hissam have been taking tablets, and the reason Hissam nearly got shot today was that, when he climbed on the ladders and asked Haj and Rifat to go with him to throw a B-7 or grenade, they refused as he had been taking tablets. Hissam was in a better humour tonight, thank goodness.

Nawoosh was not allowed a day off to grieve for his daughter, who has now died. Ahmad said this is more sensible. Thirty-one gross of cigarettes were stolen from his stores whilst his daughter was dying, as he gave them to Salah's brother to hide and someone saw him secreting them away, then stole them all – 15,000 Lebanese lira worth. They all say there has never been such widespread theft before in a war. Most of the thieving is done when there are *howens* as people are too frightened to investigate who it is knocking at the door whilst bombs are falling.

Yesterday all the doctors walked out in protest at the political organizations all using electricity from the hospital generator, thus overloading it. It failed three times during Monir's operation. Unfortunately they all marched to the mosque during Friday prayers and so had to stand outside until they were finished. Pauline had to go to the house next door for tea and a cigarette, being a woman.

Arsan nearly got shot again yesterday. He'd just used the toilet at the front of the *mahwar*, and when he stood up near a small window, the bullet went through his hat.

The food will only last another twenty days. The bread is finishing as there is no flour now. Three trucks of food went into Rashidiyeh.

4.1.87 Day 68 Sunday
Woke early with a streaming cold and made custard as it's the only thing I feel like eating. Spent a lazy day. I suppose I describe it as lazy as out of twenty-seven people who came into the clinic, I only saw seven, and there were four of us working today. Usually I see over half the entries for one day, so to do only my share of the work was nice indeed. Then I sat in while Ben went out, after doing Taisear's dressing which was small; his shrapnel fracture dressing won't be done for another two days, on Dr Saleh's say-so. He looks a lot better than a few days ago, although he needs more analgesic and Ampicillin. Then Rifat suggested walking through the camp so I proposed going to see my yellow baby as I needed a sniper guide to get past the bad roads that I don't know. We went to visit little Mohamad who looks less yellow than four days ago and much healthier.

Then we went up to Rifat's for tea and met his brother, cat, and cousins or nephews. Haj arrived, so we all went up on the roof to look at the trees, moon and stars, and aeroplanes taking off. Felt alive again, breathed and talked and talked.

Later I sat outside the clinic trying to encourage the cat to chase rats. Listened to the rats frolicking in the garbage heap and cats scrambling after them. The sky was full of stars tonight, constellations laden on top of each other, sparkling and shining bright white in the blue-black velvet night sky. The moon, the stars, the trees made me feel alive again, awake from the half-dead sleep of work and war.

Nawoosh's daughter was buried yesterday near Samed in the main cemetery. His other little girl keeps asking where her sister is. Tariq's brother was also buried yesterday and whilst the family was burying its child the house was broken into and many items stolen. More people asking for vaccines we haven't got and having to be turned away like sweet Bashar and his little 3-month-old daughter Maryam.

Shatila was shelled heavily today, again, and the artillery in the mountains shelled Amal positions around the Kuwaiti embassy. The mysterious Beirut Martyrs launched a rocket-propelled grenade at an Amal position and opened fire on it.

We received a summons to Borhan's *mahwar* about problems at the clinic. Apparently a great rumour had been going around that someone had been improper to me, and there was also a clothes-stealing rumour. So we went off with our Hebrew-speaking guide, stumbling in the dark, to a council of venerables in a secure room, with a stove from the Italian Army who had come after the invasion in 1982 and beds from the Lebanese Army. Then we explained that there was no important problem, except theft. So after turning down the proposal of an armed guard at night,

Borhan accepted the daytime guard on the front doorstep only from tomorrow.

Hissam is being completely anti-social and badly behaved; we think he is taking tablets again as his behaviour is quite strange.

Assad wants a ceasefire. Ha, ha.

6.1.87 Day 70 Tuesday

A house near the mosque has been opened to accommodate convalescents and people using the hospital shelter space and living quarters, leaving more room for really injured people. This was also done in the 45-day war.

Full of cold, aspirin and sinusitis. Had a snow fight in the square today while it hailed down; needless to say someone ended the snowfight between the bigger men with gunshot. Little Ahmad Morrah cut his hand, the withered one, on glass inside a 'snowball'. Rained heavily again, thank God. (Rain now precious to provide water for drinking, washing, etc.)

Rifat came in with Haj and Hissam, who were drinking spirit cocktails!

7.1.87 Wednesday Ten weeks

Thought of all the old wives' tales of Nada not being able to have children because of the shrapnel in her thigh, from people who should know better.

Lots of little children in the clinic and two small kittens, whom Haj Abu Taher fed 'safari' meat after Ben had moaned at me about giving the cat a tiny piece of the fish we were eating last night. I left them both to escape into the dark as our cat isn't getting fed enough, let alone two kittens. The children all sat until 19.00 folding little squares of gauze for dressings to the distant sounds of Palestinian *Thawra* (Revolution) music.

Banan and Bahia came looking for escape from their mothers and sat in the corner out of sight. Zeinab is contemplating suicide as her mother is depressed and constantly tells all the children she hates them. Then the hordes descended in the shape of countless members of Haiduce *mahwar*, and Borhan's father, and at least six more, not including Ahmad Aishey who had come looking for Ben earlier and sat folding gauze with the kids until Ben came back. He came with me to give an injection to Dr Saleh's sister, laughing while I came to a halt on the road in the pitch dark saying, 'Basically the *ajnabiyah* can't see'. He gave me his torch, saying that he could see in the dark. Nawoosh, Assad's brother, Nasser, the manic giggling Samir and Ahmad all sat drinking tea whilst the *howens* started again.

One person died and two had traumatic leg amputations when a 107 came through a sniping hole, exploding amongst twelve people sitting in the *mahwar*. The 13-year-old who was injured was at the *mahwar* for the first time today. Both boys will probably have a second below-knee amputation tomorrow. They were appealing for blood and the first thing we saw here was fighters running to donate blood at the hospital.

I fetched water and carried it alone (at last allowed to do so), washed clothes, joking about the de-luxe Italian designer washing machine.

Someone tried to kill the prominent Lebanese politician, Camille Chamoun, with a car bomb, but failed and killed his three bodyguards instead. He had the bulletproof car and they did not.

8.1.87 Day 72 Thursday

The day after the attempted assassination of Camille Chamoun: Grad missiles and 122mm mortars shelled Beirut International Airport, destroying one Middle East Airlines plane which had landed half an hour previously from Africa and luckily had disembarked its crew and passengers before the attack. The Lebanese forces and Kitaeb are trying to blame the Palestinian artillery batteries in the mountains, claiming that, as US Grad rockets were used, it was the Palestinians who shelled the airport. But as the Palestinians deny this, and the Lebanese forces want to open a second airport in the east of Beirut and beyond, in the Christian-held territories, but have so far been unable to convince Middle East Airlines to do this, the attack seems more likely to have been from the Christians. So East Beirut was shelled at midday killing up to six people. It took Amal away from us and it was strange to hear gunfire on the Green Line again, for the first time in two and a half months. There were almost celebrations in the streets at the news of someone else bombarding Amal.

Collected water and chatted at the *mahwar*, then came back to do injections and blood pressures.

9.1.87 Day 73 Friday

Khadija and Zeinab doing as little as possible about water collection, washing dishes, food and gauze folding. Sat outside with lots of little children folding gauze; some of them took it home to be folded and brought back piles of the stuff in neat little squares. Then tried to save little Rania Salim, too late, from a beating as her mother thought she had stolen the gauze from the clinic and beat her up and down the roads, despite my protestations. Still sorting out the unpleasant rumours with Borhan, and we finally agreed no guards to be posted at the clinic (as I felt this would simply confirm the stories). Instead I'm to have a small revolver, lady's size, with lessons in its usage. Dressed Taisear's leg, praying for no bone infection.

When Ben returned we went up on the roof to watch Grads and 130mm mortars from East to West Beirut. The airport was shelled again as soon as the first plane of the day landed. The tarmac was hit. The Israelis dropped eighteen bombs on Saida; Palestinians were the target again. Apparently there was an operation inside Palestine a few days ago including explosives. We came downstairs when the shrapnel started to hit the roof.

Later, went to bed – only to be disturbed by Ben and Pauline. All three of us went to Hissam's and came home dead tired. Couldn't find solitude.

10.1.87 Day 74 Saturday
Apparently Amal are preparing themselves for a bigger war with the Kitaebs and seem to be tiring of being used by Syria to achieve whatever it wants. No one seems to know what that is, but one of the benefits Syria is reaping from the somewhat ignominious defeat is that they are getting ten million gallons of oil from the Iranians and 150,000 million dollars from the Saudis. Quieter days, it feels, as people say that the war could be ending. People in the square are relaxing a little. My fourth month in the Lebanon.

Cleaned up a little in the house upstairs hoping for peace to come soon; tried to escape the hordes of children but they all followed. Little Fahdi has taken to following me everywhere along with about four other children, so eventually they all got flung out. Then raked through the boxes and found three candles, and we also discovered ancient soap, spaghetti, Dream Topping and sardines.

11.1.87 Day 75 Sunday
Woke latish again, went to fetch water and, because of the big queue, was taken by Nabil down through even better-constructed tunnels to the front street. Looked through several sniping holes to the wreckage outside and saw the big red Amal overturned container still in place. The street looked even more rubble-strewn and devastated than ever. I sat and waited with a young child of 2 years old whose father is in Bulgaria at the moment. There was a great social gathering and talking going on inside Arsan *mahwar*, and outside there was a *muzuhera* (demonstration) by Hizb'ullah protesting against Amal fighting the Palestinians, and stating that they and the Shia with them did not want to fight.

Then to the clinic and dressings, until I did Taisear's leg and stopped afterwards to talk about films and drink tea with him. His little girl Maha sat with us and later Ibrahim brought me sheets and sheets of algebraic equations (probably measurements used in calculating the launching of projectiles) which had been thrown away, so he, Maha and I looked at them.

Took some insulin syringes up to Rifat's mother. She developed diabetes with her last pregnancy, and has also had an open ulcer on her leg for the past three years, and diabetic cataracts with one operation and thick glasses. I nearly fell asleep I was so tired; then went up to the hospital to see Hannes for a while, who we found down in the shelters, so I spent time talking to Mohamad, the young nurse with the pregnant wife outside the camp. We were trying to envisage what she looks like and how much of a bump she has in her tummy and how many weeks pregnant she is now:

probably four months. Luckily she is staying with his mother who can take care of her.

The Israelis attack near Saida–Magdoushe. Three reported dead in the third raid in nine days. Terry Waite is in Beirut negotiating for the eighteen foreigners still believed to be held by 'pro-Iranian Shi'ite groups'.

12.1.87 Day 76 Monday

Jamal, Banan's friend, who took tea here one day about a month ago, was killed today by a sniper who shot him in the chest. The day he came to tea she had told him to leave Lebanon and go to Europe or Scandinavia, as there was no life for him here, maybe being taken or killed. He had refused, saying that it is their life to fight and suffer until Palestine is given back, why should they forget their country? If he had to die for Palestine and lose his life in struggle and fighting, he would do so. Today he died. He was alone in the camp, his family are all in Sur, so Banan now has another night of tears.

Hanna Dorman was injured today in the first *howen* near Haiduce. She is 26, her husband is in Syria where she refuses to go and join him, and she has her three children here. First she was reported dead, but I saw her in the emergency room waiting to be stabilized with her head half shaved. Apparently all her injuries are sufficiently mild to be discharged home.

After visiting Banan today, I came back and was sitting outside writing when the first *howen* exploded, sending a plume of smoke into the air, then another four exploded further towards Haiduce. I heard the noise and cleared two tables and got out the emergency box. First came Walid Daud with arm injuries and skull shrapnel, then Zaida, injured again, with shrapnel in her wrists, etc. Then Haj's mother Um al Abed with two pieces of chest shrapnel. Utter chaos and shouting and panicking. Zeinab wouldn't cut off Walid's top despite me shouting at her to do so. Khadija also wouldn't cut Zaida's top to look at her, or take it off. Then Um al Abed had to be seen on the floor, so luckily the girl with me cut off her top while I was rolling her around looking for other injuries; then in confusion we padded and plastered up her two chest holes. She also had abdominal holes and then, as we lifted her out on to the stretcher, I felt another soggy mass so asked them to stop. No one listened until they were out of the door. Then we had a screaming match with Haj and Ringo, who had gone off to argue with some poor girl carrying water up the road as there were bombs still dropping, so that when I told them to take Um al Abed up to the hospital, neither of them was ready.

Then we cleared up and waited. Ahmad Aishey came by and we waited to find out where Ben had been. He strolled in half an hour later, already aware of the three injured, and said he couldn't be here all the time. I said he could tell us where he was going so we could fetch him or know if it was too far to come for him. He said again that he couldn't be here all the time.

I replied that if he had told us where he was going, I would not have wasted a lot of breath and concentration shouting to Mustafa that I didn't know where he was. He said Mustafa had already shouted at him at the hospital.

Um al Abed had a five-hour operation with liver, spleen, stomach, small bowel and diaphragm repairs; her omentum had been hanging out of one of her chest wounds by the time she got to the emergency room. I apologized to Dr Atia for not being able to send the injured up in a better condition: we had no bandages and no gauze to clean and cover with.

Later I went to see the Head Nurse Salim, and Dr Rede about their proposed plan that I visit the shelters and check for scabies and lice. They showed me three five-litre containers of benzyl benzoate and perhaps two dozen bottles of benzyl chlorate. We apparently have many bottles in the pharmacy. Dr Rede was operating, so I came back after leaving behind the sweets we had been given, which were all eaten within ten minutes. Stumbled down in the dark, having torn my shoes on the zinc and got wet feet, and arrived back. Ben went to the hospital and I climbed into bed to read. Woken by Ben coming in.

13.1.87 Day 77 Tuesday

Woken early by Ahmad Ali al Haj breaking down the door thinking he was about to bleed to death. His suture scar (laparotomy) had opened and split, and he got a terrible fright. Ben covered and plastered him.

Spent the first hour and a half outside with three ladies from Democratic Front and one nurse from the hospital. Very unnerving being led around unknown territory to their shelters, which were now empty of people as the heavier shelling had stopped until yesterday. Got tired and fed up with the disorganized chaos, running then walking as slowly as possible, then hearing gunfire and shells in the distance.

Then went to give Haji Mustafa her B-complex injection; took tea with her and another two venerable Hajis. One lady in the hospital says she was born in the Turkish wars and is aged between 96 and 102 years. Many *howens*, rockets and 107s, and we were all sitting in a one-roofed house; so I was very nervy by the time I got back to the clinic. To Rifat's for *hummus*, olives and tea. Haj and Hissam came, and we all listened to the tale of losing their village in Palestine from Rifat's mother.

14.1.87 Day 78 Wednesday

President Assad has been 'invited' to go to the Soviet Union before January 20. Hopefully his fingers will be well slapped for getting out of line and being a naughty boy. Also Clivé, the Secretary of the Arab League, was in Beirut today and has promised a solution within the next twenty-four hours. So now the feeling is generally one of more optimism and hoping that we can stay alive and in one piece until the end of the war. Although most of us feel it will be another ten to fourteen days at least, making it a 90-day war?

We saw many lice and scabies in children in the streets, and at this rate I'll get them too*. I later met Abu Salim (head of UNRWA) in the Democratic office, doing not a lot. He asked me for an infestation percentage, so I blithely quoted ninety per cent. Then, after we'd been around the shelters, using up a lot of the benzyl benzoate and DDT, we went to Fadia's for lunch of rice, *basella* (beans), *molochiya* (a green leafy vegetable) – wonderful. Then coffee. I said I hadn't seen coffee in a month. It was ground by hand and delicious. Then we passed the sniper points with Hodda back to the hospital. She is 30 years old and had her 2-year-old daughter after fifteen years of marriage. Her husband was taken by Amal eight months ago and is still being held. She's kind and practical. Her daughter is outside the camp with her mother at the moment.

I went to the pharmacy for syringes and saw poor Mahmud, the pharmacist, who was hit by one of the junkies today, causing a protest in the hospital. He looked a bit weary, poor thing. Then came back, washed and did the odd little dressing and fell asleep after Ahmad Aishey came by. Slept till 19.15 with *howens* waking me. Rifat, Hissam and Haj came. They are refusing to go to the *mahwar* as the leaders have cigarettes, coffee and whisky, yet tell them that they bought these things, not that they came from the organizations. So they are refusing to go as they have nothing. Abu Sacker came looking for them.

Saw Lydia and Borhan today. Borhan apparently drew guns with Lydia's brother to marry her, as they wanted to refuse him, and there were many problems before they could marry, ending with a threatened shootout as her brother had tried to reclaim her at the Al Khatibs' house.

I've to write in the diary that Haj has chic shoes – grey with small laces – and he wears them with white socks. 'The chic-est shoes in Bourj al-Brajneh,' we joked, falling over in the mad hilarity of these shoes being worn to fight in.

15.1.87 Day 79 Thursday

Still waiting to hear of the ceasefire in twenty-four hours, no new news. At times, when the sun shines, you could think that there was no war. People are out on the streets, children are playing games, people are collecting water, then suddenly you hear a bomb in the distance in the camp, or a sniper fires, or a rocket hits somewhere and we remember that the peace has not yet come. But people pretend that it has, and so far we are lucky that not more people have been injured this way, as everyone is getting too casual. Even me. If I hear shooting or distant explosives I don't take cover now, I sit it out until it comes nearer, nearer, and if close, then I move.

*I did.

Crazy, I suppose, but as someone said, 'If you are going to die, you die.' '*Iza be muut, be muut.*'

Went on a ridiculous tour of the same shelters, empty still, with six girls and Hodda, up and down sniper streets not knowing where the shelters are and generally standing around and not doing a lot. So I said it was crazy, the war was not finished and every day there are *howens* and we should be two only, not a horde. Just as we ran into the hospital today there were bombs exploding near Amliea.

Then I did Taisear's leg. The kids all watched and asked questions, until one of them fell into the 'clean tray' and blew it for all of them and they got thrown out. His wife Yassera can't bear to look at the wound. I came back and Borhan came running in shocked from a 107 rocket blasting into the sandbags at the *mahwar* and blowing them up, lacerating his face. Luckily, the edges were pulling together by themselves so he didn't need stitches. Poor Lydia again. He was lucky he wasn't killed; he was alone and thrown two metres by the blast, hurting his ankle too.

Ahmad Aishey came in and we sat at the door listening to the radio, then all his family, Pauline, Hannes, Hissam, Haj and Rifat came by. Hannes and I went to Hissam's for tea, messed around, played the guitar. TNT explosions and *howens*. Went out to see Dr Saleh's sister at 15.00 and 22.00.

16.1.87 Day 80 Friday

One killed by a sniper today in Marrubba. An empty day devoid of emotion except tears: row with Ben over giving the cat a little food.

Hanna Dorman appeared with her head and leg wounds. She had just washed her children and parts of herself, but not all. When trying to wash, she couldn't manage her hair which was matted with black dust from the *howen* and blood. Filthy. When the dressing equipment returned with Ben, I treated her leg and head wounds while Ben took tea with Dr Saleh's family. He had visited the three buildings which collapsed at Marrubba at 4.00 in the morning with Imad al Masri whose toe seems better and who appears, like Borhan, to thrive on the situation of action rather than inaction. People now talk of the possibility of a solution within two weeks. Food is becoming scarce, but no one is starving yet, just guarding it and feeling bitter if they see their neighbours cooking bread but not giving it to them.

Nabil Shehadi came up tonight, behind the beautiful Abir, aged 16, the lovely girl with such grace and beautiful eyes. I had thought earlier this week when I saw him looking at her in the clinic that maybe he loved her, as an incredible warmth went out from him towards her and she to him. And tonight he said in front of me that she is his first love, and he hopes to marry her*. I said as they are both so pretty they will have lovely children.

*He did.

He said to look at her eyes! He had asked her for a kiss, but she had refused him. They are lovely and obviously very fond of each other: he romantic, bookish and handsome, she slender, graceful, elegant and kind.

Haj, Hissam and Rifat came round and I made a birthday card for Pauline and Haj helped me to sew her birthday present, a potpourri.

Heavy shelling at Shatila – one bomb every second at around 22.45; here also.

17.1.87 Day 81 Saturday

One shot in the chest at Amliea today. Writing by a spirit lamp, as the Lucas lamp is creating problems due to running on diesel and not spirit or a cleaner fuel. I have just listened to my lungs, front only, trying to decide if my cold has gone on to develop into a chest infection? My throat is sore and I've been coughing up stringy rubbish with great effort all day and generally feel dreadful in addition to my worms/amoebae.

Stayed in the clinic today apart from dressing Taisear's leg. Then visited Maryam, Mahmud and Mohamad and Samira who gave us *manaeesh* with *basal* (onion). Mahmud played the bagpipes. He's a teacher when there is no war, along with his brother who is in Abu Dhabi. The pipes came from Saudi, but he accredited the Scots with the invention, although I thought it was the Greeks.

Came back to babies with swollen feet, cut heads and a hungry cat. Later, I sewed Pauline's birthday present, and had a wash and hair wash. Then sat around coughing and trying to read. Driven indoors by a B-10 blast which we all thought was a mortar coming in as the pressure popped our ears and sent debris falling.

The Syrians have moved a unit up to the airport to maintain security. We are worrying that this may be a Tal al-Zatar beginning. No news from any peace initiatives apart from the Iranians refusing to attend the Islamic Conference as Kuwait supports Iraq. So we may still be here after ten days, regardless.

Listening to Billy Idol's 'Eyes Without a Face' makes me homesick, now that the BBC World Service has closed transmission from the Middle East relay station.

18.1.87 Day 82 Sunday

Rifat's cousin Kamal was shot through the heart at the Abu Musa *mahwar* at Sianni next to Haiduce. I had gone to Zaida's house to do her dressing and, on hearing the noise of an injury being moved, had run up to the clinic, but they had panicked and taken him to the hospital. (Ben had run after them, but could feel no carotid pulse.) After ascertaining that there was nothing to do I went back to Zaida's. Shortly afterwards, Ahmad Jishi came storming in, tears in his eyes, and climbed through the hatch in the wall into Haj's house to fetch his Kalashnikov. He loaded three clips full and got his pack on, took the Kalashnikov and ran out of the door to the *mahwar*, alone, I thought. They said if one of us dies, two to three Amal have to be killed. I asked her what Ahmad could do alone, she said there were others at the *mahwar*. Then we heard shooting. I said that now I understood the ratio. Her 4-year-old daughter Maisa started to make the little dance gestures that are our language to each other. Zaida and I both said that children don't understand war. 'Thank God,' she said, 'the *howens* fall, they are frightened; then when they stop, they forget.' I said, 'But when they grow up, they will remember everything they see in their childhood,' pointing to Khaled, Walid and everyone in the room.

I remember Kamal for his eyes; all through the war he was complaining of a headache which sat over his eyes. We decided that it was probably eyestrain and that he should go to see the ophthalmologist at Akka Hospital after the war, as maybe he would need glasses. We said '*Insh'Allah*', but now he is dead, a lovely sweet young man with sparkling eyes, even when he did have a headache.

Banan cried and cried again, another night, after a day of tears. I will remember this war for the tears in Banan's eyes. Every week another of her friends is killed and she cries all night and day. She went up to the house and everyone cried, and I cried and grieved. Rifat was there, near to tears. He is stubborn and proud. Haj and Hissam came in and sat around looking angry and sad, then left abruptly after ten minutes.

22.00 Those two have just come in to say hello and, after dropping off Kalashnikovs and bullet clips, they will come back later. They say Rifat is all right. Young Amer came by again and I told him that he should catch Pauline and play the 'Happy Birthday' tune for her tomorrow on his musical watch. Then Ben asked if he could borrow it for midnight as it will play automatically at 0.00 and on the hour all day tomorrow. This took much fiddling about with digital bits and pieces to achieve. I gave her the two earrings of bronze and cut metal like titanium (from Maryam Hallimi's mother), and a heart-shaped potpourri with 'Palestine' that we had embroidered (badly) on it, in unfortunate colours of blue and white, but it was all that I had. I also gave her the picture made from my Women Artists' diary of 'sipping soda at the Mall' with some of my scarf sewn round it by Haj and me, and the 'A big kiss from all the boys on your birthday' card, with Ronald and Nancy Reagan, the Pope, and the Saudis, art and lots of lipstick, and Day of Peace bodyguards and batik.

The rest of the day was flu-ridden with my first inclination being to stay in bed, but despite Khadija's efforts to cosset, spoil and nurse me, I had to get up as too many people wanted injections, etc. I dressed Walid Daud's arm, and his scalp suture fell out leaving an open laceration which again proved the 'do not suture shrapnel' point due to the unevenness of internal tearing. He asked me to go and do Zaida's dressing so I completely abandoned the idea of returning to bed.

There is no food left in Rashidiyeh now. Reports are that in Shatila Chris Giannou is sleeping in the shelters. Shatila was pounded again today at the rate of ten shells a minute. Rashidiyeh was also shelled.

19.1.87 Day 83 Monday

Beirut has gone crazy with fighting in Ouzai after the Syrians and Amal tried to kill Mustafa Sa'ad, the Nasserite leader, yesterday in an ambush there. Assad had asked for all Fatah to leave the camps, including Saida, Ain al-Helweh and Mieh Mieh, Bourj and Shatila. Mustafa Sa'ad refused as Arafat is paying a lot of money to the Nasserites, so they tried to kill him, but did not succeed. Terry Waite is now stuck in Beirut with the rest of us as the airport road is also closed along with the Ouzai and Saida roads.

17.00 The news is that 1,000 Syrians will now be stationed from the airport road to the museum crossing (on the Green Line). We wondered whether the Syrian plan for total intervention via the camp wars had failed so that now they had tried another tactic of an assassination attempt. A thousand Syrians could easily mean another onslaught on the camps, instead of, as people hoped, the opening of the airport road exit for women and children and supplies. Wishful thinking. It will perhaps be more than a 90-day siege now. The only controls on the Syrians are the Islamic Conference and Moscow. Hopefully both will exert enough presure on Assad to force him to let up for a while.

I spent all day in bed, with a filthy cold, sinuses, throat and chest; felt lousy until taking aspirin yesterday, now feel even lousier with them today. Coughing constantly. Khadija and Zeinab were bewailing hunger, so I force-fed them *mujuderra* (onions, lentils, rice) sandwiches. They refuse to eat at the clinic since last week's bust-up with Ben about the food being only for us and no one else. I later gave Hissam diesel and sugar, whilst Ben was out. Yesterday he made Hanna Dorman angry by telling her to wait for treatment while he drank tea with the boys. When I remarked on it, he said she is always stroppy, and today someone classed her as a bit crazy. She is neither, she is hardworking and intelligent, doing her best to raise three kids without a husband as he is Syrian and she refuses to go to him. So, as she defies the norm, she is called stroppy and crazy! Then Khadija and Zeinab took Ben's tobacco and rolled cigarettes for *shebab* outside. 'Why should Ben smoke all day? They are fighters, they need it, not him.'

Borhan destroyed a cannon and killed a few Amal in an Amal movement office today with a 107. His 'revenge', he called it. Amer's little watch has just played a Simon and Garfunkel tune in the drawer at 17.30. I wonder why? All night I kept waking to 'Happy Birthday to You'. Another explosion.

1.30 We listened to Voice of Palestine and an account of conditions in Shatila which are worse than here, as there is no emergency well-water supply, and the water there is dirty as Amal ruined the pipe supply by the sports stadium with a bombardment intended to flood the camp. They also had no convenient emergency fuel supply from a gasoline station.

Children are now rumoured to be dying of starvation in Rashidiyeh – two are reported to have died in the last few days – so all tales of the entry of supplies are wrong, fictitious rumours. If this siege goes on much longer it will happen here also. Hopes that the Syrians will bring about the end of the war are now surfacing. There are rumours of 1,000 to 5,000 Syrians from the airport road to the Barbir crossing. As Amal now have many wounded and dead, and are short of ammunition, and fighting with everyone in Beirut, then perhaps they can be forced towards a peaceful viewpoint despite having had a very different attitude at the beginning of the fighting.

20.1.87 Day 84 Tuesday
The three *howens* at 2.00 and 3.00 destroyed the Samrawis' house nearby. Today the hospital went on strike as – wait for the unbelievable – Salah Hammad the radiographer shot at Dr Rede. In fact he missed Dr Rede, but hit Suha (who is pregnant) in the foot instead. It was over the political organizations still using all the electricity from the hospital. After the doctors' walk-out at the mosque they had all agreed upon stopping this. But no one took down their hot-line, and the generator failed during Monir's laparotomy, then again during a Caesarean section just as the baby was being lifted out, then three times on ward rounds. Dr Rede went to see the organizations who had been told they could only use the electricity between 5.00 and 8.00 am when the hospital didn't need much, but they all persisted in using electricity at other times even though the rest of the camp is in total twenty-four-hour darkness.

Dr Rede eventually went to Salah's room where the Abu Musa line was hooked on, and told Salah to take it off. Salah refused. Dr Rede reminded him that he was the director of the hospital, but Salah still adamantly refused to disconnect the line, lost his temper and started shooting at Dr Rede with his revolver. Of course, he didn't get taken to prison as was first said as his brother is Abu Fahdi the Abu Musa leader from Beirut. But after a big meeting of the political leaders, he is expected to be sacked after the war. Hodda (from Democratia) arrived breathless to tell me this. She's just been sniped at out in the open square next to their office and was a bit shaken by it, unsurprisingly. She and Fadia and another girl sat on my sick-bed and told me this and we talked about the strike, but the hospital resumed normal working just as we were about to shut our door in solidarity with them. So much grumbling as we re-opened it.

I succumbed totally to the chest infection and flu and slept in bed, sweating with a 37.8°C temperature all day. I even slept through Haj, Rifat and Hissam, and tried to sleep through Monir, who told me he is for female circumcision, as in hot countries women get too excited and uncontrollable.

21.1.87 Day 85 Wednesday

A wet-custardy-footed kitten (Cleo) is trying to sit on this diary while I write. It was thrown off the bed this morning for wanting to frolic before 6.00, and is now grappling with lukewarm custard drink, trying to play with anything, pens, watch, custard, books and pages. Bored cat antics. The black cat has just about given up with us as it's not getting fed, whereas the little one who came to stay two to three days ago eats anything and seems to think I'm its mother, trying to sleep on my chin mostly. It's now eating my ear and hair and refuses to chase the last mosquito – now sitting on my neck, cleaning its front paws.

Still flu ridden and a bit deaf and feverish. I wanted to see Pauline and sweated my way up to the hospital with Rifat. She recommended tetracycline. The deafness is quite nice in a way as the *howens* are dulled, and even when we saw the light-flash and I heard the explosions it wasn't frightening as the noise was considerably softened. Although it does lead to mistakes. Today three rockets went overhead, two exploded within metres of the hospital and one directly on the hospital. With my distorted hearing, I thought they were going out and smiled at the thought of them exploding on imagined Amal positions.

Pauline and I had to move into the bathroom as shrapnel fell nearby from distant *howens*. There were six near Rifat's home and one near the mosque. Another has just exploded nearby again. I spent the day sleeping in bed with constant troops of people in and out of the clinic, sitting around looking, and one or two wanting me to do injections, see a spotty leg, give bandages. They were all told to come back tomorrow or see a doctor at the hospital. They all refused to go to the hospital knowing that the triviality of their complaints would get short shrift up there from the Arabic staff, rather than my lengthy Arabic-English explanations. Abu Suhail (the Fatah leader) came by to enquire after my health and later sent five packets of soup over for me – kind man.

Øyvind was on the *jihaz* and asked if there were any problems, and Pauline asked for Lebanese money, films, batteries and cigarettes when he came to the camp.

Three men from Abu Musa got caught in what looks like an Amal-set trap last night. They had gone far out of the camp to pick up lots of flour near Ouzai and as they were coming back Amal ambushed them. One is injured and in Haifa Hospital, one is thought to be in a hospital near the camp, and the other is feared dead or prisoner to Amal. No one knows what happened to him.

No sign of any agreements, just more shelling, waiting, waiting, waiting, waiting.

22.1.87 Day 86 Thursday

This is going to be longer than ninety days. Food is running out and now all we can talk about is when we will have to eat the cats and rats (the latter are not such a good idea as they are very dirty). The hospital does represent an experiment in sensory deprivation, as Pauline commented yesterday, no light, water everywhere, no noise except when working, and nowhere to go. To walk through it is like walking through Kafka's *The Trial*, as filmed by Orson Welles. Dark imperceptible shadowy humans standing in whispering corners, against whispering walls, impossible to see unless they brush against you; wet underfoot, darkness, relying only on memory to guide you through the labyrinth. Sat having a dismally ironic conversation with Hisham (brother of Salah the radiographer) about food, more food, the hostages, the war and the deteriorating situation over the past year in the Lebanon. Then we sat in the alternating dark and light, as the generator went off, dreaming of all kinds of food, from cheeseburgers, chips, salads and coffee to cigarettes; *taboulé* (parsley salad) with *mogarabiyeh* and chicken, roast beef, Yorkshire pudding, potatoes, horseradish sauce, etc, a bottle of whisky, coffee and more cigarettes.

The kitten is lying in the crook of my arm, squeaking and purring. Previously it tried to sit on my neck, its favourite place, sandwiched between my ear and my collarbone like a pelt.

I went to see Pauline to read the statement she'd drafted last night about the deteriorating conditions in the camp; lack of food, water dirty and hazardous, bombs, children undernourished, babies drinking tea and water now instead of milk, pregnant and breastfeeding mothers severely malnourished, thirty-five per cent of all homes damaged, no electricity for two and a half months, and a call for the immediate lifting of the siege and allowing in of all supplies and medicines. She also stated that repeated shelling of the hospital has caused injury to patients and nurses, and noted the running out of medicines and baby milk. At last we are able to make a public statement. (We had first thought of saying something to the outside world about camp conditions in November, but Pauline had vetoed the idea as it would reveal the weakening state of the camp.) Pauline, Ben and I*

*Pauline had included my name on the statement, although I had not actually seen it before it was sent out, as she knew that I had wanted to act as a witness before. Since all calls from the Palestinians had been ignored by the media as so-called exercises in propaganda, the situation about our releasing a statement was now thought to be altered.

have our names on it and it was released via the walkie-talkie through Dr Mohamad Ossman in Akka Hospital.

DECLARATION FROM FOREIGN HEALTH WORKERS
IN BOURJ AL-BRAJNEH REFUGEE CAMP

We, as foreign health workers, living and working in Bourj al-Brajneh refugee camp, declare that the situation in the camp is critical and conditions inhumane. The camp has now been under siege for more than twelve weeks and the 20,000 residents are being subjected to conditions of deprivation and misery. Drinking water is the most basic human need. Most houses do not have running drinking water and it has to be collected daily from taps in the street at great risk of personal safety. Several women have been shot and killed collecting water for their families. Foods stocks have been completely depleted. There is now no baby food or milk and babies are drinking tea and water. There is no flour and therefore no bread, no fresh food, so pregnant women and children are suffering undernourishment. People are eating stale food and suffering vomiting and diarrhoea. Many families now have no food. It is winter and the electricity was cut off from the camp two and a half months ago. People are cold and have chest infections. There are huge piles of garbage which cannot be cleared and rats are thriving. One old lady who was bedridden was unable to get help when her foot was eaten by rats for three consecutive nights before she was rescued. The constant bombardment of the camp forces the people to crowd into poorly ventilated shelters with no sanitation or to risk being blown up at home. Hundreds of children have scabies and many have severe skin infections. Approximately 35 per cent of homes in Bourj al-Brajneh have now been destroyed. In the hospital, many medicines have run out and we have no more gauze. The hospital building is being rendered unstable by repeated shelling and patients and nurses have been injured by shrapnel. Water is dripping down the walls and mould is growing in every room.

We declare these conditions to be inhumane and on humanitarian grounds we call for the lifting of the siege and the admission of food and medicines by the international relief agencies.

Dr Pauline Cutting – British Surgeon
Ben Alofs – Dutch Nurse
Susan Wighton – Scottish Nurse

So now we wait to see which papers will carry it. I now also have to think about a future outside the Lebanon due to the lack of safety for foreigners and inability to continue working in Beirut in the short term as freedom of movement would be so limited. Perhaps I could move to Saida or even Rashidiyeh?

Rule 1 If there are no snipers, there will be no *howens*.
Rule 2 If you can hear ambulances, there will soon be *howens*.

Then I walked the longest way home in the dark through the camp via Hisham's house. It's like a wasteland now, people out amongst the rubble, and garbage fires, and remains of destroyed houses. Very eerie even in daytime, as sniper and *howen* fire often lands there. Every house now has a *howen* or shrapnel hole. The rockets injured two nurses last night with shrapnel and glass from a shattered window, which also became embedded in the corridor wall opposite the nurses' station. One *howen* landed upstairs, and as that floor is unstable could easily have come into Pauline's room. She should move down a floor, as we all told her.

I dreamt of phosphorus bombs and the Golan Heights and Pohsie getting a diploma in silversmithing instead of a degree. There is none of the awful fear of my earlier anxiety dreams, just puzzled acceptance of everything in them. The illness seems to have had a final fling. The flu is better today, although my nose and ears are well blocked.

Hisham told me today that Darwish al Masri sold his stock of UNRWA milk to Abu Musa for 1,700 Lebanese lira?! His children have no food and he's not taking care of them well. He seems to have gone to pieces, although Hisham says he has only been like this in the past seven days. All the children are being fed at Hisham's home.

People are telling the story of the brave Abu Musa men. Apparently there was a secret raid for flour by three Abu Musa men outside to Ouzai the night before last. When the men tried to go a second time, everyone, including Amal, knew about it, so the first man approaching the pick-up place was shot. He sent a message back by *jihaz*. The other two stayed hidden and opened fire, then one tried to rescue his friend, who told him to leave him and not to die with him or for him. Amal opened fire and shot him too. The third friend tried to rescue them both and they told him to leave, but he was shot in the chest by Amal. He managed to run 240 metres before collapsing just outside the camp. The exact fate of the other two is unknown. All for flour . . . brave, brave men.

Hannes dreamt last night that he was skiing and now he dreams of *Wiener schnitzel* and snow and his family.

23.1.87 Day 87 Friday

The West German embassy evacuated fifty West Germans to the East last night. PM Bob Hawke refuses a Palestinian UN Conference in Australia as it would mean the Palestinian UN delegation attending. I'm sitting in the miseries of sinusitis and the inability to smell. Also run down like everyone else, so stuffing myself with codeine, tetracycline and aspirin. Half the camp has colds, the other half has dizziness, and many have nausea and vomiting from eating old or inadequately heated food. Many people came to the clinic saying they have not eaten since the day before yesterday; usually the children get food, not the adults. Also we are seeing many well-healed wounds breaking down again, similar to the way diabetes or kidney patients have problems. The initial healing was good, but now six weeks to two months later the wounds are opening up again. And those who were recently injured take longer to heal now.

20.30 Spent a lovely hour and a half at Arsan's home eating the most wonderful feast of potatoes, meat *kobé*, *hummus*, bread, olives and noodle soup. I was fearful of eating too much, even though ravenously hungry as I'd eaten only soup and some sweet noodles today. There was a second sitting, so I only ate the minimum – but it was wonderful, another world, as if there was no war. The whole building was lit up from inside with its own generator. Then all the *masuline* (political and military leaders) came in and ate, plus bodyguards. There were huge armchairs, curtains, glass and bronze tables, and a big balloon-like light, tiled floors and a mural of a beautiful Bavarian Swiss or Austrian chalet on a sloping green mountain with fields. The leader with the *Sovieti* hat invented his dream house of glass in the rectangular field, from which he could look at the trees, mountains, fields, cows and waterfall – everything. When Hannes asked him about the snow perhaps breaking the glass, he said that he would put electricity in to warm the snow around the glass and prevent it breaking. Then we ate sweets and Aref served coffee in a set of beautiful gold glasses, with crystal dishes on the tables and ashtrays.

Pauline described a nightmare she had last night of having been called to see wounded, not in Bourj but in a more European emergency room. When she arrived there were ten dead, all blown to bits by a bomb and so mutilated that they were practically just skeletons, and one of them was a friend of hers, recognizable by its face. As she got there and realized that they were all dead, they were being sewn together as though after a post mortem.

I thought, looking at the people who I knew at the beginning of the war, how tired everyone looked and how difficult it was for anyone to make any conversation, or raise a smile, or even a glimmer of one. Everyone looked absorbed and vague and distant at the same time, weariness and fatigue showing as there was nothing else to hide it away.

Sobhei Abu Arab really surprised me today when he came into the clinic and said quietly behind me in English, 'I am very tired.' I didn't know he could speak English and it took me a few seconds to realize what he had said. He looks drawn, with the familiar dimmed eyes that we all seem to have nowadays. I smiled in sympathy with him; both of us knew that everyone is very tired already and the prospect of being further starved when we already have no medicines or resistance left is another wearing thought.

Another two foreigners were kidnapped today from Hamra at gunpoint. Their kidnappers are being more efficient after David Hirst's escape. They sealed off the area with more gunmen, reportedly to prevent journalists seeing! That's a farce: as if hundreds of journalists are casually strolling around Hamra by the hour these days. They bundled them into a blue BMW and drove off. No claims have been made yet, and the third rule of survival is now 'Never trust a blue BMW in close proximity'. At first it was thought that they were West Germans, but now their nationality is unclear. 'Irangate' has backfired in a big way as now everyone thinks they can deal with America by taking hostages for guns and money.

Terry Waite is still around in the Bekaa and may bring two hostages back with him. I wonder if he will hear of our statement before he leaves the country, calling for the end of the siege and telling of the old lady whose toes were eaten off by rats before anyone could go to help her?

One boy was shot from side to side of his humerus and into his chest today at the Abu Musa *mahwar*. We also had a boy with a fractured right leg from a B-7 landing in Haiduce *mahwar*. He had badly torn flesh wounds, all below the knee, so even though I couldn't feel a crunch on putting his leg into traction, we splinted him and sent him up to Haifa after cutting off his trousers. The little cat is complaining as it was her blanket that wrapped him up for the journey. We are running out of gauze; now on the last lot.

Khadija got sugar and made us some sugary noodles today. She said she and her family will go back to Tripoli after this war as the Syrian *mukuberat* (intelligence) is preferable to being killed by Amal which she thinks likely, as she is a woman and her husband is lame with one leg. What harm could this family do? She too looks worn and tired. Zeinab is coming into her own at last and the kitten is grabbing at the pen.

Rifat found some toys: a plane, a car, a jeep and a tank for little Bilal Shabib who was shot and paralysed, and Khadija wrapped them up. Children were folding gauze today, the last of it, with much squabbling. All the children were out in the square, playing with bats and a shuttlecock.

1.15 I had a hair-raising walk or stumble back from Arsan's with Aref and Dr Rede; there were *howens* falling, but we couldn't run as only Aref knew the roads home. So we stopped, fell, and started in the dark, listening to the mortars exploding. Three landed next to Rifat's house and Drs Nasser and Atia just reached the hospital before the bombs fell around that area.

I dreamt last night of a self-service restaurant, gateaux with chocolate and cream and cherries, salads with lettuce and tomatoes, but I arrived too late and was not allowed to eat anything.

Collected water, standing outside for half an hour listening to the *doshka*.

24.1.87 Day 88 Saturday

Quiet day. Three killed and two died from natural causes. The two were an old lady who claimed to be 107 years old, and an old man. The other three were shot dead. One boy called Adnan was shot in the chest early this morning. The next was a boy who was shot through the heart at Marrubba and died instantly before being brought to the clinic. I had just gone to do Um al Abed's dressings when Haj came running, yelling 'Quickly – there is injured', so I put on my shoes and ran up through the crowds to find Ben trying to resuscitate him. It was hopeless, even with the mad panic for suction; he was very dead with no pulses, no respiratory effort and dilated pupils. His name was Ahmad and he was 17, a friend of Nabil Shehadi's. I didn't realize this, and was giving Nabil a graphic description of how quickly you are likely to die from various injuries, then he told me 'Oh no'.

The third person was the mother of Adnan from the hospital. Poor Adnan, no one thinks he has a father, and there are younger children in the family – and he was in a pretty sorry state today, wet and dirty from working outside, and now his mother is dead. As Pauline says, Amal have some good sniping positions this time, better than in the 45-day war. But as we both also said, with the constant demolition around the camp outside, no one knows now which areas are exposed and which are open to sniping until someone gets shot. (Although the one who was shot twice had been walking down a street where he had repeatedly been shot at before.) As Dr Rede says, people are also being very stupid, but there seems to be a fatality about the situation now, probably linked to the weariness of being subjected to constant stress and lack of adequate food. 'If you are going to die, you are going to die.' And consequently, many are playing a form of 'Bourj roulette' with snipers now, who are always shooting to kill, aiming at chest, head and femoral arteries. Respect your enemy; you must, but many don't care any more.

Molochiya for tea, only the second green vegetable that I've seen in almost three months. Pauline refused to eat hers as she dislikes it, so I got some more. Dr Darwish saves the remains of his hospital food for a family who have none.

Arafat is now coming in for criticism. Many feel that Magdoushe was the uniting victory for the Palestinians, but when everyone else but Fatah pulled out and there was no further military advancement, the whole situation stalled and after a week Magdoushe was forgotten. Now many feel any solution will do, we have to accept anything we are given as we cannot hold out indefinitely. A besieged camp or town is a defeated camp or town, until the time when the siege is lifted. We are against the wall and no one should be fooling themselves; either a relief and lifting of the siege, or a massacre. And any political sacrifice would mean losing up to 130,000 people in three camps. Assad got this 'blunder' on a plate without having to do anything for it. What also has to be taken into account by the PLO leadership is the endurance of people who have already withstood one and a half years of war, suffering and hardship and a continuous cycle of grieving. People can only take so much and no one wants this to last any longer. We will be reduced to welcoming the Syrians now. Assad's mandate will be renewed to restore order, not removed for instigating murder and terror. The Islamic Summit only agreed to discuss the 'Camp wars' yesterday when it was put on the agenda, that's how much they care about us.

The two foreigners kidnapped yesterday are one Rumanian and one Bulgarian. Today, four American professors were seized on the Beirut University College campus by gunmen masquerading as extra security police for their protection. That's eight hostages taken in seven days. Any old *ajanib* will do for dollars. Terry Waite is still 'lost' in the Bekaa.

A bullet was seen hitting the lower wall of the clinic today, so at last someone has paid attention to the protestations about the inadequate zinc barricade and two barricades were erected, one from the gate of the clinic and the second at the kitchen door. Øyvind got our statement yesterday. My reaction to grief at death is now one of confusion as happened today, perhaps because self-survival instinct is continuously foremost so that everything takes secondary importance.

The boy who was shot yesterday had his blood-stained boots stolen from outside the clinic. When his relatives finally came for his clothes his boots were gone.

25.1.87 Day 89 Sunday

Still a sniper shooting on both sides of the clinic today. Even writing out the day's events is becoming a monotony, like the rest of this bloody war. What happened today? I awoke with a coughing fit at 7.00; cold and unable to get back to sleep for coughing, so I got up, raked around in Ben's trousers for the lighter and tried to make tea. One lighter had gas, the other only a flint, but I couldn't figure out how to use them together so after half an hour of cursing and cold I went back to bed. Three dawn *howens* nearby.

Woke again at 10.45, still achy, still have sinusitis and feeling unwell after almost three weeks. Dressed Fahdi who looks so like Fouad now, and opened a blood blister on a boy who wants to be a student of engineering in Scotland, and treated his handsome and voluble friend who wants to study medicine there.

Ziad kicked a rat to death and the little kitten started to devour it. Hissam and Haj came to tell me and asked if they should shoot the cat. I said yes, if they could catch it, as it was unclean now, although many cats are eating dead rats. But then a sheikh passed and they asked his advice as to whether they should kill the cat, and he pronounced that as the rat was dead it was no longer unclean and it's *haram* to kill cats. So the cat went on eating the rat until after more discussion Ben poured diesel on the rat and burnt it. The cat is now barred from the clinic, but alive.

Got water, then did Um al Abed's dressing; a nightmare of holes, with not enough gauze or plaster or anything, and she also has an infected purse-string suture from her chest tube, one of many. Awful, no light, squashed in a corner and very unsterile. Gave her some tablets to help her sleep (maybe) and told Wissam again how to take his worm medicine. Came home to sleep as feeling awful still. Zeinab didn't come as her mother is 'ill' after fighting with her father.

All hopes pinned on the Islamic Summit. The previously unheard-of Organization of the Oppressed on Earth claims responsibility for the four kidnappings and says it will execute one hostage unless the West Germans release Mohamad Ali Hammadi (the TWA hijacking – Beirut 1985).

26.1.87 Day 90 Monday

The continuous monotony: two more foreigners kidnapped at gunpoint from a photocopying store in Hamra where more gunmen were waiting outside to take them away – no nationality, no claims. The other two initially thought to be West German, then query Rumanian or Bulgarian, turned out to be two blond Lebanese Armenians who merely looked foreign and were kidnapped for that reason. Hammadi is still detained in West Germany and no signs that a hostage has been executed yet. He comes from a large Shia family in the Bekaa, half are Amal and half are Hizb'ullah. The Americans have now stated that all US citizens still remaining in the West Beirut area are responsible for their own safety and the state cannot help them if they refuse to heed its warnings to leave West Beirut now. The ICRC is evacuating twenty-three of its staff from West Beirut today. A general school and university strike is to be held in protest at the kidnapping of the four professors. Arafat, Assad and Gemayel are in Kuwait. Arafat wants to keep Magdoushe and Saida as the PLO presence in Lebanon. That's why he stayed there. Assad and Gemayel do not want any PLO presence in the Lebanon, so what will happen? Pauline thinks the wave of kidnappings is a repeat of the last Syrian entry to restore order to West Beirut.

Our statement has been broadcast, most of it on Kitaeb and one other Arabic station, as have our names.

Ibrahim died today. He was very toxic and stopped breathing. Pauline ventilated him for two hours, but he couldn't breathe alone, *ma fi nefes la halo* (no breathing on his own), so she had to make the decision to stop and let him die. He had fixed dilated pupils and Dr Saleh had earlier looked in and said no chance of recovery. But Dr Atia wouldn't assist and Dr Rede just carried on playing chess all the way through, while she was badly needing advice and support. The neuro-surgeon on the *jihaz* said that all the meningitis treatment and drugs were correct. Poor wee boy, thin and with a lovely smile. He was alone in the camp, no relatives as he came with the Abu Musa fighters (like the little boy with his dad from the Bekaa). Pauline is very upset and depressed and wants to go home. She keeps talking about the Syrians constantly.

(If we die, it will be through the monotony killing us.)

Borhan still hasn't managed to put out the sniper who covers the clinic area yet, despite running down the street to kill him the other day.

As *howens* went out today, *howens* came back in reply. Shelling with tanks at lunchtime for a while and a 107 that went over, sending little Feraz into a state of excitement.

Apparently the war will stop within a week now. Still full of cold with running eyes, sinusitis, aches, sodden hankies and a painful set of ribs from so much coughing. Wonder if Taisear will arise again for a dressing tomorrow? He too said he had switched off from the war and lay happily in a darkened bedroom for over three weeks, listening to songs and reading poetry. I envied him, don't blame him at all. Little Amer came by. I wanted to give him a cigarette but there were too many people around; he looks frail and tired.

Went to the *mahwar* to fetch water, but it was way down at the front street and Khadija scarpered leaving me on my own. I stayed, looked at the street and counted at least two cars, one burnt on the street, which looks even more devastated than before, with rubble and wreckage – really surrealism is taking hold. Then I saw the charcoaled rat's remains. Maybe it's reading Golding that's doing it? Pauline feels that the war is really affecting our psyches. I agree. Having bad dreams again about chases and spontaneous pools of blood.

Dr Nasser was in Tal al-Zatar when he was 17 years old. There were eighteen months of war, then a short ceasefire, then more war. He said food was not the problem as the camp was near an industrial area and the Palestinians made raids outside; but there was no water, and in the end most of those who died inside were killed by dehydration after seven months of siege; the rest were massacred. His brother was married to Eva, a Swedish nurse who lost her arm; her husband was killed and she then had a miscarriage. She lives in Sweden now and he wants to go there after this war.

Looking from Ahmad and Zaida's house at blood splattered down the wall. I looked at the little trees in what remains of the square and found new shoots and buds on them.

Reagan calls the current wave of kidnapping in West Beirut 'a declaration of war against civilized society'. He is considering a full set of options, including military action – against terrorism? The Church of England are checking reports of Terry Waite's kidnapping after statements from the Kuwaiti News Agency. Radio Free Lebanon claims he is still in the Beirut area and is keeping in touch via an intermediary. I wonder if Reagan will bomb Libya, Syria or both?

The two boys from Abu Musa who were missing outside the camp (the ones who went for flour) are both dead. Amal dragged their bodies on to the airport road and displayed them, threatening all who saw them that this is what happens to Arafat supporters; the irony is that they were not.

The mosque was hit by a *howen*, four people were injured, but none seriously.

Example of a one-way conversation with myself after the sniper shooting at the back wall again at 2.30: 'God, don't they get bored sitting over there

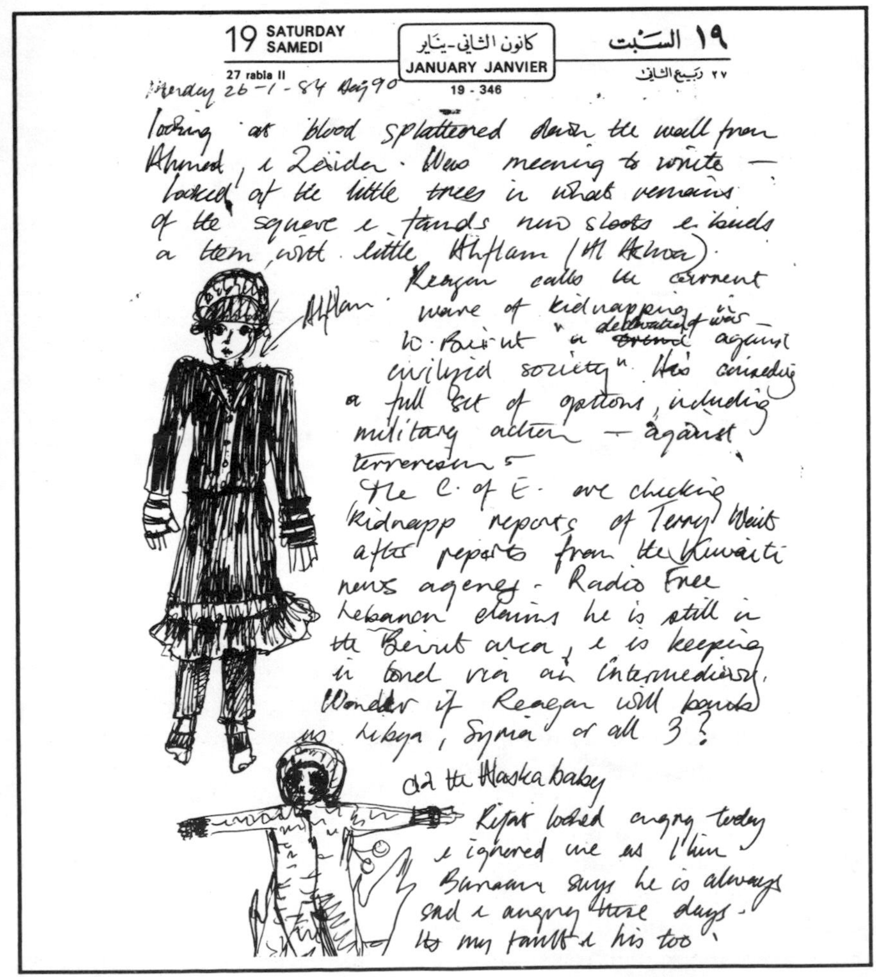

19 SATURDAY SAMEDI

كانون الثاني-يناير

JANUARY JANVIER

١٩ السبت

27 rabia II

٢٧ ربيع الثاني

19 - 346

Monday 26-1-84 Day 90

looking at blood splattered down the wall from Ahmed, & Zaida. Was meaning to write – looked at the little trees in what remains of the square & [illegible] new shoots & buds on them, with little Ahflam (Al Aklwa).

Reagan calls the current wave of kidnapping in Beirut "a declaration of war ~~[illegible]~~ against civilized society". He's considering a full set of options, including military action – against terrorism.

The C. of E. are checking kidnapp reports of Terry Waite after reports from the Kuwaiti news agency. Radio Free Lebanon claims he is still in the Beirut area, & is keeping in touch via an intermediary. Wonder if Reagan will bomb us Libya, Syria or all 3?

Did the Alaska baby

Rifat looked angry today & ignored me as I him. Banaan says he is always sad & angry these days. Its my fault & his too.

shooting into a dark street every night? . . . They must get bored, even fired by Nabih Berri's rhetoric; they must get bored. Or maybe they don't. Then again, maybe Nabih Berri is a saint. Oh heresy! – Saint Nabih Berri! Or maybe they are as bored as we are with this boring monotony. I wonder how much they get paid? So, Sultan, what now? The 90-day siege is past and we go on to day 91. What now? Until it stops, the killing will go on. Why do none of the "*big*" men get killed, only the ordinary people?'

27.1.87 Day 91 Tuesday
So maybe it's finishing at last. The word is that the Fatah fighters will leave Magdoushe at 17.00 and there will be a declaration made. What now? Still sniping, *howens*, *doshkas* and 500s heard. What now?

Saw Pauline a minute ago. She listened to my chest and heard nothing, but as the cough is still relatively non-productive, thinks I should have a chest X-ray in case of atypical mycoplasmic pneumonia. I've to go back at 17.00 when the electricity comes back on. Awake all last night with coughing and chest pain, only producing phlegm when I practically choked to death. Ben suggested loudly that I should take Phenergen, but that would only sedate me and do nothing for the cough or the pain.

0.30 Well, no further news of the supposed withdrawal. People say that if it's the end of the war then they could shell us a lot tomorrow. Already many more *howens* than for a long time, and shooting. And we can hear Amal and the *mahwars* shouting at each other. Saw a little of the Islamic Conference on TV at the hospital in the operating room, with the Kuwaitis and Saudis looking fabulous. Saw Abu Ammar (Yasser Arafat) for a second, then the electricity went out and the TV went off.

Fed the cat and Khadija after she stood in tears from hunger at the front door today, having not eaten for two days. Rifat, Haj, Hissam and Abu Sacker came and went. I'm still feeling miserable and ill. My chest X-ray was clear, with my left lung a little full; chest pain still severe at times.

Where is Terry Waite?

28.1.87 Day 92 Wednesday
This new jotter appears to mark the beginning of the end of the war, *Insh'Allah*. Today the first people in three months were allowed into the camp despite Amal attempts to discourage them by shelling the camp quite heavily at 14.00 with 107s, *howens* and gunfire. We had a little boy injured by shrapnel: three pieces, one in each shoulder, then one in his leg. After we had probed and cleaned his wounds, we sent him on the shoulders of the men who carried him to the clinic, running to the hospital. Then we got Amer al Khatib, shot twice with an M-16 near Haiduce. At first it was too dangerous to bring him out of the *mahwar* due to sniping and shelling; he arrived shocked but still conscious, covered in blood from a bullet

injury. No exit hole could be found, but, as it later turned out, the bullet was sitting just under the skin in his other buttock. We thought he had a severed artery and I thought maybe a rectal injury, so I scrambled/ran to the hospital pressing both arteries just in case. He spent seven hours in the operating room, has been transfused with thirty units of blood, is now critical and in traction.

While I was at the hospital the rumours that the Iranians had been coming with ambulances and food turned out to be true. There were four ambulances to evacuate wounded women and children only; it being too dangerous for men to go outside, even wounded men. In fact, it was Hizb'ullah and Iranians. They came to the square to take photographs of the destruction and conditions in the camp. They also tried to bring in 500 big cans of milk, but Amal shot up the truck carrying the milk into the camp and it had to be left at the top end of the road in from the airport road. They also shot and wounded the drivers, and dropped *howens* and sniped while they were on their way out of the camp.

The Palestinians are half out of Magdoushe into Ain al-Helweh, and the rest will go by the morning. A hundred and fifty of Mustafa Sa'ad's men, Nasserites, have replaced them.

Think I've torn a muscle with all this coughing, as for the past twenty minutes the pain is almost intolerable when coughing, let alone just breathing. Much worse than earlier.

29.1.87 Day 93 Thursday

Woken at 6.30 coughing and crying with the pain. Got up which helps the pain, as being flat seems to aggravate it and, of course, the coughing. Think I'll try to concoct a cocktail of aspirin and God knows what. I feel too selfish if I go and take one of the DF118 tablets as others have put up with serious pain whereas this is just an awful clicking muscle pain.

Listening to aircraft taking off and landing, and can hear cars, horns and engines for the first time in weeks, maybe because if the sniping and shelling stops, it's usually by 11.00. Looking at the disgustingly dirty state of the kitchen. Blue skies and very chilly morning, a little sun and no water at the *mahwar*. Getting a letter together to the Ross Institute about nutrition and the state of the camps.

17.30 Gave up on the pain threshold and went to see Hannes and Pauline. Had made Hannes fish and rice for breakfast, but Khadija and Zeinab got their hands into it and ate it all before I could even get it out of the door to him. Watched him treating a little boy with a nerve injury from the 45-day war; his brother had been injured in the leg also. Both had been shot and were aged 6 and 8 years old approximately. Then sought out Pauline who gave me a strong dose of DF118 in the hope that it would shift some of this chest pain, but it's only taken the edge off it slightly, so that I can cough again but nothing else.

Saw Dr Rede who like everyone else now looks so washed out and drained. There is a permanent dull-eyed look to many people here now, beyond tiredness into exhaustion, dull lacklustre, big brown bags under the eyes, that facial expression and complete apathy similar to photographs of long-term war victims or people who are very depressed.

Efforts are continuing to find Terry Waite who disappeared more than a week ago while seeking the release of hostages in Lebanon: BBC World Service.

Slept most of the afternoon and woke again with severe chest pain, so much for the fabulous analgesic qualities of DF118! Now little Ahmad has wandered in, silent after his cut finger was dressed. He has one arm, big scars on his back and legs from *howen* injuries in the 1-month war in 1985; he is 6 years old. His father has just died and his mother has remarried, leaving him with his grandmother. He refused to speak at first, but drank three glasses of tea. He also tires of people explaining about his one arm and dead father, leaving the room when they do so. But when his buddy arrived they sat playing with stethoscopes, lugging the cat around and sitting on my bed looking at a medical textbook.

I am wearing a lovely pair of handwarmers knitted by Um Mohamad Da'ah in a beautiful dusty blue in a kind of knot stitch – my hands are lovely and warm.

Visited Fatima on the way back here, who despite her fast from morning until 17.00 made me drink copious amounts of tea and made me a *hummus* and olive sandwich. We discussed the quantities required to make a store per person per house, and a rough approximation based on her mother's calculation is twenty kilogrammes of everything per person and one big tin or box of milk: twenty kilos of rice, olives, *addas* (lentils), and fourteen kilos of onions and garlic. Also thirty kilos of flour per person, and many tins of *zwan*, safari meat, sardines, tuna and soups. Plus rarities such as twenty kilos of coffee and thirty kilos of tea. They are very kind and sweet. She and Shahina are knitting me a pair of red and black socks, not before they had donated a pair of woolly maroon, grey and white socks to keep me warm in the meantime.

All the Palestinians in Magdoushe have returned to Ain al-Helweh, but now Berri is saying he wants Amal to retake Magdoushe from Mustafa Sa'ad. This is a big problem as from Damascus, where he has been hiding with Assad for the past three months, he cannot pull Daud Daud and the rest of the warmongers into line and get them to step up the war.

I've done a drawing of little Ahmad with his wellie-boots on the wrong feet. But the side view is much more revealing – of a little orphaned boy with one arm hanging limply inside an empty sweatshirt sleeve. When this war finishes I want to take many photographs just of the state of the children here after the war.

It is now illegal to travel to the Lebanon from America without government approval. Persons violating the law now face a 2,000-dollar fine. They're outrageous.

I've just swallowed a handful of chemical junk, but if I can sleep and wake up relatively pain free I'll rejoice.

Another person sniped in the pelvis with rectal injuries, a six-hour operation but not such a dirty rectal tear as Amer. He is a little better today, but he will need ten days to be certain. Little Um Aoni seems to want to die; she's refusing food and water and now is getting quite dehydrated. Maybe she'll have to be admitted for a few days to rehydrate her and take care of her.

30.1.87 Day 94 Friday

As Borhan says, we are now entering the fourth month of the war and today it's beginning to look like the end is not so simply near at hand as first supposed.

Mehdi was sick tonight. After coming twice for Ben, Borhan came and asked if I would go to the *mahwar* to see him as he refused to come up to the clinic. At first the description of his shivering made me think of withdrawal symptoms, but when I fell down into the *mahwar* I found him vomiting and covered in heaps of blankets, shivering. He had drunk some water and was promptly throwing it up again. He'd eaten nothing all day and had not passed urine since this morning. His fever was 38.8°C and I tried to take his blood pressure but found I'd gone too deaf to hear anything (much to my embarrassment). As he had no pain but there were these symptoms, I thought he should go to Haifa to see a doctor, but he refused. So I gave him drugs to bring his fever down. As no one has come to call me again, I assume he must be sleeping or slightly better.

No news apart from a car bomb in East Beirut, and Terry Waite still missing, and apparently the Red Cross tried to enter the camp, but Amal refused and promptly shelled us to frighten them away. No news about a ceasefire, although there were rumours which even little Rania, who was helping us to fold gauze and roll cotton balls, had heard. The Iranian plan is supposed to be being implemented.

The milk from Hizb'ullah was being distributed today and half a big can ended up here. I asked why and had all the children in the camp received milk before we accepted it. Apparently the mosque committee had remembered us: God bless them. (Perhaps they heard our report.) The hospital is running out of food; in three days it will be finished.

31.1.87 Day 95 Saturday

The siege goes on. The latest news is that Amal will be given back

Magdoushe tonight, then a ceasefire will be implemented. The only snag is that Hizb'ullah don't want it handed back to Amal. Their forces are equal in size to Amal, but do not enter into fights so rashly.

The other news is that three fighters from Mar Elias-Nidal bought their way into the camp last night by bribing a 6th Brigade soldier. They had to follow his instructions, and to purchase Lebanese Army uniforms, then he drove them to Ouzai in his car and they had to walk up from the sandlined street to the airport road with huge army kitbags with cigarettes and flair. They got lost and ended up coming into the camp through the cemetery instead of the assigned place. As soon as they reached there they started shouting to the fighters in Samed *mahwar*, 'Don't shoot, don't shoot; we are friends, we are Nidal.' Monir and the others told them to come quietly, and not to make a move or they would shoot them, until they got them to a light where they could see their faces. They were very distrustful as the second set of fighters to leave from Mar Elias camp had been captured trying to come into Bourj. One was killed.

Mehdi continued to have a high fever all day of 38°C but he's not taking his aspirin or drinking as directed. Also he refused to go to the hospital, but thankfully peed in the afternoon, refusing to move from his bed in the *mahwar* so that even his tribe of children had to go down there to visit him. After falling all the way to the *mahwar* to see him, I found his temperature was down slightly to 37.9°C, so Pauline and I discussed it. She says she has now seen four people with nothing more wrong with them than hunger, presenting itself as stomach pains and dizziness. One was the wife of Mohamad al Khatib who hasn't been eating as she is giving what's left of the food to the children. There were more cases of dizziness and lightheadedness today, but now there are no vitamins left in the hospital. Monir's family also have no food left and he is stubborn about requesting help, but they have no relatives in the camp. All families with children under 10 years of age got milk from the mosque.

Amer is slightly better today after his thirty units of blood; there has been no further bleeding today. He is coughing and conscious.

Got dragged off the street by two ladies trying to feed me today. At first I tried to refuse as many people have no food, but the second lady dragged me in and gave me a huge bowl of milk and rice.

1.2.87 Day 96 Sunday

Ate two *falafel* with 'Evil' Mahmud, Madam and Naamat who is turning into a beautiful little girl. She has learnt to walk and clapped when she saw me. Madam is pregnant and looked happy on it.

Quarrelled with Pauline over Ben's unhelpful behaviour which she seems unaware of. Went up to the hospital with Hissam, Haj and Rifat with the battery for recharging as Ben had dumped it on the verandah and they refused to carry it for him.

We visited Amer who looks much better today, *Insh'Allah* he will continue so, and I gabbled away in broken Arabic to Hachik. Then I went to Banan's with some *mujuderra* and milk. They took food to Juma's family who have none as their home is outside the camp, but whenever there is going to be fighting Juma's wife comes into the camp. They are staying with friends here, but have no stores or supplies and the children are going hungry. Like Khadija's kids; I met the youngest boy Abed in the street, who said nothing but 'I'm hungry', then the middle boy, so I sent them to the clinic to eat custard and whatever food was there.

There was a warning about shelling and we were shelled from 15.30 to 16.15, but not many; also some tonight, but again, not many.

2.2.87 Day 97 Monday

Many *howens* all last night and Borhan's big TNT explosion as planned at 4.00 which blew out the windows in Banan's house. Awoke before 8.00 with women and children collecting water and everyone in the camp awake before 7.00 except for the foreigners.

Amer got his shoes back today and is better but he still needs help. Hissam and Haj came at 18.15 to ask me what blood group I was and when I replied O-positive they told me '*Jalla*' ('Come on') to Mustafa, the lab technician. I told him that I had finished antibiotics a week ago, but 'no problem' as the other person who was O-positive refused to give blood. He gets my blood tonight, and one bag tomorrow.

The generator failed twice whilst I was giving blood and I thought, 'Oh no – not now, don't let it give up now with hot blood trickling down a tube down my arm.' Later, the second time, while Mustafa tried to pacify my mental state, thinking I was overly worried, I tried to tell him there was blood running all down my arm as the needle had dislodged a little. The joke is now that I'll give all my blood to drink Tang* every day afterwards. The story about Dr Saleh today is of him refusing to remove a bullet from a man's neck unless he gave him a cigarette. No cigarette, no bullet removed, so goes the joke.

Two people came from Mar Elias and were killed and a further two were captured and will probably be killed also; they were trying to come into the camp with food and flour but without a guide, and were promptly caught by Amal.

Amal shouted last night to the fighters in Rashidiyeh to surrender. They shouted back, 'No surrender'. To surrender means to be slaughtered. Us too, I suppose. The news today is getting grimmer. The Americans have ordered all their citizens out of the Lebanon or they will have their passports confiscated.

The food situation is now worse in Bourj than it is in Shatila as there are many more families living here than there, especially those with children.

*Tang – fortified Vitamin C – was given to donors.

Shatila has more fighters with some families and they have more resilience. There is talk again of going out of the camps to force some sort of solution to be made; although Berri is now talking of a solution, at least, this is better than nothing.

My allergy has come out in big lumps again, as it does every time I am near the ground or my bed, which is filthy. Huge red itchy swellings.

The food has run out in the hospital but the Abu Nidal group has given its food to the wounded. So a list was drawn up today of those who really need proteins and foodstuffs. They will get cheese and soup and tea; completely inadequate, but it's better than nothing. Khadija and Zeinab still constantly ask for things which now we can't give them after today, as there just isn't any more left: tea, sugar, milk, food in general. Now we get a lot of our food sent us by neighbours and that is beginning to run out. We are accepting anything available. To hell with pride and to hell with hoarding. Everyone is hungry. Although I'm still eating approximately 1,200 calories a day with a bowl of rice and milk, two biscuits, a little *kobé*, a little *mujuderra*, *borgol* (bulgar wheat), bread, sugar and sweet *leben*, it feels like being on a permanent diet, constantly hungry yet not wanting to eat.

A patchy peace with Pauline. I just have to keep my mouth shut until after she and Ben leave the country. Pauline says she needs a holiday after this. Don't we all. If we come out alive.

Noting the signs are coming of an end to the war. Girls are wearing brighter colours on their hair scarves and jerseys now. Drank coffee with Rifat. Terry Waite now under house arrest in the Bekaa.

3.2.87 Day 98 Tuesday

Jumblatt fears a joint American-Israeli action to free the hostages with two American aircraft carriers off Lebanese waters, although Shamir, the Israeli foreign minister, denies this. Dr Rede made a declaration calling on the Syrians to allow food and medical supplies to enter the camps. The Swiss embassy is closed and moved to East Beirut temporarily, and its nationals have been warned to leave dangerous areas.

Speculation is high about the joint American-Israeli action as the Israelis are amassing troops on the Lebanese border. Monir thinks they will bomb Mieh Mieh, Ain al-Helweh, the Bekaa and the mountain, but not here. 'Oh lovely,' as he put it, 'the situation is getting more and more worse.'

Amer had another crisis and started to bleed, so another urgent call for O-positive blood. Many women are having odd menstrual cycles, except me and Mahmud's wife whom they think is pregnant. One girl had a fifteen-day period which is still going on, so I've sent her to see Pauline in case there is a cervical problem.

Johina offered me tea or milk. I took tea so she also gave me a package of milk. I have hidden it and we can use it tomorrow for breakfast. I waited all day, then went to get the remains of the *kobé* but Ben had eaten it all, so Khadija and Zeinab and I went hungry until Khadija begged some lentils and herbs and made about six spoonfuls each of this mixture. Then I went to Fatima's and begged rice and beans which the four of us ate when I got back. I had to take her outside and explain that all of our food goes several ways, not just one or two, and could I come up to collect the food. I also tried to explain this to Maryam Hallimi: if she could give me a plate of food to take to the clinic I'd take it to share out, but could not eat it in her house by myself.

Went and discussed politics with Mohamad and Maryam Hallimi today whilst seeing their sister – and drank coffee again! Luxury, and now I know not to say '*dimé*' during a war as it means 'always'. I have just to say '*shukran*' (thank you) until the end of the war. And learnt the word for 'socialist': '*ishterakié*'. They are a lovely family and the older gentleman came in again and sat for a while at the back of the room. The other three girls in the room had all started at the American University of Beirut and had spent only one day at university after paying a term's fees of 1,000 Lebanese lira when the war started. This term all the money is lost; next term they will have to pay another 1,000 for the next three months.

Juma has told his wife and children to leave the camp to get food as they are going so hungry. They are to go by the airport road and risk being shot walking out by Amal – her two babies and three other children under 10 years old. He is so desperate, what can he do?

Ate a vegetable soup of tinned vegetables, the juice and salt, and made a lemonade of sugar, lemon and water to up everyone's blood sugar today. Got a huge saucerful of olives from a Dabdoub lady who I unashamedly took them from, sharing them with all of us and Banan, Juju and Mimo also. Then Shehadi's mother brought us a lentil cold broth and bread! I ate half the bread. Approximate intake: rice, beans and noodles – 300, olives and oil – 200, milk and sugar – 200, bread – 150, soup – 100, teas – 100, 1,050 Kcals daily.

Woken up at 9.30 by Abu Mohamad getting a Kalashnikov shot through his shoulder. He was very lucky as there was no fracture and no chest wound – checked and discharged. Then Walid came in half an hour later shot through his arm and right hip. Luckily it was a puncture in his arm and a glancing hip wound. I was going to debride his hip, but I thought the instruments were too dirty. As usual he was handsome and obstructive – refusing to lie down, refusing to let us take down his trouser belt and then refusing to go to the hospital.

Fetched water and stood for half an hour watching Borhan trying to destroy a building with a *doshka*. There's an organized system at Arsan *mahwar* for water collection these days.

Many *howens* fell at 1.00 after the ceasefire was supposed to have been implemented. No lights as all the lights had broken; no candles and no battery.

4.2.87 Day 99 Wednesday

Ceasefire from midnight last night. Again bombs are falling behind the Al Khatib house, causing Taisear and his plaster of Paris to lunge out of bed on to the floor as shrapnel hit the wall and came through the window while he was asleep. A rude awakening, like me who woke in the dark with mortars falling all around and no light. Thankfully I'm still a bit deaf from the cold, and not sure how close by they were or not. Khadia went into states alternating between joy and despair at the news as there was no confirmation of the ceasefire on the radio except Radio Monte Carlo. So we waited all day until 15.00 for any outside indication. Iyad, her son, showed up, slightly bashful after a three-day absence, when people thought perhaps he'd gone outside the camp – all except Khaled, his father – then her two others, Abed, and Mohamad, were said to have been eating bread from waste scraps thrown on the street.

Mohamad al Khatib's wife and three other women left the camp very early this morning and were later taken to an Amal office and questioned before being taken to the Iranian embassy. They told them that there is no food and that people are eating cats and dogs (and the cats are eating rats), so now Amal really know what stage we are at. It's reported that the siege will open for food and medicine tomorrow and will lift at 16.00. No solutions, just time to stock, flee and rest before the next war. Slowly, slowly, until they are annihilated like Tal al-Zatar.

I saw most of forty people and two cats injured by snipers, who had broken their legs.

Made vitamin packets, and Khadija and Zeinab cleaned out the kitchen and washed and dried bandages in the sun. I tried to feed Zeinab, Khadija, Abed and Mohamad. Zeinab fainted from hunger last night. Saw three people with headaches, dizziness and stomach pains; and three healthy babies with good weights.

Amer al Khatib has started bleeding again. He's now had fifty units of blood. As they moved his bed away from the shelling, it started more abdominal bleeding. He desperately needs platelets as he has a crisis almost every thirty-six hours. The generator in the hospital is running out of fuel and on the verge of breaking down.

People now say this is the worst war so far, as the siege and shelling, although lower in percentage of shells per day, is draining us all mentally and physically. The new saying is *fa'ah rasi* (exploding head). 'So, how are you?' is responded to with '*Taban* (tired), *jouane* (hungry), *fa'ah rasi* (and an exploding head).' We talked about food and Arabic cooking for about thirty minutes to stop us feeling hungry. It was Rifat's idea and it works to a certain degree.

The women who left the camp were on the TV news tonight, saying that the organizations refused to give people food from the stores, which was true until a week and a half ago.

If Ben and I don't have enough food to eat here now, we can go to the hospital. Today's intake: spaghetti – 200, *borgol* – 350, tuna – 100, milk – 200, olives – 100, teas – 100, total – 1,050 Kcals.

5.2.87 Day 100 Thursday
Well, it's rumoured that the once-fat black cat was eaten two days ago at the *mahwar*. More people are killing dogs and cats and eating them. Today I fetched wood from the roof by crawling on my stomach with a plastic bag laid under me – in daylight. (I must be mad.) I wanted to make a fire as the *babour* (pressure stove) had broken, so Khadija saved the day by getting Fahdi to make a stove out of a big Nido milk tin. Then we heated the milk that we had smuggled out in my bag (but Ben woke up and caught us), giving as much as possible to children hanging around, Juju, Abed and Co.

Zeinab is still persistently refusing to eat or take iron tablets, yet sits around every day bemoaning a headache and stomach pains and dizziness, so I'm trying to be angry with her, to get it through her thick head that she *must* eat. Khadija has more sense and eats, when possible, a little of what is being offered, but I had to leave her at the top of the road to the hospital today as she was too tired to walk up and back down to the clinic.

There are rumours that the US and Israel are exploring the idea of a joint assault on Hizb'ullah. Many people fear military action by the weekend as foreigners are being evacuated. The airport is closed and there is now a virtual blockade on West Beirut. The PFLP have had a sit-in to lift all the sieges in the Palestinian camps. The Israeli Army killed two in the 'security zone' after a clash with an Israeli patrol. Israeli planes dropped flares at Magdoushe at 7.00. The town has now been handed back to Amal by the Nasserites. Rashidiyeh bombed again.

Managed to get a bowl of rice and green beans. Contemplated eating some grass I saw growing in the rubble, wondered if I could cook it or not, as it was next to the sewage. Then shared the rice between four of us and went to fetch some water. I had to wait for three quarters of an hour. Met the mother of Mohamad Suliman, who was dead on arrival, shot through the chest, two weeks ago. She just stood crying and crying in front of me, tears streaming down her face with nothing to stop them, in the sunlight, with the boys at the *mahwar* now too lethargic to talk or pass the time of day, and the rest of us sitting waiting for the water – and the end of the war.

Came back to the clinic and I fell asleep or literally dropped on to the mattress and slept through exhaustion, as I had only had six hours' sleep last night. Dreamt of Shatila but it looked like Hampstead. Better than the nightmare that I woke with this morning, of a woman naked, dead and decapitated – lying beside her head in a lift.

Tonight Imad al Masri and sixteen other men from the camp are going out to bring food. They have already brought a BKC gun to the clinic and are going out prepared to attack with many weapons. There will be four to carry supplies and raid the building, and six sets of two guards each posted. They are going to steal chickens from a Shia family's house. Imad is taking the BKC with him (it's his own). Also two other boys are going out as Banan came to borrow a bag for first aid. We found a red rucksack that we think must have been Lieve's, judging by the medicines and cards in it. We also found one chocolate and two candy sweets in it. Banan took them for the children. Then we fixed up the straps in the twilight, on the clinic floor. I hope they all come back alive and safe. Imad has just produced his cheques for the past three months' wages, which he is carrying in case he is killed tonight.

Two of Khadija's children are in hospital having more of the useless drips with bright yellow vitamins in them; useless, but people feel it works and so the hospital is full of hungry people waiting for infusions, hopelessly thinking it will cure the stomach pains, dizziness and headaches that we are all beginning to get from hunger. No food – only a mouthful or so every so often – constant hunger and fatigue. My calorie intake today: milk and sugar – 200, spoonfuls of rice – 100, *kobé/leben* – 200, soup and lentils – 200, teas – 100, milk – 150, total – 950 Kcals.

Climbed the stairs to the roof and my pulse was up to 130 a minute. God, that's healthy. Rifat came by later bringing Kleenex, three boxes of matches and all in addition to the tetracycline earlier in the day. The food in his house will run out tomorrow or the next day. His mother has to see a doctor as her insulin has to be adjusted if she's not eating enough. Then we discussed the situation here, as I was very, very tired and it all looked a bit bleak to the foreigner. The Palestinians are the best to be with as they have always lived with this sort of threat over them and have a philosophical approach to it. Take your pleasure only, because if you continuously think about the way of life here, you would go crazy as there is nothing you can do about it. Later he asked me how I feel about being here. Was it the first time I had experienced this sort of thing? I said yes, of course, as in Europe maybe hunger strikes some families due to unemployment, but on the whole life is kinder there than here. It made people selfish and aware only of their possessions. Because of the fragility of daily existence here, people are more generous, giving and accepting, also more sensible about the war and the siege than we are.

6.2.87 Day 101 Friday

No news today – still waiting. People are now looking a little dejected as we linger around, tired and dizzy. Too lethargic to hold a conversation and not much to discuss except the latest proposals and speculation and rumours. Sitting in the sunshine in between the *howens* today. Thank God for the sun. At least the winter is lifting a little although the nights still get cold, and then I start coughing again. I'm stiff and a bit headachy, but I'm getting so used to it that I've forgotten what it's like to feel full of energy and lively.

Banan is talking of leaving. She wanted my advice: to stay or to leave? If they leave it will be in two days, after Ghadaffi's deadline of finding a solution to ending the camps war and also after the meetings in Damascus, which at present are very unproductive. She is very undecided, and one of the factors helping this is that there is a story circulating about one of the girls who left the camp two days ago being raped by Amal and that she is now in hospital. One other story is that the women who appeared on the news broadcast were beaten into saying that they were grateful to Amal before the broadcast. But now the organizations have all forbidden the women and children to leave the camps. Today a demonstration of women gathered at the edge of the camp wanting to leave when the offer of leaving by the Majnuk (airport) road exit was made between 14.00 and 16.00. They were dissuaded and told to wait a few days for a solution. The ban was made after that.

7.2.87 Day 102 Saturday

Woken today by shelling from the mountains, from around 8.20. Intensive shelling round the camp. Then it stopped apart from Borhan's *doshka*. We listened in our beds as it went on, then suddenly the whole camp was listening. It was absolutely quiet as the whole of the camp ran indoors, then listened in silence. It was the first time we had heard such a bombardment happening to Amal, instead of us or Shatila being bombed. Then we heard that they had been shelling to facilitate the entry of supplies from Mar Elias to the camp, but all of Amal did not go down from their positions, and the driver of the truck bringing in the flour was shot dead in the truck with two others on the Majnuk road. It was carrying flour and rice.

Fatima gave us all *molochiya* so Ben, Monir and I ate. I sat for twenty minutes on her balcony and felt more at ease than I have in a long time. Khadija's daughter, Sabrine, came with me for food to the hospital today and again later at night for the soup; little Abed came for some extra food so I gave him the *borgol* and some rice. We ate with Monir, and Ben took soup to Pauline. Gave Ahmad and Banan sugar, swapped earrings with Um Bilal, and got given a pair of black shoes with shrapnel holes by Juju.

Amer is still bleeding and when he was taken to theatre they found his artery had a huge haematoma, so after two hours he needs another eight units of blood. Zeinab lied about her age and gave blood.

Today's intake: beans and bread – 200, olives and tea – 100, rice – 150, tea – 100, milk – 150, soup – 100, *molochiya* – 150, potatoes and rice – 200. The problem arose of how to feed seven people on the *molochiya*. I think the worst part is seeing hungry children getting very thin, for example Khadija's kids. Haj and Hissam sat around but refused food. We bulldozed Monir into eating.

There is no emergency feeding left for children at the hospital and within two weeks they will start to die of starvation. The attitude of the organizations is that Amal doesn't know that there is *no food* left and therefore will not starve us out. This is gross unreality. They also believe it is better for us all to die within the camp than cause a camp to fall and then the slaughter of all Palestinians inside and out.

There was an occupation in Vienna of the Arab League offices calling for an end to all three sieges, and also at Mar Elias camp as Amal refuse to lift the sieges and have a ceasefire. Hizb'ullah were fighting the Israelis last night and Amal today in the southern suburbs.

Samira is four months pregnant and Bassam has now no cause for complaint. Three months ago we talked as he was giving her a hard time for being married three months with no baby on the way. She didn't realize at the time she was pregnant, and she's not too happy and wants to leave the camp as she's sick, dizzy and vomiting, and there is no food.

Monir's little brother left by the cemetery today. They made a deal for four of them to go, and edged closer to the hills with a crowd of people picking grass to eat. When out of sight they ran for it, but were caught by an Amal patrol almost immediately, and now no one is sure what has happened to them. Some say that they have been handed over to Mar Elias. He is 17 years old and got too tired of the war.

The heavy shelling will continue over today and tomorrow. But at the moment the shelling produces retaliation shelling of the camp. There were many *howens* at 11.10 and then shells from the mountains, then more at 12.00. The clinic was full of children, neighbours and the video-shop owner, a Dabdoub, Ali Mifli, who was having his bullet injury dressed. Shrapnel was hitting the door and the walls. In between the first and second lot Khadija and I ran up to the hospital to fetch lentils from the kitchen. All of the top of the road towards the hospital had been hit by the *rajmehs* (rockets) that went overhead, and there was a lot of rubble everywhere. The third set came about 13.30 and hit around the clinic and the Al Khatib house. Another boy got shot with a leg injury.

There is talk of two more trucks waiting outside the camp with supplies of food, but the first truck only got as far as the first gate to the camp and the three bodies are still inside; they are going to try to bring the supplies in tonight.

It's said that the mountains were told that the fighters here want to fight, as if they remain sitting all day waiting in the *mahwars* they think of nothing but how hungry they are, so after tomorrow the decision will be taken for a military solution (maybe/maybe not). Yesterday ammunition was smuggled into Rashidiyeh for five million Lebanese lira, and food supplied for two million Lebanese lira.

I came back from Banan's quickish as two mortars fell and we could hear the trucks moving outside, signalling more *howens* to come. I reached the clinic just in time as another one fell. Then Mohamad Ali al Haj came running into the clinic yelling that he was injured and holding his arm. He was hit by shrapnel on the road and also had two shrapnel injuries on his legs. His arm was bleeding quite heavily just above his wrist, so we cut off his clothes, which turned out to be Rifat's trousers and Hissam's jacket. When I put traction on his elbow to the wrist, I felt his bone slide away under my hands, so we splinted it, took his trousers off and sent him up to the hospital on a stretcher. He's in plaster, with a window for dressings to be done for a week, then it will be changed. Rifat and Hissam carried him up. He'd been in earlier joking with Khadija whom he said has a 'white heart'. I felt bad, worrying so much about the food last night and how to share it among seven people, that I didn't talk to him at all. And the food finishes in the hospital on Monday. It *finished* tonight. We got a can of safari meat between two; some families got one between seven. One woman was shot collecting grass to eat, and the queues at the hospital are already bad with families scrambling around with plates for food.

One man was refused food for his family by Dr Rede and flew into a rage, went into the kitchen and kicked over the pot of rice and beans, the whole lunch for the hospital, all over the kitchen floor. He was put in jail, as he has no influential connections, yet Salah who shot at Dr Rede and has connections did not get put in jail. His wife is reputed to have been threatened and beaten into speaking badly about the camp's situation on TV, yet what she said about foodstuffs for leaders only was true.

Pauline wrote out another communiqué about people starving in the camp and the talk of stores entering to relieve the situation. Amal have repeatedly refused UNRWA entry with relief supplies since the siege started. So we put our names to it again. She ate dog meat yesterday thinking, somewhat naively, it was one of the suddenly abundant mythological rabbits that are appearing everywhere. Khadija ate cat the day before yesterday thinking it was one of the rabbits, and Ben ate some of Moghrabi's mule today after nursing it through its shrapnel injury in the 10-day war. Moghrabi had had it for eleven years and sold it for 10,000 Lebanese lira to Abu Musa. It was in the hospital today.

Contemplating the prospect of being too lethargic to work after Tuesday if there really is no food after Monday.

Now all manners are going out the window and people take food on the first offering, instead of all the refuse, refuse, refuse, refuse which is the custom, and they devour it ravenously in front of you. Me too, I'm too hungry to refuse food from anyone. It's almost impossible to produce food now if other people are around as we are eyeing each other's food enviously, with empty stomachs. Today's intake: milk and sugar – 200, lentils – 100, soup – 400, milk and sugar – 100, tea – 100, more milk and sugar – 100, total approximately 1,000 Kcals.

The Israeli military towed a ship from Cyprus with fifty Palestinians into an Israeli port and is now interrogating them. The PLO says it was carrying supplies and medicines to the destroyed camps in Lebanon. Berri declares Waite will be released soon and may release the 'Israeli five' in return for 400 Arab prisoners in Israeli jails. He also wants Amal to facilitate entry of food supplies to Rashidiyeh. New Palestinian artillery moved onto the mountains today. Amal took the six-wheel truck from yesterday.

So we wait and wait. The radio is now attached to the big battery and acting in a similar fashion to Valium: soothing us into believing that it may all end and that we may come out again to the normal life of clothes, shops, food, restaurants, discos, cigarettes, all of it, that's going on outside – without us.

When I hear the tanks, sometimes I forget and think I'm hearing a car, then I gather my senses and think I should move soon as there is always a tank shell or *howens* shortly afterwards – usually five to ten minutes later – as today. All day. Twice I heard the tanks moving, then shortly afterwards we were shelled. The square was full of children until the mountains started shelling, then, for the rest of the day, it was empty again, devoid of people just as in the beginning of the war, and usually only people running in with emergencies or to see us – three people with shrapnel wounds. The last was one of the Dabdoubs, who was injured coming from the hospital but refused to go back, although we have no gauze or clean cottonwool, and no light. So much for trying to sleep: four interruptions, no, five in half an hour. Ridiculous things really, except for little Abed, Khadija's largest, wanting tomato paste for the safari meat. Later Iyad appeared looking for his mother; someone had said she had been injured in her head. It turned out that she'd banged her head in the shelter, so I think she must be sleeping there, as the kids were all ordered into the shelter with the rocket attack. Abed and Sabrine had appeared earlier to take me up to hospital for food, but Ben had already gone to collect it.

We ate 'the soup of the fat' (one can of vegetables and a tin of *zwan*) with a very anxious Monir, tired and worried about the fate of his brother as he had been promised he could speak with him in person on the *jihaz* today in Mar Elias, but there was so much communication with the mountains to organize the shelling that he wasn't able to try Mar Elias. Yaq'ub the cat came back.

8.2.87 Day 103 Sunday

We have to keep Yaq'ub indoors as the boys are rounding up all the cats to eat them. So we need to guard him despite his thinness and obstinate refusal to eat rice.

I am writing by my *dulsanna* light which I fashioned yesterday with a wick from Ben's old jeans, *mazot* (diesel), and Rifat's help in splitting the top to pull the wick through. It works well and gives a long light, but a lot of smoke. But the problem with using the jeans as a wick for the light is that the cotton, despite being double thickness, seems to absorb the fuel too quickly, as it was very soaked and crumbling when it finally extinguished itself. Great inventions part three. Ben is still making the rotten-smelling *samnia*, fat candles with our last can of Dutch fat (or is it Arab beef fat?), wire and cotton.

I boiled and washed bandages today, then made about five litres of Gentian Violet as all the dressing clinics are finished in the hospital and it's now soap and water, or soap, water and salt. But if there is a real need for an anti-bacterial agent then we can give out the Gentian Violet in little bottles. We're a regular pharmacy, what with wrapping packages of vitamins and making medicines.

I wanted to write yesterday, but couldn't bring myself to put it on paper that when Haj was injured I felt nothing. *Absolutely nothing*. I've noted this before during this war, but I always thought it would be different with someone I knew well like Haj, Rifat or Hissam. But it's not. I'm as remote and detached in an emergency situation as ever before, even with friends. It's strange, this absence of feeling, and yesterday I was ashamed of it and could not work it out or write it down. But I think it's partly because of work and partly due to the 'thank God it's not me' sensation that has taken over, and also a numbness and acclimatization to the war that prevails. So that now, if someone is seriously injured, I don't feel the adrenaline panic that I used to get earlier on in the war, perhaps because I'm adjusting to death being easily accepted, as it could happen at any time to any one of us. Haj had always told Hissam and Rifat that they would be injured together as they were forever wandering around the camp and up and down to the hospital. Yesterday, when he and Rifat left the hospital, Rifat said to walk, as there was shelling. Haj said no, let's run. When they heard the *howen* go out from Amal (with eighteen seconds counting until it explodes), Rifat yelled at Haj to wait in cover to see where it landed. Haj again yelled no and they ran on arguing, Rifat urging shelter, Haj yelling to run for it, when it exploded on the building above them, on the water pipes near the shops. They were showered with huge pieces of bricks and stones, but although they were next to each other, Rifat only got small pieces of shrapnel in his hair yet Haj had multiple shrapnel injuries and a fracture. I think his body must have covered Rifat's.

Then I did his mother's dressings again, mostly in the dark as the safe room and sick bed is very dark and still a nightmare to do dressings in. Now I've seen three of the family in the 'sick bed'. His mother is fine apart from the big 'in and out' shrapnel hole on her leg which seems to have closed from the middle down. There's a big hole inside that's not well closed at all.

Food was reasonably abundant with rice from Um Mohamad al Ashwa, and *addas* (lentils) and rice from the hospital and some red stuff from Um Sami with coffee. So a milk and water mixture for lunch, and a lentil and rice mixture for tea. I gave food to Khadija, Zeinab refusing to eat as usual, yet eyeing up the rice suspiciously.

The most annoying part of all the hiding of food and cigarettes, etc, is that in most houses friends come and go who know the score with each other, whereas in the clinic we are constantly surrounded by people who are not friends, often not even acquaintances, who seem to think we have never-ending and eternal food supplies which only Ben and I eat. Yet Monir eats with us at night and before that everything that can be given away is.

The 500 has just gone into action and now there have been *howens* for the past hour or so.

I listened to a review of the latest book on Mary Stuart on BBC World Service. She was a talented seamstress, leaving over a hundred pieces of embroidery.

Three PLO men sentenced to life imprisonment in Israel after the grenade attack at the Wailing Wall last October. Israel refuses to release the 400 held in jails, claiming not to deal with terrorists.

Ben went out to see one of the Dabdoub girls who had fainted when she woke up and got out of bed, having not eaten at all. She was advised to stay in bed and eat, if possible.

Many people keep telling us '*Bukhra Insh'Allah, yom* and *yomain*' – one or two days, one week. Why? What is going to happen tomorrow that will distinguish it from yesterday, or today for that matter? Will anyone tell me so that I can get excited about it? Anyway the reason is given as being a meeting in Beirut between everyone and a solution being worked out over Magdoushe, and the admission of supplies to the camps soon; even tomorrow is muttered about, but I don't believe it, I've heard it so often. Tomorrow, after two days, in a week's time: for a solution that, after three months, I don't place any faith in them reaching.

I experienced another bizarre happening today when going up to the hospital to collect food with Abed, Khadija's son. I saw a woman carefully carrying out a big tin dish and, thinking it was food, I looked hungrily in; seeing it was bright red, I tried to reason where we had got all the strawberries or peppers from, as it was *so* red. Only after a few seconds of mental confusion did I realize that I was looking at a dish full of clots of blood and a few rags from the operating theatre. I was hungry enough after a small dish of *addas* today and only soup yesterday that I really was envisaging a red treacly meal for the evening.

I was woken at 7.30 by Sabrine this morning who had let herself in and was helping herself to the sugar in the kitchen.

Four were shot today near Zeinab's area. The mountain artillery was in action at Haret Hreik, Zenadine, airport road and Ruwais, and some shells hit the first floor of the new airport building, and also the runway.

Palestinian women from Mar Elias camp demonstrated at the Soviet Embassy in Beirut to end the war of the camps. Hizb'ullah, Amal and the Palestinians are on *instanfah* in Magdoushe tonight; the Palestinians refuse to let Hizb'ullah leave the positions to Amal as the Iranian plan is based on Hizb'ullah holding Magdoushe. The French are asking for an end to the siege of the camps. Shultz has criticized the people of Beirut for failing to take responsibility to end the spate of kidnappings in West Beirut. He said that by failing to exercise their responsibility they are isolating themselves from the rest of the world. Terry Waite is claimed to have had a tracking device planted on him which has revealed the whereabouts of some of the captors in an operation named Probe or River depending on what radio station you listen to. Nabih Berri says he will reappear soon. Ha, ha. We've been on the receiving end of Berri's 'soon' for the past three months. I wonder if the Archbishop of Canterbury has any idea of the scope of a Nabih Berri 'soon'?

We sat listening to the mountains shelling Ouzai and nearer. The rumour that one Grad rocket hit the camp yesterday was true. But, although a few *howens* shelled us today, we don't know why the mountain batteries were used tonight. Rifat says perhaps to pacify us in the camps, as, if they were really to shell heavily, with each launcher setting five shells per minute, they would shell at a rate of 200 to 300 shells per minute. But they are politically prevented from doing so by the Syrians and Jumblatt.

The food finishes tomorrow. Intake today: rice and beans – 300, rice and *addas* – 300, soup – 400, *paste* – 50, tea and sugar – 150, total 1,200. *Wow*, what a luxury!

9.2.87 Day 104 Monday

The mountains shelled sporadically all through the night, but not as promised.

A premature baby girl was born yesterday to Wassella Eskander and she died as she had had no proper nourishment during the pregnancy. There was no food for the midday meal in the hospital, so a small bowl of food was to feed three people. Mohamad, the nurse from the house of paraplegics, and his brother would not eat so as to give it to their grandfather. Khadija's kids are always looking for their mother; they are hungry. The little boys who were eating off the garbage piles yesterday and today arrived just as we finished the soup, so Abed and Mohamad scrabbled for the spoonful that had been put down to try to keep the cat Yaq'ub alive, eating anything they could find. Sabrine was standing like a little thin ghost on the road to the hospital this morning, looking for her mother too, and has just gone off in disgust when I told her there were no tins of vegetables left (having sleepily misunderstood *basella* (beans) and thought she wanted onion, I'd split our only onion in two for her).

Khadija wants to feed Yaq'ub to her children now. That's something as she's been so *haram* until now and has abandoned the laws of Islam to eat. I don't think Mohamad and Allah would mind so much. I'm drinking sugary tea and am now looking at the Gevral Instant Protein emergency food – concentrated, only fifty-seven calories and fifty per cent protein and twenty-two vitamins – wondering who should get this. Them or us? It also says on the package to add water or milk! Weak laughter offstage in the wings here.

There was a plan yesterday to have three hours of heavy shelling from the mountains to cover fighters and women going out of the camps to raid for food, but Abu Ammar told them to wait only two days. Yet *another* two days, it's always two days.

I don't feel so hungry since yesterday as I know now there just isn't any food left. That's that. A mental acceptance. So I eat if I get it. So far most days have not been too bad, although when carrying the (twenty-five-litre) gallon canister back I had to stop on the road, and Mustafa al Khatib caught me and took it back to the clinic and up the stairs, despite protestations to the contrary. I'd taken it because Khadija has been eating much less for a week longer than me, and is really too feeble to carry it. I'm also looking at two iron tablets and wondering, when the food stops, how long the tablets will keep us going?

Abu Suhail said that if we heard really heavy shelling from the mountains the women and children were to go to the bomb shelters, but nothing happened – again.

The rains have come again; I woke up feeling really cold and am now wearing two jerseys.

The doors of the hospital are closed now to all, and the place is empty, gloomy and dark, devoid of all the usual noise, bustle, guns and squabbling.

17.10 Listening to the call of *Maghreb* (dusk prayer call) from outside. It sounds as beautiful as the call from the camp and it's hard to believe that, for us, it's a call of hatred – singing through the dripping rain and grey sky.

Yesterday we all thought and talked of the life outside, of food and stores in shops, of restaurants, cars, buying food or clothes, cinemas, books, services. If this war ends on a temporary stop, and I get the visa secured as soon as my passport comes back, I would leave immediately for London after ordering supplies and stores of baby foods, a milk supply for six months, vitamins, vaccines, rat and mosquito poison; ready to come back when the stores and orders are ready.

The days are getting longer again. It's still light at 17.30 now instead of darkening at 16.30. *Howens* at midday and some through the afternoon, not many though – yet. Hannes commented today on how white I was looking and was I all right? I said, yes, just a little anaemic like everyone else now. Caught sight of the big black circles under my eyes last night in the mirror. I look dreadful, especially when I'm tired (and that's about four hours after I get up now). Reading *Stars in the Sky of Palestine* which is a book of short stories I've borrowed from Fatima.

I think the most striking thing I remember so far of this war is the sight of nine-months-pregnant women running, and women running with water pitchers on top of their heads, at the sound of the mortars exploding nearby. And of mothers collecting their children, screaming at them and chasing them at the sound of the first shell. The most noticeable thing here is the children – they were the first thing I saw when I came here on the road down from the hospital – hordes of children out playing in the muggy, grey heat.

The water was weak today – a trickle rather than a gush into the can. Arsan al Habet was sitting out with Aref and a few others; Aref follows him almost everywhere, hero worship of his brother. Even Arsan, well fed, looks tired too, rousing a faint smile and greeting in the pale day and skies with clouds. He was sitting on a bit of rubble, or was it a chair, at the edge of the *mahwar*. I'm hungry now – we're all hungry, but the only ones who say so openly are the children, who don't let us forget it. The cats are hungry, but the people are hungrier and will eat them all soon. We cried when we heard the people of Rashidiyeh were eating grass, but look at us now after waiting another two days, always another two days. We fed four last night, plus Ben, Pauline and me – Amer, Monir and Imad, and Rifat, who'd been waiting outside and had hungrily wanted to come in when he heard the plates. So I forced some of the soup into him with weak and precious coffee. Being bloody fussy, he refused more as he didn't have a cigarette. There is nothing, yet they all complain when they get something, instead of being grateful for it.

For the third day women from Mar Elias camp demonstrated in Beirut. Tomorrow they will try to come to Bourj al-Brajneh. It could be another bloodbath and massacre, as Amal have no qualms about shooting women.

One young girl crawled into the camp through the sewers clutching two bags with ten bags of bread in each. She gave them to her mother then crawled back out of the camp again. Boys were reported to have been seen roasting and eating six rats today, and when Abu Riyad (Sultan) spoke to Abu Ammar today his daughter asked Arafat to send more cats and dogs to the camp as we had run out of them to eat. Sultan apparently did tell Abu Ammar that the situation is serious, and the mythical six-wheel truck from UNRWA is supposed to be coming tomorrow. But, as the ICRC and UNRWA do not bribe their way through Amal *mahwars*, I really doubt the validity of this new, placebic story, as the only way out of this is (as usual) money.

Yesterday a truck took food into Shatila under cover of the shelling from the mountain, but on the way out they shot the driver dead. A game of food and martyrdom to prevent volunteers. Sheikh Shamsidine says he will personally come with the truck to make sure it enters the camp. But some of the Popular Front want to prevent the entry of any supplies, and end the war and the siege altogether. They should try it from inside, without food.

Borhan got injured again by a bullet exploding near him and throwing up sand and stones into his neck and face. A lot of swelling but no signs of entry. Shocked again and his poor mother too. Later I got called to see Lydia who was lying shivering and semi-responsive to speech. Borhan said that she'd complained of blurred vision and had become like that very quickly. I wanted to take her blood pressure, which had been fine earlier on, but as she'd just gone into her seventh month of pregnancy, and with the visual problems and the fact that she looked as though she may start having fits, I sent her straight to the hospital on a stretcher. In fact she just had a hysteric and hyperventilating attack. Pauline in tears at the scenes of desperation outside the hospital kitchen again. One can of safari meat per family.

Came back after having left the sewage well blocked, but discovered that it wasn't just the clinic but that the sewers must have blocked totally further up the camp as they were now flooding through the square with the most awful sulphuric smell, on a moonlit night.

Listening to the radio about Celtic and Aberdeen's closeness in the Cup. It's bizarre that just when you are listening to something interesting, off goes a *howen* or the 500 or the M-16 and the rest of the programme is lost in the sounds of the war.

Listening to Alistair Cooke's 'Letter from America' when all hell let loose yesterday, just as I'd lulled myself into thinking I was at home in the kitchen and the garden was outside, with Dad, Mum and the dog in it. Then today the constant mention of bread and butter on a game with Frank Muir, Dennis Norden and Antonia Fraser nearly made me swoon, as I've been contemplating how to cook paper and other siege delicacies. (In oil?)

I think I may have worms but we only have tinea medication, and I think I've got *Ascaris* (a kind of roundworm) by the size of them.

Thirty women tried to leave the camp today. When they could not be dissuaded, the fighters deliberately opened fire on the Amal *mahwars* to get return fire making it impossible to pass through and out*.

Haj had his track shrapnel removed today in the hospital by Dr Saleh.

*Although individually men wanted their families to be safe outside the camp, collectively it was clear that it would be easier to define the camp as a military target rather than a civilian one if the families left.

Food intake was very good today: *mujuderra* – 300, soup – 200, tea – 100, spaghetti, fat, corned beef and a little bread – 1050, total 1,650 Kcals. A five-Lebanese-lira bet on the admission of the truck tomorrow, and tomorrow spaghetti again, then it's all finished. The *mazot* (diesel) is also finished, with the hospital generator functioning now only for emergencies as the fuel situation is desperate.

10.2.87 Day 105 Tuesday
King Hassan of Morocco has offered to send supplies in a Red Crescent plane to two besieged Palestinian refugee camps in Beirut where thousands of people are said to be starving. Sheikh Fadlullah of Hizb'ullah, a spiritual leader, has ruled that if necessary people can eat the flesh of dead animals and also that of human corpses. They also talk of UNRWA supplies coming today and that there is a big meeting in Syria to press for a ceasefire. Anyway, it's good that the BBC World Service has altered its version of the sieges since last night and knows that there are thousands of starving people.

I was reading the statement draft when I heard that Hamoudi, the lovely little boy whom I first saw at the Beit Atfal al Somud, had been shot. I first watched him during the *dubké*; now he is dead. He always went everywhere with his uncle, Said Nasser, the Abu Musa leader, with his little brown polo-neck pullover and his three- to four-bullet clip pack. At first I thought it was his father, but his father died a long time ago. Hamoudi was shot through the head this morning, near the cemetery, collecting grass to eat. He was a charming boy, always smiling with a cheerful 'Hello, Suzy'.

15.00 BBC World Service: I've just listened to David Hirst in Nicosia playing down the level of starvation in Bourj al-Brajneh. He's been speaking to Chris Giannou, who stated that Shatila is militarily weaker but has food, whilst Bourj is militarily stronger but has nutritional problems. He said he felt the need for the inhabitants to eat human flesh was probably propaganda. Why did they not ask if we were eating cats and dogs? We are and it's not 'publicity' as he puts it.

21.00 BBC World Service: well, at last the outside world knows! Thank God. They spoke of another dramatic situation taking place in West Beirut, that of the sieges of three camps by Amal. Then they read a statement sent by telex to a London news agency from foreign health workers in one of the camps – *us*! – quoting, 'We have seen children searching the garbage piles for scraps of food to eat . . . and a woman was shot on the periphery of the camp collecting grass for her seven children to eat as they have no food at all.' It also mentioned people fainting from starvation, then interviewed the head of UNRWA in Vienna who has been getting information from Abu Salim. He has appealed to Nabih Berri to allow supplies to enter, and the BBC pointedly asked why he should have any hope of success, if King Hassan thinks it is necessary to parachute supplies in if he wants them to enter by road. So it's also on Radio Monte Carlo at 19.00.

Rifat told me that four people went out from the camp today – two were his friends – for a price of 2,000 Lebanese lira each. They did it by making contact on the *jihaz* on the same frequency as Amal, and arranging a pick-up point and a price with Amal people who operate this escape for money. They arranged a certain point to be picked up on the street which is safe and the Amal people drove up in an armoured jeep and took them away from the camp. There are two or three of these points that people have left from.

Today's intake: sweet stuff – 400, rice – 300, vine leaves – 200, *leben* – 100, soup – 150, tea – 100, total 1,250. Hannes and I went for food at Fatima's of vine leaves, *leben* and tea. It was lovely to sit and play with Rajah's three children and eat and talk. We took some up to Pauline and Ben, and waited for the abortive entry of the stores. Abu Ammar said if it takes fifty million Lebanese lira to get food into Bourj al-Brajneh, he will pay it.

11.2.87 Day 106 Wednesday

A ceasefire – sixteen injured, one dead.

Summoned to the hospital at 11.00 by Mohamad al Ashwa to speak on the *jihaz*. They wanted a doctor and a nurse to speak to a press conference in Mar Elias, but we had to wait for Pauline to finish cauterizing a colostomy. While waiting, Abu Salim told me to go and fetch food upstairs. I said I had no plate, to which he replied that I should run to the clinic and get one. He said to Ben to tell me to go for the food. I'd already been up to the hospital and back to the clinic once already, but Ben said, 'Go quickly'; I replied 'How can I go quickly? I'm anaemic.' As I ran back the *howens* started and got closer and closer, so I ran into the houses for shelter until they stopped, and ran back to the hospital arriving completely winded. A mere run once to the hospital knackers me now, let alone twice. I got back and we went to the *jihaz* room where Pauline spoke to the conference in Mar Elias.

The BBC World Service quoted last night's statement about rats, cats and starvation. Later they quoted the fifteen weeks that Pauline had mentioned and the many infectious diseases, malnutrition, rats and dogs. At 14.00 they spread the news that Amal were refusing entry of the supplies to the camp until the Palestinians withdrew from two villages near Magdoushe and that the trucks had been detained outside the camps since 9.00 this morning.

The camp of Mar Elias spent all day and night preparing food supplies for us, and UNRWA stores worked from 6.00 to 20.00 yesterday to prepare the trucks which are to be carrying one kilo of flour, one kilo of potatoes and 400 grammes of rice per person. After I heard about this I dreamt of eating potatoes last night; after the night before's dreams of eating cake with Hissam, Haj and Rifat, and the Prince of Denmark.

17.30 Mehdi al Khatib has just been shot, once again; I was called from collecting the water and ran to the clinic, where we suctioned him and tried to put the airway in, although he was resisting. We ran with him with pressure and airway to the hospital, Walid carrying one side of the stretcher, Ahmad, Ben and I, with me sandwiched in the middle, the other. We got there just as the motor cut out, having organized the electricity in advance. Dr Saleh and Pauline were waiting and tried to entubate him. Luckily the lights came back on and his colour was better than the blue look he had had when we tried to breathe him on the road, having to stop and blow. By the time we got to the hospital he was blinking and breathing and could talk a little to answer questions. I tried his leg reflexes and felt nothing, and watched while they put up intravenous drips and took off his boots. As there was no water to wash with, I left for the clinic, covered in blood, carrying the airway. I met Walid on the road and asked him how he was, as he had carried the stretcher with a bullet wound only a week or so old; he said that he was fine. Stopped at the Al Khatibs' house and explained that Mehdi was breathing, but that I thought that he had no movement from his waist down at least. They thanked me, and I came back to find another shrapnel head injury from a *howen* that had exploded whilst we were in the hospital.

Then about four other people to see. What a day! What a bloody massacre. The day that the world thought we would get food and medicines, Amal shelled us and killed one woman in a house where five other women were also injured. Another woman lost her eye. Sixteen in total injured, and Mehdi may die soon. He is quadriplegic and we are all shocked by it. The one thought that crossed my mind was, 'Oh my God – all his kids will be standing as usual on the road and will see him like this,' and worse, his wife was watching from the window, as usual, as we ran past. Yassera saw him and screamed as she recognized him. And today I'd thought that for the first time one of his children was standing smiling – usually they are quite a solemn little bunch. And all of the treatment was done by doorlight and the homemade *dulsanna* lamp, as the battery is flat and we can't recharge it now as the generator is so low in fuel.

19.00 We were still the first story on the BBC at 17.00, but Amal is still said to be wanting the Palestinian gunmen to leave Magdoushe, which they did over two weeks ago. So today we had three casualties and no light, little gauze and blood everywhere. Amal are playing with us. They know we have no fuel, medicines, food or gauze, so they shell us again on the excuse of a ceasefire. And this could go on for days or until the world's press forget about us, that will be within a week or so. And Mehdi got shot where Ben and I, at the beginning of the war, had edged around a corner to look at Amal. The sniper had not used that position until today, and Mehdi had been warned not to go there as there was a sniper today, yet he went and got shot. It's not as if he can run with his lame leg either. Even Mohamad moves faster on his crutches than Mehdi did with his stick. He'd abandoned his crutches for the war.

One 10-year-old boy was shot through both legs and two men were shot at Samed.

If the trucks come in and Amal shell again like today, it will be another slaughter.

20.00 BBC World Service: Amal accuses Arafat of obstructing efforts to make the ceasefire; he replied that the UN should help end it, or give him the means to do so. Ghadaffi appealed to Assad to end the siege at Bourj al-Brajneh as thousands of people face death there. Mitterrand is organizing relief from France and hopes that the EEC will contribute to this effort to help the camps. (We could eat well. . . .) The Israelis mock-bombed Saida, Ain al-Helweh, and Mieh Mieh this morning.

Then obstructive but lovely Walid came back for a dressing. I asked Zeinab to tell whoever it was to go away and come back tomorrow, but he was persistent, and when I saw it was him I did the dressing in the middle of trying to cook and feed people. Then he got insulting again and told me to speak English as when I try to speak Arabic he doesn't understand me. So I said, 'Okay, Walid, if you want to fight, let's fight,' and he, fast as a shot, replied, 'What – boxing?' He speaks fluent English! So I asked him if he speaks French, but he only studied it for a year at school. He's a contrary bugger.

I saw the sad man, Mustafa al Khatib, looking so determined, although distraught, on his way to the hospital to find Mehdi. As Ahmad said, 'they take Mehdi to the second floor and leave him there; they do nothing for him.' Rifat said that Mehdi didn't care, which was why he had gone out in front of the sniper.

Today's intake: bread and olives – 300, soup and rice – 200, spaghetti – 350, soup – 250, tea – 100, total 1,200. Good. Dr Nasser fainted from hunger during an operation the day before yesterday.

12.2.87 Day 107 Thursday

The Israelis bombed Mieh Mieh again this morning, killing one person and injuring many others. Amal refuse to let supplies in until the Palestinians evacuate positions in Magdoushe. The Israelis are also now playing with us: three planes flying over every half hour or so, making spirals in the sky. Another child was shot dead through the chest this morning.

Wissam was shot through the abdomen. There was chaos, with old men falling over in the square and a lot of screaming. I heard the screaming first and ran out to see, then ran back up the street with her. We got her inside and Banan cut her clothes off while I brought the suction and the oxygen, and with a struggle put the airway in, and started to blow and suck. Then I put the thin tube down through the airway with Mustafa's help, and we lifted her onto the stretcher and ran with her up to the hospital. When she got there she was so collapsed that they couldn't even get a cut-down in. She went to theatre and had a nephrectomy, partial gastrectomy and a small bowel repair. She lost two litres of blood before going to theatre. Everyone is giving A-positive blood now for her and she's said to be dangerous but stable.

14.00 The Amal news said that Magdoushe has to be evacuated, but the BBC's Jim Muir finally recognizes that Magdoushe was taken previously to end the sieges of Rashidiyeh, Bourj and Shatila. The BBC quaintly puts it that Amal has refused supplies unless UNRWA deliver equivalent supplies to the Shia population. UNRWA have agreed in return for safe conduct through the Amal lines. According to the French Press Agency, because we are in Beirut camps, after the massacres of Sabra and Shatila we are getting a lot of attention that unfortunately Rashidiyeh did not get.

Two hundred women and children left the camp today. I watched five families trying to leave, including Hassan Abed's wife and child, Juma's wife and children, and the woman with the ten children and the new baby. But they were deterred by Fatah and Abu Musa fighters, and later Arsan and many leaders went for a meeting, which is still going on in the mosque at the moment. So the families turned back and then left from further up the camp. There was a lot of shouting to deter them and a couple of B-7s sent out too. Then a couple of *howens*. One landed behind Banan and me sending us half deaf in through the clinic door, to be greeted with 'Thank God you're safe' from Rifat, Hissam and the others who were indoors.

It was so strange to hear the voices from outside yesterday on the *jihaz*. A sensation of not being so isolated swept over me, similar to looking out past the camp from the hospital kitchen to the cars and buildings the other day.

I screwed up my courage to go and see Mehdi this afternoon after reports that he'd died, having tried earlier in the morning, but he was having a dressing done. I had met his eldest boy aged 10, Hissam, on the road this morning. He told me his *baba* had been shot through the face and out of his neck by showing me with his hands. I said I'd seen his *baba* yesterday and he asked me how was his *baba*. I didn't know what to say, so I shrugged my shoulders and said '*Noos-noos*' ('So-so). But later when

Mohamad stopped me just outside the hospital and asked how Mehdi was, little Hissam crept up on the conversation as I was explaining the breathing problem. So I asked Mohamad if he spoke English but he didn't and Hissam overheard.

I met Bahia crying and crying almost hysterically on my way back from the hospital, covered in blood as there was no washing can for the water; she was asking me about her best friend, Wissam. When I went back up, washed and changed, to collect the food for lunch, I met Hanna's sister, whose other sister had been shot in the arm. She was distraught, and was weeping and crying about Wissam and her sister; crying and crying just outside the hospital wall with the stretchers drying outside and crowds of people waiting. When I came back again in the afternoon, Wissam was still in theatre and Bahia's aunt asked me to go and find out how she was, so I went and met Nooha who told me what we already knew. Bahia came running out again to ask was there hope: '*Fi amal, fi amal*?' ('Is there hope, is there hope?'). All the doctors were still in theatre with Wissam, who lost four and a half litres of blood, and so far has had fifteen units of blood replaced.

No tea, no sugar, no detergents left. Life-saving food from Um Sami and Um Mohamad al Ashwa.

I watched the people leaving the camp with Nigar's girls and the usual gang of three or four. It was eerie watching the women and children, desperate and bewildered, but driven to face shootings or beatings by Amal after they left starvation, by no means a road to safety. It's easy for us, young and healthy, relatively speaking, to mouth off about political sensibilities, when we are not trying to feed our children and small babies, whilst going hungry. That's near impossible. I felt total sympathy, not the hostility I was hearing from men around me criticizing those leaving. How can we know?

Then I fell asleep for two hours and woke when Rifat came. I washed and cooked the *molochiya*. He told me that in the first war he and Haj were injured and left in the same room to die, as those so seriously injured were all put together; he was bleeding to death and so feeble that he could only move one leg, and Haj was in a coma for five days. He was evacuated first by the Red Cross and taken out in the first convoy of ambulances; Haj was evacuated in the second and last ever convoy to be allowed in by Amal during a war. The second set of injured were beaten up in the convoy: they were asked where they had been injured, then were kicked or hit on the site of the injury. Since then no ambulances have been allowed in and no fighters or men are ever evacuated.

Samir Dibsi, a 14-year-old, died today from his injuries from yesterday; another of the children from the house hit by a *howen* yesterday died tonight.

13.2.87 Day 108 Friday
More bombs. The first was up in the camp so I stayed where I was collecting water. Then just as I carried the first gallon to the clinic, another one landed nearby. I left the second water carrier and stayed put in the clinic. After an interval of approximately fifteen minutes came the news that there were fifteen injured in the hospital, five people were dead, and several had had their legs blown off. Ben went up to the hospital to fetch food as I finished a few dressings. Next we heard shouting and voices screaming. As they came closer we heard they were pleading for all people with *mazot* to take it immediately to the hospital, as they had no fuel for three operations. Everyone started running to the hospital with any sort of containers with fuel in them. Then more people came running, shouting for *mazot*, gauze, anything in the houses to be taken to the hospital, as there was nothing. I stopped to think and, as people started running to the clinic with first aid boxes, spirits and bandages, I sent them all to the hospital and decided to send our precious stores up as well: one drum of sterilized gauze and cotton, two boxes of sterilized instruments (the suture and debridement sets), the gauze package, eight bandages, and the cotton-wool, plus some pads. I stopped one of the boys from Arsan *mahwar* and asked him to fetch someone to take them to the hospital. I kept four gauze bandages, six pads and some unsterile gauze for emergencies. More people came in saying that they were cutting up nurses' dresses for gauze to stop bleeding.

As I went up for food at 15.10, we came to the *rauda* Najdeh road and saw the road was destroyed and a *howen* had blown the lower wall in. The small children yelled at us to run round the side road as the *howen* had just landed, injuring seven people, and there would be more. Little Mohamad, Mirvat and I ran for it into the hospital. There we found two had been killed, one of them Mohamad Zaid, Salah the Destroyer's brother. They had just left the hospital and were walking down the road when it landed, killing them outright. I had seen him earlier today in the emergency room when I went for the gauze. The scenes by Hannes' room at the fridge were terrible: Mohamad's sister and friends and Ahmad being helped up from the shelter to see him. The floor was still strewn with clothes and big puddles of blood from the fifteen injured earlier. Mohamad was lying dead on the stretcher and I didn't know him until I came back to the clinic and had it explained to me. He was very good and religious and quite young. We had missed being killed by ten minutes or so, as had Rifat. The grieving was awful to hear and watch; all day people went up and down the stairs to weep and scream and cry at the deaths. Mohamad's sister had to be carried away from his body distraught, but she forced her way back to look again, half carried and dragged to the screen around him. Little Ahmad with his one arm stood watching it all beside the nearest fridge, and Zeinab also came. It was awful.

When we heard the rumour of the Iranians entering the camp and one being injured, Rifat and I ran to the hospital; rashly, as there was bound to be shelling to deter their entry. So we ran and ran, and just as I reached the entrance I heard the whizz as a shell landed on the hospital. I ran inside with everyone else. As I tried to go into the corridor, since I could not get to see the Iranian, a shell landed next to the lab, blowing in the window; dust went everywhere, so we sheltered in the corridor. The shelling lasted for over an hour (and doesn't sound half as bad as down in the clinic), and then Dr Darwish saw me, and took me aside to say that he'd saved some food in the metal box, so I fetched it with Rifat, Hannes and Ahmad. Then Rifat and I had to screw up all our courage to run down again in the dark, without torch or moonlight, as there were clouds. We ran out to look at the front of the hospital, but there was only smoke and rubbish; no wagons of food – they were said to be at Samed. Then we scrambled over the road: the other two *howens* had both also landed on the road to the hospital and there was rubble everywhere. Ben was thankful to see us alive – as he put it, we'd run out 'like chickens without heads' as they had heard the *howens* being launched, and they had run out to stop us, shouting after us, but as we were running, breathless and talking, we hadn't heard them calling.

Imad al Masri also had a bilateral traumatic amputation of both legs at thigh, and is said to be in a coma. Another two people, one a young boy, had the same, the young one above the knees, and one person was decapitated. It was just an absolute bloodbath today. Then the Iranian embassy staff member being shot through the head and another man injured with the *howens*.

Ben again spoke of closing the clinic despite having dealt with three serious emergency cases in the past four days, and two shrapnel injuries also. Mehdi and Wissam both required resuscitation and were fitter for it by the time they reached the hospital, and Fawzi and Jihad also required care. But he said we were sitting around here all day doing nothing and there were five seriously injured now, all requiring nursing care. I agreed with him, but also said there were still a lot of nurses sitting up in the hospital not doing so much. It was a question of motivating them to nursing care. Then, when I went up to the hospital one woman started shouting at me, 'Why are you here? You should be in the clinic, the people need you there. There are *howens*.' As they were shelling I asked her if she wanted me to run back right now. Rifat and Mirvat both said we still need the clinic in that part of the camp as people now bring the wounded to us first, if there is shelling, and not to the hospital. So I suggested to Ben that he go and work in the hospital and they send me a nurse from there to work here, for example, the Dabdoub girl (all thoughts of a lovely security in the hospital going out the window).

The fifteen were injured as they were sitting outside in the sun and the *howen* landed in the middle of them, exploding, and injuring and killing them; like Wissam and her friends who were sunbathing the day before on the third floor of her house when they were shot. A Hizb'ullah official overseeing the delivery of supplies was among the dead. Abu Salim (the head of UNRWA in the camp) fled with the Iranians – first out.

19.00 BBC World Service: first story – relief lorries fired upon by militia men outside Bourj al-Brajneh. Two UNRWA lorries carrying forty tons of food were shot at and one driver injured, the tyres shot flat, and the vehicles abandoned. Two other lorries laden with food continued to Shia areas around the camp. The Israelis attacked Ain al-Helweh again with gunships; much damage and two people killed.

19.45 Lebanese Forces radio: the Iranian who came in with the food truck was in fact shot in the head and after assessment in Haifa was sent out of the camp, but the news reports the ambulance received a direct hit and he died. The Palestinians said that it was a massacre; people came out of their homes for reports of a ceasefire and food supplies and were served with bombs instead. Italy has sent two planes with food worth 7.7 million dollars for the Palestinians, particularly those in Beirut. Nabih Berri has called for a ceasefire. Ha, ha, as today 8 dead and 19 injured between Bourj and Shatila.

20.00 BBC World Service: Amal refused to allow medical supply trucks to come to the camps, so only four trucks set out, but as they approached they came under fire and the drivers were injured and the trucks abandoned.

Today's intake: onions, bread, olives, tea and *zatar* – 350, *borgol* and olives – 200, soup and meat – 300, *molochiya* and rice – 200, total 1,050. Luxury.

Hannes says that Mohamad, the nurse from the house of paraplegics, and Hassan, the one with the contractures, walked out of the camp with Hassan's wheelchair last night at 22.30 from the Majnuk Road.

14.2.87 Day 109 Saturday

The supplies finally came in at 0.01 this morning: four lorries (six-wheel) with flour, sugar, milk and rice. The Iranians brought them in and they were unloaded immediately into the hospital. Ben and Pauline spoke to the Iranians and Pauline also telephoned to her parents and to Swee Chai Ang. Apparently everyone is very worried and was sure that we were going to be killed. Well, after yesterday's three narrow escapes I may well be.

Today I went, as usual now, to Fatima's for a breakfast of bread, *zatar*, olives, tea with milk, and onions, with the six Chekhovian sisters, Amné, Intisar, Waf'a, Shahina, Fatima and Seeham. Came back to the clinic, washed it out, fetched water and did the dressings as Ben was working in the hospital that day.

As we were listening to Pauline being quoted on the radio – she is on LBC television and a national heroine in Britain, as MAP are promoting Bourj and now have enough money to rebuild the hospital – Sultan came in to offer me a phone call home. I waited all night, but there was so much fighting and shelling and B-7s and flares around the clinic that it was impossible to go for a line; there was also too much going on around Saida.

We got flour and yeast stores from the supplies, plus what came in yesterday, three kilos of flour. It was lovely to watch Bashar and others running up and down the camp with the eighty-kilo sacks of flour on their backs, with 'UNRWA, packed in bags by the Federal Republic of Germany' stamped on them. Everyone was yelling to children to get out of their way and to take their hands off it. We were told later to keep the doors open as the milk may be coming, but the fighting started immediately afterwards so no one came.

The difference between Ziad, the injured fighter from Mar Elias, and the rest of us was striking. He was full of energy, still tanned, and had shining eyes, not the tired look and big black circles under sallow, dull eyes that all of the fighters here have, or the lethargy. He seemed full of energy. He kept sitting up as I tried to look for his shrapnel, really the difference was very apparent. Then we sat listening to the *howens* falling all around us, and so much shooting. Monir's brother is safe and well in Mar Elias. His mother also, now, too, with the rest of the family having left the camp yesterday.

The UN and USA have appealed for an end to the war around the camps. Amal warned the Palestinians to avoid expansion. The Iranians evacuated Amer al Khatib.

15.2.87 Day 110 Sunday

Mehdi died today about 14.00. I had just gone up to see him; he was unconscious with laboured breathing and his wife was sitting beside him, her head on her folded arms beside his pillow, weeping. When we asked her about Ben's washing him she said, 'Why? it's finished.' (14.30 Amal versus PSP and Communists, heavy fighting. Armed men out on the streets in Hamra, people sheltering in their homes.) As soon as we heard he was dead, we ran back down the road to see if she knew, but we already guessed that she did, as all the Al Khatibs were coming into the hospital. Mustafa was already there, standing in the corridor looking very sad as he had done all day. Then we saw little Hissam, with all the rest of Mehdi's children, standing on the street screaming and crying, '*Baba, baba*,' and his wife being helped down the stairs to go and see him. (15.00 BBC World Service: large numbers of people have been allowed out of Rashidiyeh to buy food since Amal lifted the siege for a few hours each day.) She had just left him a few minutes previously in the hospital, and was also crying and distraught.

I used to think that she was unhappy with him and that it was a difficult marriage, as the children also looked solemn whenever I saw them. Shows how little I know, as she was so sad and the children too. He was a very good cook. The other striking memory I have of him was of the night that the *howens* landed when I was sitting in the Al Khatibs' house with the whole family. Mehdi and his wife had left with the youngest baby, who is about 1 year old, and just as the noise of the explosions died down Mustafa started shouting, 'Mehdi! Mehdi!' until he heard the answer and the affirmation that Mehdi was all right and no one was injured. He was also worried and concerned for them, almost shrieking to see that they were safe. Mehdi's little boy was sobbing with all his heart, as a 10-year-old boy cries for his '*Baba, baba*'.

Good news of Mohamad and Hassan who walked out of Majnuk with Hassan in his wheelchair two nights ago at 22.30. They are safe and well and in Mar Elias camp too. I was so worried for them both; Mohamad's new wife is now five months pregnant, and Hassan has such awful contractures in what's left of his arms that if they kicked him or threw him out of his wheelchair he would be helpless, and would have died if left on the roadside. But thank God they are both safe.

The fighting last night was from an attempt earlier in the day by Amal to place TNT near one of the *mahwars* at 16.00. They assumed all the fighters would be sleeping as we are all so hungry by now. But they were soon shot at and two were killed. So they fled taking the bodies with them but leaving the TNT. So Borhan's *mahwar* that night fetched the TNT, approximately fifteen kilos, and after crossing the road placed and detonated it. The problem was that they were seventy metres out from the camp on the wrong side of the street, and so had to return fire to cover themselves until they reached the camp again, hence all the shooting. (Oh! A huge TNT explosion has just shaken the building, shaking the poor battered front door well and truly on its hinges.) It's a real miracle no one was injured as they also shelled us quite heavily for over an hour and put up at least three flares, 'light bombs' as they are called here, with the eerie *whee eee eee* dropping noise that they have as they come down. The whole camp was lit up again from the sky. I was so convinced there would be injured that I put the *dulsanna* light in the front part of the clinic, waiting in case something happened. Borhan said the type of detonator the TNT had was so complex that it must have been made by a 6th Brigade Lebanese Army explosives expert.

Well, today Ben skipped working in the hospital after only one day and stayed in the clinic.

There are reports of a temporary lifting of the siege tomorrow for five hours, like Rashidiyeh is said to have been open for women and children to go out of the camp and buy food. I wonder if it will be similar to Amal's previous behaviour to women who leave after the siege, of harassing them about being Palestinian, destroying the precious food in front of them and shouting filthy things at them. Fatima says this happened after the 45-day war ended.

We may get milk tonight or tomorrow from the mosque. It was handed out this morning in the middle of the camp – a half kilo per two adults, one kilo per family of four or more people. The rest of the flour, approximately one and a quarter kilos, has gone to Fatima's mother who is going to bake it for us tomorrow, half *manaeesh*, half bread, and can give some more to Ahmad. His brother stays in Sabra; they used to live here but left after the Ramadan war. His arm still has a bad nerve injury from his fractured humerus in the first week of the war; his shoulder has only partial movement and his arm is very floppy, but at least he tries to use it to shake hands and carry things. I'll never forget his groaning in pain as I pulled it into traction for the splint to send him up to the hospital, after he was shot. Ate at Fatima's late today. We all looked at Paris fashions for winter, Swiss watches and air company adverts in a magazine, miles from the camp and the war. It was like Khadija's letter to a pen pal of Iyad's in Switzerland, with no hope of posting it, and Monir's insistent translation last night of a German recipe with pictures of apple *torte*. Oh, it was appetizing, looking and listening to descriptions of apples baking, lemons skinned, sugar, egg, etc, etc, etc. And all completely crazy and drove us almost insane with hunger for the impossible.

Talked with Pauline about the need for a prosthetics team to be sent out, at least as far as Cyprus, to deal with the bilateral amputees, all four of them that are left alive now. Abu Ghassan, the old man, died this morning, it is said after he had seen his two sons, Yusef and Hamoudi Sahnini, who also had immediate traumatic bilateral amputations.

Rafiq is still detained in Jordan, that is six months now. Pauline had talked to Swee Chai Ang, who wanted us all to leave immediately if it was possible, which it is not; also none of us want to leave until it is peaceful and others can also go out of the camp. Well, it's completely impossible anyway.

Thirty-five women and children left the camp today. They will appear on radio and TV to make wild statements about the conditions inside the camps and Amal's generosity and kindness to them, and their gratitude to the Amal movement. (And Nabih Berri who said last week that if he wanted to make a massacre like Tal al-Zatar here, he could, but that he doesn't want to, and yesterday that he is starting a new pact with the Palestinians from today?) We think that they are held and threatened maybe with death unless they say these things, as the only pressure that could be put on them is extreme fear of torture or death.

I really wanted to speak to Mum and Dad on the phone to reassure them that I am all right so far, and to find out how everyone is, safe, well, etc, or not. Just for any contact with the outside world directly, instead of word of mouth. Øyvind came through on the *jihaz* today, but it was so weak that they could only send greetings.

19.45 Lebanese Forces: with the war of the camps grinding on in the background, there is 'open fighting in the streets of West Beirut' between Amal, the PSP and the Communists. Failure of mid-afternoon ceasefire agreement. Shatila shelled by Amal and the 6th Brigade since dawn. Pauline spoke to Jim Muir of the BBC in Cyprus yesterday.

There is a meeting in the mosque tonight of Incas (Salvation Front) (the six coalition pro-Syrian organizations of dissent) and the respected old men of the camp and Sultan. The meeting is to decide whether the two Fatah leaders should change allegiance from Arafat to Incas (Salvation Front), or leave the camps and go to Saida. In every war this meeting takes place and includes the Imam (spiritual leader of the mosque) and other men of the mosque, but so far Sultan has always refused to leave, saying that the Syrians want all the guns and the Palestinians to go under their direction or die. But this time there is real discontent, and the decision of the people may go against them and they will have to leave. Many people now perceive the camps wars as a feud between Arafat and Assad; the only point is whether a Palestinian leads the Palestinians or a Syrian. Haj looked worried and dejected this morning and said Arafat wants to kill us all. This was because of the retaking by Fatah of villages around Magdoushe. Dr Rede feels that this state of semi-starvation could go on indefinitely. Rifat says the country is to be carved up between Syria in the north and Iran in the south. So both are hurrying for a prestigious solution.

UNRWA supplies from Europe have been stolen at gunpoint in Saida by men saying they were taking them to Rashidiyeh.

Today's intake: olives, bread, onions, tea – 350, milk – 150, *borgol* – 200, rice – 200, bread – 150, onion and corned beef soup – 100, onions – 100, tea – 100, total 1,350 Kcals.

16.2.87 Day 111 Monday

18.00 BBC World Service: demonstrations in Gaza Strip, Bethlehem and Ramallah against the sieges of Palestinian camps in the Lebanon; dispersed by the Israeli Army with bullets at the University of Bethlehem. Another Palestinian university has been closed on the Occupied West Bank, the third in the past month: Al Najah, Bir Zeit and now the Islamic College. This is the second or third demonstration in support of the camps in the past few days.

Great rumour of the siege lifting tomorrow and supplies coming in: first heard on Radio Monte Carlo, now on all Arabic stations, excluding Amal radio. I have a ten-dollar bet with Banan on eating bananas tomorrow.

The Al Khatib children in the Al Khatib *mahwar,* Bourj al-Brajneh, with Kalashnikovs and a photograph of the PLO leader, Yasser Arafat.

Women running back into the camp from the airport road, after having been turned back by soldiers at the checkpoint. Just out of the picture, a young woman lies dead, picked out by snipers.

'Bloody Weekend' in East Beirut, scene of yet more destruction.

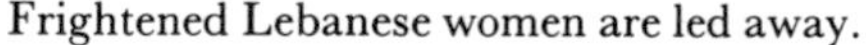

Frightened Lebanese women are led away.

The men of Shatila emerging from the ruins, at the end of the camp war, 1987.

Plain-clothes Syrian Intelligence and troops round-up civilians in West Beirut. The fate of most of these men would be uncertain: torture, jail or simply being 'disappeared'.

The front street, as a Syrian soldier patrols the Marrubba *mahwar*: a typical everyday view in Bourj al-Brajneh . . .

Dolly Fong, Suzy and Dr Swee Chai Ang, on the occasion of Suzy's first return to Beirut since the end of the war, July 1987.

Pauline talked to David Hirst who is now in East Beirut from Nicosia, and he is very bleak about the prospects as the allegiances are changing and the whole situation is very volatile. He thinks we may only get a half-siege situation like Rashidiyeh, which was said to be open again today and sold a hundred tons of food outside to women and girls. Ninety-seven dead there and people were eating grass before we did.

Amal attacked a Communist party building today and fighting continued. Jumblatt has refused to disown the Palestinians in his area, and has called for a resurrection of the old National Movement. Amal is not receptive to calls to regroup as it would lose its control of the city. Jumblatt has been summoned to Damascus by Assad's second-in-command; Berri is still there. A bomb under Barbir Bridge. Fighting from Kola to Ouzai, and in other areas.

Went up to the hospital twice: with new *manaeesh*, and to get food from Hannes and Ahmad who came down to invite me to go up to eat 'Ahmad's corned-beef cakes', wonderful stuff, like meat *falafel*; he took away the awful safari meat and transformed it into edible food. We took Taisear the Arabic New Testament that Hannes had bought for him; he was sitting outside in the sun with Borhan and Mustafa and Ahmad. Then we danced around, excited by the news of the siege lifting, the whole square smiling and happy and hopeful. The first smiles seen in ages.

I came back to the clinic and talked politics. It's becoming more and more obvious that I have to abandon any plans for after the war. After the declarations from the camps and if we want to tell the truth, then I can't come back for a while afterwards. If I go home and keep silent then it would be possible, but none of us can keep quiet about this.

Mehdi is reported to have said he wanted to die before seeing his sons go very hungry. I saw his body wrapped for burial outside the fridges, waiting to be taken to the cemetery, and heard of Mustafa washing after the burial.

Today's intake: *manaeesh* and tea – 350, *mujuderra* – 500, rice – 200, bread – 100, total 1,150 Kcals.

Listened to the skiing results with Hannes. Austria collected a few medals in the Winter Olympics. He's pleased.

17.2.87 Day 112 Tuesday

Everyone jumping around at the early morning news of Amal being taken over by a new version of the National Movement of Jumblatt's PSP, Communists and Murabitoun, including some Palestinians from Sabra, Tunis and Cyprus. Jumblatt declares that he will not stop the war in West Beirut until the siege of the camps is lifted and that his alliance with Amal is over. Nabih Berri has said that from tomorrow the ceasefire and lifting of the sieges in Beirut are to be effected by his Amal militia. But today Rashidiyeh was closed again and placed back under siege after only two days of relaxation. So who knows? The food is completely finished, the half piece of bread left is for lunch with the *leben* tomorrow.

Fighting all around Ouzai to Corniche, Hamra, Vardun, the Arab University and Kola. The airport road is open for the first time in months since the war began. Perhaps Amal may get what they deserve.

Went for breakfast and talked of Sweden with Fatima and her brother Ali; beautiful ideas of everyone leaving this hell-hole to study and live, especially the young men. They have to if possible.

Many people are beginning to complain of the first signs of scurvy: severe gum pains and some bleeding, all due to vitamin C deficiency. After the initial dizziness and fainting, there are headaches and stomach pains, and diarrhoea and vomiting after eating a reasonable-sized piece of bread and drinking milk: more signs of vitamin depletion are now emerging. Many people also have very low blood pressure and anaemia. Most of the camp looks yellow or white instead of brown and healthy. The food runs out again tomorrow as the flour has been eaten and the milk also.

Waiting for the gauze and instruments to be sterilized in the hospital, as there has been no electricity used since last night, and it went on at 11.00 to do two operations, so all the dressings have been put off until after 15.00. Went to give the third of Haji Rabba's useless vitamin B injections. Walking the Bermuda Triangle near Um al Adnan's house, Banan's house, and the sniper corner where three boys were shot at one time and killed in the 45-day war). All that area is very badly damaged and I took Rifat with me, as to go there alone unnerves me and if someone is with me, I stop feeling quite so afraid.

I was so tired of it all today with the gauze not being sterile until 13.00 and a pile of people heaping up outside the clinic; I couldn't really be bothered but dragged up the last remnants of willpower to attend to them all. Then Lino came by and started demanding that I go and see his mother, but he didn't know what was wrong with her. I told him to bring her to the clinic as Ben wasn't here. He refused so I said he could either wait until Ben came back or take her to the hospital. Hissam then came in and I told him the same. So he went to look at her and came back with a perfectly described hysteria, so I told him this was what it was and said either to wait or to take her to the hospital. When he said she couldn't walk, he was told there are five people in this camp who can't walk at the moment and it's because none of them have any legs left now. If they were so worried, put her on a stretcher and take her up. So Lino stood outside swearing and cursing me, and in the end I went out and said, okay, let's go and see his bloody mother. As he was waiting for Dr Rede to finish his wash in the house next door, he refused and started to shout, then was going to fight Rifat who was trying to get me to go inside. Then Abu Nadir appeared and told me to get inside and they took him away and started shouting it out. Ben appeared and Hissam turned up shortly afterwards and asked me to go to see her. Ben went; nothing at all wrong with her, not even hyperventilation or tachycardia by this stage, but he gave her a Valium injection to shut her up.

Ben described Chris Giannou's method of dealing with hysteria, which was to slap the person out of it, or to grab them and hold ether over their mouth and nose until they started to really struggle to get breath. Lino later came in to apologize (the reason for his touching concern was that if the camp opens tomorrow there would be no one to go out and get him cigarettes and food).

I played chase with the children outside; drank milk with the Yunis kids, little Ahmad tipping the cup for bigger sips and little Shehadi al Ashwa cleaning the kitchen up. Really the place smells so badly with the permanent cold water and no cleaning agents for the past month. And the fat and diesel and gas blackening everything. And many people don't even have soap left. (We've only run out of shampoo.) We've suffered from 'tomorrows' since before the Islamic Conference; every day a certainty that's destroyed, bringing disappointment with it. Shahina was so tired and fed up that she was in tears in the kitchen and explained that her nerves were tired of the war. She then cheered up a little and showed me how to make *leben*. Milk is heated and a small cup of *leben* is added, wrap it in blankets and leave for twenty-four hours in the covered pot.

I'm waiting for contact with the outside world, I've had none at all for three and a half months. Rifat says that it feels really strange at first. I went to watch the women going out of the camp. I hope that food comes in, all these stores they promise us. I've to make a list of what we want and give Banan the money. They think that many stallholders will come to the front street as they did at Rashidiyeh.

Today's intake: *manaeesh* – 200, tea and olives – 150, rice pudding – 200, *kobé* – 200, bread – 200, milk – 100, total 1,050. Ahmad Aishey has also only lost three kilos. We sympathize with each other about our usual lack of martyrdom to weight loss.

18.2.87 Day 113 Wednesday

This morning started with Banan trying to come into the clinic at 7.40. We had heard a lot of noise outside, but assumed it was the usual disappointing fuss of no lifting of the siege. But she came in to say that it's possible to go out. A woman had walked out of the camp and been given bags of bread and cigarettes by the Lebanese Army and had then returned to the camp. So I dressed quickly and put together a shopping list as she ran home to change. I wanted to see the women going out, so Juju and I wandered about collecting Nigar, Juma's wife and the new baby, and meeting many others on the way, including Khadija, Darwish and Mohamad. We walked the 'most dangerous route', over the hills, to come up out on one of the highest points in the camp, and started scrambling down to ground level over ankle-breaking rubble from the shelling, with everyone saying, 'There's no sniping today.' We were overlooking the corner mosque, and the sea and the airport road, all renowned for sniper deaths. It was surreal and quite, quite stupid even to think someone would not try to shoot us up there on a bright sunny day – but no one did. Then we well and truly broke our ankles scrambling along and ended up near the first entrance to the camp. There was a sniper shield near the entrance to one of the *mahwars*, now an unrecognizable sandheap with a tunnel entrance to it, and I watched the women run through the zinc barricade between here and the camp. When Banan, the last to run, had gone, I turned back to walk into the camp again. As I walked along, I saw only the men standing or walking, having watched their women go out, unable to accompany them. I walked along the road until I came to a break in the buildings and when I saw people running the sniper gap, I gestured, '*Fi shi*?' ('Is there something?') 'Run!' came the shouted reply, so I ducked my head and ran for it. I came to the garbage pile at the hospital – I had not left the camp for ever, as someone had told Pauline – and passed the growing mountain of garbage, that now had an orderly everyday appearance to it to make way for the trucks and ambulances.

I later learned that some of the women were taken by the Lebanese Army to Amal, and was worried for Banan, but thank God she was in the clinic when I came back. Apparently, she and other women were prevented from leaving by the Lebanese Army, who said they had no orders to let people out of the camp. They loaded their guns and told them they could come out for good, or return to the camp. They took Juma's wife, who was with her smallest baby, to the school in the airport road, and said they had orders to take them to Amal offices. 'Berri is not here; we are here.' Then they loaded their guns. They asked Banan, 'Do you have food in the camp? Are you Palestinian or Lebanese?' Then, 'Come with us to Hamra alone and we will get you what you want.' She refused.

Three women were shot on separate occasions by Amal with M-16s when they were trying to get food. Two, Um Wafiq and Fatima al Ashwa, were shot in the legs and feet, another was shot in the legs and taken out of the camp; and one 13-year-old girl was shot in the head and died shortly afterwards in the hospital. Rifat saw the girl shot. She and her mother were just coming into the camp with bags of food. The men waiting for their return yelled to them to run; she and her mother tried to run, carrying the bags, and she was shot in the head just three metres from the camp. She staggered two or three steps and fell down. The men had to lie on their stomachs and pull her into the camp by her hair. When Dr Saleh tried to entubate her, she still had food in her mouth. She was so hungry she had been eating and running. Rifat felt her head; her skull was smashed and he could feel her brain hanging out from the exploded fracture. He had her blood still on his sleeve. All for some food while the world believes we are being fed.

So everyone thinks we have some food now and no blockade, yet all the women and children have run the danger of imprisonment or being shot. All have been shot at around their feet and told to go to Amal militiamen or return to camp. The Lebanese Army attitude is that we have had two trucks of food, why do we need more? All the women who got through were escorted to a nearby supermarket and the Amal escort took the same money from them as the shopkeeper, who raised the prices anyway as the women are Palestinian. Mahmud's wife paid 2,700 Lebanese lira and Bahia paid 4,000 Lebanese lira for very little. Women have also had their jewellery – their necklaces, bracelets and rings – and all their money stolen.

The women who made it past the harassment came back with boxes of foodstuffs on their heads. I ate half an apple, shared with two adults and five children: absolute bliss, the best apple I ever ate, even though the amount was about the size of a thumbnail. Later I had an equally small piece of cake. The children spent the day telling us what their mothers had brought in and what we may eat tomorrow, so much so that I had to ask them to stop – it was driving me crazy. At the clinic we had a plate of *leben* each, and some fat, milk, flour and salt cakes. Ugh. Then a third of a saucer of *borgol* each, and a third of a small onion and salt. We saw other people with orange peel, eggs and bananas, spaghetti, *halva* and biscuits, and kids with mouthfuls of food – swoon, swoon, swoon.

19.00 BBC World Service: a Palestinian taxi driver has been killed after being shot by an Israeli Army patrol after ten days of unrest now. The Israelis claim he died after crashing his taxi trying to ram the army patrol. The reason given for the lack of UNRWA foodstuffs entering the camps is the fighting for the third day in West Beirut (fifty dead, 200 injured). Lies, lies, lies. Amal claim that the Palestinians have been shooting women leaving the camps. More lies. *Lies.* The BBC says that Amal is fighting the Communists and their allies; Syrians are massing east of Beirut.

19.15 Lebanese Forces radio: some of the 6th Brigade gave up fighting and went home.

22.15 BBC World Service Middle East correspondent, London: Syria puts itself forward as honest broker even though it is itself a participant through the Shia militia Amal. Assad does not want to be seen in the Arab world as the man who caused the starvation of 20,000 Palestinians in Beirut. 'Syria does no longer want to support the losing side.' 'When Amal could not take the camps militarily, they had to try to starve out the camps.'

Rifat and I talked of the Palestinians from the mountains who are now in the east landing strip of the airport, and the PSP with them. They came round from the south and into it at night. But although the estimation of the time to reach and seize Shatila is only two to three hours' fighting, they may wait for a political decision to pacify the Syrians. This could take two weeks, but it would mean a safe Beirut from the airport upwards. The camps are prepared to starve another two weeks to enable this. The same holds for Bourj al-Murr which is just up from the NORWAC flat. It's estimated that 400 to 500 Palestinians and Sunnis are held there in underground jails, but, although it could easily be destroyed with twenty-two kilogrammes of TNT, this option is unthinkable as it would mean killing all the prisoners inside, not liberating them.

Interrogation papers for some of the foreign hostages have been found in one of the Amal offices. It's said some may be held in the Murr Tower; we are hoping that they may be found.

19.2.87 Day 114 Thursday

A bleak beginning with total pessimism. No fuel left, no ether left to make ether fires, rain, the camp is still blockaded, and absolutely no prospect of food.

Dealt with one stupid girl who refused to go to the hospital to have her head sutured. Then the most wonderful Banan appeared with two big bags loaded with fruit, chocolate, sweets, sugar, tea, Kleenex, a packet of cigarettes, cakes, bread cakes, bananas, apples, cheese. I was really very fed up and despondent as I had envisaged a whole day without any kind of food, and I'd been so wiped out last night that I'd slept through breakfast and woke at 8.30. It was so wonderful that we crammed one banana, then another, then some cake or biscuit and half a small cake loaf each, with tea and sugar and a piece of cheese. Last night we'd been joking about the food that we would become obsessional about, full food cupboards and fridges of food in the morning; and also about washing: soap, shampoo, electricity. And the desperate desire to eat junk food, so much so that the end of siege shopping list now includes cheeseburgers, chips and pizza to bring into the camp; with batteries and films for cameras, candles, Lebanese money and cigarettes.

We shared the food out between us, half for Pauline and Hannes in the hospital and half for us. We also got five candles, so sent two up to them as well. Then we hid the feast upstairs. Used the last of the ether and prayed for more fuel of some sort. Gave tea to Juma, as they could not carry any more in and ran out of money to buy all the food. Because of the fighting, the bakers are shut and it's also impossible to change the money, so all our food was bought with money from Banan's grandfather. They ran round the shops to collect the food and met people from Amal who yelled at them to 'Eat, eat, Palestinians' when they saw the food, and asked if they had enough money to buy the food, so they were frightened and ran and ran, carrying as many bags as possible until they came back to the camp. On the way in Amal opened fire on them and Noora got so frightened that she dropped her bags of food and ran on. Banan saw her drop them and yelled, 'Where's the food? Where's the food?' and panicked, and ran stumbling into the camp covered in water and soaked in mud with the heedless dash back inside. Mimo (10), Juju (13), Banan (22) and Noora (38), all under fire, all of them.

Three women were shot; today they were not only shooting to wound but to kill. One woman, Amira Muselmani, aged 50, was shot in the back as she tried to go out of the camp and get food. Another woman was shot in her chest, another in her arm – all M-16 injuries.

Others were taken to Amal offices and their names taken, then to a supermarket; some were body-searched by Amal women. Only food, clothes, candles and fuel were allowed in. Batteries were not allowed, as these are used for the *jihaz*. Prices have soared in our five and a half months inside, although by European standards they are low.

Everyone was eating all day, and once the women returned the men stopped lingering worriedly in the square and went to eat. Ate pea pod peas today, bananas and apple. Feel full up and a lot better. Today's intake: cake, biscuit, bananas, spaghetti, pancakes, bread and cheese, milk and tea, total 2,100 Kcals.

Saw another crying baby who, at 27 days, is being given 'S26' milk at night to drink. Their little guts are too new to cope with it and they all start throwing up. Also now there are no washing agents left, no fuel to boil, no cleaning materials, how can the milk possibly be clean enough? Saw little baby Fatima who has put on a whole two kilogrammes. She is now completely unyellow and weighs 4.3 kilos instead of her birth weight of 2.3 kilos with jaundice. Little Mohamad is now pushing through his gums at 3½ months. He is a happy little baby: like all the children here, cleaned, fed and left with siblings, cousins and uncles, or taken naturally on their mothers' hips, or carried by fathers or bigger cousins, a circle of constant affection and love; kissed and cuddled and played with all the time, or sleeping on knees, arms, chairs, the floors, or in a hammock as I saw today in one house.

Visited what turned out to be the house of the leader of the Abu Nidal group. We were going to have coffee but there was no fuel or wood and we listened to excited contact on the *jihaz* with brothers and relatives in Mar Elias: 'There are trucks, they are not entered. We ate apples, oranges, bananas. What's happening, your brother's injured, your aunt's in the shelter, how is it there?' It was so lovely to listen again to outside contact; then Amal cut in and started asking about boys in the camp and the leader cut the frequency. His wife asked why I didn't go out for food, and he turned round and said that we couldn't leave the camp as Amal will take us as Arafatists and hold us as hostages. It was a two-storey flat with a view of the mountain and East Beirut, past the zinc sniper barricade.

19.45 Lebanese Forces radio: assorted security forces deployed today – 200 Syrians, 100 assorted leftists, 100 Amal, 100 servicemen, mostly 6th Brigade Shia. Two hundred and fifty injured and 175 dead in five days. Berri: 'continue the fight until victory.' Seventy-five women and children went out of the camp. The UNRWA chief (Giacomelli) arrived in Beirut, but went south. Israel and Syria accuse each other of preparing for a war on Lebanese soil. Calls in Congress to close the American embassy in Beirut. Amal turned UNRWA supplies away twice from Rashidiyeh and thirteen tons of flour were stolen.

I saw Said Nasser today walking up towards the vegetable shop with his *keffiyeh* tied around his head tightly like a turban. I felt as though we were both looking for little Hamoudi to come up behind him with his Kalashnikov and bullet clip around his waist, with a smile. The street looked empty without him. Felt so tired and sick of it all today. One man sniped in the camp: an M-16 injury to his thigh.

20.2.87 Day 115 Friday
Woken at 6.33 with the thought of Banan going out again today to buy food. I'm worried about her as we can hear M-16s shooting sporadic rounds at the exits of the camp.

Again a 'can't be bothered' day. Fetched water from the *mahwar*; no great queues today. Then Banan arrived back with tales of herself and her two sisters (aged 10 and 13) being shot at. She was searched seven times by Amal militia who told her, 'Go back to the camp, or we will kill you.' Many of the women and young girls were shot at around their feet with M-16s; one girl was shot in the hand, and one woman struck with a Kalashnikov butt and her groceries destroyed in front of her by the militia men. The motor in the hospital is broken today, so there is no electricity to take an X-ray to see if he fractured her bones. Another woman had cigarettes and groceries stolen by Amal.

Then we did the dressings; saw Walid's very bad foot which, because of a two-year-old bullet injury in the thigh, has no sensation: I lifted off two toenails effortlessly. The rest of the foot is a mess of blisters, so I pared and deroofed them, and treated the foot as a cross between leprosy and a burn. Swathed it in Silvadene and cotton, and told him to use crutches for at least a week. I enjoyed that one. Then ate and washed clothes; it's amazing the energy and the psychological lift after eating for twenty-four hours.

We have now progressed from the 'what we would like to eat' to the 'what we will eat tomorrow, *Insh'Allah*' conversations. Much better for us. All our stomachs are so full that we are positively bloated and swollen, looking pregnant and complaining of stomach pains from eating again.

One boy was brought to the hospital having collapsed after eating seven whole round breads at once; he had severe abdominal pains. Had the much-talked-about coffee and cigarettes tonight. It's strange not to feel hungry and to see full ashtrays instead of picked empty ones. Ali, the deaf boy, produced a big handful of seeds for me after offering me a cigarette yesterday. His little dog is still alive after being looked at enviously as he walked it past the hospital. The black cat got safari meat to eat from Ben.

Talking to some of the boys about where they will go after the war. Hissam got word of a Saudi visa from his father, but he doesn't want to go; he's for Sweden if possible. We looked at maps of Scandinavia.

I wrote a letter about what's been happening (the harassment and shootings of girls and women) to journalists: there are many outside the camp who can't get access. I hope that Mirvat can take it out in her shoes: she's a daredevil and quite fearless, whereas the others are a bit 'girlish' and overawed.

I am *full* of wind tonight!

21.2.87 Day 116 Saturday

Got up at 6.40 to fetch money to take to Shahina to buy supplies, ate cake, tea, cheese, a little bread and a banana. Gave her the money and drank some of the coffee I'd taken to her. Then went up with Ali (their brother) to watch the women leaving the camp. The men were standing in a corner behind the little courtyard that led on to the side street at Saiqa. All the buildings have holes from tanks, mortars and bullets. Under a bright blue sky, next to a sniper barricade of zinc with a green Renault 5 in its shade, we sat and waited: old toothless women, mothers in their forties, girls, little boys, young women with small children, clutching assorted bags of UNRWA and shop origin, waiting to go out, with all the men in military greens behind the next corner. A sniper was shooting intermittently from the Binni building. And we waited.

At 8.00 they had been told the road would open at 9.00. We waited. At 9.00 the way was still closed. So Ali took me up to Amliea *mahwar* to see where the women would go out. We went upstairs and peered through zinc and shell holes and sniper tracks (concrete diagonal tunnels) at Amliea buildings. We were looking at the Amal *mahwar* of sandbags, while his friend shouted at one Amal man he knew by name, 'The women want to go out. Let them go out.' 'Don't be afraid. go out. Go out,' the Amal man shouted back and occasionally raised his head. Behind the buildings were tank sandhills, where the tank was resting, or maybe it's now in Beirut. We waited, shouting exchanges, and looking and dodging. It was quite unreal in that we were unarmed, and the Shia women we saw strolled right in front of us, careless of Palestinian snipers. They walked slowly, in long dresses and *hijabs* (scarves), in full view of the Palestinian *mahwar*. When I asked why they moved so slowly and did not run, the boys replied that they knew they wouldn't be shot by Palestinians. Then we saw a jeep pull up behind the building. The shouting and peering continued. There was a smoky haze over East Beirut's buildings shining in the sun, and snow on the mountains, melting in the sunlight and warmer spring days, a helicopter flying over the city. The unearthly calm remained all over the deserted streets, towards the rest of the city that looked empty of people.

Then came the news from women coming back that Amal refused to let them leave the camp, after being kept waiting there one and a half hours. The reason given is that the Syrians are deploying 3000 to 4000 troops from here to the airport and into Beirut, so no women are allowed to leave to collect food. A senseless excuse. I was reminded of the similarity to stories and photographs of the treatment of Jewish people hounded by the Nazis. Women herded in corners, waiting, waiting, being shot at and knowing they may die on the way in or out of the camp, just to collect food.

We have no gauze or sterile cotton as the motor was broken in the hospital. Some Beirut hospitals are now running out of finished gauze already; we've managed almost four months like this.

Banan was shot at twice today. First she was refused exit and told to get back into the camp, and then when she and her mother went up to the airport road the conversation with Lebanese Army soldiers went like this:

'We want to go outside the camp.'

'You can go but not come back.'

'Okay. We will not come back.'

'Are you Lebanese?'

'No – I am Palestinian.'

'Are there any Lebanese women inside the camp?'

'Yes – there are many Lebanese women in the camp.'

'Tell them to come out so that we can give them food.'

'We have lots of food inside the camp. We are not hungry.'

'You are *not* hungry??'

'No – we are not hungry!'

He opened fire on her and yelled at her to 'Run, run. Go on, run.' Then on her way back into the camp she was stopped and searched for batteries, and a gross of cigarettes, both of which are not allowed. As she had batteries, Noora said, 'No, no, she has nothing. Come on.' As she ran on, they yelled, 'She has batteries in the bag,' and opened fire on her, missing her as she ran blindly, but they hit the woman running behind her in the legs. She was taken to Haifa Hospital with a complicated fracture.

Another woman was shot in the left arm on her way back into the camp. I saw her at home; she is pregnant. Another injured woman was taken away by Amal. She had been shot in the abdomen and died six hours later outside. She was 23 years old. They also took two fat, elderly ladies today, by signalling to them at gunpoint and yelling, 'You! Come over here.' They then made the two women put their hands in the air and run several metres whilst shooting around their legs and feet. When the women, both in their sixties, had finished, they told them to kneel and crawl. The women, with tears streaming down their faces, begged them to stop, but they were forced to crawl at gunpoint, before being allowed to leave. The humiliation is savage and disgusting. Amal are behaving as any savage army behaves, terrorizing and subjecting entire populations to fear and terror. I want all this to go to Amnesty International.

Fatima, Shahina and Seeham were all subjected to abuse by Amal: 'You hate Shia. We know you hate Shia. You are all no-good cunts.' This happened on the way into the camp and was filmed by foreign journalists. Staged for Amal propaganda purposes. In the meantime, Amal stole the UNRWA milk. Some say fifty per cent went to Amal, others say eighty per cent was stolen after the filming was completed. Others say 250 tins went to Amal and 250 tins to the camp.

BBC World Service: the Arab League has called from Tunis to allow supplies into the Palestinian camps. The Syrians are going to be deployed from West Beirut almost as far as Saida.

I couldn't get my letter to the journalists. Today there were some others, but working for whom? The Syrians are coming (4000), but clashing with the Druze now in the mountains in Sofar; Gemayel calls it 'unconstitutional'.

Banan was unable to bring eggs or vegetables, no one is able to get far enough to buy them, so we had food and fruits but no vegetables. Lots of psychosomatic illnesses now, due to the severe stress of getting food. Wafiqa (Um Akram) wants both Akram and his sister to go out of the camp. Noora (Um Bilal) had a Kalashnikov held against her chest and was threatened. I remember the sight of an old man with his *keffiyeh* and his folded bag clutched next to his stick in his hand, walking very slowly back up the hill from Saiqa having been unable to leave the camp. He was in his seventies and it was a great effort for him.

22.2.87 Day 117 Sunday

Woken at 8.15 by Seeham shrieking through the window as though someone had died. She had been sent by her sweet mother to fetch me for breakfast and I had slept in. So I scrambled into my clothes and went up to Fatima's and ate *European bread* and white cheese and olives and tea and cake. Fatima came back from fetching water and then we sat up on the verandah, from where we saw an injured boy being carried past on a stretcher. From above it looked like an M-16 stomach injury.

We went up to the hospital as there was a call for A-positive blood and Fatima thought she might be able to give blood. The doors were shut and we had to request entry through a crowd of people. I saw Dr Rede sitting down and then Pauline looking wiped out in the corridor next to the labs. So weak was the electricity generated by the one functioning motor that it was a half light. She told me to go and look at the boy. He had been shot through the chest and needed two operations, but could not be taken out of the camp as he was a young boy and Amal might well kill him. There was also a choice of only two hospitals, neither safe for him to go to. He couldn't be operated on in Haifa, with slime and sewage now pouring down the walls, no water, no clean instruments for operations, no sterile sheets or gowns, no cautery as the electricity is too weak. But he was being ventilated with a unit of blood and his legs raised. He was paraplegic and unable to breath unassisted. Hopeless.

Fatima's neighbour, Alia, who was shot yesterday, has been immediately buried by Amal in a cemetery for Palestinians near Shatila – hiding the evidence before her family or anyone else could see her. Another two women have been shot near Saiqa today. Yesterday thirty-five women got stranded outside the camp, too frightened by militiamen to try to come back in. Shatila was shelled quite heavily by Amal and the 6th Brigade Lebanese Army yesterday, and it's not finished yet. The Syrians are now reported to be near Khalde and the airport: lots of car and tank noises from the airport road.

I feel that Jumblatt has lost his chance by bowing immediately to a Syrian invasion and not securing the safety of the Palestinians from Amal. Perhaps Assad would not have allowed it, but a socialist control of West Beirut would have been preferable to this non-solution, non-implementation of the ceasefire. After a few months pro-Syrian forces will re-group and re-strengthen Amal, and then the war, under Syrian encouragement and supervision, will start all over again.

The idea of a month or two in Denmark or Norway, drawing and reading, is absolutely delightful and tempting escapism. But apparently our names (Pauline's, Ben's and mine) have been read out on TV. Is the airport safe to leave from? Are there boats from Saida to Cyprus or is Jounieh (the port east of Beirut) the only option?

I went with the shopping list to see Shahina and Fatima, and was fed on fish and lemon, chicken, bread and chips. I spoke to the young woman whose hand was smashed by Amal the other day. She had collected her shopping when an Amal car drew up, men got out, struck her with the butt of a Kalashnikov and destroyed all her shopping. This woman is another example of failed emancipation in the name of either traditionalism or Arafat's call for every Palestinian woman to bear ten children to fight for and continue the revolution. She had persuaded her father to let her continue her second baccalaureat and go to the Arab University, but was only allowed to study experimental sciences for six months before she was taken away to marry, and became pregnant immediately. She's the second woman I've met who has told me she was 'married off' by her father. The Sununu girls, who are 14 and 16, are refusing their father's efforts to marry them by saying that they are too young – so far successfully. Fatima's mother Sofia was married off to her father in Palestine in 1948 at the age of 13. Her husband was 26, double her age. She also thinks it's not a good practice.

She's lovely – feeding me the fish she'd saved since yesterday for me, and the chicken. Shahina is very similar to her in kindness.

As I drank tea with them, the noise of stretchers came past for the second time and, looking out of the window, I saw two badly wounded men, one with an airway in place, being rushed up to the hospital. I was putting on my shoes to hurry back to the clinic, when Shahina ran in saying there was another injured person in the clinic. I hurried down there, falling over people all the way, and met Ben running up to the hospital to fetch the stretcher and airway. He said the woman in the clinic was fine, only a flesh wound; he'd just got her on the table when the first man arrived outside in a pool of blood. They couldn't find the injury and he was so shocked that he was airwayed and sent straight from the square to the hospital. Then the second man arrived, also with abdominal injuries; he was also too shocked for them to have time to stop the bleeding. The square had large clots of blood in it which we washed away, and I put the injured woman on the stretcher and sent her up to the hospital. The two men are both in the operating theatre together to save electricity: two tables now *in situ*. They are looking for O- and A-positive blood now.

As we collected water in Arsan we watched the little Israeli spy plane circling above us, photographing lots of destruction, Palestinian children and the Syrian Army. They only photograph when the Syrians come in to strategic areas, taking pictures through the new leaves on what remains of a willow tree on the terracotta sandy soil, and the stump of what was once a tall palm tree in days gone by. Now the willow's leaves are coming for the spring, the days are getting warmer again and the nights longer. It's dark at 18.00 now. Nice.

Listening to more of the disturbingly obsessive love songs that constantly spill out of Beirut radio stations, always wanting eternal love. Had my coffee cup read again by Waf'a: the same three points from the reading in Abu Dhabi and earlier here came up:

1 A long road that I am on (three times)
2 An aeroplane (twice)
3 A paper (twice)
4 A lot of money (to or from me?)
5 A meeting – a big meeting.

And again the 'fish' came up; it's a good sign. Amer's mother saw a journey or a plane, and Shahina also saw a bride. What does it all mean?

23.2.87 Day 118 Monday

So much for the Syrian security plan, hand in hand with Amal. The airport road is supposedly safe for exit, provided the women go before 7 am. And it's said that 200 left to get supplies by that route today, but at Saiqa, where I stood with Fatima and Shahina and their mother, the road had been blocked by Amal since 8.00. They said it would reopen at 9.00, but at 9.00 they opened fire on the women, with M-16s. Although reassured that there were no snipers, I didn't believe it, and as the bullets hit off the walls I dragged Fatima round a corner into one of the sniper positions that was in a recess and had zinc over the roof. Maybe this was dumb, but it was preferable to remaining standing outside in the open, in full view of at least three tall Amal buildings, with no protection when someone starts shooting at you. They continued to shoot at us and a woman trying to return into the camp from outside. So we stood exposed in the sunlight and under the bright blue sky again, and I saw trees blossoming into the green of spring here. That beautiful vivid lime green of new leaves. It was strange looking at bushes and trees flowering, and continental apartments and terracotta sand, and shells of buildings with light blues and pinks on the remains of their walls, and women cowering with their children, scarves and shopping bags, some pregnant, some already injured as the thugs outside shot at us. The road was closed from 8.00 and no one was allowed out again after waiting two hours.

The snipers *are* still working, as the bullets have just come near the clinic again. So today the Syrians are deploying in the southern suburbs, are they?

Zaiqa Um Mohamad, aged about 50 years, was shot through the chest at the gates of the camp at 11.00 this morning trying to ask to be allowed out. One Amal said come out, so she stepped forward and tried to take Banan with her. The other shouted to go back inside, he wouldn't allow anyone out, and shot her through the chest with an M-16. She was very lucky, but needed a chest tube; Ben pasted her chest up and sent her to the hospital

The Syrians are now definitely deployed only into PSP areas: Bourj al-Murr, Bashir. They are making no attempt to enter al Adahi, Janoub (southern suburbs). Last night Shatila was shelled at the rate of one shell every five minutes from Amal positions near the sports stadium where the Syrians are. Today we were shelled with 120mm, thirty over a twenty-minute period. Three people were injured – minor shrapnel wounds. The shells came from near the airport where the Syrians are also in position, and Amal areas behind the camp, towards the Green Line. Nothing is happening in Rashidiyeh now as the Iranian plan is being enforced and so the shelling has stopped over the last few days and the siege has been lifted. Thank God.

0.00 BBC World Service: Bourj al-Murr has been taken by the Syrians;

Amal have 'packed up and left quietly'. We are still wondering about a real possibility of a Tal al-Zatar yet.

There is talk of an evacuation of all the wounded from the hospital and new doctors coming in tomorrow. What is needed now is new nurses as half of them are not coming into work and Salim the Head Nurse says it is impossible to function properly. Some of the doctors are very tired, like we are, but not finished yet. But the generator *is* now finished and there can be no more operations, or X-rays, or anything. The motor worked yesterday to give one light but no cautery and gave up ten minutes before the end of the operation. Pauline was working by anglepoise lamp.

24.2.87 Day 119 Tuesday
The Syrians appear to be rampaging through Beirut arresting over a hundred PSP and Communist Party members and killing at least four people by firing indiscriminately. There has been a murdering and looting spree by Amal in areas of Syrian control. Over fifteen bodies have been found bullet-ridden and dumped, and one in a pick-up truck and another of a pharmacist called Najjal who was kidnapped from his home on Sunday. There were Israeli mock raids on Khalde at 5.00 to 6.00. Syrians took over only PSP and Communist areas yesterday (the Murr Tower is the only Amal position taken), and their convoys withdrew from Beirut by the coastal road. A Hizb'ullah office is to be closed today. The Amal killing spree goes on. The Syrians are arresting everyone they can, of course, except Amal. Things are going to be very similar to Tripoli at this rate.

15.15 Fathallah Barracks burnt down by Hizb'ullah at Basta at noon, before the Syrians entered it. Syrian operations with Amal – 16 bodies. Joint killings this morning and against Pro-Palestinian southern suburbs later, after the Iranians meet in Damascus. Assassination of Communists in the south. The PSP say Amal are forcing them to flee from the south. The roads are closed to the south and Bekaa. Trying to get supplies into the camps. UNRWA and camps security is part of the general security of Beirut and the issue of the camps should be settled soon.

17.15 We have just been shelled again, first with RPGs mounted on a jeep; Rifat and Haj counted them through to twelve rockets, then we heard the jeep skidding and speeding away. Abu Nader grabbed little Hamoudi who had been eating *taboulé* with Rifat and me, and ran with him downstairs to their house as fast as he could, whilst Um Mohamad walked slowly through the dust with little Ibrahim al Khatib. Then we heard lots more jeeps and truck noises and the first *howen* going out. I said to Rifat a *howen* was coming. He laughed it off saying it was the zinc blowing in the warm wind, then after a delay of about twenty seconds it exploded, followed by others. We couldn't figure out where they were being launched from, unless from Syrian-controlled areas, as the count was twenty seconds on the watch or twenty-seven counting them aloud, instead of the usual twelve seconds/eighteen aloud. No injured here, but five in the hospital. Two men shot today trying to leave by Majnuk building. They say the roads will be shut again tomorrow.

We have heard a lot of jeeps, truck and car horns blowing for the last hour and a half. A piece of shrapnel pierced the flag on the Martyrs Memorial as it rained down on here for quite a bit – one or two of the *howens* fell close by.

Twenty-three Hizb'ullah were apparently killed by the Syrians when they stormed the Fathallah Barracks, shooting at random. 6th Brigade Lebanese Army raided apartments under Syrian supervision. The PSP doubts Syrian impartiality. The PSP military office was broken into by the Syrians. Palestinian artillery in the mountains came into action after shelling of Shatila and Bourj al-Brajneh. One million Swiss francs are to be given to victims affected by the fighting around Shatila and Bourj al-Brajneh via the ICRC to both Lebanese and Palestinians. Amal troops have left by sea to Sur today to clear the way for Syrians.

Rifat believes that everyone knows now that the use by the Syrians of a war against Arafat is no more than a pretext for war against the Palestinians as a people. He says they all know this now, but are refusing to admit it to themselves.

25.2.87 Day 120 Wednesday

The winds brought the rain and clouds last night and it got cold. Fatima's mother got out of the camp early this morning with Waf'a and Seeham, but, after leaving via Majnuk, it is now doubtful that they will be able to come back in via Saiqa later on today, as the camp is now said to be closed. They are incredibly brave to go out through all that harassment, and then walk the distance of the airport road (approximately two kilometres) with thirty kilos of food in their arms or on their heads for several hours, and always subject to intimidation at any point, from Amal or the Lebanese Army force. It's more than words can describe to ask people to bring supplies in like that for you. I feel sometimes it's *too* much to ask.

11.15 Khadija has arrived in tears. Her two daughters left the camp reluctantly at 6.30 this morning to buy food. They had not wanted to go, saying they were scared, but their father told them to dress and go out. They had turned to their mother for support, but their father had insisted. They were let out of the camp by the Lebanese Army, but outside Amal were rounding up all the women and taking them away. One woman managed to get back into the camp, and said that they are being beaten with Kalashnikovs, including Hissam's mother and sister; the air is filled with tears and worry.

19.30 Well, none we know were taken, but many were hit with Kalashnikov butts and beaten, and their groceries were stolen and destroyed. Seeham was hit and her eggs destroyed and she was crying. Sabrine (Khadija's daughter) and another girl got knee injuries from shrapnel from the M-16s that were fired at them over their heads, and which hit and injured two women again.

Car bomb at 18.20.

19.45 Lebanese Forces news: Hizb'ullah gunmen are hiding from the Syrians in Basta and the Holiday Inn.

A paralysed man was shot today after being accused of being a Communist. Many Communists are being arrested and murdered along with Hizb'ullah men. Rifat had talked of a list being drawn up of a hundred men who needed to be assassinated to bring peace to Beirut. But now there is a purge of Communists by the Syrians and Amal.

We got more candles, and more supplies will come in tomorrow if, contrary to the usual threats, the roads are in fact open. Today lighters and coffee were forbidden at Majnuk, although they were allowed in at Saiqa. Cigarettes are still burned along with batteries, so Shahina smuggled some in between her layers of pants, as we worked out that a body searcher, unless very thorough, never feels in between your legs, just down the sides. Bras are useless as you are always grasped there. We think that the intention is just to make life as miserable as possible. At last supplies came in, after a bleak, very wet start to the day, making the feeling of stagnation and helplessness, the inertia and immobility, ever more acute. No wonder so many people feel depressed and need anti-depressants. Took Pauline a sandwich to make her a bit fatter as the hospital is still on a diet of safari meat; a cheese, tomato, parsley and sardine sandwich, with an apple and a banana. She felt very bleak about the prospects of a Syrian arrival.

The daily feeling of tiredness and less empathy with the people here grows worse each day as people still make demands on us and we are exhausted almost to the end of our tether, especially when faced with selfishness and self-absorption. But – *the supplies came in*!!!! Flour, milk, medicines and diesel in two six-wheeler trucks. The other two trucks were stolen by Amal. Also an official from the *Austrian* embassy who said he saw Hannes, and a healthy lady from the UNRWA who took photos, looked clean and gave Pauline her card! And MSF (Médecins sans frontières) have sent a 'team' of Belgian surgeons who are waiting to come in. We are rather scathing of their motive as MSF jumped in when the publicity started and not before, plus one remembers that they refused to work in a PRCS hospital in 1983, when they were in the Lebanon before, as they didn't want to be associated with the PLO. Lots of grim quips going around, like 'Don't tell them to bring soap and shampoo – we don't have any water,' or 'Wouldn't it be funny if they came in and got stuck for another four months?' Anyway, as the Syrians are refusing to deploy around here they may not be able to get in for a while yet.

The sewage smells extra foul in the rain for some reason, and when I went to the hospital it reminded me of Govan sewage works in the summer, the same distinctive odour of sewers and dank in the rain.

Shahina bought me a pair of slippers outside and will try to buy a pair of jeans tomorrow, if possible, and some socks for Pauline. They gave us candles that we hadn't asked for from their own supply today; and they will buy us a chicken tomorrow and I can use their gas to cook it on. And their mother and father keep stuffing me with food whenever they see me. Fish, chicken, Mars bars, bread, cakes, anything edible.

The little cat is sitting on my knee making grabs alternately at my nose and lip (she's just been flung away for that), and the purr making it impossible to write. It's just beginning to dawn on me that we may be minor celebrities after this for a short while. Pauline and Ben are used to it, but I'm not really prepared for any sort of praise just for sitting out a war and siege with the rest of a population I am working with, and to whom it happens at frequent intervals. The exit from London was so disorganized and low-key, with me catching the tube alone out to the airport, that the fuss on our return or at least on the exit from the camp will be strange, and I hope I don't say anything stupid or pompous. All this occurred to me with the advent of the MSF doctors and hoo-ha that always accompanies them when they go anywhere.

I got a terrible fright today when I thought first that I'd lost all my films, then some of them. Aagh! pure panic as that's approximately a hundred photos, all carefully documenting this war.

Voice of Lebanon news: funeral ceremony for the Hizb'ullah dead attended by 18,000 people, accompanied by 2,000 armed men to the graveyard on the airport road. 'The Palestinians are the Trojan Horse responsible for admitting the Syrians to the Lebanon since 1976 and this cancerous tumour should be eliminated.' The Guardians of the Cedars, quoted on the radio.

22.15 BBC World Service: Faisal Aweida, the PLO representative in London, spoke of Syria fighting in the Lebanon via Amal, and the PLO being worried about Syrian intervention as the camps continue to be besieged by Amal and they have been regularly supplied with Syrian arms. The rest of the world asked Syria to intervene on behalf of the besieged camps for fifteen weeks, but it was not until the PSP and other socialist groups became discontented with the continued besieging of the Palestinian camps and fought with Amal, who began to lose heavily, that the Syrians mobilized their forces and entered Lebanon, with four days to rescue Amal from defeat. Then he stated that Syria wanted concessions from the PLO who were not prepared to give them any as they had thought the Syrian intervention was not made on the basis of concessions. Of course they wanted an agreement, but not an 'agreement of slaves'. Although PLO men had come back into the camps, it was purely in a protective role, and it was done legally not illegally as the PLO had always negotiated with the Lebanese government and would continue to do so. He spoke very cautiously, and it was heartening to hear him talk of continued daily contact with the camps, and that the international world was watching both Assad and the camps.

One of the nurses went out of the camp to Mar Elias to shop. When they heard that she was from Bourj al-Brajneh camp and that people really had been eating mule, etc, one of the people cried; then they gave her all her shopping at low prices and some of it free.

Pauline noted that Imad al Masri has gone 'quite psychological': it took her long enough to see this. I remarked mildly that ever since I'd first met him, I had thought he was crazy. She says he's really gone quite off, but maybe he's just highly strung. In fact, the guy's loco, that's all.

A car bomb went off at the mosque beside the petrol station just next to the camp where it demolished three Amal buildings used as offices: nine dead, fourteen injured, and all the camp shook. Another man shot in camp today by an Amal sniper.

26.2.87 Day 121 Thursday

10.30 A woman aged 50, sister of Ali al Ashwa's wife, was shot dead through the chest entering the camp at Amliea building. A girl was injured and is in the hospital. Amer al Khatib died yesterday in the Maqassed Hospital, of post-operative complications. Shit, after all that effort. Because he was so strong, it took him a long time to die.

Noora collected letters from her son Jalal in Denmark after seeing her other son Bilal in Hamra. Whilst bringing them back into the camp along with three watches sent by Jalal's friend, Amal searched her and stole two of the watches which she hadn't hidden and two cassettes of Jalal speaking to the family. They said they will return them tomorrow and just want to listen to them. Yesterday it was egg smashing, and hitting and kicking women with Kalashnikovs, and shooting at them with M-16s. Today it is downright robbery.

16.45 Another attenuated day of waiting, waiting, to the sound of a 500 that has been shooting all day. But the children were loud, playing the handclapping and chanting game of *Roz, humus, roz, humus, fool, fool, batata* (Rice, chickpeas, rice, chickpeas, beans, beans, potatoes), a game that would have been unthinkable even only a week ago, but now was being yelled from end to end of the street with extreme vigour and giggles. 'Fatso' is still Yaq'ub's nickname despite his complete lack of fat these days.

Loud hammerings and bangings and for one dulled moment I thought that perhaps people were repairing their damaged houses until I realized that, of course, they were taking all the inflammable bits for fuel. Then I saw this confirmed by window frames being carried past the clinic and UNRWA bags filled with wood. We should get flour and milk distributed tomorrow.

I felt today, a sometimes common feeling, that we are here now for an eternity. That it will never stop. Sometimes this hits me, and other times I feel full of optimism (rarely pessimism), but on the odd occasion, it just comes to me that it's always been the reality and will never change, one way or the other. Arsan has just waddled past in his tracksuit, combat jacket and half boots into which the very baggy pants are always stuffed, carrying his *jihaz* in the rain. He reminds me of Charlie Chaplin: the same self-absorbed little comic walk. I can hear sounds of military vehicles, jeeps and a far-off explosion. The noise of intense activity outside on the roads makes the feeling of stagnation inside the camp far more acute – especially when we know that all these military forces and jeeps, tanks and trucks are conspiring to prolong the situation of deprivation inside here.

I met one of the first children to be injured in the *howens*. She is 6 years old and came back into the clinic two days ago with her mother. Her new glass eye has been fitted and, as everyone said, you wouldn't know it was there, it matches her other eye so well, and in the half light I couldn't notice the lack of movement. She was quiet and hugged in between her mother's knees, and listened to us, examining her dollies, one blind and slightly bald, one dark.

17.30 Just heard two *howens* launched and before I got inside they exploded nearby. At first I thought they were too close to be coming here, but no such luck. Shrapnel flying everywhere again and people running. No end in sight yet by the looks of this. They are shelling us at a rate of one shell a second, all over the camp, with 120s landing and showering shrapnel around, masked by the call to prayer. Everyone is listening to the plopping raindrops and Shia call from the safe mosques outside. I was trying to listen to BBC World Service choral music, but as you can't hear the mortars being launched with the radio on I found I couldn't get into it at all. So the radio is off and the shelling seems to have stopped for the moment. Thinking of home, of the house, Pohsie, the dog and cat, Mum and Dad, Ruth, Ghillie and Stewart and Pepper.

Another young woman, aged around 20, died today after being shot in the back. The other woman shot through the back was dead at the gates of the camp. They had both been told by Amal militiamen to enter the camp without any problems and then were both shot. That brings the total of women dead to five in eight days since Wednesday.

At last Pauline is going to make another declaration about the shooting and terrorizing of women, girls and children when they are getting food.

19.45 Radio Free Lebanon: Syrians are rounding up their opponents and have made restrictions on Hizb'ullah in the Bekaa. The pretext is the arrest of supporters of Yasser Arafat, but there is mounting disagreement as Sunni, Hizb'ullah and other Shias and Leftists are also being rounded up. The Basta 'massacre' was 'barbaric and premeditated'. 'Victims were beaten up and tortured and shot in the back at close range': medical reports from Hizb'ullah. The deployment of Syrian troops in the southern suburbs has been postponed for the time being. One Syrian captain was killed and seventeen injured in the car bomb last night. Syrians are arresting and looting, looking for supporters of Arafat in hotels and apartments. Forty PSP members have now been missing for five days. All posters and stickers in Beirut are being removed and replaced with photos of Hafez al Assad.

27.2.87 Day 122 Friday

Seeham banged the door down before 7.20. Pouring rain and freezing weather, so got dressed, put on boots and an anorak, and carried up a small water bottle to have breakfast with Seeham. We drank coffee and ate, then came the news that Abu Bashar had been shot. He was shot at the top of the camp along with two women who were trying to go out. Two more women escaped injury. After I got back to the clinic (after comparing Shahina's photograph before the war with her tired worried face now on her green ID card), I found out what had happened. There is a rumour that there is a Syrian order to shoot the women bringing supplies to maintain pressure on the Popular Committees to expel the Arafatists from the camp quickly, and to facilitate their control of the camps. There is another meeting in the mosque now to decide whether the Fatah leaders should leave, and now they are demanding also that the military commanders of the *mahwars* leave as well. That means Abu Riyad, Abu Suhail, Arsan, Borhan, Sobhei, Abu Arab, Nawoosh, etc, have to go to Saida which people are already leaving in anticipation of the Syrians and Israelis waging a longer war here in the near future. If this meeting agrees with the meetings of Incas and General Q'anan, the head of the Syrian forces, the siege could be lifted soon. All the camp knows that Syria is demanding this and controlling all negotiations.

Apparently Bashar had been holding serious conversations with Amal for many days. He was Syrian and had escaped from Syria after finishing his military service over seven years ago. The Syrian army had wanted him to continue to train in tanks, but he had refused and fled to Lebanon. So today the Amal fighters had invited him to drink tea. He hesitated and made them give assurances not to shoot him if he came over. They promised and as he stepped into the road they sprayed him with M-16 bullets, not shooting first at his legs, as he may have been able to escape, but all over his body to kill him immediately. His body, bullet-ridden and dead, is still lying in the middle of the road. Four women pleaded with Amal to let them collect his body and carry it back into the camp, but they were shot at also and two were injured. So he lies there in the mud and the rain. He had refused to extend his military service in Syria as he said he did not want a fighting life but one of peace.

Rabiha and her little son left for Saida with Hassan, Hissam and Mohamad. Her husband ordered her out of the camp. But she was warned against going to Saida now that the Syrians have come in force, as it is the Arafat camps that they and the Israelis wish to destroy.

Now Rashidiyeh is open people have started to arrive from there. There are several points that have been clarified. First, that no families left, no fighters came or were evacuated, and no supplies arrived by sea, as was rumoured. Second, that the food situation was never as serious as it was here, as the camp held out on its rural produce and sheep, cows, goats and chickens, orange groves, orchards and fields, so feeding was not the problem. There were no medical facilities whatsoever and consequently 130 people died during the siege and fighting over almost five months. The women who have arrived said that as the siege lifted it was similar to here with sniping, shootings, harassment and intimidation, thieving and beatings. But it has eased off to searches of groceries in the streets by Amal, and now the only forbidden articles continue to be the small batteries used for *jihaz* and cameras. There was one doctor originally, and another managed to get in, but all the seriously wounded died.

Supplies entered Shatila from UNRWA yesterday and today.

Fighting off the small cat who again is being over-amorous and playful with my left shoulder and her favourite toy, the pen. She's always booted out, and frequently this expulsion is in the small hours of the morning, or she waits to get in along with Yaq'ub who also either breaks the door down by scratching, or meowing to be let in or out.

Bashar has just been mentioned on the radio as one dead Palestinian. He is now referred to as a corpse, or to be more accurate 'the corpse'. The two women wounded are referred to as 'two others wounded', omitting the gender.

Had a game with the children before they were all finally evicted, and Feraz had an English lesson. Mohamad and Ibrahim al Khatib were also evicted after too much noise. Ibrahim fell noisily flat on his face and lay like a little stranded whale, arms and legs sticking out, completely immobile until Maryam's brother, with his red wellies, picked him up and comforted him. Children were playing behind the clinic today oblivious to the snipers' barricade erected there.

Vivid dreams: last night I dreamt of a wonderful open-plan shelter which had open grille spaces, like a studio garden. They started to shell us, but I felt completely safe as I knew it was a shelter. Then people were running, but towards the open grilles, so I kept running and shouting at them to come away from the bars as shrapnel would come in. But in the middle I found lots of wonderful medical supplies that we hadn't known were there, especially double-headed airways which I started to gather up as fast as I could and ran with Banan as the 120mms were exploding on the roof of the shelter, yelling and running with Banan to keep away from the open garden doors. This must have been because they lost our airway in the emergency room. I also dreamt that I was in a garden with Fatima and one other girl. I needed to stop and had to take a lie-down. They were faintly disgusted by the idea and left. I realized it was Ghillie, Robin and Betty's old garden, so I went to the water pump where the roses and beans are and washed my hands. At first I thought they were away, but then saw a light in the kitchen window and Aunt Betty. I knocked on the door and was asked to come in, and stood in the warm doorway, and I asked if Ghillie was about. Uncle Robin came in from the outhouse and Aunty Betty said, no, she wasn't here at the moment, but that she would be back soon. It felt nice.

20.15 News: Sheikh Fadlullah (Hizb'ullah) has called the Basta murders a 'downright massacre'. The Syrians are continuing searches in all areas of Beirut and are rounding up everyone opposed to the Syrian regime. PSP claim that over 200 people are now missing in West Beirut since the Syrian operations started.

Shatila got food today, not yesterday: UNRWA got in two lorries of flour and milk, but Amal stole the truck with medical supplies. A doctor who entered the camp has now verified eight cases of typhoid. This comes from all the water and shelter problems they have been having, compared with our situation of lack of hygiene but a good water supply, rather than extreme overcrowding.

My period has come again explaining the feelings of extreme lousiness over the past twenty-four hours. We all weighed ourselves and have all put on two to three kilos: Ben, Hannes, Pauline, me, Hissam and Rifat, all.

We also discussed the new statement sent out by Dr Rede on *jihaz* today, the great lack of security we face once this is over, and the realization of the danger we are now in from Amal having a free hand from Syria to do as they will, with corpses being found daily in West Beirut since the 'intervention'. We are all quite apprehensive and don't talk now of where we will go, but how we will get out, and security measures for films and diaries.

Yusuf, who got shot at the beginning of the war and showed off one day doing his arm physio with Hannes and Pauline, chatting up all the women, died today, shot through the head by a sniper – another death. Every day death, death. It's becoming a circle of death in the middle of a cycle of terror that's increasing by the day as the Syrian security forces rampage on with Amal. We heard more about the girl who died yesterday. The story is that someone from Amal grabbed her by her hair, beat her and shot her at close range. As the women tried to get her into the camp, they were shot at again, so they had to tie a rope around her and drag her into the camp, so that she arrived filthy and oozing, and covered in sand and dirt.

28.2.87 Day 123 Saturday
Ahmad Hayek came in to the clinic for a finger dressing and told us that B-10s and tanks had also been used. He said that there was no news from the meeting in the mosque yesterday except that the Arafat leaders, including himself, had been asked to leave the camp. Fifteen out of a total of thirty names. The rest could choose to become Incas, Salvation Front, pro-Syrian, Saiqa, etc, or leave the camp for Saida. There is another meeting and decisions today outside in Beirut about the expulsion of the Arafatists.

Bashar's body still lies where it was shot yesterday. It is in the middle of no-man's-land and no one can go out to get it in. He had apparently drunk tea with the Amal militiamen and given them money to buy bread and other food for him, then left, with their worthless promise of safety. It's against all ancient traditions of Arab hospitality to kill someone after you have eaten with him.

10.00 BBC World Service, 'Reflections', by a rabbi. He says 'As a Jew, living in a city gives me an identity problem, as if you read Hebrew much of it is placed in agrarian society.' 'Much deals with the displacement and dispossessions of peoples' – is this rabbi a Zionist, or naive and unaware of the foundation of the Israeli state with the displacement and dispossessions of the Palestinian people as its foundation?

'When and if we decide to enter the southern suburbs no one and nobody will have special treatment': General Q'anan talking to the BBC and *Sunday Times*.

Sobhei Abu Arab's wife has just passed crying and carrying her new baby Sara, followed by her relatives. She was outside when her other little daughter, looking at the Amal man's Kalashnikov, said quite defiantly, 'Your Kalashnikov is not nice, my daddy's is better.' The innocence of a 6-year-old girl caused her mother to be hit, and poor little Abir won't know why.

Attempts are now going to be made to rescue Bashar's body. Apparently they asked the Red Cross to try to remove it, but it was not possible. He had been over to the Amal *mahwar* a couple of times before to request that they let the women leave the camp by the Balbekeyeh road, as it is better than leaving by Saiqa, but this time they shot him. His body is still lying in the mud and rain. The attempt will be made when the time is right. Four *doshkas* have been moved into positions near that corner of the camp, and they will start shooting with them and B-7s as cover to try and get rope around the body and drag him into the camp. His wife and little daughter are in Mar Elias Camp.

Just been visited by Sammar and three other little nurses from the hospital; they are all on night duty from 20.00 to 8.00 in the morning and, having just woken up, they are collecting water in the twilight. All are wrapped up in ponchos and talking of after the war, and their families. Sammar, aged 18, is engaged to Hussein; her sister, aged 17, is also engaged, and Hussein's sister, aged 15, is engaged to Sammar's brother. They all weighed themselves, then set off into the dusk to collect the rest of the water.

Listening with Saturday afternoon nostalgia to the BBC World Service Sports Round-up: a football commentary by a Scot, of Dundee and Celtic playing and goals being scored, and thinking of Mum, Dad and the dog asleep in the lounge in front of the TV and the fire, whilst the football is on. It's so bizarre listening to it in the freezing cold clinic, with the *doshka* firing in the distance. I'm supposed to go home in ten days time. I guess we get paid for the extra; I just hope to God that they keep the insurance policies up to date at MAP, that's all. I hope also that the Agence France Presse office gets messages out.

Dr Rede is discussing with Dr Mohamad Ossman in Mar Elias the plans to get the MSF team into the camp, and then the plan to evacuate women and children patients to hospitals outside – and to evacuate us! Via Mar Elias, then to Saida, and leave by boat to Cyprus. This is to safeguard us and the journals and films we have recorded, as the questioning at the airport might result in confiscation and detection. Rifat says getting to Saida is no problem past Khalde junction, as beyond there is the Druze 12th Brigade Lebanese Army. He suggests buying our way there as everything is done for money. Before the war the price to Saida was 500 to 1000 Lebanese lira. He thinks it may be different for foreigners. His mother wants him to leave the country now.

Amal smashed all our groceries on the ground and broke our candles, leaving only five. Bashar's brother-in-law is said to be a Syrian chief in Beirut and has heard of his death and that he is still lying where he was killed. Amal wanted to bring him into the camp, or the Red Cross, before the Syrian threatened to come and see with his own eyes. But Bashar's group refused to let anyone move him. Even Fatah refused so he's still there.

The last memory I have of Bashar is him running up and down the camp with the fifty-kilogramme sacks of flour on his back – four or five times from the hospital and back when everyone else was flagging, but he kept running, full of energy, shouting at people to take their hands out of the sacks, smiling and laughing.

1.3.87 Day 124 Sunday

'There was a further outbreak of violence yesterday between the Palestinians inside the Bourj al-Brajneh camp and Shia Amal militia men' – this was the BBC World Service at 15.00, explaining the Syrian efforts to bring peace to West Beirut by distributing leaflets 'in an effort to win support', after meetings in Damascus today. Where *do* they get their reports from?!

Zeinab was body-searched by a Shia Amal woman calling herself Nabir, who accused her of working in the *jihaz* office, claiming first she had heard her voice and recognized it, then that she had seen her carrying water from the *mahwar*. This quite bewilders us; perhaps the lady has a vivid imagination. Poor Halla, Zeinab's younger sister, was reduced to tears again from fear when they were signalled to come over to the Amal check-area. Coffee, matches, candles, gas and batteries were taken from them.

Writing by the warm firelight of a tin-box fire-holder brought by Um Mohamad al Ashwa. We broke up the wood, and charcoal-cooked potatoes, onions and apples for tea. Abu Salah's children brought us rice and milk and *falafel* to eat now that the *babour* (stove) is broken forever. So it's choking woodsmoke and choking fuel *dulsanna* lights, as the candles are finished again today; all very rustic.

Our statements are apparently in the press with old and new pictures of Pauline from the day that the UNRWA lady gave her the card when the first few trucks entered, and they have been trying to send letters and films and batteries into the camp for us with other agencies, but so far none have entered. Bashar still lies bloating in no-man's-land. His wife came back to the camp from Mar Elias with his little daughter Maryam. The story about his brother-in-law being a big Syrian chief seems to be unfounded. Nabih Berri is back after three months in Damascus to try and sort out his Amal dissidents' coup. Iran states that it will not ignore the Hizb'ullah killings and clampdown by Syria.

2.3.87 Day 125 Monday

Mohamad Ali, brother of Hossam Ali, is dead. Adnan is a paraplegic for the rest of his life, and Um Ahmad Maleji was shot in the chest bringing in supplies of food. All three were sniped in the camp or at the entrance today. Mohamad was taken straight from where he was shot at the front street to the hospital. He had just greeted his wife and new child, who returned to the camp today from the war outside, when he was shot whilst holding the baby, and was rushed to the hospital. He lost his blood so quickly that by the time he was brought into the emergency room he had stopped bleeding, and he died afterwards. He was only about 27 or 28, handsome, quiet; his poor mother now has two sons dead and two fatherless grandchildren here in Lebanon and another child in Canada. Mohamad's baby was injured when he was shot. It happened on the slope that we all climbed up and down every time we went to and from Saiqa to see the exodus of women from the camp. Only once has anyone ever been shot there before, and that was in the First Camp War.

Then Adnan, motherless Adnan with a host of little brothers and sisters, was shot through his spine. He is also about 27 years old. What will his family do now? He can't earn any money any more to support them.

It was also a hellish day as, when I was removing crust from around Noora Azan's bullet haematoma, I suddenly got a warm gushing spurt of blood all over me, in my mouth, eyes, hair and face. I called to Ben for help as she had a spouting artery which continued to bleed profusely at the slightest let-up of pressure. The woman's husband, whom we'd already tried to calm down earlier, went into a flap and it took a lot of shouting and more shouting, to get him to stay quiet. I went to the hospital with her, walking her up the road at a reasonable pace until her husband caught us up, flapping. While Pauline examined and prepared her for theatre, he got worse, accusing us of negligence and having a heated argument with Dr Saleh who at one point was saying in the three-way conversation between Pauline, husband and himself, 'No, no, Pauline, you don't understand – the point is that he is accusing us of negligence.' Then when she said the wife needed a unit of blood, the husband said three units and was there none in the fridge? Then tried to give her his O-positive blood. Just as she was almost prepared for theatre, Mohamad arrived. The husband then asked if they would do the two operations at one time. I replied possibly, but I didn't think so, and they would do Mohamad first as he was a serious case.

When I returned to the hospital later, I learnt about poor Mohamad and Adnan from Hussein, who was sitting dejectedly in the warm gloom dressed in his theatre clothes for Mohamad's operation. I collected the drum of gauze and came back to the clinic. On the road I was so absorbed with the awfulness of what I had just been told that I didn't see Mehdi's widow and children standing on the road. She invited me to drink tea which I had to turn down as a horde of dressings were waiting in the clinic. I asked her about the tale of little Hissam aged 10 being beaten by Amal yesterday and she said it was true, they had grabbed him, asking him what he was going to be when he grew up – a fighter? – (rhetorical bullying questions), and beat and kicked him. The poor little boy was crying as he was kicked and hit with Kalashnikov butts. First her husband dies, before he can see his children eat again instead of starve as he had feared; then her son is beaten while she fetches the food from outside.

As I did Haj's dressing, and we were joking seriously about how to get him out of the camp and country, Rifat came in to say that two UNRWA trucks had come into camp and there were foreigners with them. So I ran up to see if there was any mail or messages for us. The scenes were fantastic: hordes of thin, thin, scraggly, dirty and dusty people, and two trucks with big blue UNRWA flags on them, containing milk and flour.

The Chief of Lebanon was there, Piers Grodnan, who was clean, corpulent and dispassionate about the whole scene, and oblivious to the fact that he was standing at the exposed end of the street where Sultan's bodyguard was shot dead which had started the war. So I introduced myself and he blandly told me that no, they had no messages or films for us (as they are searched too), that they had no control over what foodstuffs they could bring in (they could only suggest what to bring), that we would now have flour for a few days' bread, that he did not think it was possible that we had 1,000 children between the ages of 0 and 10 years old in the camp, and to Rifat he made the bold statement that Sweden and Denmark are closed to refugees now. Then he disengaged himself from the conversation and went away to collect a fattening Abu Salim, then left the camp.

We hurried inside, fearing a shelling for Amal's wrath at the entry of supplies under Syrian protection into the camp. The Syrian foreign minister pledged to let supplies into the camp in adequate quantities, and the Swedes pledged to try to bring in supplementary baby-feeding kits to the clinic after I'd searched Dr Salim's book for the numbers of new babies born into the camp during the war. Sixty-one delivered, seventeen miscarried or stillborn.

Ahmad Maleji's mother was shot, so we took the remains of our oxygen cylinder up to the hospital for her, torchless and in the dark. Ahmad and Rifa his wife were looking very drawn and worried. The two women had been outside for food and, coming back into the camp with hamburgers for us, as we had talked so often about them, Amal stopped them, then told them they could walk into the camp. Then they shot Ahmad's mother through the chest from the back as she walked in. Poor Rifa had to half-carry her into the camp from where she was shot; she had small and large bowel and pelvic injuries and fractures, now she has a colostomy.

Noora's arm went to theatre at 19.00, not before much teasing from Doctors Saleh, Salim and Rede about the husband's stories, circulating both camp and hospital, of my cutting his wife's artery and nerves, etc. Dr Saleh repaired it very neatly, saying '*Merdi*' and telling me not to do it again. I said I would try. Then we ate lemon, onion, *zatar* and lettuce, and listened to the news with Hannes and Ahmad in the dark, open-windowed candlelight of Pauline's room, before coming down in the dark again to the clinic with them both. We sat outside by the fire with Haj and Rifat until about 22.25, lit by the flames of the *dulsanna* lights, talking and listening to the first cricket of spring (like the first cockroach the night before).

I went to inspect the damage from the 500s and M-16s which had been shooting up the square for an hour earlier. We'd sat cooking and watching it from 17.00 to 18.00, sheltering in the doorway as bullets took holes out of our wall and the house next door and on the corner. The top wall is full of holes and rubble, and bullet remnants are everywhere. I collected a few. Rifat fetched the spare wood from the roof; we looked onto the street and saw that Amal have hung it with very bright neon lights. Very eerie, as before there used to be no sign of electricity until well into the Shia Green Line areas further back to the east. We looked down on the black and twinkling lights and the murderous light on the street and scuttled back downstairs over the rubble.

Pauline and I talked about our increasing dependence on daydreams to keep our sanity. Not nostalgia, just a longing for normality and peace, art galleries, friends and animals far from all this.

They say the war is ending.

Abu Fahdi, the Abu Musa leader, came into the camp with a package deal for peace, by force. If the Fatah people do not agree to go underground, close their offices and stay silent or leave the camp, there will be a larger and harder extension of this war in the camp until they agree to do so – either by Amal, Syria or Incas – so the Fatah leaders must be forced by convincing argument from the responsibles to do so. With that little arm-twisting 'instant' solution, he entered the camp with a white flak-jacket to save us all from his supporters – the Syrians. He has another meeting with them tomorrow in the Beau Rivage Hotel, their Beirut headquarters.

Mohamad, the nurse from the house of paraplegics, is reported to have been taken by Amal and to be held and tortured by them. He is so frail anyway, it's awful. Poor Hassan Ablawi, paraplegic since he broke his neck during a swimming-pool accident in 1978, was taken from his wheelchair and beaten. They thought he had been made paraplegic in this war and jumped up and down on his stomach.

This is being written in the light of one flickering fat candle.

3.3.87 Day 126 Tuesday

Woke today with my face swollen like the moon, all puffy and round. At first all we could think of was a reaction to getting Noora's blood in my eyes, and Ben got up at 7.00 to give me a very painful injection. It still hurts now fourteen hours later as it is oil-based. Ouch. As the swelling was still there at 12.00 I went to see Pauline, who immediately thought it was an aspirin allergy, as she'd noticed it beginning last night. We figured either that or tomatoes. So I'm now on Piriton. Good grief! I'm becoming a walking pharmacy.

I slept almost all day, going back to bed from 9.00 to 11.20 then from 14.30 to 19.00. Fatima came, but I was so drowsy that she left after a few minutes. Woke to a knocking on the door by someone handing in a food parcel from the sheikh: tea, bread, a few potatoes and apples, and a slab of compressed dates. Then Pauline came. She spoke on the radio-phone to

Jim Muir of the BBC World Service, who is now back in West Beirut with several journalists. This is quite incredible as they were waiting outside the camp, trying to come in. Maybe they'll phone again tomorrow.

4.3.87 Day 127 Wednesday

The team of MSF doctors are not awaiting entry in Mar Elias, but have been ordered from Cairo, so God knows where they are at the moment. The question that perplexed Jim Muir yesterday was how the hospital was doing for fuel. To which Pauline replied it was difficult, stalling him. In fact, all the big trucks coming in since the Iranian Hizb'ullah trucks have had whole tanks full of petrol siphoned off to feed the motor at the hospital. That's how the motor has been able to keep functioning over the past two and a half weeks – stealing and siphoning. If Amal found out they would send in the tanks empty.

Borhan used our roof for sniping at the M-16 and 500 sniper. He went up yesterday to inspect the damage from the day before and said he could see the new holes that the sniper was shooting from. So he fetched an M-16 with a telescopic lens sight and tried to shoot him from upstairs. I of course slept through it all. Hannes had let him in. Pauline is not too amused as the Hilal (PRCS) buildings are not supposed to be used as it could return fire into the buildings.

No news today, again everything seems to have stagnated. All the political meetings are going on, but producing no results. The Syrians are constantly talked about as deploying soon but not until they get concrete guarantees that Fatah will leave.

Gas, diesel and other fuels came into the camp again yesterday and today. The road from Majnuk, which is often open but by no means all the time, let gas in and any goods including batteries and candles without any searching today. There have been service taxis on the airport road for two days now also, so the women don't have to walk the entire distance and back with cylinders on their heads. Signs of returning to normality?

More flares at 19.00 lighting up the camp for half an hour. One fell right behind the clinic, not exploding, falling slowly with an eerie distinct *whee* as it spiralled down, altering the shadows of the camp walls and buildings with black and yellow circles. Then at 22.10 came a series of explosions of TNT, mingled with mortars. This went on again for about twenty minutes with no sense as to why, shaking the buildings with every explosion. At least we weren't out fetching the water by torchlight again like yesterday, when we went out torchless to find Mohamad al Khatib balancing on one leg turning the water tap to fill the hose. Little Ahmad was standing dwarfed by Mohamad's crutches that he was holding while his father worked with one leg and a torch among the shells of buildings left next to the *mahwars*. We used the slide projector as a torch, flashing it in everyone's face.

5.3.87 Day 128 Thursday

When will the Syrians call off their dogs? Ghazi Q'anan now declares that he will not enter the southern suburbs as there is no fighting there(!) Amnesty International have submitted a paper to state that many people have 'disappeared', assumed to be prisoners in Iraq, Iran, and from Tripoli in January at the time of the Syrian massacres of the Sunni population and Murabitoun. Good. I hope these diaries are of use to them when we get back.

We ate beans, cheese, tomatoes and onions, tea and cake for breakfast wondering what is going to happen to us all. 'Evil' Mahmud came by, feeling better, still without his one unit of blood, to say his shop was open for all sorts of chocolates and sweets – things are returning to normal. You can get batteries again now at Haj Abu Taher's. I'm still thinking of our electric ambulances. What will NORWAC think when they hear that all the wires, lights and batteries were removed long ago to help the hospital run, all those little carlights hanging twinkling all over the hospital.

So today: thunderstorms, lightning all day, pouring rain and hailstorms. Wet, but not too cold. The swelling on my face has gone down and been replaced by spots. Went up to Fatima's and sat for half an hour watching her mother, Amné and Intisar washing clothes. Then Waf'a was slightly injured when a mortar exploded in the houses near us as she was hanging the clothes out to dry upstairs. Amné charged out of the door into the dust and smoke running madly. I thought someone was injured and wanted to run after her, but was restrained and told she'd gone to the shelter.

When I got back to the clinic, I was immediately taken by Seeham to get our supplies, which included three pairs of socks and all I had hoped for in batteries and slide films: six of these, and the 36-exposure that we had asked for. Wow! It was like Christmas, so I immediately loaded my camera and took photos of them all, including one of Ben and Zeinab working on the woman's leg, Zeinab and little girls fetching water, some of Saiqa *mahwar* in the rain, and a boy waiting by the gate. I took two of the car on the sandheap marking where the women keep getting shot. Rifat and I will go back tomorrow to take more. We came back in the pouring rain past heaps of rotting rubbish and broken zinc and overflowing sewers.

A dried-up dismal day of monotony. Now we are not exactly fighting for survival we have time again to think about boredom and get a little fed up with it all. We walked past the sniper hill and the side alley where Mohamad Ali was shot holding his baby, only metres from his home. And past the place where the mortar landed on Friday February 13.

Our plaster disappeared with Aref al Habet and I had to press for the return of any sort of plaster to the clinic. It had been taken to tape up TNT as usual, but we really had none to spare and so it had to be returned. Heard the tale from the other night that Nawoosh was going to divorce his wife if the fifth child had been a girl. It shows what a complete lack of understanding he has of his biology, it being up to his sperm and not her eggs!

The Syrians have discovered the PLO telephone connection in Beirut, so no more phoning out or home. They also probably control the exchange in Masra which means all calls could be monitored. A sinister warning came by megaphone at 23.00: 'All residents of Bourj al-Brajneh camp, do not leave the camp tomorrow or your lives will be your responsibility.'

6.3.87 Day 129 Friday

Today is not so bad for leaving as it's pouring with rain, grey and bleak, and the sewers are running over and flowing fast over everything including the *hamman* floor and the kitchen, which now smells dreadfully of sulphur and rotting eggs as the drains have been blocked for one or two weeks now. It makes a terribly fed-up morning of it.

Oh God, there is a dreadful woman wailing and croaking about the 'look of love' on Magic 102 radio station in a supposedly 'sexy' voice. She's flat and 'ooh-ooh-ooh'-ing in a very dire impersonation of the early sixties cocktail crooning. The phenomenon of Beirut radio stations has to be heard to be believed. All but a few of the DJs are women who put on this disembodied transatlantic accent, and either make constant 'hot sex' statements whilst playing the blandest ballads or swoon on about love, longing and being lost, and occasionally about lust, but rarely. And the bizarre thing is that all these chic DJs are looked up to by their brothers and husbands in East Beirut as they are in West, and it's all a constant outpouring of fantasy only. Like the neutral pulp musical Valium that churns out twenty-four hours a day, constantly urging beauty, Moulinex Electrics, dentists, hotels and restaurants – all fantasy.

A cold lethargic day on antihistamines and waiting. The slump period has happened again. It does this every so often but now I'm hitting a low more when it does. Not bad after four months and more of this unreality. Although, as I said a week ago, another three weeks of this and I too will be finished; like Dr Darwish, getting terribly apathetic and short-tempered, not myself.

20.15 The Iranians have dispatched an ambassador to Lebanon to take office within forty-eight hours; they are supporting Hizb'ullah and are unhappy about the Basta massacre. International concern over the lack of Syrian entry into the southern suburbs and the camps situation, which is seen as a Syrian failure to combat problems. EEC aid of 169 million Lebanese lira of food and medicines.

Sent for at around 12.30 by Dr Rede to go and speak on the *jihaz*. Went with the man with the artificial leg (which I didn't notice until he mentioned it), who had visited Yugoslavia, Cyprus, Athens and Bulgaria to get his prosthesis. He should have it reviewed every six months but it's too expensive and difficult. At present he has a fixed leg and wants to get a flexing knee soon. Anyway, he led me up to near Rifat's home and it was the Fatah office *jihaz*. There Pauline and Dr Rede were waiting for me. It was ITN news, Brent Sadler on the line from Mar Elias; apparently he'd been asking to speak to me as he had heard there was a Scottish nurse in the camp.

He asked me for a little biography and said how come no one had spoken to me before, so I replied I was usually in the clinic at the other end of the camp, that's why. So then he said that now I'd been discovered (both Pauline and I thought that this was rather a bizarre cliché sort of thing to say, as if I'd been waiting all my life for stardom) could he ask me some questions. Then he ran the tape and asked me about work in the clinic. So I replied that mostly it was dressings and for the past week and a half it was fresh bullet wounds of women aged 16 and 50, who had been shot bringing in ordinary supplies of foodstuffs now that the blockade of the camp was partially lifted for a few hours each day for women, girls and children to go out and bring foodstuffs into the camp. I said that although UNRWA had brought a few trucks in, the supplies were selected for them and it was only flour and milk that came into the camp in sufficient quantities for the camp's population.

He asked me what it was like now in the camps and I replied that it was getting a bit difficult after four months of siege as things were beginning to run out, for example the oxygen here and in Haifa. Then he said how did we find the situation? So I said that we were horrified at the continued harassment, intimidation and humiliation of women, girls and children trying to go out of the camp to buy ordinary foodstuffs, and also by the fact the International Red Cross is still refused entry to the camp to evacuate the wounded.

Then he asked what I expected to be doing for the rest of the day. I said we'd be doing dressings, seeing small children as there are many infectious diseases now as people are debilitated due to the food situation of the past four months, and waiting for any emergency, and that we were the first aid clinic for wounded people when it was too dangerous or difficult for them to be moved immediately up to the hospital. And that many of the injuries we see are either removed to Haifa or we see them first and send them on to Haifa afterwards; that we worked with many women and small children.

He asked how it was now that it was quieter, so I said it was as good as it could be when you're being shelled and shot at. He said that in spite of it all we sounded in good spirits. 'Ha, ha,' I replied. Silence from ITN. He then asked what were my plans afterwards. I said that depended on the security situation. He'd earlier asked when we thought it would end, so Pauline and I quipped, 'You tell us!' Then he signed off and asked Pauline if we would be able to come out to speak to him; we replied no, but could he come in? He replied that he didn't think so, so we ended with Pauline saying he didn't need to eat dog now.

At the beginning he heard that he was my first contact with the outside world in over four months so he said he would get the London ITN office to phone home and let Mum and Dad know that I'm all right.

I didn't tell him about my lesson from three little girls all aged under 8 in how to find a flare-bomb casing without parachute in pieces behind the clinic yesterday and scattered on the rubble. I'd never have found them alone, not knowing what I was looking for. Or that Dr Nasser has lost his skeletal look and now looks a lot healthier, or that Dr Atia will not be able to return to his house in Sur for the next five years after this war. Or that Dr

Rede will not be able to leave this camp after the war, or that we may never see the flat in Hamra again, being taken immediately to Saida, with perhaps one night in Mar Elias, or that many people died here for nothing but other people's dirty money and games, and many will die after this. But I did tell him that the sewers are flowing over and smell today.

Dr Rede, Dr Atia, Pauline and I joked about fleeing this war to be in Saida for the new war together, and about the two old ladies, stooped and dressed in black, leaving the camp together muttering farewells in German to the waiting crowds. No one knows where the Belgian MSF team are, and a British team is supposed to be arriving tomorrow, obviously not by plane as the planes don't arrive on Saturdays and anyway the airport is closed for the moment, so I guess by boat.

Dr Rede was quite firm about us not seeing Hamra again and asked us what things we had to pick up, as they will be sent for when we escape at the first opportunity to Saida or Mar Elias. It's strange to think I will not see West Beirut again after waiting all this time, thinking of relaxing days there; strange to think that all the plans of working for Hilal after the war and all the foundation of that work may be for nothing, almost like a waste of time. It makes me confused to think of it.

7.3.87 Day 130 Saturday

Got up late at 8.00 fighting off the little kitten; fell over her while dressing, as usual crawling over my feet or ankles. Ate at Fatima's: cheese, bread, eggs, and 'Spring is in the air and summer is just around the corner, at Rays Sportswear' (radio from East Beirut).

Took photographs of the operating room staff having coffee for breakfast: Nooha, Sooad, Nadia, Dr Salim and Dr Saleh. Then to the nurses' station where Hannes the physiotherapist was at work with Hamoudi, the young boy whose father died after his traumatic amputation. The boy is very brave and is in the wheelchair they found, his legs still very painful after three weeks, but he is uncomplaining and gave a wistful little smile when I asked him if he had no voice, as he just looked at me when I asked him questions.

I took two photos of the emergency room in the dark by candlelight with Dr Nasser; and Mohamad by candlelight in the gloom at the pharmacy; and then upstairs to take three pictures of the laundry and cooking ladies, the deaf lady and the little bossy one by the big wood-log fires; then to the remains of the third floor up a staircase. Then I came back to the clinic for more film and Rifat came. So we went back to Saiqa and took pictures of eight women coming into the camp with children and one old man. I hope the film speed was up to it, being only 100, but you could see real tension in everyone's faces and gestures as one woman was shot dead this morning at the exit. She was a relative of Rifat's mother, and the story is that from today all women leaving the camp are being forced to buy the Amal magazine (once weekly) for twenty-five Lebanese lira. She refused, some say because she couldn't read, and they shot her as she walked away. She was taken away by Amal and a message came by *jihaz* that she had died, shot through the chest.

Then we scrambled and ran snipers to a point across the garbage and up two alleys to a sandbagged first-floor position where we waited for more women crossing the zinc barricade at the edge of no-man's-land. Like yesterday we had to dodge our heads from the sniper. We left after a short while, running up the sniper alley.

I came back to the clinic and sat trying to write, then went to hang out the bandages to dry and got shot at twice by the M-16 sniper. I was shouted at to get inside, and there is much argument as to whether he is shooting blind into the street or he has a telescopic lens on a Brezhnev and could see me through the zinc barricade, although I thought I was screened by it. The bullet was found by Rifat at the kitchen door. So the streets and the square were blocked again, as the bullets were hitting the shop corners.

Banan and Pauline came, and we tried to solve Banan's mother's attempts to force her to marry a good educated man she has never loved. That's why she's been locked up in the house for the past month by Noora, who is trying to make a good marriage. She has four suitors: two are 6th Brigade Lebanese Army and Shia, and out of the question; the other is thin Ghassan who she liked before. But Noora is being awful and putting pressure on her, to the extent that Hanni's mother arrived from Saida today and wants Banan to go back to Saida with her tomorrow. Rifat thinks she may have to marry this one, although he says most of the mothers from Tarshiha are pushy and socially aspiring.

Rifat came back later; he'd knocked earlier but we'd mistaken it for gunfire. We sat and talked as Ben and Pauline played chess. We discussed Banan, and Rifat's sisters' and mother's weddings, and the custom of arranged marriage. He says that things are less strict now, although the camp has been like a prison since 1984 and Arafat's leaving. No joy or parties, only fear and death. Then he left, going off into the pouring wet and dismal night, tired and a bit empty feeling, like me; Pauline and Ben left soon afterwards. I feel as if I have to get everything down on paper and do everything, as if we will be leaving very soon, within a short time. No rational explanation for it. I'm tired again, but not so thoroughly fed up as I took all the pictures today that I've been mentally planning for the past four months.

Made a birthday card for Dr Rede from us all.

8.3.87 Day 131 Sunday

A dull, cold and very very wet day. Slept badly after the disturbed evening last night, the kitten getting in the way. My arm has stopped hurting after yesterday's aches; I don't know why it started up again.

As we sat in Fatima's house, I had my premonition of doom, and four *howens* exploded, the fourth being nearer than most with shrapnel falling nearby. They were 120mm mortars, defying all complacent expectations of 'no *howens* as it's raining', yet fulfilling our gloomy expectations of last night when we all decided that after two days of no mortars we were due for a shelling today.

Cheering news that the Fatah films are already in Cyprus being developed, having been smuggled out of the camp. When we are in Cyprus, we can also have our films developed and reproduced for PLO archives. Goody, goody, I think that thought excites me most, as the detail on a projected slide is greater than on the average photograph.

The feeling of damp stagnation and hopelessness continued until Rifat came to the door at 15.00, followed by Borhan, who later sent round a plate of charcoaled chicken and fish, salad and chips, cooked on the wood fire in the *mahwar*. The cats had a feast on fish head and bones, and chicken bones. Pauline appeared, happier for having her room back at the hospital and for speaking to her friend Liz Sly from *The Times* who is in Beirut. Dr Atia's wife had left the camp again with the children, finding the grim reality of life in Haifa, water-less, electricity-less, etc, worse than Akka Hospital, which has been bombed out.

Pauline says that she and I are regarded as national folk heroines back in Britain, beleaguered humanitarians adrift in the mayhem and bloodshed of the southern suburbs of Beirut. Anyway, a return via Cyprus sounds lovely, if we get out of this alive and in one piece rather than pieces.

We speculated on the news that the Syrians are trying to keep the lid on the camps, and the fact that all questions about entry to the camps are met with 'no comment' replies. No reasons are given, so much so that Liz Sly is contemplating returning to London as nothing is happening here. Although apparently Jumblatt, Hawi and Co. are beginning to make noises about the continued bombardment of Shatila which is in the area of Beirut city and still besieged and frequently attacked. We decided on a campaign of persistent belligerence publicizing our situation which includes getting Øyvind to call John Grey, the British ambassador, weekly to pose the question of our continued besiegement in the camp, to Amin Gemayel, and also to 'phone' Mar Elias and speak to journalists weekly on the situation in the camp. Then after we had nostalgized about Cary Grant movies and listened to Saint Alistair Cooke's scathing 'Letter from America' (about Reagan's Conservative journalist critics on the Tower Commission), I fell asleep.

Today, I saw my first up-to-date newspaper in four months, *Al Asifir*. On the front page was Margaret Thatcher clutching a small girl. Inside was the greeting of the new Iranian ambassador at Ouzai by lots of Shia, their heads covered, and dressed according to Islamic clerical dress code, whilst the smiling new ambassador was well dressed in an expensive silk suit, shirt and tie with glasses that looked fairly Yves St Laurent. He looked an approachable sort of chap.

We talked for a long while last night about when the Israelis came as far as the Majnuk building in the 1982 invasion, and fought an eighteen-hour battle for control of the airport with combined Leftist and Palestinian fighters. Rifat told me that when the first reports of the Sabra and Shatila massacres came from a woman who had escaped to Bourj, they didn't believe her. When the news came that the Israelis had arrived, the entire population of the camp and the southern suburbs fled, as far as East Beirut in some cases, fleeing to the combined savagery of the Phalange and the Israeli Defence Force – more than 10,000 people running from the prospect of a second massacre, or a Tal al-Zatar. Bourj was almost flattened by the aerial bombardment of the Israeli Air Force and the mortar bombardment of the Phalangist Forces, who used 155mm shells, which would completely destroy a breezeblock house. More than half the camp's houses were destroyed and had to be rebuilt with strengthening pillars in the corners afterwards, but many of the population were spared that way.

Rifat also told me that at the time the Israelis came he and his friend (now dead, killed in the 10-day war), were in the cinema in the front street. The cinema emptied as people learnt of the Israeli advance, until only he and his friend remained as they wanted to watch the end of the film. Eventually the cinema owner and staff implored them to flee also, saying that the film was finished as they too were closing the cinema and fleeing the advancing armies. He also says they were stopped many times. Even though he was only 14 years old he was very tall, yet somehow always escaped arrest or murder by the Lebanese Forces.

9.3.87 Day 132 Monday

16.00 One woman, six months pregnant, was shot and later died returning to the camp through Saiqa with food for her family. Another, Khadija Dibi, was shot through the chest. Khadiji died within an hour. She had been left outside shocked for quite a time and was brought in on a stretcher with everyone thinking she was dead. Her mother had died and her father left the family and went to Syria. They say that no one loved her in the family. Now she's dead, despite Ben going to Rashid, her brother, to tell him not to send her out of the camp for food as her foot was badly infected and needed rest. If only he'd heeded Ben's requests, after all Ben's work and running the snipers near Saiqa to get to her house. The other injured woman died along with the unborn baby after attempts by five doctors in Haifa to revive her. Three dead.

Ben and I were so angry that we immediately decided to abandon humanitarian non-accusing statements, but after much rage Pauline came down to the clinic and vetoed a lot of what we had written, saying that Dr Rede would also refuse to send out what was in our statements, so we all argued vehemently about the content but decided in the end not to split on our issuing of statements at this stage and also to maintain the impartiality of our previous messages. We adjourned to the hospital to see Dr Rede. Rifat, who was also in on the argument, agreed with Pauline.

He and I then fell all the way up to the hospital, torchless and with me getting irate as I'd lost the argument, knowing full well that Pauline was right, and also because Rifat walks too slowly for me to avoid falling over him in the dark and if he uses the lights it makes it even more difficult for my eyes to adjust. Then I sat with Hannes in the doctors' room watching a chess match by candlelight played with an un-cool style of flamboyance and enjoyment between Dr Rede and another man, who was being noisily coached by Dr Atia over his shoulder and kneeling by him alternately. They shouted, finished the match and then replayed several alternative moves.

Dr Atia invited me to stay for tea in an effort to salvage manners and civility in this war, so I sat and thoughtfully drank it, then shambled out into the watery dark of the hospital. Rifat came back again and we stumbled out past two old men, *keffiyeh*-clad and heavily coated against the damp, cold winds blowing down the corridors, past the candlelit emergency room and out through the door, passing men sheltering against the cold with a smoky wood fire. We fell down the camp to the clinic.

We discussed why I don't feel so fed up and bleak now about the siege, whilst the staff of the hospital talk in very depressing terms about their continuing difficulties.

We accepted everything early on, and as everything happened to us in a regular succession as in the rest of the camp apart from the hospital, we have lived through the siege like this. So rather than everything suddenly appearing to get worse, as at the hospital, making everything appear dreadful (even the gauze and cotton folding), the introduction of fuels, food, light and batteries has suddenly dramatically improved our working conditions after a very bad period.

I fell asleep fully dressed after hearing the regular midnight call for the boy next door to go on guard duty as he does every night at that time, being woken by his friend, their Kalashnikovs rattling together. My arm still hurts and is a bit duff from the cold. Four mortars today.

10.3.87 Day 133 Tuesday

Rumours persist that the Arafatists are stalling for time by offering money to the camp. Arafat himself is rumoured to have sent a message saying this from Baghdad to Abu Riyad. So, with Incas sending its recommendations to the Syrians, including the removal of Fatah from Beirut, and Fatah claiming that that wasn't a Syrian demand but an Incas demand, the ball bounces up and down between the old men of the mosque, the Popular Committees, etc, and the Syrians. Abu Fahdi, after his grand entrance into the camp wearing a bulletproof white flak jacket of peace, has left again and gone back into Maqassed Hospital with a heart complaint. The Syrians do nothing, but today there is a lot of talk on the radio about various parties wanting a solution to the camp wars: the Iranians, people in Damascus, etc. Wonder if it means anything, as for a long time absolutely nothing has been said at all about the camps.

Khadija and Zeinab tried to go out today from the Majnuk exit, but were told by Lebanese Army soldiers to come back tomorrow at 6.00 to leave early, as a captain of the Lebanese Army, a high-ranking Amal official, was at Majnuk, so they wouldn't be let out. We hope to have letters, etc, brought in, along with some money.

Later Pauline and Hannes came down to the clinic and gave me the fright of my life. Hannes sidled up to me and said, 'We may be leaving today.' Pauline confirmed it, and my heart hit the floor and my stomach went into my mouth, or the equivalent. Last night's dream about leaving Beirut seemed to be coming true. Pauline told me that in two hours an Italian-motivated evacuation of the wounded was supposed to take place and there was a remote chance that it might include us, but we would probably go tomorrow if the promised team of new doctors come in. So I contemplated packing my things, then decided against it. We sat on the steps deliberating and Ben arrived as we drank tea. At this point Juju ran in saying he'd heard a *howen* going out twice, so I ran to the door to call the children in from the square. They all hesitated, then ran into the clinic, all but Ibrahim. He stood, so we shouted at him, then he about-turned and started up the hill towards his house, saying he was going home to find his *mama*. So I ran out, grabbed him and ran into the clinic. Thank God, there were no explosions and it was a false alarm.

Pauline went back up to the hospital and I wrote a letter to Øyvind for broadcasting about the state of the children here, then Hannes and I went up to the hospital to await the evacuation. We waited and I photographed the hospital again and East Beirut and Amal positions, and took tea offered by one of the cooking ladies, and we talked about awaiting the evacuation and the past two days of waiting, and the Syrian escorts. Then I waited more and looked out of Pauline's window and heard the noise of troop carriers and tanks outside on the airport road and saw silver linings on clouds in the setting sun and blue sky, counted the number of shell holes per building and wondered at the miraculous survival of the roof garden nearby with its hanging ivy, tended at risk by its loving owner who crept onto the roof, despite threats of shells, to feed it. Then I went back to the clinic. But as I was tired and worried, I tripped over a tap on the water pipe saying hello to a young boy, and went flat on my face into the mud and sewer in front of an audience, grazed my face and hand but nothing else, and felt very stupid as I was helped up and offered a wash by kind onlookers. But I was near to tears at the thought of leaving and this was the last straw, so I stumbled back down to the clinic, listening for *howens* all the way.

Pauline and Hannes returned and we tried to discuss whether to leave the camp, Hannes wanting to go (prior to his arrival, he hadn't realized there had been wars here, and the whole thing has been a big shock for him), Pauline also wanting to go as she's had enough, Ben not wanting to go as his stuff is here and he doesn't want to leave the people before the end. I don't want to go before the end. Pauline wouldn't have a civilized discussion about it, so later, after the food, for Hannes' and her sake, I tried to get a discussion as a team about it. I said that just because two of us wanted to stay the others should not feel coerced into staying. It was not a question of morals about staying or not, it was just up to each of us as individuals; it would be stupid to make it an issue of morality. If we were all to get blown up the next day and killed, then it would all have been a waste of time. If they wanted to go out and wait for us in Saida, they could go without worrying about us until we came out at the end. I said I didn't think she would worry, but she just said no. I said again I didn't think so as she was sensible, but she tersely replied that, no, she wasn't going out alone, and wouldn't discuss it further.

There is said to be more than the first rumoured team of three, a surgeon, anaesthetist and nurse, trying to come in tomorrow. Doctors Atia, Nasser and Saleh want to go. Dr Saleh is leaving to assist on all the orthopaedic operations on his evacuated patients; he doesn't want to miss any of them. Dr Abu Nadir is said to be coming in. The new theatre will be almost finished and ready for transfer as soon as the new foreigners arrive. Among the patients, Ghaleb refused to give Pauline his surname as he didn't want to be transferred out to an outside hospital. He said it's better in Haifa (even after three and a half months bed rest). The paraplegics Wissam and Adnan are going out. We think an eight-bed field hospital has been set up in Mar Elias.

Nabih Berri now wants to capture the position east of Saida taken in September by the Palestinians before lifting the sieges of the camps. The Syrians raided American University of Beirut dormitories this morning, taking from their beds fifteen students who have PSP, Hizb'ullah, and possibly Amal political involvement. Shatila have five injured in the attempt to take supplies into the camp with a *Syrian* escort. So what happens now?

11.3.87 Day 134 Wednesday

Emotionally traumatic morning. Went up to Fatima's, but when I arrived at the Al Qassam house, I heard Ali and Intisar arguing. I didn't quite understand the context, but he'd apparently just hit her and she was asking why did he use force, why hit her and not settle it by words? She was a woman, she felt the blows, why hit her? It got more heated as she argued with him, refusing to be passive. Then I heard Intisar scream as Ali hit her again and again, and I sat still thinking surely he will stop and heard their mother go through and try to reason with him. Then I got up and saw him hit her again as she cowered pleading and weeping in the corner. As he kicked her in the stomach I went to grab him and yelled, 'Ali, stop it!' Intisar was on the floor cowering under the window weeping and there was glass from a shattered photo frame of Mahmud, their elder brother in Abu Dhabi. Ali stopped and shouted and marched out of the room glaring at her and her mother and their father who had come in from the 'men's' room. I held Intisar and tried to comfort her as she cried and cried in my arms. Her father retreated into his sanctum and her mother shook her head. After she had stopped crying and I had wiped her tear-stained cheeks, she looked at me with water-filled eyes and said, 'God, God sees all, God sees everything. Is it like this in Europe? – only here? No! It's only Arabs!' She then picked the glass from her hair and the hairpins that had gone astray as her head was beaten, and wiped the tears from her eyes, sitting on the floor, as her mother picked up the pieces of glass and playing cards that had fallen by the door during the beating of her daughter. Fatima led me away from the room to the kitchen and, shaking, made a pot of coffee. As she poured it into the little cups her body was shaking so much that she had to stop, and I took the little metal tray from her knees and put it up on the kitchen sideboard. She was shaking whilst trying to drink the coffee, and gave way to tears as she stood up to take the empty cups and pot away, saying, 'Why is it like this – and I want to cry?' She then said that Ali always hits Intisar if he's angry, always Intisar, because she and Fatima refuse to cower before their father. When he hits Fatima, she stands up to his bullying by asking him why does he hit her? Because she's a girl? Why does he think girls are different to boys and hate them? She says Ali behaves like this because of watching their father beat their mother all her married life; she said when her mother was married to their father she was 13 years old and did not know if he was good or bad. He always beat her, and once hit her so severely across the face that he wounded her in the right eye, and she had to have an operation to restore the sight. I asked if her three other brothers were like this. She said no, if they hear that Ali or their father has been brutal towards the women in the house, they are very angry and argue by telephone with them. She said they have learnt that women are human beings and not different from men, that women can learn as men do, and can move from one thing on to another with this knowledge. They treat women well and try to help their sisters, especially Mahmud who is trying to help Fatima to learn and grow and does all he can for her.

She also said that her father is ruining all their lives and futures by blocking all proposals of marriage to his daughters. She said there is someone in the camp who wants to marry Intisar and she him, but they will wait until the end of the war, so that they can telephone Abu Dhabi and, by enlisting the help of the three exiled brothers, force her father to agree to the wedding. Her suitor has the gold, money and house necessary to marry her, but her father always automatically rejects suitors and tries to make marriage deals that his daughters don't want. This happened to both Amné and Shahina, who at 37 and 29 are now getting too old, according to their culture, to be married. She then asked, 'Where is it written that men are better than women? Nowhere! Not even in the Q'uran that they could behave like this towards women.'

We went up to the hospital to see Hannes; after our discussions the night before, he'd decided to leave, and so had packed up his bags in the smoky dark, and we brought them downstairs to await his departure from the camp at the first opportunity with the Red Cross or anyone who could get in to take the ready-and-waiting wounded out. The hospital was in darkness as usual, and I found Dr Nasser sitting in candlelit gloom and asked him what was happening, was the ICRC to be allowed in? He said, '*Yumkin*' ('Possibly'). I said 'What is this "possibly"? Four and a half months of "possibly".' 'Okay', he said, 'I don't know.' Then we met one of the sheikhs who greeted me with surprise: 'Oh, I thought you were dead.' I said, 'No, I'm not dead. I fell in the mud, but I didn't die.'

I came back and tried to tape-record the children's stories of the war, but it was impossible as the battery is too weak, so a search now begins for six small batteries, as ours went into the flash on Ben's camera.

Fell asleep in the cold, huddled up in my sleeping bag, and then Pauline came and said that in three to five days, if peace comes, foreigners and the injured can go out, and she too will leave. She took a wash and I fetched more water with Rifat's help, then Ben made a fire which we all sat round relaxing and laughing. Later we talked about the necessity for a third statement and got down to composing it as we all felt we should follow up Arafat's appeal to the UN.

So we appealed in one of the 'half-baked, wishy-washy, wet, liberal' statements from Bourj al-Brajneh for intervention to end this misery. We mentioned those who are pregnant, the women being too frightened now to leave, the frostbitten child, the rats and garbage, the conditions in the hospital and the exhaustion of the staff. All without argument!

Pauline and I started discussing the baby quota during the war, then theoretically how to plan a live-births survey for one year of the camp, as most of the births are now in Haifa, except for the odd one or two; so we decided that if you followed up all the hospital births for a year, you could conduct a very representative survey of the pre-natal statistics of the Palestinian camp population in the Lebanon.

12.3.87 Day 135 Thursday
One woman was shot dead today after arguing and being beaten by an Amal man; she was put against a wall and shot. Many women were beaten with hands and Kalashnikovs by Amal at Majnuk exit, but this is the first time that this exit has been unsafe for use. Previously only Saiqa was known to be dangerous, but now no exit from the camp is to be regarded as even vaguely secure. Nawoosh's wife testified to this as she saw it happening.

Afterwards many women went to demonstrate at Ghazi Q'anan's office in Fakhani, near the Beau Rivage Hotel. They filled the street from Kola to Fakhani and one woman went in to represent them. They told of the nine deaths and over thirty injuries excluding today, and he said that after one week things would be normalized at the camps. Should we place bets? Khadija and Zeinab came back in at 16.48 to tell us this and had only managed to collect a pile of letters for Pauline. What the hell has happened to all the mail waiting for Hannes, Ben and me? After four and a half months! Really, we are very pissed off with the Norwegians, as Hannes was also told that his mother had contacted Mar Elias by phone, and was crying and very upset and thought that he was dead. So he went immediately to Dr Rede to make a strong request for contact immediately to Austria. We are very angry and bewildered by it.

Four thousand Lebanese lira were stolen from a woman today, but as Fatah, with Amal help through bribery, brought in thirty million Lebanese lira yesterday, some in gas cylinders, it's not too awful.

I met Imad today who now refuses to speak to me although he looks well. He muttered a reply to a greeting as I passed him the first time, perhaps because he didn't recognize me, then afterwards, when I met him several times as he was moving around in the chair, he refused to speak to me, just stared. This is despite Pauline thinking he is saner again having stopped all his addicted use of Pethidine. Today they took his two severed legs out of the fridge to burn them. After one month Hannes said they smelled awful.

Little Ahmad got taught to use the camera with one hand and instinctively balanced it against his stump to take three pictures of me.

13.3.87 Day 136 Friday
A bleak cold day – wind and rain after the incredible thunderstorm of last night. Still lightning today, maybe we'll have to light the fire to keep warm. Wearing jerseys and jackets; the clinic reminds me of a wind tunnel.

News came that, amongst the many women beaten yesterday, was Fatima's and Waf'a's friend who I met at breakfast the other day. She was trying to bring food into the camp for the organizations and was first beaten then shot in the legs at Majnuk by Amal. She and Waf'a, we think, are back in Mar Elias, but we are not entirely sure where they are and are worried for them. As Rifat said last night, 'Really they were too Fascist today.' The arbitrary controls were back in force: no coffee, no candles, no cigarettes, no gas and all the money being stolen.

10.30 Radio Free Lebanon news: talking of strong attacks on the Syrians again. Christians in key points to preserve the values in which they believe and to prevent the others imposing their will: Geagea's speech to the visiting French delegation. In London, Amnesty International calls for an inquiry into the massacres of people mistreated in Tripoli and West Beirut by the Syrians who continue to raid apartments. A statement issued by the Revolutionary Justice Committee states that Jean-Louis Normander's execution is threatened within forty-eight hours unless Chirac clarifies French policy on Iran and arms to Iraq.

The largest galaxy in the universe has been discovered 300 million light years away from Earth – lucky galaxy to be so far away.

I'll go up to the hospital now to collect medicine for Nawoosh's cherished son and see if there is any gauze yet. Some hope.

11.40 No gauze, no electricity, nothing, and the question *'Fi shi ijdid al yom?'* ('Is there anything new today?') produces wry smiles all round. A glimmer of sun disappears again behind the clouds.

The full story of Fatima being shot is that, as she came in the Amal man stopped her and stroked her face. In correct response she slapped his face, so he hit her, then shot her in the legs. She ran to a service taxi which Amal tried to order to take her to Sahel Hospital. She bravely shouted to the driver that she refused to go to Sahel and that he was to take her to Akka, repeating that she would not go to Sahel Hospital. When she reached Akka the doctors from Mar Elias came to collect her and take her back there. This was because she had been coming into Bourj from Mar Elias with food supplies or money for the organizations. She had 100,000 Lebanese lira strapped around her waist; other women and girls have also carried money into the camp.

Good news of Banan, who I scurried down to see whilst I knew Noora was out of the house. She's not going to marry any of the four suitors. She told Noora that she didn't want to marry, so Noora replied that was as she wished. She looks very relieved.

I heard the story that two of the amputees who are fast becoming Pethidine addicts have got their guns by their bedsides and are getting Pethidine on demand now. Abu Tha'ir had five hundred milligrammes of Pethidine and sleeps with his Kalashnikov behind his bed; Yusuf, the other prospective addict, is sleeping with his revolver in his locker. Abu Riyad has been requested to disarm them as he is the military leader responsible for them and apparently it's up to him to take the guns away.

Pauline is very angry as she and Dr Atia have been trying to control their intake, but others have given them free rein to take as much as they want, which is completely at odds with all their hard work to keep them from addiction.

Imad and little Mohamad are weaned off it. I suggested taking them up to the third floor of the hospital which is very unsafe, and leaving them screaming and unable to manipulate their environment by making it unbearable for everyone else in the room, until they dry out. They make it a life of misery unless they get what they want, which is the Pethidine.

No water tonight as all the pipes are empty, so water purification tablets were used in the *hamman* water to make banana custard. No food in Shatila. Chris Giannou, as a Canadian doctor working in the camp, is still issuing declarations every Sunday to explain the terrible conditions. They still have typhoid there.

There has been a PLO message to the UN Security Council saying Bourj, Shatila and Rashidiyeh have insufficient food. Arafat appealed to France, Britain and Italy to intervene to stop the suffering in the camps. Three Palestinians have been arrested in West Germany after trying to hold a forty-person meeting in defiance of a ban; the meeting was broken up by 300 police.

Amal refused all women exit from the camp until Arafat supporters leave the camp. About ten women passed us on the way to Saiqa to protest against Fatah: noisy slogans and shouting, also at Majnuk and Amliea.

Fatima says her father is beating her and her sisters every time he wants food and it doesn't come quickly enough. I was told, too, about her cousin who is 18 years old. Her father, mother and brother all beat her and refuse to let her out of the house even to visit friends. Her brothers are all young men and her life is made a misery by them all. Apparently both sexes are beaten until they are about 12 years old, then as the young man grows up he in turn beats his sisters, older and younger, as does his father. Fatima and Banan both estimated that ninety per cent of families in the camp behave like this towards their women. This is much higher than Rifat's view that only some old-fashioned families behave like this.

When Ali beat Intisar last Wednesday, it was on his father's instructions and with his encouragement. Today I visited Intisar to make a recording of the women's experiences going out of the camp, but when the men arrived the atmosphere was charged: all the women went silent and then suggested I returned the next morning.

My plan is to record the women and children talking about the situation of being under siege. I had been searching for batteries all day and eventually found some at Banan's. While I was there Juju came running to tell me to go quickly to the clinic to have my photograph taken by a 'foreigner'. I scrabbled up to the clinic to find Pauline with a crowd of people and a very chic UNRWA photographer who had just come into the camp. He took photos of us with the children and examining people's injuries, and then of the UNICEF trucks being unloaded.

At the hospital I met a very nice Irish UNRWA official, grey-suited as they all seem to be, and very warm and friendly. We immediately got talking about the clinic, the PHC programme, pregnancies and new babies. We estimated that there were about 400 small children in the camp, although the birth rate is dropping because of the wars; so far sixty-three new babies had been born during the siege: approximately one new baby every two days. We then had a meeting with Dr Rede, when I talked and talked about daily life for half an hour or so. The Irishman offered to phone outside for me, so I gave him the number at home, with clear instructions about when everyone would be there, quite forgetting today was Saturday so no one would be at work.

We were on the BBC World Service news three times today: good reports, mentioning our appeal to the United Nations, supplies entering the camp, Syrians keen to show the world their good intentions, Amal insisting on having the same supplies for themselves before allowing the trucks to enter the camp, and the casualty figures, cited as thirteen rather than ten dead. The reports really cheered us up as the amiable Irishman had said he knew nothing of our statements to the UN and we feared they might have disappeared without trace on an official's desk. As the world seemed to think things were back to normal, I had felt despondent about our efforts to get news out about the murders and terrorizing of the women and children.

15.3.87 Day 138 Sunday

Spent the first part of the morning looking wistfully at Intisar's suitcase of travels and souvenirs from Abu Dhabi: cutlery, place mats, ceramic dishes for the corridor, batteries, books, each Q'uran bound by Waf'a, picture frames from Samed, dresses and the most exotic collection of bras and pants that I've ever seen. I refused a gorgeous pair of the palest blue panties of transparent nylon with a silver embroidered heart on them fastened with a little clip above the heart – beautiful; and little flimsy pale orange tie briefs, and bras of palest salmon pink or silver, and spotted blue scanties; with a fabulous transparent blue lace nightdress, frothy and wonderful, from Abu Dhabi. All this she keeps upstairs locked away under a bed, waiting for her hopes and dreams to come true of escape from her father's brutality to the house of another man, who will see all these romantic expectations encased in the lingerie and hopefully fulfil some of them. They were carefully and lovingly displayed and then stowed in a travelling manicure case within the suitcase, under a blue prayer mat with Mecca depicted on it, also from the Gulf. She also had towels and Chinese embroidered dresses from Abu Dhabi, handkerchiefs, presents from her brother, and beautiful bead woven tapestries of the Prophet Mohamad's names to hang on the walls of her future house, the intricate tapestries in bright fluorescent colours. She is waiting for her good man to be able to marry her. She doesn't want 'the gold', only a kind man to take her out of the misery of her father and brothers' selfishness. We sat looking at everything, including a little beaded bird and some table mats which she had made, carefully edged with gilt lace and with fabric sewn on the backs to cover all the needlework on the reverse side.

After recording Fatima and Intisar's stories of Amal brutality I visited Banan. We sat for an hour talking of the ways of men, and the necessity for a 'good' man; drinking tea and screaming with laughter while dunking biscuits into the tea. She told me she would be going out of the camp tomorrow. Recorded her story of walking into the camp, praying and praying she would get inside safely without being shot.

Later I went back to Um Bilal's as I thought that I might not see Banan again. Shortly afterwards Abu Suhail and Ghassan, Samir and Issam arrived. Abu Suhail told Banan that I could ask him anything about politics that I wanted to know. So I asked him first about the situation in Beirut and the situation in Saida and whether they were expecting the Syrians to go after Saida or East Beirut soon. He said no, as before the Syrians can make any war, they have to do it by political negotiations so as not to offend the Israelis, Iran or America. Although Assad knows that Gemayel's army is weak, he can't go into East Beirut without the correct political manoeuvres. The idea is still that of cantons, and the south is for Amal so eventually they want all the Palestinians out of Lebanon. Then I asked him about Terry Waite, was he in Beir al Abed as everyone previously thought? He said no – he had been in Bourj al-Murr but not any more, as when the Syrians came to rescue Amal, they took all the prisoners out of Bourj al-Murr, the 400 Sunnis and Palestinians and Waite, and moved them to another hiding place.

And we ate and talked about Arafat, and how all of them had come out alive from Tal al-Zatar, and how they had had their studies interrupted, and Juma's wife said that Amal were asking whether it was true there were foreigners in the camp, and about Pauline.

I came back to the clinic with a full escort of three Kalashnikovs: very impressive in the moonlight. All the bombs (grenades) and TNT had stopped but the 500 and M-16 kept shooting at the clinic, and I stood at the window for a while, watching the bullets exploding off the walls next door in the moonlight. Big bangs and flashes; *ta, ta, ta*. All the little children here, because, unlike European kids, they know the sound of guns well, instead of saying '*Bang bang*', yell '*Ta, ta*', the M-16's *puck* sound as it hits a wall.

17.3.87 Day 140 Tuesday

Fatima told me a story of a young fat woman we met, dutifully scarfed, but looking blank and sad. Apparently her husband told her this morning that he wanted to marry a nurse as his second wife. His first wife was married to him when she was 15; she has had four children by him, one boy and three girls. She cleans, sweeps and looks after him, so why should he want another wife, as Fatima put it. She wants to go back to her parents, leaving the children with him in accordance with Islamic code, as she is frightened of him. She also wants to tell the woman's parents about the love affair with her husband as she feels they would disapprove. In fact her husband theoretically cannot take a second wife as he is with Abu Nidal, which is the only organization which disallows two or more wives, feeling it to be anti-revolutionary. If he divorces her at 25 years old, her life is finished, as the children customarily stay with the father and she is once again locked in her father's house and probably will not re-marry because of the children.

Pauline, Ben and I talked about the 'fake' photographer who had miraculously walked into the camp on his own, waving a Newsweek card, and looking for Pauline. He kept taking photographs despite her requests that he wouldn't and was eventually thrown out of camp, still with his film, to everyone's horror.

18.3.87 Day 141 Wednesday

Apparently we were mentioned on Voice of Palestine last night at 20.00, quoting our statements about the camps and saying how bad things were in Shatila. Arafat said last night that 'Shatila is dying', and that the Palestinians have evacuated the villages east of Saida, and Amal were now in control, after killing two Palestinians and injuring others. So we wait for Berri's fulfilment of his promises.

Today, despite Amal agreement and Syrian observers, when UNRWA trucks of supplies entered Shatila they were sniped and shelled with mortars, killing one Lebanese employee of UNRWA while they unloaded the supplies. Apparently Shatila is now so devastated that it's like working in a landscape of rubble and anyone outside a *mahwar* or shelter is an instant target. So now UNRWA have become targets for Amal along with the Iranians. That's two neutral figures killed now trying to bring food into the camps. Perhaps, though, the outside world will doubt the efficiency of the Syrian peace for West Beirut if even they fail to get urgently needed food supplies into a starving camp within their jurisdiction. I hope the world questions it.

The same journalist as yesterday has turned up. He was in the Fatah office with a video camera, leaping around on the roof in front of windows, seemingly blissfully unaware of the dangers of being shot or blown to bits by *howens* landing on the roof and sending shrapnel into the room to pockmark the walls. Pauline and I sat in the office talking to him, then it was thought that the light was too poor for photographs, so we decided to go to the hospital, after he had requested that she and I stroll around the big streets of the camp and we looked dumbstruck at his lack of sense of impending doom and death on the streets. More squelching around in the mud and water at the UNRWA store and the old Haj's house which was blown to bits. We sat around and he photographed and recorded Pauline telling the men's story, and photographed us examining our bombed-out ambulance. Then he went away.

We wanted to ask Brent Sadler if he ever appointed this guy to represent ITN in Beirut. Apparently he came over the route described by Monir, near the cemetery and Majnuk, after paying a Lebanese Army soldier a large sum of money and giving his video camera to Sultan instead of taking it back out with him.

I did some more recording. Banan has left now for Saida with Juma's wife and babies. Then I visited Fatima. Her father has had a fit after his authority was questioned by his son. What happened was that Intisar had been left alone early one morning as all the others had gone to try to go out of the camp. The old tyrant tried to beat her, so she ran away from him to a neighbour's house. When Ali returned, she came back and told him. Ali confronted his father with it, as he himself felt extremely guilty after beating her and had apologized to her. He told his father not to beat her and if he wanted anything to ask Waf'a, Fatima or Ali himself. With this the patriarch took himself into seclusion, developed his rage and then fell into hysteria. So we all laughed a lot, and even more when I told them to keep giving him the Librium very regularly and then he would be smiling and zonked most of the time.

19.3.87 Day 142 Thursday

I felt pessimistic all day, as if the world wanted Syria and the Israelis to kill us all as there is no sympathy for the Palestinians, and as if all this inertia had world backing, even though we heard that the UN Security Council was called today for a discussion on the camps wars and sieges. Pessimism also after news from Shatila. One truck was completely set ablaze, but the Saudi supplies of boxes of tinned foods for the Palestinians had been emptied beforehand, so at least they ate last night.

20.3.87 Day 143 Friday

Freezing all night. This is being written on Saturday as yesterday I was so cold-ridden that I slept and slept (and snored) all night. Hassan and Amira Muselmani's daughter Zeinab was shot dead at 9.20 at Saiqa. She had been waiting for her mother with shopping by the destroyed car in no-man's-land when the one-armed man yelled to Amira to get out of the way and leave the boy alone. They replied that she was not a boy, but he had already shot her through the left eye. It is a blatant lie that he thought she was a boy as she looked like any young woman in jeans, which are standard dress here. She was 17 years old and clever, preparing for university after the war. When I last saw her at her house two weeks ago, she was sitting on the steps reading a book with her little brother Yusuf who is 11 and Adnan who is 4 years old, after helping her mother to prepare food for me. All her sisters were educated as well as the boys, as her father believed his girls should also study. Yesterday I saw her dead on the stretcher on the way from Saiqa to the hospital. What I at first took to be brain hanging out all over her face, which was unrecognizable, was in fact her left eye, which had been shot out and was hanging down her left cheek. She had a totally fractured skull and there was no bullet exit site. Women screamed and turned away as she was carried, jolting and shaking on the stretcher, up the road which was said to be covered in blood.

Did dressings, feeling hellish and grumpy about Zeinab's death, and seeing her little brother Yusuf being led up the empty street by an older man with his hand on his shoulder shortly afterwards. Went out to do Mohamad and Yusuf Sahnini's dressings which were very dry and good. It seemed quite normal to be at their home with the two boys with no legs and a dead father who died also having his legs blown off. Then I went up to Ahmad Yaqub's lovely pastel house, and sat with the pastel granny with her double-wrapped white head and pastel blue dressing gown and river-tiger-patterned skirt and thick socks and soled shoes. She laughed a lot describing how she'd had the old man, his head wrapped in his red winter *keffiyeh*, out in the sun earlier in the day, on the bright whitewashed upper verandah, with its potted yucca plant and little gatepost over the steps. Her grandson, aged 6, had met me on the road and accompanied me up to the house, disappearing at intervals to buy seeds for one lira in a paper cone wrapping, or to get *cak* to eat with our tea. He'd spent all day asking when I was coming, every hour it seems: 'Has Suzy come, has Suzy come?' He described his family, and new little baby sister as being 'long', with his hands about one foot apart.

21.3.87 Day 144 Saturday

Mother's Day – usually celebrated by all-day parties and gateaux and presents. Today four women were all shot simultaneously; shortly afterwards the 35-year-old sister of Abu Tha'ir, the amputee, was shot dead through the chest. She bled to death from a simple injury because Amal refused permission for several minutes to the nurse who tried to collect her, so she lay outside the camp bleeding. The brave nurse refused to take her to a hospital outside and carried her on her back into the camp, shot at by Amal as she did so. Abu Tha'ir's sister died, as all these women are dying because none of them are being resuscitated quickly enough, and simple or fairly simple bullet injuries are killing them all, as they get shocked in the five- to twenty-minute wait before getting them into the camp, and it becomes irreversible. Almost all the fighters from the *mahwars* have survived these injuries, even double bullet injuries to the chest, because we can get to them sooner.

Amal are getting more and more sadistic each day, despite Q'anan's flight to Damascus to see Assad after the UN Security Council passed a resolution yesterday calling for the lifting of the sieges and the admission of foods and medicines into the camps. Today we heard that of the one million Swiss francs donated by the Swiss government through the ICRC to the Palestinians, half is to be given to Amal for permission to give the other half of the money to the camps. This was said to be being negotiated at the Beau Rivage Hotel headquarters of the Syrians.

The telephone is out of order so we can't make any contact with the outside world except by *jihaz*. Another fed-up day with a cold, although I still haven't written the 'in the event of my death' letter that we were all considering two nights ago, as it sometimes feels we will be very lucky if Amal let us out of here alive after this, with or without Syrian collusion.

22.3.87 Day 145 Sunday

Pauline struck down by flu, but had to struggle up to do an appendix operation with Dr Saleh, then back to bed. I too collapsed into bed with a cold, and heaped blankets on in an effort to get warm; fell asleep eventually to the clamour of Ben losing his contact lens on the floor of the dressing space, with many helpful grannies trying to find it for him. I then awoke to the sounds of heavy shelling every few minutes and, after three or four fell with people crowding into the clinic for shelter, I somehow reasoned that it wasn't going to stop and there would be injuries and got up. The kitchen was full of people, a granny had shrapnel in her arm and was led in, and the sleeping and dressing area filled with people as the shelling went on.

Then screaming and screaming started; Rifat grabbed the stretcher and ran out, and the screaming intensified, and women crowded up the stairs with the stretcher. I had cleared the table when the screaming started, and got the suction ready, yelling for the scissors which I couldn't find. The girl came in looking dead. I helped put the stretcher down, put in suction and the airway when Ben said she had a pulse, and blew after thumping her chest. We decided on immediate removal to the hospital, but as we took her out we noticed a huge pool of blood, but didn't know from where. Her eyes were fixed and dilated and she wasn't breathing, chaos followed, and I yelled to get them to turn the stretcher round so I could breathe her, but they ran off without letting me get in between the handles. They refused all the way to Fatima's, where I managed to breathe her a few times as they stopped to change.

Then I decided it was useless and ran up to the hospital at a stagger pace because of this bloody flu. Usually I can run up to the hospital purely on adrenaline (and fear), but today I sweated and had very wobbly legs, and could hardly speak when people asked me what was up. I staggered into the hospital where two minor shrapnel injuries were being seen by Pauline and Dr Saleh and Dr Atia. I gasped, 'There's another one, there's another injured coming on the stretcher; she's not breathing, she's nearly dead.' I tried to get them to clear her a space, but she came in just as I said this. They took her to the end bay and discovered that her skull and brain were terribly damaged. Her torn brain was hanging out of the huge fracture. I stood winded (with pain) against the wall and took the airway. They bandaged her head and then her family came in screaming, her father weeping. The doctors started an obligatory resuscitation on her for her family's sake. I excused myself as I knew there were more injured in the clinic, but Pauline called me to feel the extent of the girl's fractures. The whole of her skull was fractured into tiny little pieces like an eggshell on a hard-boiled egg, or crinkly paper in your hand: completely hopeless.

Big pools of blood outside the clinic. Then Ben showed me what else had landed: thousands of little one-centimetre cylinders, like bigger slices of steel bullets. No one could decide what these bombs were, some say B-10, others 107s. Then they found a base similar to the 107 bases at the *mahwar*, with the imprints of these deathly little cylinders still on them. We found about fifteen on the clinic stairs and in the rooms upstairs. Anti-personnel bombs, a new weapon, last seen in the Israeli invasion of 1982 when they were dropped from planes. It was figured that a shell fell every two to five seconds, a total of thirty or so shells in five minutes in our vicinity alone. Children and adults cleared the streets which were covered with steel rain. The shrapnel sound was this metal, raining all around us. Now they are destroying buildings all around us; it's becoming more and more like the early days of the war, as the fighting intensifies again.

We wrote another statement at the request of the DFLP and Dr Rede. Copies of our statements are circulated to DFLP people and offices also.

What will they do to us tomorrow? I really thought we were all going to die on the way to the hospital today.

23.3.87 Day 146 Monday

The black depressing mood is lifting. For the first time in four days, the tears have not come to my eyes, nor have I felt angry and hopeless. I know that all I needed to unwind and snap out of it was to do things to normalize my head. As usual it comes from frustration rather than from true despair, a hopelessness at being unable to be myself, and when I tried to start the reversal progress, I was always crowded out and it got worse. It wasn't helped by having flu and generally feeling unwell whilst having to continue as Ben was sicker. All I wanted to do was to lie down, read, write and listen to a cello concerto on the radio.

Haj Abu Taher again told us the story of Bourj being tents from the fifties until the 1960s, when zinc structures were built; the solid houses were only built after 1970, and then completely razed by the Israelis in 1982, and again by Amal since 1985.

Still burning the bookcase for fuel; lazing around coughing and sniffing, the smoke makes me cough like a dog.

24.3.87 Day 147 Tuesday

Pauline thinks I should have a chest X-ray when I get home. Query TB, or pneumonia that didn't show at first? Can you imagine, after all this, if we get out alive, now that we're planning our staged exit with lots of foreign journalists in attendance, to wind up with TB and being in isolation for several weeks – ugh! I hope not, although there's a lot of wet coughing and nothing coming up. It's made much worse by smoke or fires. Apparently internal shrapnel quite often sets off airport X-ray metal detectors, so we'll find out what type of metal I have in my arm when, or should I say if, we get to Cyprus.

Today the hospital came practically to a standstill as the motor finally gave up when the fan belt broke, so absolutely no X-rays, operations or sterilizing as no electricity of any kind.

Banan came back today. She forgot that she should run for cover when she sees Israeli aircraft in Saida, and had to be dragged to cover when they bombed the other day.

25.3.87 Day 148 Wednesday

The grinding monotony and harshness goes on. I feel disturbed by the cruelty of the domestic tension between men and women. I have no patience left for the brutal chauvinism and autocratic patriarchs masquerading as gentlemen, sitting all day in the sun doing *nothing* whilst the women clean, cook, wash, cook, wash, serve, serve, clean and risk their children's lives daily to bring in food. I've no patience at all with men who ask me if it is not *ieb* (culturally wrong) that women smoke, question their fathers and brothers, or make their own choices.

Today there is a demonstration of women outside at the Majnuk entrance, but although they called journalists to Majnuk, the Lebanese Army prevented them from taking photographs of the women and their protest over the repeated abuse and killings.

Visited Haweida and Abu Iyad, as they call her husband, in the hope that the baby will be a boy*. Drank coffee and was given new biscuits to take home with a few apples. Looked at her engagement pictures of a very pretty 14-year-old dressed in blue silky *lamé* and high-heeled shoes, and a handsome husband-to-be, cleanshaven, and both of them obviously besotted with each other; as they appear to be, although he looks a bit worse for wear with the war, wearing a beard and long hair.

A close friend has agreed to smuggle my diaries out of the camp to the

*Father of male children are given the honorific title 'Abu'.

safety of Mar Elias, and to try to bring the mail in for us. She's also going to get me a pair of shoes and sandals, I hope; they are so elegant here.

Pauline and Ben told me that the women's demonstration was reported on the BBC World Service with Jim Muir saying that he'd seen one woman being shot in the legs. It was also carried on Beirut's radio stations, and the PFLP fighters are being quoted again as saying twenty-one dead and over sixty wounded, instead of over fourteen dead and over forty wounded. Why exaggerate by thirty-three per cent? It's bad enough as it is.

26.3.87 Day 149 Thursday

A further wet day with some sunshine. Alternating with the weather there have been mortars every fifteen to twenty minutes since 10.00. Every so often Amal shell us in the rain as well as on dry days, trying to catch us out moving around in the wet. We think the reason is the big news coverage of the women's demonstration: impotent rage at a group of very brave women results in the shelling of the camp.

The Palestinians now refuse to evacuate any more positions east of Saida until *after* the sieges are lifted, as so far all these concessions have done is to provoke violence and mindless brutality. I hope the outcome of these meetings is more positive.

Returning from shopping, Fatima and Suhair were sent by the Lebanese Army to Saiqa from Majnuk, where they were touched and body-searched by Amal men, who found the gauze they were carrying wrapped around their stomachs. They were accused of carrying it for fighters and then heavily questioned about makes of weapons and the camp, before Amal took the gauze and fifteen packets of cigarettes. Then they were ordered into the camp and shot at with M-16s for trying to bring the gauze in. They were covered in mud by the time they reached the camp. They had had half the groceries tipped into the watery sand and had stood in the pouring rain and hail storm as they were searched.

14.00 It's true; three women and a 4-year-old boy have all been killed by the shelling of the demonstration. One woman has also been shot dead. That makes five dead and seven injured. The worst day of the war so far, but by now we are all so jaded that we can only speak in tones of numbed blank resignation. Abu Mohamad al Khatib and I exchange the news in matter-of-fact voices, as though that's the way things are. No more, no less. No grief, sorrow, shock or horror. And as though these are our own private deaths, as we know that all the foreign journalists were forbidden to come to the edge of the camp, so the killing and maiming, as usual, were perpetrated without witnesses. God – now we've become unshockable, even to the extent that the numbers fail to move us. I hope my diaries reach Mars Elias safely.

20.30 Well, they did arrive safely. The girls made a spectacular and wet entrance back into the camp. They brought two films and two sets of batteries for us, two pairs of small, half-moon earrings and a pair of sharpster 'Viennese' shoes and *letters*, *letters*, *letters*, *letters* from home. I went down in the rain clutching a cheese and lettuce sandwich and got the first word from home in over five *months*!! Pauline, Hannes and I read the letters from all the people in Britain who were sending money to MAP, and read and reread our families' letters, some of them two or three times, everyone reading in sequence. Looking at the photos of Ghillie, Ruth and Stewart – wonderful photos of Christmas and tales of snow ploughs and drifts, pictures of presents etc. They all think we need help!

Had tea with Lydia, who was at the demonstration banging on car bonnets and shouting on the airport road today, despite being nine months pregnant! She said the Lebanese Army warned the women that they were going to be shelled, but they refused to move, having stayed despite being shot at. When the first shells landed they ran for shelter and safety into the *mahwars*. She sat full and round, knitting and telling me the story. One shell killed two women at the bend in the road out of the camp where Amal thought they were all standing, and another fell on a house next to the hospital. There a grandmother, mother and daughter were all killed instantly – three generations wiped out. The man who died lost his four sons in the Sabra and Shatila massacres; one was just a baby, the others were teenagers, and then he was killed yesterday. The worst day of the war. I went with Pauline to photograph one of the women after she was washed and wrapped for burial. I felt terribly intrusive but took four photographs.

27.3.87 Day 150 Friday

Uneventful day with my cold still bad. As I settled to write, Pauline, Dr Rede, Ben and Brent Sadler, the ITN reporter, walked in. He got smuggled into the camp twenty-four hours after Dr Mohamad Ossman at Mar Elias camp said he would come, with the Lebanese journalist who'd been in a few days ago, and with a flak jacket that his TV company insisted he wear. There was a lot of confusion and Abu Musa are very put out that he had Fatah introductions instead of theirs and want to guard him all round the camp. Anyway we talked until 0.30 and then I took him up on to the roof to look at Amal on the street which was still partially lit up. He's sleeping now on the floor. He said we have to work on my speaking voice as it's too faint for broadcasting.

28.3.87 Day 151 Saturday

Got up at 5.30 and gave Brent a cup of coffee. Then I took him up to the roof to look through the little holes at the street and the Amal flag to get his bearings a little. Then we chatted to people in the square, Seeham and others waiting for the Lebanese journalist to appear. At 6.30 we gave up and went up to the hospital. The PFLP brought the journalist up and we looked at the house where all the women had been killed by the mortar two days ago, next to the hospital.

Then they started shooting film in the streets, including Ahmad Yaqub's grandchildren, and me and Nasmia chatting, and then we went on to Saiqa at 7.15. There was no road out, and I met Maryam Hallimi and her mother, Mirvat, Sitti Samira Mifli and others. We waited; Brent went to shoot elsewhere and missed the M-16 shooting at us and around us. Later Brent interviewed us about the situation in the camp.

29.3.87 Day 152 Sunday

Woken by a very fresh Brent and the Lebanese journalist who'd had a good sleep and wash and shave and looked bright; not kept awake by my cough and the cats all night. They wanted to film my arm again, so I wandered bleary-eyed into the square, and droned on about the 'scratch'.

I pottered around doing dressings, washing bandages and folding gauze, and Brent came back and filmed us all on the steps, from the top of the rubbish tip. I tried to write letters to Ghillie and Stewart, Mum and Dad. Then Pauline came with the tape recorder and we recorded messages for home, giggling and describing food; Ben and Dr Rede made messages to go out also. I finished my letters and we sat nattering on the stairs inside the clinic.

Sooha came in for an injection, Brent was crawling all over the clinic as usual for a picture, and the journalist was photographing, when Amal timed it well and dropped two bombs on the camp. We carried on. I gave Brent my seven films and tape of women describing what had happened to them with Amal, and a letter to the PLO press office in Cyprus; then they left us. Felt a bit flat.

Pauline looked at my bumpy ribs and thinks it may be a callus from a healing cough fracture. I should have an X-ray at home. I went up to find Dr Rede to see if Brent and the journalist had got out okay. They had been led to the edge of the camp, run through the sandhills and ruins and had immediately found the journalist's pre-arranged car waiting for them on the airport road. They'd gone directly to Mar Elias and *jihaz*-ed back to us that they and all the films had got out safely. Dr Rede looked elated, so was I. I ran back to the clinic as an explosion went off in the *mahwar* and told Ben and Pauline. We all breathed sighs of relief.

Brent had given Ben his contact lens solution, Pauline his big Duracell torch and batteries, and offered Lebanese money. Very kind and unassuming for a TV news reporter. He goes east and straight out of the country today. By now I hope he's in Cyprus. He told us that the BBC and the British ambassador had been making plans six weeks ago to rescue us, which would have been farcical as they'd have negotiated all the way to get us out and when they arrived we would have refused to leave! More farce from Beirut.

30.3.87 Day 153 Monday
No signs of the Austrians who are supposed to be coming in today. Watched Brent's film of the little girls being shot at by Amal as they came over the hills by the cemetery yesterday with gauze and bandages and medicines. It's very powerful as you see sand flying up as M-16 bullets shoot around them, on a bright sunny day. There is shouting and confusion and people go running out to fetch them in. It's brilliant that at last the journalists have got filmed proof. They all knew where and what was happening but had not been able to prove it. It's the same for Terry Waite. They know exactly where he is, even down to the room, but can't prove it. They even know who is interrogating him.

Pauline and I looked like complete zombies on film and the jokes are now about Estée Lauder gift sets, Jaegar clothes and health farms.

31.3.87 Day 154 Tuesday
Today started at 5.45 with me waking to the sound of chaos and shouting. I went up to the hospital to find that there was no electricity, since there was no *mazot* left to run the motor. So Dr Rede had called up lots of women, mostly middle-aged, to go to Mar Elias with twenty-litre containers to fetch the *mazot* from there. So for today there was no electricity, no sterilizing, nothing. I came back to the clinic, leaving them trying to negotiate with Amal and the Lebanese Army to let the women out of the camp. So far there was no road open. Back at the clinic I was faced by the usual load of impatient people, so in exasperation at having to repeat everything *ad nauseam* I got Ben's friend Hisham to write a notice explaining that as there was no motor fuel there was no electricity and therefore no clean gauze for dressings, perhaps tomorrow. At first he refused to put 'no' as he said everyone would be frightened, but I said they had better be frightened into trying to get some, somehow, into the camp.

Thinking about Brent's film constantly as we hope it may put pressure on the Syrians. There is also speculation that the Syrians may have to do something for their Incas people before April 20 in Algiers, the PNC meeting; they have let them rot so far, apart from Abu Fahdi, the leader in the camp, who has pointedly not been suffering with his people in this siege.

Pauline and I were called up to the Fatah office at around 17.00 to speak to journalists; we thought it was Brent on the phone from Cyprus and went up quickly to find two people sitting in Sultan's office: a tall young woman with curly hair, Marie Colvin, and a plump sweating young man called Tom Stoddart. They were full of London newspaper jargon and looked high on adrenaline and anxiety, having just come running into the camp.

They had met Brent in Cyprus. He was so excited that he eventually let slip where he had been. He said it was the most important film shoot of his life and if they could get in they were to try as it has to be told. 'The price here cannot be paid for in Lebanese pounds but in blood; the people here feel forgotten' – very well said. Marie and Tom had tried all ways of getting into the camp and had been told they could just walk in, but Amal either started shooting at them or threatened to shoot them in the back if they went a step further. Finally they did a deal with a Lebanese Army soldier to show them a road into the camp and look the other way, then take them back to Mar Elias where he would be paid. We took them round the camp, showing them the destruction and going to Mohamad Sahnini's house so they could take photos of his mother and Yusuf's baby, in a room with glass lamps, flowers and ribbons and family photographs.

We came back to the clinic with Dr Rede and a guide and arranged food from Um Mohamad al Ashwa and we cooked it up with eggs from Ahmad. Tom photographed everyone and everything that moved. Then we went for coffee with Haj, Hissam, Rifat, Shabati and Jalal. Haj was telling Marie that Hissam's brother Iyad's last words had been 'Shit for Arafat' just before a B-7 landed on the *mahwar* and killed him, when a huge flash and explosion of TNT went off. I clutched Marie's jacket and we all jumped – except for those hardened to it.

I had arranged with Abu Mohamad for Marie to sleep at his house; he invited us to tea, so we went over, and as Marie was tired they took her upstairs to sleep immediately. We found ourselves in a lovely self-contained first-floor apartment flat which turned out to be Mustafa's home. We were led through a sitting room, into a bedroom with a double bed and a small kitchen with shower and *hamman* just up a step from it. Um Mohamad said I should stay there every night, as she always does; she had decided I was staying that night anyway. Mustafa and Lydia prepared the room, bed and tea. They offered us nightdresses and when I accepted for Marie, Mustafa opened the wardrobe which was full of his dead wife's clothes, all still carefully wrapped and preserved with much love. He took out a long beautiful pink nightdress, then offered us a choice. I refused because he looked so sad as he took them out, and I felt too sad also.

Then we drank tea with Um Mohamad firmly wedged between Marie and me, giving us squeezes and laughing and holding our arms. I told Marie how she'd had eight children, despite doctors advising against it as she had a serious heart complaint. She ignored them and carried on, having her children – six boys and two girls. Borhan came back from the *mahwar* and sat next to Lydia and talked about the war. He had spent every night in the *mahwar* for the past five months and three days. Eventually at Abu Mohamad's and Mustafa's gentle chiding, Um Mohamad left and went to bed. We talked for quite a while until Marie said she had to sleep.

I told her how Gamili and Yassera bring food for twenty people as Um

Mohamad is too sick and Abu Mohamad doesn't like Lydia to go out now she's so heavily pregnant. And how Mohamad had his leg blown off in the last war, and has three young sons aged 7, 4 and 2, and a new baby, Hinnit, in this war. And how I used to see Iman running when she was very pregnant also. And how on late visits I used to find nine little bodies sleeping on the floor of the safe room, seven of the children rolled up like little sausages in blankets and the two little babies on beds with their mothers. And how Ibrahim and Mahmud both got shrapnel when they were sheltering on the floor and the 120mm exploded outside sending shrapnel through the shutters and into the wardrobe where it embedded itself. And of Mustafa's wife being shot. And Ibrahim jumping the boat from Cyprus as it was attacked by the Israelis with his friends and swimming back to the island off Lebanese waters. And Abu Mohamad leaving Palestine when he was 17 years old, thinking he was just going out for a short while before returning.

Then eventually we fell asleep, me crammed up against the wall and listening to bullets and explosions. I didn't tell Marie that four mortars had landed on the house and one on the house behind our window, as I thought it might frighten her. I woke with the usual coughing fit and fell asleep again.

1.4.87 Day 155 Wednesday.

Woken up at 7.00 instead of 6.00 by Mustafa coming in and saying 'Oh' that we were still asleep. It was a beautiful sunny morning with the cockerel near Fatima's house crowing. He pottered around his kitchen while we got up, dressed and folded the blankets.

Marie was anxious to be on the move despite her wish to see a Palestinian family, so we refused food and set off with Marie annoyed that we'd risen late and wanting to find Tom. His plan had been to go solo to photograph, instead of with a crowd. We met Ben and set off with Mustafa up to Majnuk to watch the women going out, Marie chafing to find Tom and stomping on up the road when Mustafa stopped to find out how many had been injured at the exit. She continued to march on up the road as greetings were exchanged, and both Mustafa and I signalled to each other that she may get shot doing that.

We reached Majnuk and she was really angry at having missed the women being shot despite the fact that Tom missed it also, as he was further up the road. Then we stood watching, as a woman tried to run back to the camp, all the while seeing traffic only a hundred metres away in the traffic jam on the airport road. So bizarre: we were surrounded by Amal and women were being killed, yet traffic jams were happening yards from us.

They next took us to Amliea. We went up to the first floor to look at a woman who had been injured previously. Then we got the shock of our lives, as there was a woman lying on the ground about fifteen metres away from us, just outside the exit gate. She was bleeding heavily and faintly moving her arms. All hell was breaking loose around us, as Tom and Marie tried to get photos and the story without being shot, keeping our heads down. (Like Tom photographing Pauline and me on the roof of Dr Wissam's paediatric clinic, which is now full of holes from tank and mortar shells.) We went down again, crawling along a narrow alley and sewage to get closer to her. They were all talking of how to rescue her. She'd been there an hour or more by the time we got her in. There were hoses, then ropes, and strings, then a Haji with a bad limp came by and tried to bring her in and look at her. Then there was talk of Kalashnikovs and bullets and how they'd return the cover fire, so we'd better get out of the way.

Then the screaming and the crying started as the two brave women, who had persuaded the men they should go and fetch her, brought her in. She looked dead when I got to her: dilated fixed pupils, blood everywhere, over her face and thighs. They ran on with her to the hospital.

We walked the long road to the hospital, in the sun and warmth and sand, with the smell of sewage starting with summer. I went into the emergency room and found Tom taking photographs, Marie writing, and doctors Rede, Atia, Nasser, Pauline, Salim and Mashur and the nurses trying to resuscitate her. Tom photographed me, fed up, covered in blood. He was upset and sweating.

Later we went to Saiqa, scrambling down to the front and then back to the clinic for final words and farewells. Photos of all of us at the hospital for Tom's mum. Then more kissing and we took them to the exit route. Pauline and I left to avoid Amal or the Lebanese Army perhaps seeing a big fuss. Tom and Marie looked very worried and scared. Hussein asked why were they going out at 13.00 *by that way*!!! We all worried and wandered around waiting for news. The PFLP girls tried to contact Mar Elias without success on the *jihaz*. We were worried as they had told us of the threats Amal were making to us, and felt anxious that the same might happen to them. Pauline and I agreed that death seemed nearer than ever again, but directly at the hands of Amal this time instead of by bombs. We discussed how they might take us, and what excuses they would make to the outside world for killing us. Then we decided that the tactic of intimidating us was working, so made resolutions to ignore it until it happened.

I slept at the clinic for three hours, exhausted with excitement; then back to the hospital for news, but still no word. Worried sick for them – they're both so sweet and unsafe. We worried and worried, thinking the films would be taken even though we calculated that they may get shot. We also worried that Marie might get shot as she's a woman and they may think she's Palestinian. We hoped it wasn't a trick.

News that Shatila has no water and they are drinking rain water collected in bomb craters and sewers; no food and children are reported to have died of starvation. We are very pessimistic as we feel there will be no intervention and once they kill everyone in Shatila if it has to surrender, then they will come here and kill all of us, Tal al-Zatar all over again.

2.4.87 Day 156 Thursday

Indirect word that Tom and Marie got to Mar Elias without problems; awaiting proper confirmation. Their safe exit to Cyprus is our last chance for international pressure to stave off the complete destruction of Shatila and perhaps Bourj. I don't care so much about Amal's threats to our lives but the thought of another massacre in Shatila is awful. God, I hope Brent's, Tom's and Marie's films and reports have some impact.

News that Shatila's Popular Committee has appealed to Gorbachev to intervene in Beirut as conditions in the camp are 'inhumane'. We hope for Soviet intervention: anything to stop this, to save Chris and Régine and everyone else in Shatila from being slaughtered. We are so frightened for them all; it seems that no one cares, no one will help and no one will stop it. Everyone here was running around in terror yesterday thinking that the *howens* we could hear being launched were coming here, until we heard them explode on Shatila as it was pounded again and again.

3.4.87 Day 157 Friday

Well, another exciting day! Noora Bustani, foreign correspondent of the *Washington Post* and *The Financial Times*, came into the camp with the women from Saiqa. Tom had got film of women being beaten at the Jalbout exit, but Noora, along with another woman, was put against a wall and the Amal man started to shoot around her feet. She got into the camp disguised by a scarf and thick tights and wearing a bulletproof vest – an essential part of a journalist's uniform here! She interviewed many of the women.

After meeting Noora at the clinic, I went off to sort out shopping lists with Fatima and arrived to find her curled up in bed sick, because her brother had hit her. He thought she and Intisar had been talking too loudly, so he punched and beat Fatima around her head, neck, ears and back, near her kidneys. Her eye and cheek were red and swollen, and she had pain behind her ear, neck and spine. She said he'd punched her, and she told him not to and hit him back and said he was weak to beat her, so he kept telling her to shut up. Salah, their friend, told him to stop and so did Fatima's mother who also hit him, and then took him outside the house. She is so miserable, she keeps praying to God to let her die. She feels that even if she escapes him to Mahmud's in Abu Dhabi she will not be comfortable there as she will be away from her mother. Her mother would like to leave him and go to Mahmud's also, but cannot and is frightened to leave Intisar, Waf'a, Shahina, Amné and Seeham alone with him as he beats them all. When one woman recently asked Fatima why she doesn't go out, she replied that if she saw a sniper she would ask him not to shoot her in the legs but in her head, to kill her. When I commented it would be better for all of them if her father were dead so the women could leave, she told me I couldn't know how many times she had prayed God to stop this misery. She feels that all her life she has been miserable and that she will always be unhappy and sad.

One supply truck got into Shatila despite shelling – *hurray*!!! Apparently Marie and Tom are safely out. Marie was so shocked by what she had seen that she got very drunk and was ordered out by *The Times* the next day – just as well. The UNRWA man tried to sell all his films for 50,000 Lebanese lira; his boss, the woman Pauline met, tried to sell the photos for 20,000 Lebanese lira and was only giving information to reporters for money! It's disgusting and completely despicable and I hope Noora succeeds in getting her fired. Noora's reports are to go out on Sunday, the same time as Marie's and Tom's. God, I hope this works, something has to.

4.4.87 Day 158 Saturday

Abu Mohamad al Ashwa went out of the camp yesterday. The Al Ashwa name is so renowned for being with Fatah that when they took Imad al Ashwa after the 1-month war, he was beaten so severely in the Amal jail that he nearly died from his injuries. Fatima's friend, one of the girls, went to get a passport to travel and when the man in the passport office found out she was Al Ashwa, he told her to get out of the office before he put her in prison.

Again the plainclothes man is selecting from a rooftop the women to be searched. This was confirmed by the woman who had the 75,000 Lebanese lira stolen. She was first searched for cigarettes, got past his check, then was told, 'You there, in the jacket, come and be searched,' and the money was taken. The next two women, carrying 13,000 and 20,000 Lebanese lira, were also signalled out, searched and the money taken. This is in spite of a deal with Amal of money already paid to let the women into the camp. The price to stop them shooting a woman is not known. No one injured today.

Called on Adnan's little sister Abir for her dressings. They had bought *fool* (beans) and lemon and gateau for me. It's so sweet of them as they have nothing at all; a very impoverished house, with this wonderful collection of bound books on a desk, very beautiful well-looked-after books. It was a bright sunny day and we wandered along the alleys with trees blossoming and the rubbish piles and sewers beginning to smell awfully. Blue sky over the ruins at Haiduce and that bombed-out street behind it, little puffy clouds in the blue, blue, safe sky.

Invited to eat at Borhan's; Mustafa's Lebanese friend Abed had come in, in the middle of the war, with bread and cigarettes from Mar Elias. The whole Al Khatib clan gathered and we ate; Mustafa had done all the cooking. We sat talking for two hours; revolvers and bullets on the table and babies being played with. Really I love them all very much. I went to fetch Fatima to join us; she is completely miserable and morbid at the moment, wanting to die. She refuses to pray now with Intisar; men say they are God, but the women hate men for the way they see them behave and so refuse their religion. Later we walked her back in the light of the crescent moon to her house of sadness.

5.4.87 Day 159 Sunday

Newspapers are now also banned from entry; the only paper allowed in, and bought, by forcing it on frightened women, is the Amal paper. So we have no idea of the impact of Tom's and Marie's stories in *The Sunday Times* or Noora's reports in the *Washington Post* or Reuters.

The Syrians were seen moving at Majnuk yesterday, and the sandhills are reported to be either being taken down or reinforced; no one knows which, although Amal reported via one militiaman that after April 15 things would be normalized from Majnuk. However, others fear that they are removing them in order to give the tanks a better position from which to shell the camp, or that they are heightening them for fear of shelling from East Beirut. The B-7 that hit the truck trying to enter Shatila apparently destroyed the foodstuffs; all the people got was the smell of burning sugar as the truck went up in flames. There was a wonderful BBC World Service report last night by a news correspondent none of us had heard of before, Tim Llewellyn. He expressed 'innocent outrage', as Pauline described it, declaring that Shatila is suffering terrible deprivation and the people are facing deplorable conditions, starvation and disease, and that Amal blew up a truck attempting to enter with relief supplies. He asked whether Syria had the will or the capacity to enforce the entry of supplies to the camp. Oh, we said, he must be new and he won't last long if he reports the truth like that. But he was immediately removed from my hit list of BBC correspondents.

On the 11.00 reports of the Sunday papers, I waited for mention of Marie's and Tom's reports; it was mentioned that either the *Telegraph* or *Times* carried a report that 'A British nurse working inside the camp of Bourj al-Brajneh has written to the Queen, asking if she can use her influence to gain entry by the ICRC to the camp.' Whoops, all socialist credibility blown! Pauline found it very funny, and so do I. So will Dad if he buys *The Sunday Times* this morning. I imagine it was *The Sunday Times* as Marie carried the letters out.

17.15 The trucks came in, six with food, blankets and clothes; just as winter finishes we finally get blankets. I went to watch them unloading. It's incredible when they enter the camp. It's like the scene from *Close Encounters* when the little beings send messages by music, then they finally land and come out of their spaceship and meet the people on earth. It's just

Top: Syrian troops parade in front of an Amal militia mural, with their logo top right.

Above: Devastated graves at Shatila Mosque after the 133-day war.

Overleaf: The red tracer bullets in the West Beirut sky at night.

The evacuation of Fatah fighters from Bourj al-Brajneh, 9 July 1988, prior to disarmament and being loaded onto waiting buses. Women and children surround their brothers, fathers, friends, cousins, fearing that they will be shot as soon as they have put down their weapons

Four hours later, after being kept outside Saida, they are finally allowed to enter the city.

like that when the big decorated six-wheel trucks come in to bring us things from outside. But today I did not feel the usual elation as, in my heart of hearts, I wished that these supplies had gone to Shatila. I did not want them to come to us. We can wait, Shatila cannot. But I guessed that they would come here, as psychological torture to the poor starving and diseased people of that devastated and destroyed camp. Today all I could ask was, 'Did they go to Shatila? Did they get into Shatila?' The standard answer was, 'Don't know, tomorrow, tomorrow.' How long do they have to wait for tomorrow? Do they all have to die before that tomorrow?

Sobhei Abu Arab got very enraged with Ghassan today, when Ghassan refused to let him in to see Abu Suhail, so he beat him up well and truly, then tried to shoot him before being stopped by others. Tonight Abu Suhail is making peace with everyone and Ghassan is recovering in bed. So if another journalist comes again and asks why everyone is carrying handguns, or has bodyguards, I can truthfully answer, so that they can shoot each other if they feel like it during an argument.

The Lebanese journalist sold his film for 3,000 dollars; he deserves it, and more. It was on LBC yesterday and today. A young boy came up to Pauline and told her he'd seen her on TV yesterday. One little girl came running up to me to tell me she'd seen me on Lebanese TV. I said 'When?' She said 'Now!' Jokes about fame abound, for example, 'You can't do that, she's famous,' or 'Shut up, you're famous at the palace,' etc.

Tim Llewellyn is still in the country and reported from the airport road that the trucks came into the camp, that the Lebanese Army and Amal are besieging us, that Amal are hoping they can take Shatila, that Amal are demanding half of everything that goes into the camps – as ever – and that the camp was bombed with mortars and rocket fire after the trucks left Bourj al-Brajneh: reported on BBC World Service at 20.15. Jim Muir tells us that we will have a ceasefire from 6.00 to 8.00 Beirut time at Bourj and Shatila. We heard that a big meeting in the Beau Rivage Hotel has produced this agreement. All we want, we agreed, is for food to go into Shatila, just that, no more for tomorrow. Suffering, starvation and disease – it's too much.

23.35 Well, the news of the ceasefire is being heralded by gunfire, bombs and a lot more gunfire by comparison with the past few relatively quiet nights. Today I moved downstairs at the first bullet in the nick of time with little Ahmad and Hannes, as our M-16 sniper opened up on both sides of the clinic for a while, bullets bouncing and whizzing overhead and cracking on the walls. *Ta, ta.* I still have an instinct about shelling which is good – I thought I might have lost it.

6.4.87 Day 160 Monday

Well, the ceasefire started at 8.00.

Supplies finally got into Shatila: five trucks from Kuwait with food, clothes and blankets, and the Syrians made a checkpoint to allow the women out for food, whilst Amal looked on. But one person was shot dead unloading trucks, and a woman and a boy were shot early in the morning here today, the boy at the *mahwars*, the woman coming into the camp at Saiqa. The Syrians and Amal still put the east of Saida condition on the lifting of the sieges of Shatila and Bourj. The BBC World Service falsely reported that medicine came into the camp at Bourj, but rightly pointed out that the admission of supplies to Shatila didn't necessarily mean an end to the siege. Good old Tim Llewellyn – his days will be numbered re visas for Beirut.

We are all so numbed by the fact that Shatila got food today, at last; we are just numbed by it, what else can I say? Food (and fuel from trucks, perhaps, to cook it on). Someone from the PFLP was killed unloading it. What can I say? Relief? Too numbed by suspicion to say anything else. No mortars today – yet – the first day of the war like this.

Venka at Mar Elias was *too busy* to send us our letters with Nadia. She says she'll do it on Saturday! Bloody hell, do they think this is a picnic?

Rumour is that Ben and Pauline are about to marry; Hisham's naughty sister told her not to wait, just make a baby now.

7.4.87 Day 161 Tuesday

The Syrians have gone into Shatila. They reached agreement to enter earlier today, and deployed in what is left of the camp. They are reported to have had an 'entrance welcome' by women and children crying *Allahu' Akbar* (God is Great) – in relief, I suspect. Several people immediately walked out of the camp to waiting relatives. I can't believe it all – after so long and such destruction, such a length of time; Rashidiyeh, Shatila, only us left now. They say that agreements may be reached soon to lift the siege here. The PNSF and Amal and the Syrians met to arrange it.

So today we waited and waited for the Red Cross, yet no Red Cross came. We waited outside, walked up to the PFLP office next to Samed and talked to a man who suggested that if I wanted a cross, I could draw one on the ground; then after pointing to the sand, walked off into the camp with his Kalashnikov slung at an odd angle over his back.

Quiet day, visiting, sleeping in the sun; went to sleep overnight at Banan's.

8.4.87 Day 162 Wednesday Ending

Spent last evening with Banan, Ghassan, Hanni, Samir, Abu Suhail and Noora. We sat with the new M-16s that Ghassan and surprisingly Samir also was carrying, which is very unusual for him. They had been acquired from the Lebanese Army, or I think stolen, to be more precise. Nice weapons from the elegance point of view as they are longer than the

Kalashnikov which looks quite stumpy in comparison. Gives them their high velocity, even the ghastly bullet is elegant.

We listened to news of Shatila on Radio Monte Carlo. After they had drunk cocoa and left, we went to bed and snuggled up like four little sausages on the mattress in the big room. Noora slept next door, now restored to its former glory of curtains and a long rug, turquoise blue couch, big covered matching chairs, swan-headed matching tables and a feeling of airy comfort.

I woke early thinking that it was daylight, as the light is left on all night. Then Noora called Juju and Mimo and they went out of the camp at 5.30.

Rumour of the Red Cross coming here and to Shatila today. Who knows? It's incredible to think that it's just stopped there. Just like that. As it did in Rashidiyeh. Just stopped.

19.35 Well – it's happened here too. It just stopped. We heard the ICRC were going into Shatila, then we heard that they were in Shatila. We heard that Venka and Elizabeth had also gone into Shatila; then we heard that twenty-three people had been evacuated from Shatila. At around 14.30 we heard an uproar that the Syrians were coming. The Incas leaders went marching through the inner streets, then all of a sudden the crowd cleared into many armed Syrian and Lebanese troops, some with helmets and the distinctive pink of the Syrian Army, looking distinctly nervous and glancing all around them. They quickly rounded the square and at Haj Abu Taher's went into Arsan's *mahwar*. One muttered '*ajanib*' as he saw Ben and me standing with Banan and others on the clinic steps. Then Arsan and Nawoosh went past, furious. According to reports, Incas did not consult Arsan. The Syrians went on into the front street and are now stocking up on weaponry there. I turned away from a photographer. No rejoicing like Shatila.

I asked Dr Rede for a job and he said, of course, I was welcome to come back any time to the Palestinian people.

17.45 Haider Juma, the Amal spokesman, says that the sieges of the Palestinian camps will continue until the Palestinians evacuate positions east of Saida. General Ghazi Q'anan says the war of the camps has ended. Amal and Palestinians involved in clashes near Magdoushe. A convoy of Amal weapons transited through Saida with a twenty-Syrian escort. Pauline still waiting in Haifa in case the ICRC come, which they didn't, being bureaucrats. Lots of reporters came for example, *The Sunday Telegraph*, and others with radios and big microphones.

BBC World Service at 20.00, Tim Llewellyn: 'Amal refuse to let in medicines and have physically assaulted journalists. Amal doesn't like it; its fighters are angry at and frightened of the Palestinian guerrillas.' More ambulances are to go into Shatila tomorrow. Films and equipment were confiscated from journalists at Shatila as the Syrians and Amal claimed they would use them to make Palestinian propaganda! People in Shatila are very thin, like we were.

Ran up to the hospital as promised for coffee with Ghaleb, who is going out with the ICRC if they come, to Saida then Cyprus, then to a good hospital for a bone graft operation. He's sweet; so is Haj who came with Rifat to carry all three water containers back to the clinic for me. Electricity at the hospital now from 19.00 to 23.00 each night.

Got a beautiful card from Rafiq via London; he expects to be detained in Jordan for at least a year. Also had anxiety letters from Ghillie, and funny ones from Mum and Dad and Pohsie. Pauline had messages from Tom and Marie to say they were safe; my letter to the Queen has been published!

22.00 The BBC World Service correctly reported that there were no scenes of rejoicing at Bourj as there had been yesterday in Shatila. Perhaps we weren't hungry enough. We are said to have looked thin and starved after a long siege and many residents are reported to have stayed indoors; the welcome to the Syrian troops was restrained.

Haj came in and said that he was very frightened by the fact that the Syrians were here, and he did not like it one little bit, nor the Syrians either. Saw Mustafa earlier looking anxious, especially when the Syrians arrived. At first we thought they might be rounding up Fatah leaders and were very worried.

9.4.87 Day 163 Thursday The end

The new doctor arrived today, Alberto Gregori, of Italian origins, from Greenock. Born and bred in Scotland, bilingual in Italian and English and trained at Glasgow University, finishing in 1982. He worked in Zimbabwe in a field hospital for six months. He's spent the last two weeks working in Saida at Ain al-Helweh. Says Kirin is back for a year and is doing magnificent work teaching there.

The Israeli helicopters and gunships bombed pro-Syrian Palestinian positions east of Saida today, killing two and injuring six people. Incas and Abu Musa forces went to Saida to supervise the withdrawal of positions tonight.

Sat on the roof as they cleared up the camp, then I went to Borhan's *mahwar* as I wanted to see the Syrians. Haj took me down there and Borhan invited me to sit down. So we sat still, then we'd stand up and peer round, like all the others who were standing up on the roofs, even the hospital had people standing on the roof. Washing was hung out again on the rooftop washing lines. We are somewhat dazed by it all, no guns, everyone in training shoes and spending time with the Syrians, who were boredly combing through the rubble for copper from bullets, and watching Amal men and civilians picking through destroyed shops for silver. They also take the electric wires and old copper from bullets to sell – looting.

We sat first with a Syrian lieutenant and then with some soldiers. There are no Lebanese Army soldiers, only conspicuous Syrians as the Palestinians refused to have any 6th Brigade Lebanese Army deployed around the camps. The Syrians have strong accents and are very uninterested in foreigners. Borhan and I giggled like children as I asked him if they spoke English. 'Speak English? They are animals!' He looked at me, and I laughed and slapped his hand. Then we giggled more as I described our future plans and we made anti-Syrian jokes. Forty-seven people were evacuated and I went to the edge of the camp to watch them leave, looking at the traffic and the grass and all the buildings Amal used to shoot us from. Afterwards lots of Syrian force-walked us back into the camp, all photographed by Ben somehow from the top of a big lorry.

Afterwards we ate chicken, rice and yogurt, with doctors Nasser, Rede, and Atia, and Ben, Hannes and Abu Kamel who supplied the food. Dr Atia let slip that some 'busy' people might be coming today. I guessed it might be Øyvind and then he appeared at the door, with a big bearded Italian, and gave me a crushing hug that hurt the rib fracture, but we all shrieked with joy. Then Amal the nurse appeared, who we all thought had been killed at the beginning of the war, and another lovely nurse also, plus a tall doctor. Then we all talked at once for about half an hour, when his driver came to take him away. He said he would ask permission to stay the night and sped off to the Syrian headquarters with screeching wheels in a fast, big, yellow Mercedes. I walked to the edge of the camp, but he didn't reappear, so I guess the Syrians didn't give him permission.

I waited sitting on stone and sand at the end of the camp. Dr Rede came and gave me a piece of orange peeled and cut. We both watched and waited a little while then left again.

I went to the cemetery for the first time in over five months. I looked first at the temporary burial ground behind the PFLP-GC office, then went into the big one filled with new graves. Heaps of sand and stone, hardly marked, yet the old cemetery has bloomed and is blossoming like a wild, colourful overgrown garden. I stood looking at all the grieving women and for the first time tears came to my eyes about death here. The futility of death, the senselessness of the deaths here. I stood looking at Hissam's brothers' graves; both had died within a week of one another almost a year ago. Mustafa came into the cemetery with a little girl of about 2½ or 3 with a red bow in her hair. He was holding her hand, and they walked over to a grave and sat down.

I sat on a pile of gravel talking to a girl who was there to mourn all the dead. From under my foot I picked up a pair of fluid-stained, discarded rubber gloves used for removing bodies from the temporary graveyard to the cemetery. I picked them up absentmindedly, twiddling them, then realized what they were and threw them away.

I got permission to take Alberto to the *mahwar*, so we clambered around the ruins of Borhan and Marrubba's *mahwars*. Someone asked where Alberto was from. We decided Italy and one non-English-speaking man said, 'No, he's not. He sounds the same as Suzy.' Very sharp, for a German-speaking Palestinian.

We crawled and clambered around ditches and saw what had happened to Marrubba *mahwar*. The sniper trenches are all full of water, and there is a pond of water now with a wrecked car floating in it and grass sprouting everywhere.

Alberto had had meetings with Nabih and Madam Berri. He was sent from Ghazi Q'anan to them. They uttered the famous statements:

1 They did not need foreign doctors in Bourj or the camps.
2 The supermarkets in the camps were fully stocked and open.
3 All supplies were getting into the camp, including medicines etc.

Madam Berri said that she'd like to let him come into the camp, but as it was all propaganda, he might be used by the Palestinians for their own ends. Alberto replied that if she let him into the camp and the supermarkets were open then he'd come back out, say it was indeed propaganda and bring her back a Mars bar! Berri said it was all lies and propaganda. Yet the press tried for over five months to get into the camp; and the Associated Press woman tried to get into Shatila yesterday and was beaten up by the Syrians and Amal.

I met Mustafa on the road with the little girl in his arms. He stopped to speak and I asked if she was his daughter. He said she was, and I asked if she could talk. 'Not a word, not a word.' My Arabic was awful today. Then he smiled as I walked off and said, 'Really, she does speak.' She was very quiet and he looked so right with his child in his arms, instead of lonely, sad and empty.

Pauline is talking 200 to the dozen about surgery with Alberto, eagerly brainpicking, talk, talk, talk. MSF have got 200,000 dollars from the EEC, in a blaze of publicity. They may come back with a neurosurgeon and a plastic surgeon. Hurray! The new anaesthetist went to Shatila today.

10.4.87 Friday

Woken again earlyish by Pauline and insomnia, both of us not sleeping very well now that peace and calm has sort of returned. I went out for water and stayed half an hour at Um al Abed's to pick it up with Alberto and Pauline. Drank tea, went to Fatima's, arranged Hannes' birthday party and then wandered about on the roof, gazing again in disbelief at

Jaloul, Haret Hreik, Ain al-Ruwais, Balbekeyeh, unable to understand any of it. Later I took Fatima's mother up to the hospital and waited with her until Pauline and Alberto came down, he with a plaster on his head having collided with the iron window shutters on the way to the hospital.

Went to Fatima's for Hannes' birthday party. There was a beautiful birthday cake with candles all over it, and we gazed and gazed at it in wonder and nostalgia for normality. Waf'a, Seeham and their friend ate with us, then Pauline, Ben and I left and put on more makeup, clothes and perfume and went up to the hospital *haflé* (end of war celebration party) at 21.00. Over an hour of speeches by every department and lots of letting off steam and clapping and smiles of relief and disbelief. Then Nadia shimmering and dancing, and dancing and shimmering: she is said to be the best traditional dancer in the camp. More clapping, chaos and the Palestinian version of mayhem set in. Everyone drinking Pepsi or Miranda juice, eating cake, talking, giving speeches, taking photos or videos. Doctors Saleh, Nasser, Salim, Rede and Atia were all behaving like boys; Nasser, Rede and Atia are going out tomorrow morning.

Very tired and exhausted. Feeling strange.

Mustafa surpassed himself by shooting at me. I don't think he saw me as he fired his revolver at the clinic wall and the hot bullet bounced over and landed at my feet. I found the cartridge case and threw it over and hit him with it, saying, 'Sorry, it's warm.' He came in shortly afterwards to tell me, 'Thank God you're still alive,' and to say that he didn't realize there was still a bullet in the upper chamber. I asked was he trying to kill me after all this war? He said something I didn't understand and, when no one could explain, he said, 'Here six months and you still don't understand Arabic,' so I pushed him out of the door of the clinic. Cheeky mad idiot. I shouted later to Borhan that his brother was trying to kill me, he'd shot at me. Borhan laughed.

11.4.87 Saturday

Imad al Masri is still dreaming of new legs from a leg transplant or a bionic leg graft; mad raving delusions. He wanted to get his gun to shoot the Syrians when they entered the camp the other day, screaming to be put in his chair, to be given his gun to do this.

Dr Atia's love letter to his wife on her birthday included descriptions of Amal's lack of Islam and barbarism and brutality. Amal took it from the woman he sent it with and gave it to Sheikh Cabalan who enquired, 'Why does Atia write these things? We have done nothing to him.' Atia replied, 'Nothing! Do they think that by maiming and killing my people, and maintaining sieges on all the Palestinian camps in Lebanon, that they have done nothing to me?'

Waited all day to see Doctors Saleh, Nasser and Atia off, but after eating breakfast with them and waiting, Liz Sly of *The Sunday Times* arrived to say goodbye as she's off to the States. We went up to the roof of the hospital which I'd been on earlier with Alberto, past all the staff cleaning the hospital and taking down the sandbags, leaving a red carpet of sand everywhere along the corridors, but letting *so much* daylight into the rooms for the first time in over five months. It was odd, and feelings of relief swamped all of us, so that much shrieking and yelling went on up and down all the staircases. Salim and the little nurses were dragging sandbags upstairs and laughing, singing and clapping every time someone came up or down the stairs. Smiling, smiling, everyone smiling, reflective and anxious smiles at the hopes for an end to the war. We clambered over the remains of the second floor, finding pieces of B-10s, tank shells and mortars, and looking where the wires for the wall had come up to protect the original wall that now no longer exists.

Later we went back to the clinic and up on the roof. There we looked at the moon and at East Beirut, at the lights sparkling and glowing like diamonds on the mountains, the layers-of-cake lights of the presidential palace at Baabda, and all sorts of golden jewels sparkling mightily, while we had sat in the dark void of mortars, destruction and fear before, and now in wariness.

Swee Chai Ang came in and brought with her letters she'd written to President Assad asking for his help and protection. So we now have Syrian guarantees to get out and be escorted to Mar Elias in safety. Dr Rede told Swee Chai that I could work for Hilal (PRCS).

We got a message to go to Borhan's, so we went and sat for a while at the edge of the *mahwar* round a fire. We were joking about being the sinking ship that had sunk, and Dr Rede said he would be the last to leave, with us. I said good, because then I wouldn't miss him, which I felt I might if he had gone out before us as we had been expecting him to. He's very sweet.

Borhan's friend Khaled came back from Saida and crept into the camp from near the cemetery. Borhan stood waiting and watching from behind a clump of flowers, closing them every time a car approached. He is going out to Saida for two days soon, and admitted to having been back shooting with a *doshka* the day after he fractured his clavicle.

I went up to the cemetery again in the dark and saw the mosque at the corner on the airport road brightly lit up once more like a fairground, and the Syrians with lights near Majnuk. All this electricity and we have none still: all the Syrian points have electricity. I knelt in the sand and cried and cried at the senseless, evil waste. Then I got frightened by two PFLP-GC who'd followed me and sprang up from a roof to see that I was all right, asking why I'd come alone; was I running away or going out? I walked, still crying a little, back to the clinic. The *Newsweek* journalist had gone. Did some dressings. Very tired, some bombs and shooting around about. Ate seeds and sweeties with Ahmad and Salah, who since becoming thin in the war now looks very uncannily similar to Mohamad, just as little Fahdi now looks similar to Fouad. How do they grow to resemble their dead brothers so quickly?

12.4.87 Sunday
A day verging on tears and farewells even though it is only for six weeks. Fatima told me she was crying whenever she sat alone, and had tears in her eyes, as I did looking at her. She says she's praying for six weeks to fly, as I will.

Cleared the medicines out of the shelves and took them back to the pharmacy. Went to Banan's to escape Khadija who finally turned up for work and did practically nothing. Got summoned from a meeting with Abu Suhail, Ghassan and Samir to see a reporter. It was Halla from Reuters. The *Independent* wants to print our story tomorrow; they can't wait until we get to London – a scoop, I suppose. I talked about the hunger, the mutilations, the children, and then made tea, and a whole party of Banan, Fatima, Haj, Hissam, Salah, Ben, Pauline and Alberto turned up.

Then I went down to wash trousers and clothes, picking up 500mm bullets and having a shrapnel-on-the-roof competition with Haj Abu Taher, counting who could see the most mortar holes.

All reports of our evacuated patients are the same. Nothing good is happening to them in the private hospitals; Beirut medicine should be ashamed to call it medicine; non-practice of medicine is more apt.

Went to Ahmad Yaqub's and got a bottle of maple syrup and earrings from Mona, Fatin, Little Ahmad and Majda.

Back to pack. Banan and Ahmad Aishey turned up, with Fahdi and Ibrahim al Khatib. We all sprayed ourselves with Nina Ricci 'L'air du temps' which Banan brought for me. Dr Rede brought me and Hannes our Samoud steadfastness money: 5,000 Lebanese lira which will help pay for East Beirut.

Mancini, the Italian ambassador, is coming to get us out at 10.00 with Swee Chai Ang tomorrow and after an hour's stop at Mar Elias will take us east; two days in East Beirut or straight to Cyprus. Better than Grey who said he would meet us at the British consulate in West Beirut and wanted Alberto to go home when he learned he had dual British/Italian nationality!

When Mohamad al Khatib heard I was going tomorrow, he said not to go; this was my home, not the clinic but the Al Khatib house which I was to return to.

Two wedding parties today and more planned before Ramadan.

13.4.87 Monday
I'm writing this on the boat from Jounieh to Larnaca in Cyprus.

Got up at 5.50, washed and made tea, after sleeping on the veranda. I had had a coughing fit at Banan's and left after lying awake for an hour;

came back to the clinic at 1.50 and lay on the balcony with the cat, reading *Wuthering Heights* in the wind and rain by candlelight until I fell asleep at 3.15.

Laughed with Alberto about 'holiday package siege deals' and 'special offers' on death threats; went to the cemetery where the men were up early digging the graves, and then on to Fatima's for breakfast. Luckily Alberto kept our spirits up and even Fatima stopped crying for a while.

Packed and went up to the hospital, then out to the gate to wait and wait. We finally left the camp at 12.30 in total chaos, having waited from 10.00. There was a hold-up because one of the wounded who had been transferred outside had died and arrangements had to be made to bring his body into the camp for burial. Syrians came and went, trucks, bulldozers, jeeps, guns and soldiers, telling us to get out of the way. Eventually Swee Chai came and then we had chaos over luggage, which we had to carry right up to the airport road! The first car was too small for it. The driver of the next car (Colonel Walid Hassanato, the Syrian Intelligence Chief for Palestine) was rude to Dr Salim who had no papers, and then said he was going to Shatila to get Chris Giannou out, so we changed cars for the second time. Confusion about whether the drivers were Syrian or Amal, or even Palestinian! Chris refused to leave Shatila as he had had no warning about his evacuation, but the rest of us reached Mar Elias, the Christian Palestinian camp.

After lots of argument and bureaucracy the British ambassador's two Range Rovers, one four-ton Jaguar, and a few soldiers with sub-machine guns turned up, fussed us into cars, and took us over the Green Line at the museum crossing into East Beirut. No problems at all, unlike the Syrians raking through Ben's belongings. Went to the embassy fortification/art gallery: two Raoul Dufys, a Wilkie, a Poussin, Turkish and Persian carpets, Syrian pearl-inlaid mirrors, etc. Met the ambassador's Cypriot wife and 16-year-old Marlborough-accented son, safeguarded from the civil war in the big soft pudding house. Ate very well: chicken, rice, soup, salad, profiteroles, oranges – all silver service – and wine and coffee. Then left for Jounieh.

Lots of press attention, the BBC calling us from Cyprus, press in Mar Elias, photos for LBC. Talked with Christian Lebanese Forces as we waited for the boat to leave; young serious men, talking of Christianity and whether life is normal in the camps. No! All the people were herded back into the camp at gunpoint by the Syrians today.

Very tired; cognac to sleep. Woken at 4.40 by a steward asking about the cabin key which had to be handed in; at first I completely misunderstood and thought he was muttering about Fatah and Abu Nidal, etc, until he spoke in English.

Awoke with my name and Pauline's being called over the tannoy in different variations, followed by Hannes' and Ben's with a selection of prefixes and suffixes, so we staggered down to pick up our passports and discovered that 'someone' was waiting for us and we were to go straight off the boat. We wanted a cup of tea and coffee to rid us of the first beer and cognac dehydration in six months. No such luck. We were herded up to our cabins to collect our baggage and straight off the boat, no duty-free allowances or even five minutes to eat, or even a message to ask the people meeting us to wait a while. Awful at 6.20 in the morning.

14.4.87 Tuesday Cyprus

Brent, Chris Drake of 'Breakfast Time', Tim Llewellyn and other press met us off the boat in Larnaca; we skipped customs and emigration and had coffee with the port authority chief, escaping the press until one hotel, where the next four and a half hours consisted of no breakfast, coffee or anything else, just an endless series of radio links and television interviews, with me refusing to do radio or TV link-ups with Mum and Dad, and Brent telling me to swear every three seconds and then they wouldn't use it on TV.

After a day of rushing round and coping with the press, we went to the Hilton with Brent for a drink. He bought two bottles of champagne which made us giggle a lot, while he told us the hair-raising story of how he and the Lebanese journalist left the camp, scrambling to the edge, guided by following the tail-lights of cars on the airport road. Finally they made a run for it across the road and the journalist stopped the first car going out of town. In the car Brent asked him in English what they were going to do; they both jumped out at the Ouzai road. The driver was an Amal sympathizer and went straight to the Amal office and said that he had sand in the back of his car from a foreigner. Amal immediately patrolled the camp area, catching two other men hiding in the long grass waiting to make a break for it, and beat and tortured them.

As Brent and the journalist made their way to Ouzai, Brent worried that his white foreign face in the headlights of cars would get him kidnapped or killed. Then he got 'roaring drunk' on Scotch, which he normally doesn't drink, and went into hiding in a basement for twenty-four hours with a hangover, before escaping via Jounieh. The journalist was arrested and is now under threat. After the champagne, Brent left for Jounieh again on the 22.00 boat to go and sort him out.

This is being written with Brent's pen. Throughout the 6-month war, eighteen women dead, fifty injured in fifty-two days; 135 dead and 880 injured in 163 days.

Slept relatively well in our North European holiday complex hotel, after removing an awful picture of a rustic amputee shepherd and his straying flock under a pastoral tree. The other grazing amputee was left over Hannes' bed as he could cope with its awful reminders of Death from Bergman's *Seventh Seal*. I could not. A horrific nightmarish painting to be hanging in the seventy-seven holiday bungalows above the 229 beds in the 'Rashid Karami' hotel, as we called it.

15.4.87 Wednesday On the plane home

Watching the moon over the Alps, shining white and luminous, like a blob of white paint from one of the Impressionists, over a pale pastel pink and blue icing sky, near the Alps of Switzerland, Austria or Germany – even Hannes can't tell which alps are which.

The press jamboree went on and ruined what should have been a nice day. We pottered about town, gazing in wonder at everything from the sun to the blue sky, palm trees, cars, motorbikes, people with very smart holiday clothes, naked grannies in topless teeshirts and shorts, and an old ruin in the midst of some very nice and clean landscaping. All very pretty and the kind of place we would immediately have checked out of if we had had the choice.

Too cold to swim in the sea, so Pauline and I swam in the pool. My fracture hurt a lot and my chest is still tight. We applied headlice shampoo when we came out and dripped with wet hair for a PRCS video.

Went out to eat, slept two hours, went to the airport, avoiding the press for only five minutes, and then on to the plane, where we ditched the *Standard* man who kept pestering us, with the help of the cabin director who seated him in the back cabin.

Slept one hour on the plane; woke up with diarrhoea. Got a pair of British Airways socks given to us – grey for refugees.

16.4.87 Thursday

Reluctantly landing in London, like recalcitrant children being brought home to heel. Can't be bothered with all this. They want us on breakfast TV tomorrow. Another sleepless night. Ugh to the press crowds, ugh to them all. Funny how I always get diarrhoea on planes . . .

PART THREE
The Fall of the Beirut Camps

Introduction to Part Three

In the summer of 1987, Dr Swee Chai Ang and myself returned to Bourj al-Brajneh camp. Following the threats made during the 6-month war, it was not thought safe to come back any earlier. The devastation caused by the length and ferocity of the war made the subsequent resumption of the partial siege of the Shatila and Bourj camps unbearable for many of their inhabitants. The situation was especially difficult in Shatila which, throughout its last year of existence, was subjected to a siege of almost unbelievable intensity, with military attacks on the camp population nearly every day. Many inhabitants of Shatila were killed. Chris Giannou remained until the siege was finally lifted in January 1988 as a gesture of solidarity with the Palestinian Uprising begun one month previously.

In January 1988 I visited the Occupied Palestinian Territories as an observer from the Scottish Trades Union Congress, where I continued the diary. There I heard the slogan 'From Ballatta to Beirut, one people shall be free!' It became, to quote Charles Richards of The Independent, *'a recitation of hope', heard from the mouths of Palestinians under occupation and in exile.*

Subsequently, I travelled back to Beirut to witness the lifting of the sieges at Shatila and Bourj al-Brajneh, including Chris' safe departure. At the time I also thought I would witness the peaceful rebuilding of the camps. How wrong that was.

This final section of the diaries, written in the summer of 1988, records the complete destruction of Shatila camp and the bombardment and eventual fall of Bourj al-Brajneh. What the Israelis, the Syrians and Amal had all failed to achieve – the destruction of the Beirut camps – was finally brought about by Abu Musa's pro-Syrian Palestinian faction, a grouping which remained outside the PLO after the 1987 Algiers Palestine National Council meeting which had seen the reunification of many of those previously with the Salvation Front.

6.6.88 Monday
The car is refused entry to Bourj airport road checkpoint, the Syrian soldier claiming new orders so I get out and walk into the camp leaving the bag with Ahmad in the car. All appears normal except new sandbags at the front of the camp and the Syrian checkpoint, but after passing the PFLP-GC office and shouted greetings, normality disintegrates. The dental clinic has been blown to bits and the newly painted ice cream shop's mural is in tatters with chunks of twisted metal hanging off the remnants of its simple camp-style ironwork. There is a huge bomb crater in the middle of the road and sandbags erected on oil drums block the way to Samed. The place is deserted, rubble and dust everywhere, just dust and flies buzzing in swarms. Deserted. Like a camp after a massacre in the bright sun, like a camp under curfew. The hospital gates are locked and the Pepsi shop on the corner is blown away and gutted.

At this point I felt totally frightened after finding the streets empty, and had that lost feeling of panic, with no alternative but to continue; I couldn't retreat except to the Syrians and therefore had to keep on going down into the camp. Several men with Kalashnikovs and M-16s were sitting at the hospital entrance, and I asked into the darkened emergency room of voices in the gloom if there were any problems on the road down to the clinic. They replied 'No', it was deserted and the road was safe, so I set off gingerly for the clinic, at the same time trying to make the most noise possible, clacking my heels all the way down the road to signal that a woman was approaching. Terrified, I got from the hospital through roads empty of sand and people as far as Fatima's house on the first corner. By the time I got to the Al Ashwas' shop there were people on the streets.

Met Dolly, Ahmad *et al*, safe and sound, thank God. Of the ten dead, most are Munshaqine/Abu Musa 'mutineers'. I found the clinic still in one piece with the beautiful roof garden. Sniping and shooting around the clinic later, plus one hand grenade. This was explained as people cleaning their guns and firing off a round once the gun was released.

Talked with Dolly, Ahmad and Tha'ir about the 'war of the Fridays', as this is called. A ceasefire is in progress, although the Camps' Popular Committee delegation did not enter Bourj. Later I went to the hospital where I was shown the site of the first explosion, TNT set against the inside wall of the physiotherapy room.

Head nurse Salim explained how Salah deliberately sabotaged the new X-ray machine, as an attempt to demoralize the camp, and how they will have to use the old one. He has since left. Doctors Ighlas and Nasser are outside the camp, despite Ighlas being supposed director of the hospital; she is issuing the orders from outside. The pharmacy has been closed for several days since a hand grenade was thrown inside the hospital. Many of the nurses are too frightened to enter the camp to come to work; yesterday Salim had ten, now he has just two. There is one surgeon, Dr Barjat, who has been on duty alone for twenty-one days, plus two GPs from outside. Many of the wounds are infected, and Salim asked me to send for one surgeon with good general skills and replacement nursing staff. The surgeon is the priority. The hospital is where the fighting often starts and the road is being deliberately bombed. So now a longer 'safe' route has to be used for the wounded.

I telephoned Mary to relay to Swee in Amman Sultan's 'urgent' message: tell Swee that her papers are ready at the airport arrival desk, and to divert to Beirut if possible as the situation is the same as during the 1- month war. Call her driver and come direct to where Suzy is.

I slept on the floor downstairs at the clinic. Dolly, Looi, Tha'ir and Ahmad were still sleeping upstairs. Earlier Dolly had shown me pictures of injured people being treated on the floor of the clinic. One man was very dead with his eyes practically forced out by the pressure of being hit by a B-7. There was a cat with its head completely severed by shrapnel and masonry, which was thought to be Yaq'ub until he was found drinking from the sewer tonight, more crazy than ever from the bombing. Cleo is pregnant again, filthy from living wild and quite scrawny.

7.6.88 Tuesday

Woke at 8.00 and treated patients with Dolly, Tha'ir and Ahmad. Many people are leaving the camp with their belongings. The Al Khatib house has been blown to pieces as a result of deliberate targeting by the Munshaqine from the sports stadium outside and the mountain. Mustafa's house is in pieces, as is Mohamad's, Borhan's and Ibrahim's, all wrecked and destroyed.

Dr Salim had run out of the camp as the fighting started, but appeared to be spending the night inside as he visited twice, with Mohamad the X-ray technician in tow. Hussein, one of the Lebanese from the ICRC, came in and asked us for a list of requests. We asked for everything we could think of, down to body bags to use as sandbags; we have no sandbags as yet as they are still sewing them, having run out of supplies. Hussein said everyone now expects huge trouble regarding East Beirut. There was a bomb in the Ouzai road near a Syrian checkpoint at 16.00 today; Dolly and Bassam heard the explosion: three dead and fifteen wounded. I was asleep for three hours and missed it. Nothing today except the odd shot and reports of people still constructing sandbags around the camp. Sent Swee another telex via her husband Francis that there are two demarcation lines, one at the top, one at the bottom of the camp, nurses and doctors request relief. Will send one out with Dolly tomorrow too.

Looi went out today for a rest; we walked her to the checkpoint and got a detailed description of the ear infection of the Syrian soldier. I promised him medicine tomorrow. I heard how an ex-friend from early *rauda* days stood at the Syrian checkpoint saying which person was from Abu Ammar and PFLP, then denouncing them all as they tried to leave the camp. Seventy-five per cent of the camp has left to go to safety. I saw Suhair leaving with crockery, etc, in a cart 'for a few days'. A young boy in a political T-shirt tells me: 'We forget to think of Palestine now – forty years and now we have left it. Palestinian people are stupid.'

There is the same military plan as the camp wars: more than 150 fighters from Abu Musa have been brought into the camp; originally there were only sixteen. Some are school students from Tripoli. It was meticulously planned to start on May 10, and in fact started the day before, the commemoration of the Syrian-inspired Abu Musa mutiny against Yasser Arafat five years ago.

8.6.88 Wednesday
Papers taken when the Abu Musa offices were dynamited show records and files on every Fatah member in the camp: their houses, ages, wives, whether their wife is susceptible to conversion to the Abu Musa cause or not. They also indicate that this war was planned to start on May 10 with instructions from the Munshaqine leaders to remember their glorious uprising in Tripoli 1983.

19.25 My trousers are vibrating with the pressure of B-10s going out. The whole camp is reverberating to B-7s, B-10s, 500mms, M-16s and mortars. 'The first time the fighting has restarted with bombs,' says Ahmad. It all started just as we were waiting to listen to news of Arafat meeting Assad in Algiers. Rabir aged 7 starts crying with fright and wanting to go home; we try to keep him in the clinic with us. Tariq then runs off home with him slung over his shoulder. A young fighter runs in pale and sweating; he can't get to Slieme because there are snipers on every road and door to the *mahwar*. He sits still sweating; Looi gets him a tissue and his colour comes back slowly. Tha'ir insists that he puts his safety catch on as the Kalashnikov is pointing at him; the boy takes the clip off and counts the bullets. Another man runs in also sweating from heat and adrenaline, and sits to have a cigarette, moved away from the oxygen by Tha'ir. He and the boy debate whether to leave together, but stay a little while longer to smoke. Door and room vibrate with the B-10 launching. Ahmad goes out despite our protests. Mortars dropping. We sit listening to shrapnel falling. The boy goes out, stands, loads a bullet into the barrel, listens and runs out into bullets and shrapnel all around us.

The boys in the camp want the fighting to stop for the sake of their families and homes. The same policy of bringing fighters from outside so they have no emotional ties applies here. Palestinians are brought from Tripoli to fight those in Beirut, from Syria, from all over. However, the boys and students from Tripoli are at a disadvantage even if their numbers are increased to 800 as they don't know the camp at all. TNT explodes, shaking the room. Before it was Amal from the south and from Baalbek. Now Syria is using boys from Tripoli to try and empty the camps and disarm Fatah.

M-16 bullets are hitting the clinic upstairs; Tha'ir switches off the news to listen. Cleo isn't pregnant after all. Today I found her four kittens in a box; Abed said they had been looking after them in the Arsan *mahwar*. We decided to try to send them back.

I'm trying consciously to keep my mouth open because of the pressure in my ears from the shelling with 160mm mortars from the sports stadium next to Shatila. When we flew in over the sea to the airport, I wondered why we flew from Ras Beirut rather than from over Shatila and Bourj. Now I realize Abu Musa are shelling us from above Shatila and around the sides of the camp. The bombs are falling every twelve seconds. The cat refused to go with Abed to the *mahwar* and seemed frightened, so we put the kittens on the balcony upstairs with Cleo, despite Tha'ir protesting as he thinks it's unhygienic. When the shelling started I ran upstairs and fetched the box and put it back where Cleo had left them, under the table in the safe room. She was right, it's a good place; by now the verandah will be littered with shrapnel and bullets. Ahmad and Tha'ir are in here with Looi. They still maintain that there will not be bombing around this area, so refuse either to open the windows behind the dry heater or take the glass off.

20.30 It's now almost pitch black outside except for us and a nearby light. The cat is wandering around frightened and we try to feed her soggy dry *cak* with a little condensed milk and water, but she's not interested and the kittens are squealing with hungry cries as I put her back in the box. M-16s and 500mms firing. A friend is nervously pacing around the clinic and is still here an hour later. Tha'ir is jumpy, not helped by the fact he's been taking Valium in the afternoons and evenings to try to sleep. Um Mohamad al Ashwa comes in. Haj Abu Taher went out to pray, saying he has to pray before he gets killed. Cleo goes out last, slipping round the door and into the dark. I switched off the outside light for fear of attracting gunfire to the clinic as people come in.

1.45 One person died after the B-7 was launched from Munshaqine to a Fatah position; they responded with a mortar and he died at 18.00. Then the fighting was ordered to start at 19.00 both in Bourj and Shatila, first with 160 mortars and 107s which have been brought up to the Samed area by the Munshaqine. Their weaponry is arranged ten metres from the hospital wall and the new operating room is now unsafe as its outer wall is unprotected. The fighting has been stopped by the PFLP threatening to combine forces with PFLP-GC and Abu Nidal to protect Shatila.

9.6.88 Thursday
We have been encircled by Munshaqine since yesterday from the Jalbout building to the Khatib *mahwar*, and in the streets around Mar Elias they are walking around openly without guns. I'm feeling that we are again facing the beginning of the end. What Israel failed to do, Amal failed to do; so now they are going to try to do it again, but using Palestinians. With seventy-five per cent of the camp empty, the Syrians are going to fight it out here.

18.10 Shelling starts again. B-10s and mortars with M-16 fire. Crashes of mortars reverberating around us, as frightened fighters let off a whole thirty rounds of M-16 bullets in fear at the explosion. Shrapnel and M-16 bullets landing around us, plus B-10s. A blue sky, sun and a radio. Ahmad turns the radio up in French so as not to hear the fighting. He doesn't understand it, it's the Lebanese news. A kid runs past us as a B-7 shoots with a whizz over us – going out. BBC and birthday greetings with classical pop.

Last night's shelling at the hospital was bad, with blown-in windows in the patients' room, rubble and glass everywhere, and empty beds with the occupants fled, leaving their Kalashnikovs on the covers, so frightened that even the gun was forgotten. The surgeon was unable to operate for exhaustion and fear, his hand shook too much.

Last night the Norwegians apparently passed a message to all of us to evacuate the camp for policy reasons; it hasn't reached us yet. Heavy artillery from the Samed areas around the outskirts of the hospital, blown away by last night's bombing. The 160mm mortars are being launched at us from too far away to hear them going out. M-16 bullets hitting the walls outside and above. It sounds like the camp wars, bombing the camp all around again, from outside and the hospital area.

Tonight Munzir, Nasser's brother, accidentally shot and killed Abu Khalil's brother, the owner of the fruit-machine shop near the old clinic. He was fooling around as usual with a gun, holding it to his friend's head, saying, 'I'll shoot you, I'll shoot you,' and the young man was saying, 'No, stop,' and he pulled the trigger and shot him in the head, having forgotten that there was a bullet in the chamber.

We can hear the *crump* of mortars launched at us from the mountains and at Shatila.

20.15 Nawoosh visits us to say that he is now fighting on the second floor of the building opposite his beloved *mahwar* Haiduce which is now held by the Munshaqine.

I remember when we used to rejoice at the *crump* from the Shouf mountains helping to bring us food, and now 14 months later, a driver of a PRCS ambulance from Bourj is shot dead by Munshaqine going into Shatila.

10.6.88 Friday

8.00 The fighting eventually stopped last night at around 21.30 after three and a half hours of shelling and fighting. It was ended by a telephone call from Abu Ammar in Algiers to Sultan to tell him to stop fighting, and from Abu Musa to his troups. Again, incredibly, it just stopped – just stopped – no prolonged sniping, bombing, anything. It's surreal, this wholesale murderous activity, three and a half hours of non-stop artillery, then nothing at all. Again the usual euphoric let-down after tension, people out in the square. We laugh, releasing the nervous exhaustion of several hours of worry and fear – worry that we can't evacuate the wounded, worry that the surgeon can't cope, worry that we'll get killed trying to get to the hospital. Dr Ighlas came into the camp, but is frightened by the bombing of the hospital and she may leave again today, I don't know. We sit around eating *falafel* and laughing. There's electricity in the square as we all come outside for fresh air.

BBC World Service at 8.00: the mood is that the PLO has bounced right back into the forefront of Arab politics: 'PLO leader Yasser Arafat says that he sees the Algiers Summit as a great success for the Palestinian people'; with the recognition of the PLO as the legitimate representative of the Palestinian people. With 600 million dollars over the coming year to be donated from the Gulf Arab states, the PLO has no doubts that the Uprising will continue for some time to come.

Only one new injury here last night: a boy comes in bleeding with a small shrapnel injury. It had been dressed by someone at the hospital who said there was no shrapnel in it, but there was a hole and a track, and what goes in must go down and stay in until taken out or left inside: the simple law of shrapnel injuries and gravity. We cleaned and dressed the wound properly.

11.30 A 107 rocket has just slammed up the camp with M-16 fire and mortar accompaniment. I get up to shut the shutters on the windows, close the door and shut the inner doors. Mortars and gunfire up the camp.

Dolly waited an hour at the airport road to get into the camp. Eventually she came through Jalbout, even though Munshaqine standing on Haiduce roof were turning women back. A nurse from the hospital carrying her new baby was shot at from above to frighten her away from trying to enter the camp. At first the Syrian, Yusuf, refused to let her in, saying if I was here that was enough, she didn't need to come in as well. She asked him to walk her in, but he said no, he was scared and he would only walk her up to the first set of sandbags.

What do the Syrians want? To empty and destroy the camps as with Tal al-Zatar? To force people to accept Abu Musa rather than Arafat internally? To what end? To force us to ask them to enter the camps for the sake of protection? Why attack the hospital so ferociously? Why attack

Shatila every time? People are running in the streets, with children, bullet clips, provisions, to the shelters, *mahwars*, houses, or safety.

Abed aged 14 comes in having fallen over again. In uniform now instead of the red sweatshirts of two years ago. Still uncoordinated as he runs around after Mohamad and Ibrahim al Khatib. The bomb in the outpatients' department was planted to damage the operating room, but failed.

12.15 More 160mm and 120mms exploding, with fighting in Shatila again. We've had no chance to see the damage here. Tha'ir has run off to the mosque to pray; it's been damaged again by bombs. Ahmad advises him to run up via the right-hand side of the camp all the way, and to take cover. The bombing continues. Nigar's and Wafiq's kids are still out playing on the street, despite being told to go home or into the shelter at Arsan. Nawoosh's wife is pregnant again and Yassera had another baby girl twenty days ago.

A ceasefire at 20.00, although, apart from the odd bomb, it all stopped around 15.00. Sultan (Abu Riyad) was not included in the negotiations, but he will sign anything as long as they stop the shelling of the camps.

Numbers dead: Sabra and Fakhani, eight dead from one bomb, thirty-eight injured from two mortars, which landed around the camp and not in it as intended; Bourj, none; Shatila, two killed.

Nawoosh comes in covered in bites from mosquitoes or fleas from the *mahwar*. He refuses calamine lotion at first in favour of spirit, then, after having two antihistamine tablets, falls fast asleep on top of the emergency table and is still asleep one hour later.

Arafat and Abu Musa mediations are being conducted through Naif Hawatmeh of the Democratic Front. Assad and Arafat rumoured to be meeting in Damascus. Talk of lifting the sieges and turning a new page in Syrian/Palestinian relations. What does Abu Musa want, more and more Palestinian deaths? More misery? Or weariness and the dispersal of Palestinian culture and identity?

0.15 What a sight: Nawoosh, half-dressed, face down, asleep on the couch; Dolly under the fridge charging the battery, temperature 22°C; one man about to have an anti-tetanus toxoid jab; his friend sitting watching; Tha'ir kneeling on his mattress filling his revolver clip before putting the safety catch on and putting it back in its holder; and the kittens still asleep in the box under the table.

11.6.88 Saturday

12.20 Sleeplessness from the persistent shelling all night of Bourj and Shatila with Grad rockets, 160mm mortars and 107 rockets. The Al

Khatibs all had a narrow escape as a Grad hit their position up by the hospital. Cuts and scratches to Mohamad and Mustafa, who woke us at 6.15 with rubble all over him uncleaned at the hospital, black with dust from the explosion. We cleaned up the bits we were dubious about and sent him home for a shower. He was sweating and shocked, with a stitch in his forehead, all shaky from the near miss.

We went to sleep about 0.30 after the shelling had stopped, only to be woken by an explosion and a *whoosh*; I can't work out what it was. Then at 2.30 I woke with what I sleepily thought was a 500mm shooting but worked out it was a 160mm mortar exploding up by Samed. I went to wake up stubborn Ahmad, who'd decided to sleep upstairs despite all protests, and told him they were bombing Samed. He came down and shortly afterwards the bombing of the camp started with up to six 150mms being dropped at one time.

One girl has just run past with Ibrahim and Mohamad in tow; something's happened, meetings, and everyone's discussing it. The news on the radio tells us that Shatila is completely destroyed, what was left of it, that is. This news depresses us. Is it true? We've heard nothing as yet from inside the camp. This makes us ask why attack Shatila again, using 240mm mortars? The vibration alone could bring down what is left of the buildings, which are full of holes and rubble, strewn with iron wires. 240mm mortars; no wonder they kept us awake all night.

Did it take a Palestinian to do what all others had failed to do? Has Assad really forced a deal on Arafat to sacrifice Shatila, and perhaps Bourj, for peace of a kind? There is no peace while you are on your knees.

Um Khalsum* sings on the radio on a hot day, flies buzzing in the sky over the deserted camp, swarming above the sandbags and rubble. We all seem to know each other well, all of us who are left. Are we on the way to another Tal al-Zatar? Is it Assad's wish to erase us from the face of the earth? The same camp war, the same director, the same strategy, only a different agent. I wish that the mothers of Tripoli would demonstrate again to stop their sons coming to the killing of their brothers. The demonstrations from the camp have stopped, from the women, from the mosque. Even the sheikh in the mosque yesterday told us only that it is inhuman to continue this fighting and attacks on the camps. Ahmad says the same was said last week, what else could the sheikh say?

I am having vivid dreams about Swee and people preventing any help coming to us, ignoring all our messages. The last dream was about people practising witchcraft by winding up horses as though they were mechanical, so that when they are set off all their legs shatter and break due to the pressure of the mechanized speed. It must be indicative of my anxiety? I wish we could hear some news of a surgeon or anyone coming. Listening to

*She was one of the most famous singers in the Arab world.

singing, we have all forgotten the singing, clapping, weddings, *khotbés*, *haflés*, and having fun. Abu Badir from PFLP-GC who goes swimming every day with his ghettoblaster hasn't. He's not involved in this war. It's someone else's. He doesn't understand why.

23.30 A ceasefire since 11.00, interspersed with the occasional *ta* from an M-16. Mohamad Fawzi comes by, still looking pale and tired. He says that perhaps the Syrians just want to destroy the camps and have no Palestinian population in their midst. As this fits in with Lebanese theories on resettlement it may be so.

Sitting outside with a light wind on the verandah, listening to the news of our ceasefire. What happened to all the promises of saving Shatila by the other assorted political groups? More empty promises. It is rumoured that there are only a few fighters left inside and that they have nowhere left to go for shelter. A quiet, beautiful, starlit night. The total dead in the last few days is seventeen. The population of Bourj rose last month to 15,000 due to fighting in the suburbs, now it has fallen to approximately 4,000; Shatila has 1,000. So the chances of being killed in the last four days were one in 235. Ghassan passes by to say, 'Hello, Suzy.' I can't see him as it's very dark, until he shines his torch on his face. He's as handsome and sweet as ever. His hearing is still damaged despite treatment abroad and may never be sorted out now. He says to Tha'ir that when he is fighting or shooting with a Kalashnikov he gets a headache and feels pressure with the noise in his head. He thinks he has a psychological problem and doesn't know what to do with himself. It sounds to me as if he has middle and inner ear auditory disturbance.

Someone lets off a few shots up in the camp and is promptly cursed by all, '*Charmouta ochto*,' ('His sister's a whore,') for disturbing our *esrude* (reverie) under the stars. Ibrahim comes by and asks me to write another letter to Denmark to let him get away from this place. Mohamad says, 'We should all go to Denmark before we die here in the camp.' Unusual for him. Tha'ir is still jumpy. His sister is very frightened and has gone out of the camp. His mother is also very frightened and lives all the time in the shelter.

12.6.88 Sunday

Midnight The ceasefire has held since yesterday. Rumours of the Munshaqine sending a letter saying that they wish to end the fighting. Arafat's second-in-command, Abu Iyad, is to meet Hawatmeh (DFLP), Jibril (PFLP-GC), Habash (PFLP) *et al* tomorrow in Damascus. Rumours also of the fight continuing because, in the Palestinian/Syrian unification plan, Abu Musa wished to be included as a separate group entity but was told by Arafat that his fighters had to disband and join into one of the other groupings, and not be a single political/military front any longer.

Looi managed to come in today, having tried twice yesterday and failed as there was continuous sniping, and Øyvind took fright and made her promise not to try to enter again yesterday. She brought greetings from outside and a message that disheartened us all, that Swee could not come, that she is sick (?), but that they were trying to send another surgeon. Gloom and anger. Abu Riyad comes by and asks if she is coming. He too becomes despondent about the news, and asks why. We ask Dolly to phone Swee in Chinese dialect to find out the real reason, and then Abu Riyad will phone direct to Abu Ammar. But no international lines available from Lebanon and frustration felt deeply at our isolation and the knowledge of seventeen dead in the last four days, with so many injured. After all the trouble and danger to go to the Fatah office to try to connect a line to the outside world for help. . .

Today, I woke up with mutterings of the bombs from the mountain early in the morning, confused with half-sleep and dreams. My dreams came true – Swee won't come, and the voice of the mountains, that was like the singing of the artillery to save us and bring us food last year, becomes our nightmare. Our friend for a day becomes our foe. Our cousin Jumblatt becomes again the mirror in which you can see anything you want when you are too fatigued to care.

Flour bags and UNRWA sacks collected from friends and neighbours are filled with sand by around twenty children crying, 'I am with you,' and we all shovel the reddened sand from what once was a floor into the small bags to be carried to the big bags and on to the wooden beams and holes knocked through the plaster and breezeblocks of the clinic walls by Tha'ir, Ahmad and Bassam. We all get filthy and bitten as, two people per sack, we lug the fifty-kilogramme sacks from the old entrance to Slieme *mahwar* and on to Tha'ir's shoulders. Breezeblocks line up outside the clinic waiting to form a *dushmeh* (defence position). Abu Khalil is still building at the top of the camp. We listen to the comments of others such as, 'Why are you building now? The war is over.' '*Ma fi harub, hallaset al harub*.' ('There is no war, the war is finished.') We persuade the others to continue until 21.30.

Banan, a 13-year-old girl, Hanna, Linda and Lulu are all released after being caught on the third run bringing bullets and hand grenades into the camp. On their second run, a PFLP-GC guy had told them to conceal the ammunition better under their clothing or they would be caught. On the third run a Syrian soldier stopped them and asked them to pull their shirts tight across their waists. When he saw the outline of the ammunition underneath they were all taken to the Beau Rivage Hotel. They slept in terror of 'the black room', so called because it is where the special chair is kept for electrical torture. They were all kept together and the Lebanese (Amal) prisoners and Palestinians, an estimated half and half of each, were shouting to them to pass the radio out of the window for the news.

The Syrians beat up Hanna and Lulu, but left Banan and Linda and the young girl. When they asked her where her father is, Banan replied, 'With you, sir, in Syria, for the past three years.' Hanna still has a bruise on her leg from where they kicked her.

Haj was climbing trees with little Abir for the mulberries which grow all over his roof and finding the B-7 that went through his roof leaving the rest of the roof undamaged, when I was called to the *haflé* to celebrate the release of the five women. Sitting on the water pipes in the alley, clapping and learning words, singing '*Hey, Jalla, yakhiyen itla barra,*' ('Spies get out,') and the praises of Abu Ammar and the *mahwars* and previous famous battles, clap, clap; the men dancing and the girls looking relieved to be out. With *'Al hamdo 'lillah al Sallameh'* ('Thank God to see you safe') everywhere. Clapping and letting off steam and more clapping.

Dolly and Tha'ir are away to the Fatah office to try to telephone again. Ahmad can't sleep. The kittens have been moved by their mother under Ahmad's bed. The littlest black one with the eye infection and the loudest voice died last night. *Haram*. She was a sweetie, although the runt of the litter. She didn't even know how to eat even when I kept putting the nipple into her mouth, yet she sought food from my finger. She would sleep alone in the corner and we found her dead with all the other kittens lying on top of her. Wee soul. I don't know which is better. I tried to feed her yesterday, and cleaned her eye with tetracycline. She had a lively squeak.

Tea with Banan and Bahia. We hear thunder and think it's an air raid going on in Saida or the Shaif. It turns out to be raining. A cool breeze blows and I stand on the roof getting wet, looking at the mountain and thinking how I love this place, love the people, and prefer it here even at its worst to London and all the awful machinations of ego and power. Infinitely preferable here; perhaps it's so simple, the honesty of life and death. Only.

13.6.88 Monday

Swee was reached in London by Dolly in Mandarin Chinese twice from the Fatah phone. She hadn't received any of our messages except the phone call about the 'Ramadan' war. She thought there was no entry into the camps despite my instruction to phone Ahmad and come to Bourj. She hadn't received any telexes apparently and may come next Sunday. Dolly and Tha'ir returned at 0.2.15 and woke us all up to tell us the good news.

The ceasefire held until 10.45 when the rockets started shooting over us and the one that went out apparently went as far as Baabda Palace. Then *rajmehs*, B-7s, B-10s and Ibrahim's newly installed *doshka* started. The vibration from the *doshka* caused the shutters to slam on the unsandbagged windows every time it was fired. The bombing was still continuing two hours later as I fell asleep after a lunch of tomatoes, swan meat, cucumber, bread and sweets, kindly brought to us by Haj, as all our food is still upstairs. Two injured people came in as I woke up.

Tha'ir is very nervous and worried, so is Ahmad; they are both having sleeping problems and are irritable and ratty. Nawoosh comes here to sleep on a plinth at night from 23.00 to 2.30 or 4.30 instead of going home; then wakes us up again in the morning.

Abed has a ruptured eardrum and an irregular iris, caused by being on the wrong end of a B-7 explosion up near the hospital. We removed more shrapnel, treated his eye for the third time and referred him despite his strong protests to a doctor outside the camp, perhaps in Saida, for an eye and ear examination.

Ghassan gave me the little red carnation he was wearing on his uniform. What a sweetheart. He said, 'Everyone is smiling with Suzy today.' Tried to watch *Miami Vice*, but Abed interrupted it with his wretched eye again. Then the cat got stuck next door and was wailing pathetically while Dolly and I tried to remove shrapnel sand from Abed's back. We forced the window open and she was rescued with the help of a friend and one of the kittens screaming as I picked him up.

Taisear's shop and house were destroyed by the bombing today. Several more houses in front of the Haiduce area were destroyed. They have finished the sandbags outside as well as inside the clinic and it is now safe enough to protect the injured inside during a bombardment – I hope. The playfulness of Haj and the children yesterday reminded me of the relief of seeing friends' faces in the sunshine after a bombardment.

At around 12.30, Sultan issued orders for no more return fire from Fatah positions; despite people saying yesterday that Fatah were running low on weapons it seems they have more than enough in the endless exchange of gunfire. Sniping this afternoon and this evening. Um Mohamad al Ashwa also has a perforated eardrum. No news on the negotiations in Damascus.

A clear night on the roof picking flowers, or sitting on the balcony watching and listening to the rain and thinking how much I love this place, these people. We are open because we all share the seconds, minutes and hours together, whereas elsewhere everyone is concerned only for their own ends. How can the others sleep upstairs, with 160mm, 107s, Grads, B-10s, B-7s? How can I still love this camp more and more? How can we bear this disintegration slowly, slowly, by bombing another few houses away each day? Another life and memories. So far, this is nowhere near as bad physically as the siege was for us, but if tactics change then it will be. All are getting visibly thinner – except me.

14.6.88 Tuesday

The ceasefire is still holding with a delegation from Mar Elias visiting the camp up around Samed today; only some sniping at around midnight which stopped just before Haj came to announce a ceasefire agreement effective from 8.00 today via a letter from Abu Ammar? I went to sleep and woke to queues of people waiting for dressings. All are improving, thank God. Abed went out of the camp to get his eye seen to; nothing wrong, but he's not wearing his eye pad again.

The ceasefire has technically been violated tonight by one political party hearing on the *silké* that the Munshaqine agreed to do something to Sultan when he was at Nawoosh's house and advised him to leave the area immediately, which he did. It does not augur well for good intentions.

We saw three people today with high fevers. One of them a boy who had been on the receiving end of five bombs yesterday and this was the explanation given by his family as the source of his fever of 40°C. We also saw a sweet Haji who wanted us to tell her how to get her speech back properly after a stroke two months ago. At first I misunderstood and thought it was a mechanical complaint of having all her teeth pulled. Then Ibrahim (al Khatib) came in with a fever of 38.8°C and pain in his right hip; I hope to God it's not his appendix with Dr Barjat in the hospital! I gave him paracetamol and shouted, 'Bed, bed,' at him as he left, with Ghassan agreeing with me.

The mosquitoes are breeding like rabbits and colliding with each other in their attempts to bite you. Looi, the 'mosquito sniper', kills at least a hundred a night.

I fell asleep in the sun and breeze on the verandah this afternoon. The stress of fighting makes me very sleepy; on ceasefire days I switch rhythm and sleep less, and think real thoughts again, very odd and automatic, for example, 'The voice of Fairouz (a popular Lebanese singer) is like diamonds in sunshine splashing on the water and Um Khalthoum is like the velvet of the night and silk in darkness.'

A quiet night sitting on the doorstep reading an old *Newsweek* with Ali, Hassan's little brother, giving me and Dolly chewing gum and having childlike discussions with Abed, aged 14, and his sister Abir, 10; Borhan, Mohamad, Mustafa and I laughing at them. Abed is nicknamed Moshe Dayan by Borhan because of the patch on his eye – when he wears it! Then they move off back to the *mahwar*, with little Ali. At 12, he is 'very good and very brave,' says Haj Abu Taher, 'he is fighting'.

In the dark we twiddle the radio tuner: disco, classical, news and breakdance come across the stations. Tha'ir, Ahmad and Ghassan water the sandbags and splash each other, throwing the water around from a Nido milk can. We debate who is sleeping up and who is sleeping down. Looi and the cats are up. Momma cat got the remains of chicken and beans that Looi cooked tonight, great Chinese food, and Nido milk. One little kitten has sticky eyes; they are all becoming more mobile, if uncoordinated, still sleeping under the bed.

15.6.88 Wednesday
The ceasefire still holds.

Ahmad Yunis, aged 5, is being a complete terror, pulling the sandbags to pieces and regularly being scolded or hit. Fahdi is sitting out in the sun, looking pensive; he is growing up so fast that all of a sudden he's gone from a giggling boy to a tall young fighter. I used to think of him as indistinguishable from Fadia, his younger sister, perhaps twins, but now he is obviously well into his teens. And both he and Ziad are now acting as young men of the house instead of kids hanging round with no responsibilities. His family have gone *en masse* to Saida leaving him here to fight. If he is anything like Abed he would refuse to leave the camp anyway.

Mirvat has been picked up by the Syrians at the Jalbout checkpoint on her way into the camp. She is eight months pregnant and this was her first time out since last April when her name was high on the wanted list. Samir, her husband, sent her out during the last shelling as he was frightened for her and the baby.

Hussein from the ICRC comes in from the airport road to tell us that all our requests for supplies have to go via Dr Mohamad Ossman and Mar Elias store. So we will give this tedious work to Kristine (of NORWAC) as extraction from the storekeeper is lengthy and very time-consuming. Hussein is very brave; he covers Mar Elias and Bourj camps. We wish him safely out of the camp, and to take care at the top. He invites us to the ICRC Sur beach house any time we want.

Thank God, Mirvat is okay. They promised to release her at 13.00 and she has just returned at 13.45. Mustafa tells her to stop talking and go down to see her husband and let him know that she is safe.

23.25 Fighting in Shatila today at around 12.00 leaves one dead and one injured. Julie Flint from *The Guardian* comes into the camp. Unfortunately Ahmad Aishey has told her that I am here, so she waits to see me. I tell her on the balcony that the war is a continuation of the camp wars, same sponsor, same tactics, different agents; that of course people are demoralized after three years of fighting, especially as they thought it had stopped a year ago, but now again, houses are destroyed, and relatives killed and injured. And the camp appears empty – people have fled. I tell her of the deliberate policy of attacking the health facilities to demoralize people further and disrupt the undefended side of the hospital, deliberately trying to damage the operating room first and now the water tanks. We went on the roof and I showed her where Maryam was shot in December, and told her how preferable it was to know that Hizb'ullah were around us instead of Amal who were a bunch of thugs by comparison. I finished by saying if only these people had been allowed to stay in Galilee instead of being driven out; now even their shelters are bombed, and people are frightened to stay in Ain al-Helweh because of the frequent Israeli air-raids.

Ahmad Hayek and Taisear are jumpy about the continued building of reinforcements in the camp and the placing of new rockets by the Munshaqine in Haiduce three days ago. Taisear is unhappy at Yassera, Lydia and Gamili bringing the kids back into the camp, as he feels the fighting may still continue.

Again the story is recounted of the rocket hitting Borhan, Mohamad and Mustafa's *dushmeh* seconds after they had woken up and moved downstairs with the onset of the shelling. Um Mohamad berates Mohamad in his absence for not coming home to sleep. She is worried for him.

Ahmad Hayek told Sultan of the *dushmeh* erected by Munshaqine. He replied, 'There's a ceasefire.' Ahmad told Nawoosh about two new rockets taking up residence opposite his position. He replied, 'Ceasefire.'

Two cases of anxiety in the Tosa household where a son was suffocated when sandbags collapsed on top of him in the *mahwar* in the 6-month war.

Shooting again at 1.00. Ahmad is anxious, and Dolly and I are wide awake again.

Julie Flint says no Palestinian camp demolished has ever been reconstructed. '*Fi* bloody ceasefire.' ('There's a bloody ceasefire.')

16.6.88 Thursday

Six dead in Shatila yesterday, assassinated by two members of the Munshaqine after a meeting with a Libyan delegation inside the camp. As they parted with the delegates at the border of the camp, the two assassins followed them back into the camp again and shot them dead with a BKC. And they really want to stop the fighting? Or are they turning Shatila into a living death trap for those few Palestinians left?

Haj comes in to tell me of seven dead now in Shatila. Here in Bourj Sultan maintains Arafat's ceasefire.

23.57 Another uneasy day. The camp must be even emptier as we spent most of the day sitting in the breezy sun on the steps, or in the niche behind the sandbags, talking gibberish with the children, none of them at school as the war has shut the schools down. The only teachers available are those who go out of the camp for a whole week to sit in the empty classrooms (most of the schools are outside the camp); a whole week outside the camp by force, like Tha'ir's father, who goes out to look after an empty building, unused for almost two years now.

I found the palm trees across the front street again after a long discussion with Looi on their assumed disappearance from the corner on Haret Hreik: had Amal and Hizb'ullah taken to blowing up trees and gardens as part of their military strategy? We found them whilst drinking coffee with Nasser, Tha'ir, Ahmad and Aref on our roof under the rattling

zinc and stolen vines; nervously sunning ourselves, while trying to imagine whether someone would shoot us or not, and from inside the camp or not. After the assassinations in Shatila are we all potential targets?

Much debate about the killings in Shatila; it sparked off a lot of fighting, using B-7s, sniping and grenades. Ibrahim told us that the six had gone to a prearranged meeting in the camp with Munshaqine, but were shot on their way to it: a trap. No official reprisal or acknowledgement, even *Télé Liban* broadcasting from East Beirut only mentioned the Libyan initiative of deploying 300 Libyan troops around the camp for its protection and Assad saying he had not made any intervention so far. (Ha.)

A call from the mosque for ten units of O-positive blood for Shatila. At least they must have a surgeon inside now.

I'm having the usual boat dreams and trying to reach somewhere comforting again – longing, I think is the interpretation – guitars and boats last night, and fish divers from the cliffs. In the one the night before I was near Palestine but too far to get to Nablus and palm trees. I talk to Bilal and Hossam, sitting on the clinic steps, about Palestine and Al Quds (Jerusalem). They ask me questions and tell me they have never seen Jerusalem. Haj tells me he was 5 years old when he left Palestine. Every night the Jewish planes flew over the village, so they left to come to Lebanon, thinking it would only be for a short while.

Sweating, mosquitoes everywhere. The little cat stuck somewhere has stopped mewling for its mother. Our kittens are getting adventurous. Tha'ir and Ahmad are less nervous as we sit in the sun a little bit more each day, cautiously savouring daylight and no bombs. Assad's hatred of Arafat has reduced us to this. Oh, Galilee.

The Norwegian medical workers are still too frightened to enter the camp.

17.6.88 Friday

The *dushmeh* (defence positions) up near the hospital are still getting higher. Looi and I grabbed each other's hands as we walked past the deserted streets in front of the hospital, more bombed out and shattered than before; we stepped over more scraps of twisted metal and saw the destroyed sandbags of Abed's and Sami's *mahwar*, where the B-7 hit the bags and Abed's eardrum was blown out by the pressure.

Syria has issued a warning to both factions to stop fighting; yet today there are rumours of the Munshaqine surrounding Shatila, preventing PRCS staff entering, and cutting off the main water supply to the camp. Ten people have died over the past two days, yet still we abide by the ceasefire. The feeling now is that we too should fight for Shatila; not one and each camp alone, but together. Libya wants to send 300 observer troops to divide the factions. The radio tells us that Syria wants to send 300 of the Palestine Liberation Army from Damascus. 'From where shall they send them? From Tunis? Baghdad?' asks Ahmad incredulously. Asked if there is any news, he replies, 'News? There is football – better than news.'

So perhaps another siege: guns are being moved around and there is shooting around the area whilst we are eating on the balcony, so we all drop our heads below the wall and visibility. More shots, so we joke that we will finish the meal with our faces resting on the ground. All this from Abu Musa, the man whose son was killed by the Syrians a month or so ago.

Fatah says that the Munshaqine are refusing to let food, PRCS staff and medicines into Shatila; the Munshaqine say the opposite. I wonder what will happen now? We are rested after four and a half days of peace and quiet. When I was coming back from the checkpoint, one of the PFLP-GC boys insisted on walking me back from their office to the emergency room entrance at the hospital 'in case something happened'. Well, it *was* Friday!

We stand on the roofs and look at the Munshaqine positions, wondering if they will shoot at us or not, wondering if we have violated any rules of battle, wondering if in the next round the clinic will go too, perceived as a military target? Still the camp is deserted. Still Ahmad's mother is taking her family nightly to sleep in the shelter with blankets and mattresses. Still Abu Mohamad with Parkinson's disease daily wobbles up the road with a mattress on his shoulder to a safer area. Do we have sufficient food or water for another siege? Salim the head nurse at the hospital is at his wits' end over the lack of supplies. He's asking for ambubags, laryngoscopes and medicines via Looi who went to Mar Elias.

Apathy seems to have set in. Ghassan waved to me.

18.6.88 Saturday

Nothing for days on end; a few shots this afternoon and a bomb that exploded by accident, whilst I was at the checkpoint. Looi came in het up as there is a telex from London telling me to leave the camp for the meantime. It talks of an executive committee meeting with the situation very different to the one faced before and quoting a directive, but whoever the executive committee are, the director is, and the difference in situation, who knows? They want a quick answer but, as the Norwegians imagine sniping every five minutes, and they don't expect to visit us until Tuesday, the quick answer will have to wait. Two bloody weeks we have been waiting. Dr Barjat asked me today at the hospital when the surgeon was coming. I had to tell him no surgeon was coming from London; perhaps one would come from Norway? But Looi says, on the contrary, they are trying to pull us out also now. God almighty – last week immediate aid was promised, this week Øyvind is back on his 'prepare to leave' tack! I was so agitated by Looi's agitation that I dropped the blood pressure machine that I was carrying to Ibrahim's in the sewer.

Salim asked me to go to the checkpoint to try to get entry permission for a truck of medicines from Mar Elias. We passed piles of tipped-out supplies at the checkpoint which I mistook for Pepsi and Miranda boxes. We had to hand-carry it all into the camp. All of it. No cars were allowed. Looi asked the ICRC, who were visiting the camp, if she could use their car for half an hour; they refused. I asked the *mukuberat* if we could get the ICRC car to move it; they refused. The PFLP-GC drove by in a car, as did a stationwagon full of journalists, and the ICRC drove out uninterested, saying that they were in a hurry for another appointment, and anyway we had lots of time. Poor Hussein having to work with that lot. They were all uncommunicative and looked very frightened; as though we were all animals. The *mukuberat* are racist in the extreme towards Palestinian women, calling them big and strong (gesturing uncouthly), whereas

Syrian women and we foreigners are soft by comparison. It is for Palestinian women to work hard, not for us.

I was not allowed to carry any of the medicines into the hospital and we had to open all the boxes with the soldier. Two and a half hours later, thirsty and sunburnt, I was allowed to leave. Every time I asked to take a box inside the camp or to go to the clinic I was told to stay where I was. If I left the checkpoint, no medicines would be allowed into the camp. So I stayed, not wanting to push my luck. By the time a PFLP-GC guy had helped carry a box of tubigrip in and I'd carried the cottonwool, Nasif told me that my face was very red. I was harassed and so was Ali from the hospital stores. They made him turn the wheelbarrow around and around. One boy with arm injuries had his card taken and his arm twisted round until his hand mopped the sweat from the soldier's forehead. He looked utterly terrified.

One kitten died tonight, one of the cute tiger-like ones. Perhaps these sticky eyes and cough are caused by a flu that's killing them. Tha'ir and I buried him in the *mahwar* with a stone at his grave. Another bomb explodes up in the camp.

19.6.88 Sunday

Ceasefire agreements announced in effect from tomorrow. Attachments from the Libyan Army (300?) and from the PLA (300?) from Damascus paid by the PLO are to be deployed between Munshaqine in Samed and twenty-five in Haiduce area. This is supposed to be implemented tomorrow, first in Shatila then in Bourj. The bigshots from Damascus have been back and forth, back and forth, all gone again. More meetings are to be held in Mar Elias tomorrow.

Attempts to get a lab at the clinic going ground to a halt today. I will have another go for books and microscope tomorrow. We planned a safety structure outside the clinic with Ahmad and a small operating room along the lines of Shatila. We came to the conclusion that we will have to dig underground, but the houses had all the sand scraped out and stones brought in by the truckload for foundations, but no cement, so it's not very stable. Ahmad estimated a million lira to buy a house, a million to dig under, and a million to construct from scratch, so we may as well start from the beginning as with Shatila's new hospital. But look at the remains of that after almost three years of continuous shelling. The logic is sound but we have no Chris Giannou or Ali Abu Tawq to implement it here.

The kittens are more mobile; Mummy Cleo firmly rejected the roof as a home and twice brought the kittens down. The little stray ensconced himself under the bed, and Cleo is now inspecting Dolly's cupboard as an alternative to the balcony. I cleaned two kittens' eyes and put eyedrops in. The little one seems quite stumbly and blind.

Some shooting throughout the day, but we are more relaxed as time unwinds without further shelling. Ahmad and Tha'ir are still quite depressed and uncommunicative. Dolly and I discussed how impossible it is to get either of them to give us any information about the situation, but if we persist they will tell us, albeit unwillingly and with their own ideas on the situation included. Dolly says that the fact that Tha'ir's family has been split, as has Ahmad's, with half outside and half inside the camp, to prevent the extinction of the whole family should a bomb fall on the house where they are sheltering, is depressing them both very much, this necessity for survival. Also that neither of them wants to fight in this war, and despite the heavy fighting for weeks Ahmad would not fire a single bullet.

Little Ali was hauled up by Mahmud for throwing water into Johina's house. Haj is throwing flowers from his roof to us and the kids in the square. Nawoosh is sitting on the swing seat in the corner of Haj's roof out of sight of the sniper behind the sandbags in Haiduce. Haj declares his neutrality and sits in front of the Sianni position and the Haiduce sights. We look at the Lebanese people across the road where Amal used to be and feel relieved. Ahmad works out how to avoid the Norwegians trying to take us out on Tuesday.

20.6.88 Monday

I couldn't sleep last night as my brain was buzzing with writing draft telexes and statements in my head.

Rumours of Salah, who used to run the X-ray at the hospital, now sitting out his days at the checkpoint. I want to congratulate him on doing a more effective job than the Israelis ever could in demoralizing The Revolution of the Stones (the name for the Uprising), destroying PRCS, emptying and destroying the camps and with it Palestinian autonomy in Beirut once and for all. As Tha'ir says, 'Ask anyone in the camp, even the smallest child will tell you that they hate the Munshaqine. Why? Because they are destroying their homes and killing people in the camp.' He is very depressed by it all, saying that the people will believe no one now after all these pseudo ceasefires.

Today as I was cooking and relaxing at Dolly's request, pulling off the *forfahini* (a vegetable) leaves, I thought I heard shelling far off. A little girl confirmed this below in the square and an old man below the verandah. They had switched on the news and found out it was Shatila. I had initially thought it sounded like that direction but told myself that it must be the Shouf mountains. The Munshaqine shot and killed someone from Fatah, which started the fighting. They had denied this on the radio, saying that one of their fighters was injured by Fatah, so they needed heavy cover fire to evacuate him and this spilled into fighting. It is said that both sides were shelling and that it was landing outside the camp as well as inside. It went on from 15.30 to 20.00 at least. So much again for our ceasefire.

A young man came for a quick meal with us; he is fighting for the first time with Nawoosh. Today his muscles are aching from carrying sandbags. We asked him whether he was taking them down or putting them up. 'Putting them up' was the answer. Nawoosh had deferred rebuilding for a couple of days, until now. Why the change?

It's so obvious that the Munshaqine intention is anything but good. It's not so much the attacks on Shatila and our empathy with them that upsets us – although it obviously does – but it's the symbolism involved with every attack on Shatila, a fragile destroyed centre of resistance and dignity, that is being pounded into the ground by the seeming psychopaths around her. That is what upsets us, that they cannot be satisfied with the death, destruction and misery meted out to Shatila for the past six years, but that they too love to claim their part in smashing these small boundaries and lives inside to pieces. The love we feel for our friends inside almost surpasses any other emotions we are capable of feeling under the stress of bombardment. We love the symbolism of Shatila more than we love ourselves. Tha'ir and Ahmad have always fought until now. Now new people take up the fighting when others grow sick of it.

It is a hot, airless night, with a new crescent moon illuminated as though on a mosque in the Gulf in a blue sky. Stars, Sunni call, Shia call, silence, clouds puff across as though contemplating rain in a few days. What a place. Children, noise, East Beirut's mountains glittering in the dusk, cars coming down, going up. Cars outside, soldiers, buildings, and this continued assault on the right to existence of a community in exile. A protracted form of genocide.

I'm still sleeping on the floor with Ahmad, Looi, Dolly and Tha'ir upstairs. Dolly is going out for a short holiday next week; Looi may go out too as she's been here since May, and has her shelters project to start. Both are real angels, sweet, firm, and good health workers, yattering on in Chinese and working away unceasingly. The electricity is very weak, not enough to sterilize or pump water; we think someone is tapping our line.

Samrawi was playing his flute again today at the *mahwar*, with clapping, whoops and ullulations, as though *dubké* was being danced out of sight. Beautiful village music coming up through the vines and kitchen of a refugee house. The children were also beating the drums and clapping again to rhythmic songs down the street. Sobhieh called to Wafiq's wife, Fatima, 'What are you doing? We want to listen for the bombs.' She yelled back, '*Madrisseh*' ('School'). Nawoosh, Sobhieh, Borhan and Salah all gathered looking very serious after the shelling of Shatila started. Ali got beaten again in public for throwing a bag of water into Johina's room yesterday, and cursing her. Every day Johina creates a fuss for the wave of women to surge up from inside the alleyway to see the men in the square; they come like a wave, then recede back into the alleyway and their separate life of children and the household again, meeting again in the political sphere.

We hear the story of a very brave little boy who took up twenty kilos of TNT past the Munshaqine at Samed. They ignored him carrying the ten kilos in each arm because he is a child, so he left it at their *dushmeh* and returned to the Fatah positions, whereupon they detonated the explosives and commenced the second Friday's fighting. A brave wee boy.

We got a microscope; very nice but no light source. We'll have to get one, as it is useless trying torches, candles etc, to use it.

21.6.88 Tuesday
Two dead in Shatila by the end of the fighting and three more injured. Three more new rockets in place in front of Nawoosh's position since the day before yesterday; hence the sandbags.

17.00 Heavy fighting since 14.45. The first indication was fighting in Shatila from 9.45 to 12.45, then a meeting in progress at Mar Elias. I heard this at 14.00 sitting beside the kitchen door drinking Haj's coffee and laughing as Taisear tried to take Dolly's and my photographs with the wee Syrian boy running past us every few minutes. After listening to the news in Arabic I saw four young men from Nawoosh and Mahmud mobilizing. Then Hossam shot past carrying someone's M-16, going uphill after the others. I asked Tha'ir what was happening, why everyone was running uphill? Abu Sultan explained about the fighting in Shatila and that we were now on *instanfah* again. Tha'ir came back saying, 'Nothing's up,' until I questioned him about the *instanfah.*

Fifteen minutes later Najib, one of Nawoosh's boys, came back down and smiled, waved his hand down and then away as he went past me. I took it as 'There will be bombing, go inside,' and went inside immediately. Hearing all the TNT and mortars now makes me wonder how long the middle of the camp will be upright after our walk around it last week. So much in the centre was destroyed with the first month's fighting, and the TNT vibration is even loosening our sinks from the wall, whole roofs are lying in huge slabs at the side of the road. TNT explosions are blowing out our skirts and the window shutters. They are really chucking it around. The five of us are sitting in what is regarded as the safe room.

One bomb landed off-target at the Kuwaiti embassy on a car and killed one person. Another landed in the Arab University area, killing five people, and the injured have been taken to Al Maqassed Hospital which has asked on the radio for O-positive blood donations. The ceasefire is supposed to have started now. More TNT and bombs. Salah comes in sweating to say that all the rockets aimed at Nawoosh fell down in their casing, all faulty, thank God. We are the top news item, bombs in Fakhani and the Kuwaiti embassy. A 160mm mortar goes off nearby, shrapnel raining down. This morning I joked with Aref about having a shrapnel injury and a burn, what was he going to do next? I should have kept quiet.

Have been on a psychic phase again since arriving back and the first shelling. Maybe the pressure of explosives and tension coupled with vibration makes your brain alter? What an awful thought. The dreams continue, with a dream of Shatila being empty, no one left inside it. The dreams don't seem to be realized, although the one about Swee being prevented from coming has come true. Only the thoughts – they're bad enough. All of us fighting off sleep, unable to make coffee as the stove is upstairs.

Ben's first law was 'Don't go out in the bombs unless you have to.' Tha'ir is always running out so we tick him off, saying the possibility of being killed is higher while there is still bombing; better to go when it's certain it has stopped. Quieter now after four hours of heavy fighting. We are hungry too. We need a small stove downstairs. A rumour is circulating that Abu Fahdi, Abu Musa leader of Beirut, has been shot and fatally injured by three women at Mar Elias. We all feel he deserves it. Four hours and it's still going on.

Nawoosh staged a preemptive strike – we saw him all kitted out in military plus hat earlier on, looking serious. They heard on the *jihaz* that the Munshaqine were planning to bomb the camp and so ordered him to take the 107mm rockets opposite him out of action. He used two B-7s and the rockets were tipped over and under the *mahwar*. Jubilation.

The Munshaqine refused to negotiate a ceasefire as they say that Fatah started this fighting. Technically they are right, but in intentions wrong. Haj says they are blowing up all the houses along the Terasha area with TNT, hence the continuing explosions. Dolly asks, 'Why destroy houses and kill people?' Ahmad replies, 'Why? The same as before, the same as the last three years; to destroy the camps completely.' Since Black September in Amman, the Israeli invasion and the camp wars have all followed the same plan: to drive out the Palestinians and destroy their military and political capacity and autonomous groupings.

Six hours of bombardment.

Hanan Ghale, returning from the first and last day of UNRWA School in three months, tried to come in at the Hallimis. She was sent along the camp to Jalbout by the Syrians. She told them, 'There is fighting there now.' They replied, 'You Palestinians are trying to kill us.' She said, 'You want to kill us.' And had to walk along the front street to Jalbout and through the camp to her home under heavy shelling and gunfire.

Phosphorus was found in the tips of the 107mm rockets. Mohamad al Khatib and Salah show us in the square, then bury it under the sand to extinguish it. The *mahwar* at Slieme where all the women and children and elderly are sheltering is hit upstairs by a mortar. In the gloom there are the voices of all the people who have been sitting in the sand for the past six hours sheltering from the bombardment, with no food, water or amenities until it ceased.

Odd bombs still going off around the camp. The destruction is beginning to resemble the 1-month war, they say, with so much TNT used and heavy artillery fire. All the houses near the school have been destroyed. One boy from Fatah is dead, possibly four Munshaqine left for dead, seen by women outside from Haiduce. Total of possibly nine dead between Bourj and Shatila today, including those outside the camp.

Banan is engaged. She will meet her fiancé to decide finally next week, when he comes through Syria from Jordan having obtained a visa at last. She has been betrothed for six months but refuses to don a ring until she meets him and sees 'his way', whether she likes him or not. Her future mother-in-law travelled from Jordan to ask for her, and whilst here she had a stroke 'from happiness'. Just as fever is put down to a bomb blast, so cardio-vascular accident can be attributed to happiness. It's mysterious.

A planned visit to the hospital is abandoned because of bombs after 21.00 and shooting. The last dressing for an injury is at 23.40; all the past weeks have been like this. Ghassan is injured on his thigh by a 500mm bullet. Whilst I do his leg dressing, he says he wants to marry and have a wife who is like me. I tell him to live away from Lebanon. He says, how can he? His mother and sister are here, he has to care for them and cannot leave. Really he's lovely.

22.6.88 Wednesday

A sunny and breezy morning of calm and disbelief at the extent of the damage from yesterday's shelling and TNT. Six to seven houses destroyed. Abu Hassan's and Mirvat's are completely flattened. Nine dead and twenty-eight plus injured. Nawoosh has put up a *dushmeh* with a sniper hole in it, where the zinc sniper barricade used to be at the junction going off to 'Evil' Mahmud's shop. Yesterday they shot two Munshaqine as they tried to come out of Sianni building and dynamite the houses. Confirmation of the four Munshaqine dead outside Sianni thrown on to the road and left there. Thirty-nine dead since last week. They are using 240mm mortars on Shatila to destroy the houses completely with one bomb. We visit the hospital and Salim asks me if there are any foreigners working in Shatila.

Kristine checks the death list in Mar Elias then radios the PFLP to speak to Dolly. She asks if we are leaving. Dolly tells her to ask us herself. Then Kristine tells her that no assistance will be coming after all. We all curse them and refuse to acknowledge the message as they won't help us. Ahmad is as angry as I am.

Ghassan's mother has renal colic. I was taken to see her, and gave her an injection. He's handsome and sweet, and as I was leaving he gave me three flowers that he'd brought and put on the table in front of me.

Dolly and I drank home-made grape juice in Mohamad al Khatib's little home-run clinic. Dolly told me he was taken by the Syrians a short while ago in mistake for Borhan's brother who has the same name. They beat him until they realized that he had two legs and not one.

The ceasefire lasts one hour and now the shooting has started again, with Nawoosh sniping at one Munshaqine in Sianni going to throw TNT at his sandbagged position. More shooting, a mortar explodes, and then it stops. I have written another telex to Norway and London saying, 'We despair of sending you more, as you do nothing to assist us', but scrapped it as we felt it was too emotional and dramatic.

The 13-year-old son of the ice-cream-shop owner near the hospital will have his name on a wall in Palestine one day, as will the woman who died when the house collapsed on top of her, and Wissam who died slowly after a year of paralysis aged 16, Khadija Dibi, Zeinab, Maryam, Assad (Big Mosquito), Suliman, Rifat's cousin Hassan, Mohamad, Mehdi, Iyad and Ahmad (Hissam's brothers), Seeham's fiancé, and little Ibrahim, shot collecting grass for his family to eat near the graveyard. Sweet Ibrahim, 12 years old, wearing a full bullet clip and a beige polo-neck sweater, carrying a Kalashnikov, following his uncle Said Nasser around the camp's *mahwars*, and now dead. All of them will never be forgotten on the road to Palestine's rehabilitation to the lands of gentleness and fields, fruits, homes and freedom replacing oppression. Nasser, Tawfiq and Shaher will not have lost consciousness during beatings, or had their years in prison for nothing. Ghassan's M-16 scars as a 20-year-old and pain at his brother's death will not be wasted.

The PFLP boys from Yarmuk camp in Damascus, Tal al-Zatar in Beirut and Bedawi in Tripoli, now being tortured for their operation inside the security zone by the Israelis, will not suffer for empty ideals and naivety. When we heard of their capture we all felt their endurance and thought perhaps they would be better to have died. This suffering has taken them from exile outside in Lebanon, into their longed-for Palestine for their interrogation. I think of Mohamad Salim Bakri's insistent and constant refusal to be obscured, and his existence denied in the movie *Hannah K*, a Palestinian with no right to return to his homeland Palestine.

12.50 Hisham's wife has been killed. They had only been married some weeks. He had waited all through the 6-month war to wed her, and Ahmad and I had been invited to go for coffee on the engagement. She lived in the houses that have now been destroyed next to the Fatah office. For the first time she was afraid of the mortars and ran to the shelter; as she was the last one to go in, she was killed by the bomb exploding near her. Poor Hisham, he too is ill (epilepsy from the bomb that exploded next to him in the 45-day war), and was in love with her for a long time. She was only young and I went out to cry at the call (Shia) from the mosques around us in the suburbs.

Haj comes in, refusing even to attempt to go up and pray at the mosque, as he's frightened now that they have started bombing this area. So am I. Rasmi's water tank next to us has been hit, and his roof; we have just removed the rubble from the road and from blocking the sewers. The Al

Ashwas' house and the one opposite us across the road have also received direct hits. The Syrians call to us on the loudspeakers that if 'one bullet from the Tarshiha area hits their sandbags' they will demolish the camp with bombs from the mountains. With friends like that who needs enemies? The cat returns screeching as she hates bombing. The kittens are either hiding in the cupboard or under the bed.

20.45 Nine dead in Shatila, thirty-five injured between the camps, one dead in Bourj. Total death toll – eighty-four at both camps, 437 injured in seven weeks; approximately twelve dead per week, approximately sixty-two injured per week. It's awful.

The Syrians at the checkpoint ask if there are any injured. The women tell them a woman has been killed. They say that doesn't matter. Banan is angry: 'Only a woman,' she says. We went to the hospital to pay a visit. 'Divide and disarm', sing the Talking Heads. The same message from the mosque today. The Syrians claim they will not enter the camps until they are asked, as they were in the southern suburbs and West Beirut. Asked by whom? By Amal. Is Amal going to ask them into the camps as well?

At the hospital, we talked to the anaesthetist (who I thought was leaving, but seems to be staying or is perhaps stuck?), and met two of the four Sudanese doctors sent for fourteen days, who are slowly getting used to the hospital and attempting to adapt, God bless them. But a TNT explosion was followed by a mortar and we left and ran down to the clinic. We reach the clinic sweating. Nothing happens and we feel a bit foolish, although the square is emptier and Borhan says maybe there will be bombs.

Then we go to the front street to look at visitors who came from Saudi Arabia yesterday, but who cannot come in as men have not been allowed to enter the camp since the fighting started. So we stand at the edge and wave, on the grass where the garbage is dumped. They look at us and smile and walk towards the Syrians. People come and go in cars or bicycles and walking. The decimation of the front street is incredible; derelict, shelled buildings, with a wide, carefully cleared area in front of us, the rubble piled metres high on the other side of the road. The Syrian soldier appears and tells us to go into the camp; we ignore him, so he loads his rifle and points it towards us telling us to go back in. We laugh at him, at his fear of the camp, his fear of us, only women and girls, and we return into the camp.

Later I take Looi down; we watch all the boys come back, with military trousers, boots, Kalashnikovs, bullet clips, and wander home in pairs, just five minutes after the fighting ends: Aref and Ziad and the others, all looking relieved and weary at the same time. We greet each other with '*Al hamdo' lillah a salameh*', ('Thank God to see you safe,') '*Ahlan ya shebab*' (Greetings, young men,') '*Allah maak*,' ('God go with you,') the words flying from our relief.

I try to sleep as the tiredness after tension is almost overwhelming. I dream of sitting on the roof, of friends, the cat sitting on top of me, dozing and wanting food. Then give up with the shooting starting again.

Ghassan's mother blames her renal colic on the fighting. Looi and Dolly relate the Chinese superstition of fear giving babies green diarrhoea, citing New Year firecrackers as an example. And the other superstition that fear brings on a fever. True, we reckon that if the adrenaline goes up, sweating goes up, which leads to dehydration, encourages the onset of fever and illness, for example diarrhoea, renal colic, etc. Especially from sitting in the shelters for ten hours at a time with nothing at all to distract you.

Mortars start exploding from up at Samed across the camp; dropping all over the camp. Sultan sent messages to the fighters, 'Be ready for anything.' This is the beginning of the war in earnest by the sound of today. The Fatah boys have gone from standing still for a week without reply, to active defence. More TNT is being manufactured. B-7s, M-16s, and mortars all sizes are being used. Issam and Mustafa give up trying to sell us *falafel* during the ceasefires – all the fighting seems to hinge on the half hours. The Munshaqine are shelling us from Aramoun with Hassanoto. A self-declared ceasefire at 21.00. No agreements, a restocking and repositioning goes on. Boys come down again in pairs moving the ammunition around; relief at seeing friends alive again.

After thinking hard about Ghassan he came in, shocked with extensive sand burns on his left arm and side. I asked if it was anything to do with his deaf left ear, and told him please not to get injured again. He replied, 'I will fight until the last drop of blood is left.' I said, 'So we have to stay to mop it up, then.' He was very lucky: twice bullets exploded near him but not on him, thank God.

Afterwards I went outside to see the moon and feel the fresh air. Bourj was fighting alone this time, without Shatila; it felt good to take their weight for once. Johina was sitting with a cigarette on the water pipes in the alley next to her house, telling me that the sewer is her sea, with waves in it and the moon above. I asked her when she will go out of the camp again. She said, 'Maybe in three or four more years.' She has been here for two years now, apart from going out after bribes for her operation in Saida and Abu Jihad's funeral. '*Hassarna*' ('We are besieged,') she said.

23.6.88 Thursday

19.55 The death toll since May 9 is eighty for both camps.

More fighting all night until 4.45 when the last B-7 woke me up with the thump. Dolly is sleeping with her head against the wall for some strange reason and was kept awake all night by each explosion vibrating the building and bumping her head against the wall. Banan didn't sleep all night as they shelled over their house which only has one storey, no protection whatsoever.

A new order from Abu Ammar that there is to be no ceasefire in Bourj if Shatila is being attacked. The camps are no longer separate. Rumours in newspapers of seventy-five to 130 Fatah fighters joining the Munshaqine in Shatila. We find this hard to believe as many of them came via Saida and are not run-of-the-mill fighters. Even if it's true, we assume a plot aimed at demoralizing us.

A ceasefire was agreed from 19.00 within the camp today. The five points were:

1 Stop fire.
2 Stop building positions.
3 No bullets or sniping.
4 The community leaders – men from the mosque – to inspect the camp.
5 Meetings outside and inside the camp to observe the situation and analyse it for an immediate solution.

If fighting occurs in Shatila, we are to break the ceasefire in Bourj. This is very nice and would work if this was a localized war confined to the camp. But as the fighting is again Syrian-sponsored then it will not hold, given the history of their involvement in Lebanon.

This ceasefire of good intent is broken at 20.10 by the shelling of the middle of the camp with mortars. This time there was no warning shooting, B-7s or TNT; just straight, bastard, shelling, the same as Amal. Four at a time blanket shelling for fifteen minutes or so. Then stop. Then start again. Just as we step upstairs another shell is dropped. The sounds of screaming and of children crying as TNT exploded nearby.

Everyone is running for shelter in the dark of Arsan and Slieme. I got laughed at yesterday for saying I went to Haiduce, not Sianni: wrong building, wrong war. I forgot that the Munshaqine are now in control of Haiduce. The shelling is now deteriorating into the old frightening proportions; now we'll never know when they are going to try to kill us. 'Was it like this in the 6-month war?' asks Tha'ir. 'Every day, every day,' we told him. This is worrying. We now openly joke that there will be no Bourj camp left soon if they continue like this.

22.00 Mohamad is here, dizzy from making TNT explosives, despite medical advice on safety and numerous packets of gloves being handed out at all hours last night. I give up trying to sleep and go up to wash. The moon is half new, and bright in the sky. Tha'ir's house took a 120mm mortar yesterday, and a rocket exploded in front of the *dushmeh* in Salah's house.

When Øyvind and Kristine came we were dreading a protracted conversation. We showed Øyvind the six houses at Sianni, now destroyed by Monday's bombing, nothing left. Mirvat came with us as we stepped over the rubble to Tha'ir's house, new rocket damage and destruction. Øyvind remembered her, now very pregnant and homeless, only able to rescue the bedroom from the rubble of her new home. She called after me, 'You will stay here? In the clinic, you will be there?' I took Øyvind to the shelter and showed him where they had shelled near to the women and children on the staircase. He asked me what I was planning to do. I told him I will stay as I am PRCS and he said Norway is still trying to send a team: a surgeon, anaesthetist and theatre nurse. I told him about the Sudanese doctors and their fourteen-day limit in the hospital. We talked about the same strategies being used against the Palestinians since 1971; a 'filthy war', the same as the camp wars. MSF are trying to get equipment, medicine, etc, into Shatila. Our dear friend Mohamad is still going in and out when possible. I think Øyvind now understands the situation.

Ghassan came in the middle of all the farewells to Øyvind and Kristine. I did his burn dressing and his back and arm. He came out to say goodbye to Dolly, who is going out for a few days. A small bomb went off while Øyvind and Kristine were still here and Taisear and Haj came to tell them to leave in case anything started: we all thought Nawoosh was obliging us! Then they all left with Ahmad Aishey and Abu Hassan to the Jalbout exit where they had left the car outside.

When I got into the clinic there was a gardenia waiting on the desk. Tha'ir handed it to me saying, 'This is for Suzy from Ghassan.' I nearly fell over in shock. Jokingly, I pinned it over my heart and went out for air. Ghassan came up ten minutes later and quietly asked me if I had got the flower? I yanked my jacket up above the sandbags to show him where I had pinned it and he covered his face with mock embarrassment. I laughed and went inside still laughing. I have always liked him since I met him with Borhan in the first week of the 6-month war. He used to bring his nephew, little Hamid, to see me often then. He's so sweet, when he's not being proper. I was very frightened for him tonight with the mortars and his deafness – the first true fear in a long time.

A boys' club are here with Ahmad, all watching the football on TV.

24.6.88 Friday (The seventh Friday in the War of Fridays)

9.15 We are being shelled again, since 8.00. Like Amal before, they now start early in the morning to catch us out. So much for trying to sleep with my mouth open; I forget and now I'm sitting through this with my mouth closed. *Howens* are falling around us again. Um al Adnan appears to clean the clinic. She says that the shelling is up at 'Force 17' area, and we tell her there is shelling here. She smiles, then just as she starts to clean the floor, the shelling begins on the houses around us: Dorman's? Ringo's? Ibrahim's? Ramsi's'? She starts praying and, despite our asking her to stop and sit with us, she continues, praying and mopping. As she goes to the outside area, I say, 'Enough, only one room, I'll do the rest.' She sits for five minutes, finishes praying and gets up saying she's going to do a washing. We ask her to stay but, saying, 'It's all God's decision,' fatalistic, waiting to make the Haj pilgrimage, she goes off to the right of the camp, avoiding if possible the main hospital roads. '*A yamin yamin yamin.*' Ahmad asks her please not to come when there is shelling like this.

More *howens* now – this one sending shrapnel all around, maybe it hit Slieme. Every ten minutes, more big bombs. Just to keep us unsure, unready. The women and children shout as they run with mattresses and water to the shelter, Haj comes in cursing the Munshaqine. It's a blanket and circular bombing of the camp. None of the rules which Ahmad, Tha'ir and Dolly were following; no first bullet, TNT, B-7. They are using straight bombing in new directions in the camp, positioned during our ceasefires. Shatila has also been shelled since 8.00, the same time.

We try to invent a new word for ceasefire, as in reality it is little more than a break for the attacking forces to redesign their attacks. At least the casualties of defence are fewer than those of attack. One quarter at a rough estimate: one Fatah to four Munshaqine. A standard ratio of warfare. Thank God for the sandbags, and for no Munshaqine positions to the front of us in the southern suburbs. The Syrians are going after the Shouf mountain and PSP positions to make up for their failure in the suburbs, it is said.

The more they blow us up, the more determined we become to stay until the last house, the last breath, the last drop of blood. Why? Why do we love our right to remain here more than our lives? Perhaps it is inexplicable, maybe we will never understand!

Bombs landed in a circle round us today; six bombs per minute in a small square, says Ahmad. Later, after I treated the injury from the bomb near the PFLP-GC office at the cemetery, the door opens and in comes Ghassan. He asks me in English, 'Hello, how are you?' 'Very well. How are you?' 'Fine, thank you.' All bright eyes and smiles, like yesterday when we pulled faces at each other. Then loudly he asks, 'Where is Ahmad?' I reply, 'Inside'. He asks, 'Inside?' 'Inside.' It's the first time he has used English. Then they launch into a serious discussion about his dressings and he says he will come back tomorrow for the dressing instead of making twice the work for us. God, I was so worried about him today, I don't know why. Very, very worried.

Wrote to Hadla, Mum, Karma and the ICRC, and that's the lot I think.

25.6.88 Saturday

A rest day to recharge for the next few days. We have had a quiet day so far, but Shatila is being shelled, and there is shooting. The papers tell us the hospital is completely destroyed. A bomb lands in Ghassan's house. His mother is ill again. I visit twice, and he shows me the photos of Yugoslavia, his girlfriend there, and Cyprus. A quiet day in which the Munshaqine build new *dushem* and install 127mm rockets. A new attack is awaited.

Two of the Abu Taher family try to go out, their father arranged it with the Syrians. He comes to collect them from camp to take them to Hamra; the one who was injured twice is taken to the Beau Rivage, but the other is not allowed to leave the camp. Nice moon. Mummy cat had all the kittens out playing on the moonlit balcony and I had to move them inside in case of bombs. Shame.

26.6.88 Sunday

Ibrahim said last night that the Munshaqine has installed new rockets trained at UNRWA office beside the hospital from behind new sandbags. There are twenty-five families left in Shatila.

Woken at 5.20 by heavy shelling of Shatila. On instinct perhaps, I get up and make coffee, feed the cats, contemplate doing a washing, then hear a *howen* being launched. I thought the time was 6.20. I listen to a few shells, then Ahmad shouts for me to come down. I thought it was the Munshaqine shelling from Bourj to Shatila. I come down with the coffee and ask Ahmad is Nawoosh sleeping? He complains that Ibrahim, Ghassan, Abu Ehab and Abu Sultan stayed talking until 2.30. I try to sleep again, thinking perhaps to catch two hours more before 9.00, but they start to shell the camp at 6.15 and move on to our area at 6.45.

Mortars are falling all round us and then we hear shouts for help. Smoke everywhere and a woman runs in shocked. We scramble into our clothes. We can hear cries for help, but in the smoke and dust from the explosions can't see where the cries are coming from. The injured man is too shocked to answer our calls so we can locate him. Then Ahmad and Tha'ir run out into the mayhem and bring him through the kitchen; he is soaked in blood and has a ruptured femoral vein or artery. Ahmad, not unreasonably, refuses to fetch four people and a stretcher. I ask him again where they are as the man has to go to the hospital or he will die here from blood loss. A bomb has just exploded right beside us, blowing the door open, the room filling with smoke and shrapnel; the sandbags seem to be still standing by the sound of it.

Please come out of today alive. Please, please, please, all of you come out of today alive. The pressure makes my heart go to my mouth. Tha'ir calls them children of dogs. Shrapnel keeps flying through the kitchen window. Ibrahim yesterday had suggested more reinforcements. I told him how long I had had to ask to get the sandbags. Tha'ir goes out despite my asking him to stay in as I had heard three more bombs being launched; they explode next to us.

I was furious with Ahmad, as with better judgement than me, he had decided not to get people for the stretcher. When I asked, 'Where are they?', drenched up to my elbows in blood, he replied, 'There is no one –

you can't go to the hospital now. There are too many bombs falling everywhere.' I was yelling at him, pressing the hole, blood drenching my hands and the plinth I was yelling and yelling that he had to get someone. He said, 'There's no one.' I said, 'Well, go to Slieme and get someone.' He just stood there. I yelled again, 'Go and get them – this man has to go to hospital.' He just stood there intransigent, looking blank, knowing the severity of the bombardment. 'This man has a burst femoral artery; if he does not go to hospital he will die here.' Intransigence. 'Look, Ahmad, the only way to stop bleeding like this is for me to press as hard as I can [and still a huge swelling was forming inside] and he has to have an operation – he must go *now*!' He went to bring Ibrahim and Safwan (from the Syrian camps). Finally the three of them were going to go, but I reduced it to two, so that if a bomb hits them only three are dead. We put the oxygen and intravenous drips on the stretcher and blanket, and strap him and the splint in. Ahmad decides to go up. I refuse, telling him one bomb = four dead. 'You too is stupid.' Ibrahim says he will bring back the oxygen and stretcher. Thank God, Ibrahim and Safwan got to the hospital in a twenty-minute period of no shelling.

Nawoosh gives up trying to disguise the launch of the *howens* with a spray of bullets and is back to launching them straight from the pipe – shamelessly. We count the launches out and await the retaliation.

Sounds of running in the street, with guns clanking and soft-soled boots. A great explosion that vibrates may have been upstairs – houses are being demolished and the electricity has just gone off. The sewage is blocking from rubble in the street. Abu Mohamad protested that Nawoosh should move his mortar from here, but regardless of where they are we will be shelled anyway, merely for resisting. 'No electricity, so wishes Gemayel. What a shit country.' A bomb has hit the electricity wire; luckily the boys connect it to Haj's TV line, so we are only in the dark for ten minutes. Our hair and lungs fill with dust and fumes from explosives; I am coughing again.

Boys run past to the *mahwar* as the bomb falls. Everything from sandbags to emergencies is now happening as before. Ahmad still sits by the door in the kitchen despite warnings. Crashing mortars echo and reverberate around the mountains and still a plane takes off from the airport. The artillery seems to be getting heavier. 'Fighter teatime now,' says Tha'ir. 'Take a break,' says Looi, as we hope for a short break, 'a fighters' teatime'.

The shelling let up at 14.15 with the odd bomb falling every so often after that. It was at the rate of one bomb every four to ten seconds around 13.00. Two Syrians were killed at Jalbout and one at Shatila. We go out to inspect the damage and Banan whizzes by with an apricot for me as we run out to look at the empty unexploded-bomb hole at the video-shop pavement. Issam was inside the shop sorting the *hummus* when it fell. Omer was injured drinking coffee in his house, a burnt-out shell remains. The streets are chock-a-block with rubble, the air is dust laden, the wreckage shoulder high.

Then Wafiq comes in, and tells me the Syrians are taking the women and cutting their hair. As with all bad news it is so incredible that I disbelieve him as there is no proof. Then a few minutes later we hear wailing and sobbing, wailing and crying, and Tha'ir and I run out to the street as a woman goes past us sobbing and sobbing, her head covered with a shirt and we cannot see her face. As we catch up with her, I find it's Banan. She collapses in the street and we catch her just as she reaches the ground. We half-carry, half-drag her to the clinic. And then we discover in a tale of tears and shame that the Syrians caught her and her mother at the checkpoint, beat them up around their heads and necks and pushed them against a wall, where in front of a crowd of lieutenants and officers from the *mukuberat* they cut off their hair – at least six soldiers from the Syrian Forces hacked at their hair, especially at the front of the face and forehead, to cries of 'Cut it more, cut it more, to zero, zero,' from the officers and *mukuberat*. When the PFLP send a woman to investigate she is told that the Syrians did nothing, the girls and women are lying.

We give Banan five milligrammes of Valium to try to settle her. She is very distraught as her fiancé arrives to see her for the first time next week from Jordan. And she is very ashamed. Noora appears with a less brutal version of the haircut, but shorn still. Banan was beaten around the face and ears with such force that she lost both earrings. Bahia is shaking and upset as she narrowly escaped having her hair cut also.

The Sudanese doctors are leaving tomorrow instead of in fourteen days. It is too much for them. The four placed in Shatila left yesterday and one was shot in the arm by the Munshaqine as he was leaving. The Syrians were sniping into the camp with M-16s hitting the clinic wall half an hour ago and round the women and girls sheltering in Slieme. The water is off as the pipes are completely damaged; no water all day. An awful day.

27.6.88 Monday

Shatila is finished, the twelve commanders and seventy-five fighters surrendered at midday today to Libyan delegates.

21.00 After shelling for forty-eight hours and a toll of ninety-four dead and 495 injured Shatila had to surrender. The injured were taken out this morning; the Sudanese doctors left two days ago, at the time when we heard rumours of the hospital being finished and only twenty-five families left. As with all the terrible news, we cannot believe it. Tha'ir tells me about it after hearing it on the 12.30 news; Mirvat and Samir come in also shocked, and we debate it, comparing the withdrawal and fate of the remaining fighters and the camp space with the situation here. Then

Safwan tells me that they want to take all the Arafatists to prison. Amné Jibril is still inside the camp. How are Mohamad, Abu Tito, Dr Al Khatib, Dr Iman, Dr Mohamad Asslan? What will happen to them? Oh God, three years of bleeding, bleeding, bleeding, to come to this? Some have already gone to Tripoli and Saida, the injured went to Saida. Some heard on the *silké*, 'Shatila is finished, now Bourj.' All their artillery is now for us: six dead yesterday, fires, and the Shatila fighter reported on the *silké* that they are hungry and tired. Syrian soldiers were also fighting as the Munshaqine advanced inside the camp last night, until 6.00; forty-eight hours of continuous bombardment. We are worried; the people here are very pessimistic and all but those who can't or won't are leaving or have already left. The only women left at this end, are Um Tariq, her daughters, Nadia, Johina, Looi and me.

Ibrahim says the news about Shatila is the worst so far. 'But it is good that it took them three years to kill Shatila; now it will take the same for us.' I don't think so. The end of Tal al-Zatar took six weeks. If they use 240mms then it will be the same here. Already we have water problems: they repaired the damage from yesterday, but it is a weak supply. Now they are all too late to save Shatila. 'Hungry and beaten down.'

I wrote the report on the women's assaults yesterday. Many women are too frightened to speak of it. Sixty-five were attacked from both inside and outside the camp, all from Bourj al-Brajneh.

I moved the house downstairs today, made a home with the plants from up on the roof – an indoor garden, and brought the cooker, cats, iron, plants, clocks and books down. Today we made sandbags from our blankets, Ghassan, Abed, Ahmad, Looi, Safwan and myself; we hand-sewed them first from Ahmad's cut-out patterns, then Abed took me to Maryam's mother who has a sewing machine. Then we filled them with sand at Arsan, and the boys, with Looi's help, brought the bags to the clinic. We put them at the kitchen door half-covered and on the staircase window three-quarters-covered.

Ghassan was fooling around during his dressing. He wouldn't let me touch it and yelped every time I went near him with the forceps. Then when telling me his mother had gone out of the camp, he started pretending to cry: 'I'm here alone, no mothers or sisters.' So I said, 'Me, too, alone, my mother and father are in Scotland and my sister is in London.' He said, 'No, you are not alone, you are my sister, you are the sister of all the camp, they are your brothers.' Later he comes back to borrow scissors to trim his dead brother's photograph. In it I see a young Ghassan as I remember him, thin and sitting on the step of their house with Hassan his dead elder brother during the 45-day war. 'You were not here,' he says gruffly. I protest that I was trying to get a visa to come but there were none, so I was in Abu Dhabi waiting. I also bring down the photo of Maryam and Dolly, trim it and put it in front of the photograph of Ghillie and Ru.

The Libyans declare that if anyone fires into the camp they will be invading Libyan territory. The bulldozers are said to be ready and waiting outside Shatila, already another Zatar. Abu Fahdi is quoted as 'worrying about the women and children'. We are rumoured to have 3,000 Arafat fighters left in Bourj-al-Brajneh. A woman, very frightened, comes to the Al Khatibs' home to tell of *dushem* she has heard of, very afraid. We watch a James Bond movie with Sean Connery on video at the Al Khatibs', as ammunition is being sorted and guns are greased and loaded with bullets, scattered in piles and boxes around the floor.

Tuesday 28.6.88
4.30 The defenders of Shatila left to go to Saida, ninety-six men including fighters, sixteen women and four children: 116 people.

9.30 Mustafa Sa'ad refuses to let them enter Saida; everyone is still applying for permission for them to enter Ain al-Helweh and Mieh Mieh.

21.00 At 15.15 the 116 people were finally allowed to cross the Awali bridge on which they had been waiting for eleven hours since leaving Shatila at 4.30. Such torture sitting in trucks for eleven hours in the heat on a bridge, with those who want to kill you behind you, and those who are with them in front of you, having organized demonstrations against you, mobilized all their militias against you, burnt tyres in the streets and refused to allow you access to safety of sorts, to a refuge of sorts.

Mustafa Sa'ad showed his true colours today, despite Arafat money, as Jumblatt did last year. Take the money, play the games, acquiesce with the Syrians in the hope that Syria will abandon its expansion to the whole of Lebanon. Are they mad? Do they, including Berri, Abu Fahdi, Isa, Musa *et al* really think anything will prevent Syria from uniting Greater Syria, or at least attempting to? From Tripoli to Nabatiya, perhaps on to Palestine, Jordan and down to Egypt? Issam and I joke, 'Are they going to take us to Saida before or after they destroy all the houses?' 'Why, after, of course,' says Issam, 'and not before they have killed some of us and demolished the houses.'

In Shatila apparently Nidal, PFLP and DFLP have regrets about their mistake of pulling the political organizations out of the camp a week ago, thus being tricked by a fake ceasefire into allowing the continuous bombardment in their absence that led to the capitulation of the camp. They are debating whether or not to fight and help us to protect the camp, or let their homes be destroyed also, like Shatila.

Debates over how to protect the camp; we are making bags out of blankets. DFLP and PFLP have many bags and TNT, etc, but refuse to help or hand them over or to assist, but a free ambubag and laryngoscope from MSF arrive with a visitor from outside.

Dubké is being danced by Munshaqine in Mar Elias and sweets handed out in celebration of the fall of Shatila. Random shooting and bombs in Bourj, sweets and whooping in celebrations too. Hisham al Jishi passes by, looking distraught at the death of his wife and now of his cousin yesterday in Shatila.

We sit in the street: Tawfiq al Caq, Johina, Mohamad, Haj and others. Now we're laughing. Before we were absolutely miserable at the thought of friends dying (although Khaled is alive, not dead), of Kirin's friends dead in the defence of Shatila; of the destruction of our houses and lives, the clinic, the cats, work, friends, our deaths, our hopes and happiness. Near to tears, all of us unable to voice our saddest thoughts on the symbolism of Shatila's agonizingly slow death. Ghassan passes, waves a hand in frustration and goes to sit on the far side of the square, lost in his thoughts. I think of him yesterday sewing sandbags with us. We are all lost in our thoughts.

Kristine comes in early with Looi with the MSF medicines. She is badly frightened by the Munshaqine celebrations and the shooting-off of rounds of bullets. I learnt immediately that Mohamad is out, evacuated from Shatila; safe, not dead as we felt he may be. NORWAC is deciding his future; perhaps he too, like the 116 from Shatila, wants to come to Bourj. The Libyans asked if this could happen, the Syrians refused. One hundred Arafat fighters have no refuge. To defend your self-determination is to court your death.

29.6.88 Wednesday

News not good today; although Mustafa Sa'ad is rumoured to be playing a political game perhaps orchestrated by Abu Ammar, the Syrians have now declared after their meeting in Damascus that there are to be no more PLO in Beirut and negotiations are now under way for a peaceful withdrawal of all PLO fighters from Bourj al-Brajneh. Sultan has not updated us on his yesterday's views of 'Fight to defend the camp', and no other news (or history).

Thinking about our own deaths preoccupies us from time to time, and the imminent destruction and leaving of the camp saddens us. We wait. No more Arafatists are to be admitted to Saida from Bourj al-Brajneh, so we have to stay and fight it out. Ahmad thinks we may have to go 'to the sea' as we have joked about before, and complains that the pollution scare is still on. A friend talks to Øyvind about the political solution, but privately tells him, 'We must stay to defend the camp, all of us, to the last drop of blood.' Ghassan brings us a gardenia; the kittens are wreaking havoc on the plants. He's sweet and comes back for his dressing after we finish lunch.

20.40 The same as before. Abu Fahdi tells the world that if Fatah leaves Bourj-al-Brajneh then he will help UNRWA rebuild the camp. If they do not leave he will destroy it. The Munshaqine invite the people to return to Shatila camp. As there is nothing left now but rubble and sand this is a difficult invitation to follow up. It seems he doesn't know what he wants – the continued existence of the community or not.

Hopefully Dolly's press conference in Oslo went well and people understand what is happening here after three weeks of non-understanding. The same list of eighteen Fatah people to leave the camp has again been presented to the camp population. So far Sultan refuses to leave, but if ordered by Abu Ammar will do so. He will go to Cyprus or Tunis this time perhaps, not to Saida. Also on the list are Mohamad Fawzi, Johina Akashi, Tawfiq al Caq and the others. So we wait. Meanwhile a hand grenade goes off, and shooting. And we wait, and we worry about which of us will die, who will lose limbs, who will lose friends, who will be exiled from family and friends. And still the women come and go in the morning as Shatila used to eight months ago. Silence in the camp until 9.30 or 10.00, then silence again after 13.30. Øyvind tells us the only people he and Kristine met on the road into the camp were two families with their belongings going out.

It is a chore these days to write as sometimes I wonder what use it is for a foreigner to record her version of the Palestinian experience. The world sickens me with its spoken desire to help, yet making pictures and commemorations of us once we are dead is all the people do in reality. Ziad tells me that all the people in the camp are very bored. (I think he means *za'an* – fed up.) He says that when this war started they thought it would only last one week or two. Now we are in the eighth week. We wait. Johina tells me she wants to leave Beirut, leave Lebanon, she's had enough. No wonder, the alternative is to end up like Amné, collapsed in Saida after three years' incarceration inside Shatila until the end.

Tha'ir eats olives, tomatoes, cucumber and bread, reminding himself of the days in 1982 when he, Nawoosh, Salah, Nasser and Mohamad Da'ah were fighting from the airport road to East Beirut, of days in dugouts, nights in dugouts, under the trees to hide from the Israeli planes. Of the time Salah 'the Destroyer' broke down the wall of a building they were in at the last minute to escape from the Israeli tanks that surrounded them. 'He saved our lives, we would all be dead.' Of how easy it was to fight that war as there was a clear enemy, and how difficult this war is – the psychological disadvantage of attacking fellow Palestinians who in turn have no qualms whatsoever about attacking you. He talks of how he will always want to defend the camp, and of how in the invasion his commander had to slap his face to make him leave the front and go to Hamra to visit his family for two hours, as he was so youthfully determined to defend the camp.

30.6.88 Thursday

The news continues to get worse and worse by the minute. Now there is the announcement on the radio that ten members of Fatah have to leave the camp, plus all the Fatah fighters, to go either to Tripoli or Sudan. The Syrians are looking for a fight, no settlement without disruption of the community and the PLO will do. None of us will go to Saida for another stage of the genocide at Ain al-Helweh, with the help of the Israeli air force. Abu Iyad again talks on the radio of the deal between Syria and America to clear out the PLO before the Lebanese (and American) elections.

Mohamad Dirbi, aged 22, was shot in the head with a Kalashnikov bullet at 6.50 this morning at Sianni; he died instantly. He was standing in a doorway when he was sniped.

The Syrians refuse to allow the camp to repair the main water pipe on the front street, the Syrian Army having a long history, of course, of killing people by dehydration as in Tal al-Zatar. So we all carry buckets and go through a palaver to arrange hoses and motors, etc, to get to another supply. This is okay when there is no bombing, but if we are bombed then we will run out of water in two and a half days – and that is only providing our tank is not hit.

A TNT blast while two reporters from Reuters are sitting in the clinic. How do we pass our free time? 'Folding gauze,' says Looi. Again they had been misinformed about the Munshaqine, not believing that there were any in the camp and incredulous that they are inside the camp and so near to us. 'But we were told that there aren't any inside?!'

An old lady from Shatila is interviewed on TV collecting her belongings. She says of Abu Fahdi's stated remorse about the women and children that she will now live outside the camp, leaving it to these 'new people' who have destroyed her home and her life, as she cannot live with 'them' after that. (The black kitten is eating the corner of this jotter as I write.)

We hear repeated stories of an exodus from the camp taking place at Jalbout exit; reportedly similar to the film of people from Shatila trying to salvage what is left of their homes shown yesterday. Tha'ir and I go to see. It is true. We follow an elderly woman dressed in black towards the exit at Jalbout and she is carrying two very large suitcases on her head. We are greeted with scenes of great to-ing and fro-ing at the Jalbout strip, women and girls and boys carrying out whole gas cookers, furniture suites, baby cots, mattresses, basins of crockery, pots, towels and clothing, all in the heat of midday, up and down to a stream of cars and service taxis crammed into the exit at the front street. It is like a mass holiday in the sunshine and sand and palm trees. The atmosphere is determined: determination not to lose everything owned – again. Gas cylinders and relatives. Delal's family are moving tables and chairs out, the Shehadi girls, aged 13 or 14, come in saying, 'We are from a steadfast house, we are all inside – we are not leaving.'

Later Issam shoots a bullet off in a joke disagreement about money, then Nawoosh uses the twenty-three kilos of TNT in an abortive attempt to bring down a building and we are all covered in clouds of dust and sand. We should stop listening to the news as it just gets worse and worse. A woman in Rashidiyeh tells her son on the *silké* that Amal are preparing positions again around the camp. Tha'ir says it's a big game; it's seemingly going to be the summer of the persecution of the Palestinians in Lebanon.

21.00 A seven-point ceasefire is adopted again. We heard first from the PFLP-GC as Aref and Ziad came in; they wish to leave the camp tonight or tomorrow morning and want the Norwegians' address outside in case they make it. The seven points are:

1 No more fighting between Fatah and Munshaqine.
2 All building of positions to stop.
3 All positions to be dismantled from 10.00, 1 July 1988.
4 All who have fled to return to the camp.
5 The Munshaqine to have offices inside the camp.
6 The situation to return to that before the fighting on 30 April 1988.
7 No more disagreements to occur.

Whether it will hold or not is the question.

Eight Algerian doctors arrive, Ighlas comes in, as does Nasser. Two surgeons, two anaesthetists, four others, three will stay in the camp tonight.

Ghassan comes in with his 'head exploding' from the war, the noise in his ear, the pain in his leg, and says it is all coming from inside his head, soon the whole camp will be gaga and crazy. He is in a very bad mood. Borhan, Mustafa and Issam are all called away to a meeting about 'the ceasefire'. Looi tries to remove the cottonwool stuck in Ghassan's ear.

1.7.88 Friday

So much for all the great promises. After a jolly and relaxed morning of singing, chatter, women and children coming in and out – nothing happens. Great meetings are promised inside and outside the camp; hopes go up, there was impromptu dancing in the square last night and Ahmad was dancing this morning, but then the radio tells us that Abu Musa declares no ceasefire despite the deliberations of the Beirut meetings. Jokes about going on the boats to Tunis; Nawoosh *et al* opt for a life of peace and beaches in Tunis. Johina too. We wait feeling relieved due to four days without bombs, but still Mohamad was shot yesterday. Mohamad Hallimi comes in frequently with minor complaints. He's getting more and more depressed. It's really worrying. His dressing was wet from washing the dead Mohamad's body for burial.

Twenty-nine are rumoured to have left the camp from Fatah, including Ahmad Hayek, one of the Fatah leaders, who has not only left, but joined the Munshaqine. This is a blow and is talked about and debated all morning.

Ghassan appears for his dressing, saying he is *'Al Hamdo'lillah zift.'* ('Thanks be to God – awful.') Kristine doesn't come with the emergency lab or other things we requested. The Algerians are still here, and Johina finally gets her chest X-ray and has another shadow on her lung. She had a biopsy last year in the other breast.

We all agree that the women and children should go out as the shelters are unsafe and unsanitary, and people often go outside safety to the shelters when bombing starts and get killed. But it has depressed so many people that others are leaving as it continues to drain the resources for defending the camp. As yet the DFLP and PFLP have to decide whether to stay and fight, or to hand over their TNT and sandbags. This is also demoralizing as, when they returned to Shatila, someone from Nidal was beaten, the PFLP people were all taken prisoner, and Jebet Nidal, the Popular Struggle Front, were closed down, so no freedom for others here or in Tripoli.

Al Ittihad newspaper in Abu Dhabi produced a terrifically accurate cartoon of a power-crazed Hitlerite figure waving the victory symbol as a Nazi salute, surrounded by various sycophants declaring that, 'Now he has liberated Shatila he will liberate Jerusalem in a day,' and that the act of liberating Shatila from the enemy was of benefit to the road to Palestine. The paper comments that Abu Musa has performed what the entire IDF and 6-week siege of West Beirut could not do, in making the legitimate representatives of the Palestinian people leave the camp; he achieved this despite the massacres, despite the Amal wars waged through Syria. So now Abu Musa should be called Ariel Sharon, as he has made Sharon very happy.

On the Amal radio we hear in Arabic that Abu Musa declared, 'We have cleared the shit out of Shatila, and we will clear the shit out of Bourj, and then we will cleanse Saida after that.' He says all the Beirut agreements are not valid. (Not put thus in the English broadcast.) We get depressed, and again worry about what they intend to do with us. The radio news is old news. Borhan offers me coffee in the dark, and we all joke about enrolling all the women now on *harasi* (duties) at the *mahwars*. Borhan wears a photo of Arafat round his neck and offers it to me.

I go to the roof to water the flowers in the dark as Ahmad has given me a row for doing it during daylight because of the snipers. I want to give the flowers to the fighters as the gladioli and the carnations are fading unseen in the sun, but I feel embarrassed. Everyone has tension headaches and sleeplessness, and even Issam goes shooting in the square, with laughter and fighting.

2.7.88 Saturday

Abu Musa declares on the radio that he never said anything quoted by the Amal station, and that there is no agreement reached in Mar Elias. Ahmad says that one pushes as the other pulls; one minute Beirut agreements are struck, with abuse from Abu Musa; then the next day a lessening of hostility from Abu Musa, but declarations of no agreement from Beirut and Damascus. We all sit depressed in the square, not helped by sleeplessness through anxiety, tension, fear, whatever. The camp is emptying. 'Another week of this,' says Tha'ir, 'and the camp will be completely empty.' 'We want children, children back in the camp,' said Haj the other day. 'I send the kids out to be safe and they injure each other when they come back into the camp,' says Abu Sultan after Hamoudi aged 4 has whacked Maisa over the head with a lump of wood, giving her a bleeding scalp wound.

Cleo is taking the air in the sun, outside the *falafel* shop, looking more and more like a tiger every day, after getting a few 'when necessaries' across the nose, for attempted robbery of sweet-and-sour chicken Looi has cooked and put on the table. (Tha'ir's method of cat discipline is a whack across the nose only 'when necessary'.)

Kristine and Mohamad come in and bring us the battery-run emergency lamp (MSF-donated again), medicine, autoclave paper and tapes, and camera film. They have been down to Shatila, and Kristine is shaken by what she saw. They tried to take medicines into Rashidiyeh but were refused by Amal. She says they will try and come back on Monday. I ask for more stocks, scissors for emergencies, film and food stocks in case. She asks again if we will leave and we refuse. She says that the PLO in Saida thanks us for remaining, and that they are furious at PRCS for leaving Shatila as it demoralized the fighters, leading to an earlier capitulation. They leave after an hour.

Lots of new Fatah fighters have been moved down from Samed to around the clinic. Coming down the hill, carrying mattresses and looking weary, they are being stationed around the clinic to defend the empty buildings here. Haj's girls come in to see their father and go out again. Another man brings his little daughter, telling us she was born in the 6-month war and he has sent the rest of his kids out but is keeping her with him. She is cute with a wide space between the eyes.

Lots of people are out in the square, and the noise carries of tea glasses being stirred, and leaders coming and going like old times. A letter comes in from a journalist outside who writes for *Al Nahar* (the Lebanese government paper) and the *Daily Mail*. I'm thinking about what to say in reply.

I am tired again already after catching two hours sleep from 13.00 to 15.30. My hair is falling out with the stress, as is Ahmad's. Darwish al Masri, the plumber, fixes the water in the street again, up to his elbows in black silt. He tells me Aref has gone outside with Juju and Ziad. Ahmad Hayek's house is burnt down in the middle of the night and inside four little kittens are burnt to death. The Al Jishi family also sends its boys out. The mother of Mohamad Dirbi passes us wailing and crying in the street.

One man from the Munshaqine comes past. Tha'ir yells, 'Emergency case' but they take him to prison. We set up and then dismantle the emergency gear; then he's brought back again as he has too much blood on his face to be kept in prison. He is a prisoner from the Munshaqine, although he spent the 6-month war with us, helping us to launch mortars. He has been acting in a bizarre fashion and has been drinking Septol disinfectant (equivalent to Dettol and lemon juice) by the bottle and started a fight. He was causing such problems that Nawoosh decided to release him outside the camp. So they took him up to Majnuk, gave him 15,000 Lebanese lira and told him to go to the Syrians. He refused. So they took him back to prison. Then he started a fight and someone laid into him, perhaps with help. To be Munshaqine is not an advantage these days. And he was hit, kicked on the ground as he was covered in sand, and beaten with stones. He came in with two scalp lacerations on both sides, one deep and one shallow. I cleaned and dressed the injuries and had an argument over stretchers as the guards wanted him to walk, but as he was concussed we wanted him to go on a stretcher for a skull X-ray and observation. More arguments about placing the stretcher outside the clinic or inside, etc, with us shouting at people to bring it inside. Then they threw the poor man around on it. I went up with him to the hospital to explain what had happened. The poor man was so frightened, clenching his fists in the effort not to cry.

3.7.88 Sunday

The noise of bombs, *howens*, bullets and rockets comes over from outside, bringing a bomb into the camp. 'Where is that from – Amal?' come surprised voices in the dark. Mustafa is dancing around with a fly-swat saying that all the camp has gone crazy; echoed by Issam and Ghassan. We are all crazy.

The day passes quietly – no electricity again, but as we have water from yesterday it is not a problem yet. The flowers were upright and in full bloom on the roof after the watering. Carnations, gladioli, green tea, geranium and honesty plants. All glowing in the starlit sky and shadows of the camp in darkness. How we miss sleeping on the roof, sitting relaxing and laughing in the cool breezes that are trapped in the basin of the camp below.

We clean out the clinic this morning after sleeping until 9.00. I slept from 23.00, so got ten hours! No disturbed sleep, no nightmares, but circuitous dreams of people and streets I don't know, with leafy trees and cars, and bombs exploding in them. When I wake up I ask if there were more bombs and the answer is, 'Yes': bullets and *howens*, plus one rocket in reply from the East, and hand grenades. 'They tried to make a new war here, but Fatah refused to return fire,' is the explanation.

We are reading by kerosene lamp with the Kalashnikovs for the boys' duties resting against the sandbags; mosquitoes are swirling around the mattresses and the little table Ahmad made from the stool he broke, sawing away when erecting the sandbags. What a life. Despite the bombs last night we are less pessimistic, in fact a lot of nervous tension is released through clapping, singing and dancing today, the boys dancing to the radio with a fly-swat.

After tea, Amal radio gives an account of the taking of all the young Palestinian men from Haret Hreik and telling them to register at Mar Elias camp on certain dates and times: done by the Munshaqine. It's hideously similar to the rounding up and registration of the Jews by the Nazis, before the ghetto-ization and concentration camps. The Armenian genocide, the slow death of the Kurds, all history repeating itself – *ad nauseam*.

We have a visit from two of the Algerian doctors, who speak with such a dialect that I cannot understand either their Arabic or their French; we used an interpreter who worked for a while in Algeria. One asks me why I am here and whether I prefer Abu Musa or Arafat. I reply that the legitimate representative of the Palestinians and observer to the UN is the PLO under Arafat, and as the PRCS is the legitimate health service of the PNC with observer status to the League of Red Cross and Red Crescent Societies I support the official representatives of the majority of the Palestinian people. They are sweet and want to come back for photographs tomorrow.

Rats are squeaking away outside. Ghassan is reasonably sour today, but lingers on, reading the weight for height chart outside after his friend leaves. I don't know what's wrong with him. Poor boy, his ear hurts too much – I'll send him to the hospital tomorrow, perhaps the Algerians have an ear, nose, throat specialist? I'll save the flowers upstairs for him, as he has given us so many recently.

4.7.88 Monday

The fireworks for Independence Day are filling the air with phosphorus, explosives and shrapnel. Since 5.00 we have been bombed and bombed and bombed. Over forty bombs in two minutes – one bomb every three seconds. The mummy cat came in to steal fish and then the little stray wailed to come in. We don't know where the others are, but mummy cat seems quite unperturbed by it all, she's asleep under the desk in the cat *dushmeh*. Six Munshaqine are dead in three buildings up near the hospital, all sniped as they tried to move towards the hospital during an attack. The PFLP overheard plans to shell the hospital area heavily and warned Fatah who mobilized at 4 am. The PFLP and DFLP are supporting the camp with shelling from positions in the mountain. Abu Musa is shelling from the mountains and Sports City near Shatila. We can hear them to the right and behind us as they are launched.

Mohamad al Khatib is injured in his left arm; he is sitting on the roof behind us sniping. Completely courageous and selfless, one leg, crutches, and two or three snipers shooting at him from Sianni with 500mm, M-16 and God knows what. Haj comes in. Reports are that perhaps two from the camp are dead. One of the Munshaqine is injured in the chest and abdomen and has run into Haifa Hospital to give himself up to Fatah. The Algerian doctors will be working overtime, as the hospital area is also being bombed with phosphorus and several houses are on fire and burning endlessly with the bloody stuff. Thank God they are here. (I ducked as the *whizz, whoosh* of another 160mm mortar comes over and explodes in front of us. It's very, very unnerving as the *whizz* makes you wonder if it's coming to explode on top of you this time, or go past you again. Every three minutes or so at present.) The road to the hospital is also completely destroyed – again. We found the two other kittens hiding in the sandbags outside – too frightened to come inside and running confused into the sunshine instead of indoors.

There are two factors which help. One is that Shatila is no longer fighting. This helps our morale as we used to feel so much for them, attacked endlessly with no shelter from the bombs and very tired after three years and two months of continuous attacks. Plus the fact that Abu Tito, Amné and the others are now in comparative safety. The second is that after a week of anticipating this, it has finally started.

12.15 The radio tells us thirty are injured in today's fighting and possibly seven dead. Kristine and Øyvind won't be coming in: the camp is completely closed. Still no electricity and rationing for another twenty-four hours. *Al Dohar* – the midday calls – reverberate from all around us in the southern suburbs: crying for '*Al salam al alikum*', peace to all, devotion to God and the Q'uran, and bullets and mortars crashing down around the mosques and faithful in the sunlight and heat.

23.30 Ghassan died this morning – he was shot in the head by a 500mm bullet and had the top of his head blown off. 'You couldn't know it was Ghassan by his face; there was nothing, all his brain was out,' Ahmad tells me. They are all tired from fighting, there were only three left up at

Balbekeyeh at the Jesh Tahrir road where three died including Ghassan, sniped at a lookout hole as the Munshaqine advanced. Ahmad agrees with me when I said he was talking too much recently of death, as though he knew he would soon die. I was saving our first carnations to give him, waiting just to see him tonight to give them as thanks for all his flowers; now it is too late.

The hospital closed after shelling all day. The Algerians left the camp after half the hospital was blown away, including the emergency room. A number of wounded were evacuated: perhaps thirty? It took just one day to finish the hospital. The Algerians were quoted as saying, 'We will never leave the hospital – never,' by Mr Salah only twenty-four hours before they left. We had no warning and were swamped by mortar and blast injuries. We sent out one boy with a long skull laceration line and shrapnel embedded in the bone. There were no X-ray or lab technicians yesterday afternoon, they had left the camp. Now no one is left at all. How can the boys defend the camp if they may die unnecessarily from injuries?

5.7.88 Tuesday

Two rockets from the mountain have exploded; six mortars in three minutes. 160mm and 240mm, *rajmehs* now too, from below us and up in the camp. The M-16 sniper who has been shooting up the front of the clinic balcony and roof is still going even after all-night shooting and bombs. But at least we slept.

Najib, Muammer's brother, looks worn out – grieving for Muammer. He was here last night coughing with his chest infection, swaying with fatigue from two nights without sleep and grief at the death of his younger brother in the afternoon. Najib's younger brother, Lui, and I were both outside, red-eyed with tears, at dusk; I standing on the steps crying and crying for Ghassan and Muammer. He walked past me to the memorial, just as Ghassan had the night before, and stood silently crying and beating the metal with his fists in grief. He's 15, Muammer was 17. Najib said nothing, but Wafiq looked terrible and fell asleep on the floor with only a pillow under his head until he was woken at 4 am. Lui eventually went to the *mahwar* after Borhan called his name several times.

Johina estimates that fewer than 1,000 people are now left inside. Hassan Abu Arab was evacuated with severe chest shrapnel injuries plus a chest tube. The Syrians took him prisoner as he was evacuated with the wounded in the agreed ceasefire and evacuation. No one knows what they have done with him. If they even detain him he could die, due to the necessity of chest tube, blood, antibiotics, physiotherapy and care with rest. Sobhieh is worried sick. So now we cannot even evacuate the seriously injured in safety.

Tha'ir's house had half of each storey destroyed by TNT yesterday night. Ahmad's house had the sitting room destroyed by phosphorus that burnt four houses after it fell outside. Complete phosphorus bombs are being used now, not just in the tip. 240mm and 160mm, and evidence that the Syrian Forces are also fighting and shelling against the camp since yesterday, as they did in Shatila.

The radio tells us of the arrival of Libyan and Algerian delegations, but, as before, every time the delegation is due the camp is heavily shelled to prevent entry and to continue the war. Rumours of the twelve wanted Fatah people leaving are unfounded. People talk openly of the Syrian torture methods including *al Cursi* – the chair where you can die of torture by electric shock within a few minutes of being strapped to it.

We were full with people injured until 23.30 last night, then managed to sleep before being woken by women at 8.00. At least we slept, if fitfully – I woke again earlier at 5.00. Looi slept on the table, I underneath her on a sheet as it is too hot with all the windows sandbagged and no air circulating. Johina awoke cursing all those who took Fatah money and left the camp. Um Mohamad sits on our steps sobbing. Nadia provides biscuits as we haven't eaten since breakfast yesterday and Ibrahim tells me how dangerous it is. I say, 'What do you suggest I do? Run away?' 'No, *I* want to run away.' Mustafa wants me to look at his mouth – after being shot through his lip and out.

Ghassan's mother is in the shelters with her daughters. I wish I had gone to stay the night and to eat every time I was asked. I wish Ghassan had gone out of the camp. Oh God, why does she have to lose Hassan *and* Ghassan? Is one not enough?

The hospital is empty, full of stores that we can't reach. And perhaps also the dead are still lying in the corridors where they were left yesterday. No one knows for certain, the fridges aren't working anyway, as there is no electricity.

Muammer was so sweet, pale and thin, with Renaissance looks, thoughtful and kind, and now dead and we are grieving him. I had written Ghassan's name in my mental list of things to do, in an effort to sleep the night before. I was so worried for him, I wanted to see him alive so desperately. I must have known, as he did. The last time we saw each other was in the clinic as he turned around before walking out of the door. I went out with him, looking at him completely miserable. He never brought the bloody medicine back. He was just a shadow in the dark, collecting water from the pipe, washing his face and wandering down to the memorial behind the Algerian doctors before returning home with the 'gallon' of water for his mother and sisters. I'd said a quiet 'Hello' as I passed him when I left Borhan's; he looked up, that's all. Eleven dead and thirty wounded yesterday. We don't care if we live or die now.

14.16 There is talk of an agreement to end the constant shelling of the camp. It is that all Fatah in the camp must leave to go to Saida, not just the twelve requested for the past three years. Abu Musa is saying, 'Why did all the Palestinians who fled the camp come to Mar Elias? Because there are strangers in the camp. All the strangers have to leave and then you can come back to the camp.'

Then the bombing stopped and talk of the arrangements became a reality. Boys shaved their beards which had grown during the war and made preparations to leave, with suitcases, guns and ammunition being secreted in houses, bits and pieces being carried out of the camp. A cooker, a suitcase, books. We went to look at Saiqa, and on the way we met Wissal al Jishi. I asked Ahmad what she was doing inside the camp. He replied, 'She's here to spy.' In the square Um Tariq ran past looking for Sultan, then came down with a thinly disguised BKC in a black plastic bag, an M-16 polished, cleaned and greased, and a Kalashnikov. 'Where is she going?' I asked. 'Whose are these?' 'Ghassan's,' said Borhan quietly. 'Whose?' 'Ghassan Abdo's.'

Then I went to see the road to the hospital but it was so covered with large blocks of rubble that I came back to the clinic to get proper shoes and Looi's camera. I was walking up to the hospital just past the road where Hassan's house used to be – the lunar landscape has been completely flattened. I met Wafiq and his wife Fatima, and their sisters and relatives going up the road to the hospital weeping. They told me to go up with them in case of more bombs, and we made our way through the holes in the shells of the hospital road where houses and *mahwars* had been only three or four days ago when we had last walked past it. Now it is completely demolished, with dust, sand and mattresses sticking out in brightly coloured piles where houses had once been. We went into the blackened hospital, and they went on to the X-ray room. I went into the emergency room, deserted, unlit, dust still hanging in the air from the bombings that continue up till now with TNT demolishing camp houses.

As I went through the dark rooms looking at the damage I heard weeping and cries, and walked through the corridor to the X-ray room. In the dusk coming through the dust and windows, I found them kneeling over one of the six bodies, still lying on the table and the floor as the fridges aren't working. I heard one of the women say, 'That was Ghassan, here is Muammer.' I felt so hopeless; Ghassan was lying on the table, washed and wrapped in a white sheet. He was so tall, and had his arms across his chest. He looked under the sheet as he used to when he was alive. Tall, self-controlled and impressive. They knelt on the floor as I stood numbed in a corner, watching, looking at Ghassan. Then they opened the covering over Muammer's face and instead of the usual expression of death, placid and adrift, Muammer had died screaming. His neck was contorted and twisted away and his mouth and eyes were open, screaming, screaming, endlessly screaming in fear and agony for eternity. His face was already blanched and white and he looked so terrified that I wanted to take him in my arms and cradle him, even in death, pacify him, comfort his screams of fear.

Fatima was shocked and let out a sob. We stood and cried and cried, weeping as if we could bring them back to life with our sobs for our grieving them. Oh God, we would give our lives just to make them live again. I stayed looking, straining to see Ghassan as long as possible. Lulu opened the wrapping around his face for me and I tried to make out his features as I took a photograph and then we had to leave. I could make out his face, and his eyes were closed, along with his mouth. He looked peaceful and dead. So dead.

Even his kitten was sad yesterday and she sat quietly with her paws on my feet looking at me, crying for him. And today the auriscope is broken. The last person I used it on was Ghassan to look at the ear that drove him mad with its *shshsh*. What is so strange is that you cannot recognize even your loved ones when they are dead. No matter how hard you try to see them, how much you love them, you don't see them. Oh I loved them – loved them so much – they were sweet and lovable. And now they are dead. I wanted to stay the rest of my life in that room in the dark with them.

The boys who left today for Mar Elias have been taken to Anjar and Damascus prisons, taken from Haret Hreik in a red car by the Syrians.

Nawoosh's little girl aged 8 was taken by Munshaqine coming into the camp and beaten when they asked where her father is. 'Bourj al Brajneh,' she replied, 'he's with Fatah Abu Ammar,' and they beat her again. She was released a short while later. She is very brave and strong. Nawoosh was very worried for a short while; now she is making her father proud of her in her defiance.

Abu Hussein from UNRWA had to check on us from outside and will try to come tomorrow to bring us Nescafé. One Fatah man went out and has been taken immediately by the Syrians to Damascus.

23.30 No one knows what will happen – will the Munshaqine enter and close the camp for three days as with Shatila? Will they enter with the Syrians? Will we all be told to leave while they clean up the camp? No one knows and we have conflicting reports every five minutes – and arguments around them.

Ahmad and Tha'ir don't know what to do or where to go. We wonder too: will we ever see each other again? Mohamad Fawzi advises me to leave in case the Munshaqine take us for running the clinic during fighting. Looi refuses, and I refuse if she does, so we decide to stay as there will be no hospital for three days and all the mothers and fathers of fighters will be staying, all the sisters, lovers, wives, daughters, grandmothers will be staying. We are all pensive sitting on the water pipes over the nearly dry sewer with a candle, Yusuf Diab, Johina Akashi, Mohamad Fawzi, Borhan, Mahmud and others; Nawoosh and friends passing us carrying weapons to secrete them and rejecting our offers of help, as we sit sweating with mosquitoes biting us and drinking Seven-Up, with cigarettes. All of us are so sad, with tears in our eyes. 'How can there be no PLO in Lebanon? How can there be no more Fatah in Bourj? How can all the young men leave us, our friends?' Um Ahmad's son has travelled, her daughter is dead and now her other son must leave, go to Saida, an enforced leaving. 'Worse than 1982 – worse than Israel. America and Israel are all the same.'

I go to try to call the Agence France Presse with Najib, but there is no telephone line. Abu Riyad is lying on a hot bed with several people all around him, all tense and chainsmoking in the dark. It was the most terrifying walk of my life up to the Fatah office over rubble, zinc, wires from the roofs. I nearly fell three times going up, then back. Every moment I felt we would have a bomb fall on our heads in the dark. I was too frightened and unable to see without torches in case of snipers, or to run if we heard one. All of us were stunned at the destruction we saw around us in the dark under the stars; the bright stars twinkling on so many injustices in the world, on the stars of Palestine, the living, the tortured, and the dead.

Issam al Khatib went out today and was immediately taken by the Syrians. Why? Why did he go? Good grief, he's been wanted for three years, he only had to wait a few days more. Ahmad has lost six kilos and Tha'ir is also getting thin. One of the boys complains of a headache from the smell of the dead, having been on guard duty at the hospital with Nawoosh and spooked by the unburied friends. Another comes in with vomiting and dizziness, the same cause I think: fear and love.

6.7.88 Wednesday

Everyone is waiting for news of the departure. Today? What time? To Saida? Algeria? Libya? Tunis? None of us knows.

11.00 The Munshaqine started shelling the camp around 10.00 and fighting in Amliea area. They waited until everyone had had a sleepless night and was overwrought with farewells, dressed in military clothes for leaving, all the weapons stored away during the night and many of the *mahwar* positions destroyed with TNT so as not to give the Munshaqine advantages when they enter the camp.

We are all tired, with our heads out of sync as 160mms are dropping all over the camp again: in front of us, behind us, the shrapnel falling over the roads.

A night of tears and coffee with Wafiq, Kamal, Nasser, Ahmad and myself until 3.00, then sleeplessness and cigarettes, and kittens in the dark, and more tears as the odd bullet is fired and we want peace and quiet. 'Where do we want to go?' 'To a country of peace.' 'Where is there a country of peace in this world?' 'Switzerland?' Then all of us awake at 7.00.

I crept on the roof last night and watered the flowers, terrified of being shot on the moonlit side after leaving the cover of the vines and zinc. I found by touch and smell the lone carnation that I stupidly saved for Ghassan: it's red, like the first one he gave me. (A lone cockerel is crowing and squeaking in fear at the bombing – the cat jumps at even the sound of 500mm bullets, yet sleeps inside through bombs.) I took it down, and then a boy from Nawoosh mentioned that Ghassan's guns had been distributed and also those from the Fatah stores (the food stores are now empty from damage), and that the gun, an M-16, resting against the wall next to the door, was one of Ghassan's. It had seemed familiar, the shape, colour, polish, perhaps it still had his smell, yet I never saw him carry a gun, although he would talk about cleaning his BKC to Mahmud.

I took the flower to Um Lutfi this morning and Dima met me at the door, tears in her eyes, then Ghassan's sister came out and I asked if her mother was here. She took me into a circle of women mourning and crying. Dima took the carnation and put it on top of the photograph of the young Ghassan I first remember with a soft boyish face, wisps of beard and the faded orangish sweatshirt he used to wear in the 6-month war: the photograph that he came to the clinic to cut out, of himself and Hassan sitting together. At the time I felt it was morbid of him to do that during a war, but he was in that frame of mind. Then we sat as his mother asked me if I had seen his face and had I included his head split open from forehead to the back of his skull in the photograph. I told her no, only from eyebrows down. Then she told me that the night he died he hadn't slept. She told him to go and try to sleep, but he got up saying that his ear was paining him and his head was exploding from the constant noise and that he may die, and if he did, not to cry for him, not to wear black, he would die. She said he was so restless that night, and had put on newly washed clothes and his skin had been itching. She said he was going crazy from his ear injury.

Then we heard some shooting and then a bomb, with shouting outside. Dima moved towards the shelter where I had once run in last year. I left, running to the clinic, and found Looi, and just as I arrived two people came in having fallen while running. All the positions are empty. Everyone comes in with tales of people running up to the front of the camp, yelling, 'To the hospital, to the hospital,' – not for injuries, but as a position for defence of the camp now.

The first condition of yesterday's withdrawal is that the dead be buried in the cemetery – Sultan's first stipulation.

Two bombs at a time and sounding as though coming from the mountain and Aramoun and Sports City. Every organization is now fighting to defend the camp: PFLP, DFLP and ALF (who have women fighting with them), so now we have become like Shatila. We will all be ordered out as a punishment for resistance. There is talk of even Saida's fighters being evacuated with wives and children to Algeria, to prevent a Saida war. Last night we waited for Mustafa Sa'ad's permission for those evacuated to cross the Awali bridge to Saida. The Syrians wanted to give unconditional protection to the evacuees, but of course this was refused.

There is shooting from all sides of the camp: apparently the Munshaqine want to fight their way through the camp to regain all of it, as with Shatila. It feels as though 240mm mortars are dropping also, so great is the noise of the explosions (usually two at a time) on impact. We try to decide whether to leave or not. Looi is apolitical and refuses, as she is purely humanitarian. But perhaps I should because of the statement about the women's hair. Mohamad Fawzi is adamant that I leave with them. We debate on three years in Anjar prison wasted, as opposed to three years in Algeria not wasted, starting our lives all over again if not killed before it ends. Wafiq says for the first time that he wants to leave the camp. I agree with him. Um Lutfi urges me to leave to Saida, she thinks my name may be with the Syrians. For what? Working in a clinic during a war? We are very tired and worn out, the food stock is not so great either. I just want to see Ghassan's grave before I leave, just to see him safe and sound and peaceful.

16.00 The camp is being blown to pieces around us. Literally to pieces. Bombs are falling everywhere, nothing less than 160mm. As Borhan says, 'The Munshaqine love us too much, they send us 160mms today; Amal did not love us so much, they only sent us 120mms.'

We are watching the kittens playing with each other on top of the Kalashnikovs in the cats' *dushmeh*. We hear that Aref managed to get to Saida despite being recognized and so did one other.

The Munshaqine have commandeered the PRCS ambulances and have them outside for evacuation of the injured from the hospital which they can't use as it has been blown to smithereens. But they are out, safe. Mustafa went out today, with his mother and sister, and was seen waiting at the checkpoint. He was taken by the Syrians and we don't know what has happened to him.

Theories of the Syrians agreeing to disarm Lebanon, starting with the Palestinians as a non-indigenous armed group, followed by the southern suburbs, West Beirut, unification of the city, Saida, Shouf and Tyre; then, apparently, after all this is achieved within the two months preceding the presidential elections in which Gemayel will not be re-elected, the Syrians will voluntarily leave Lebanon(?). Ghazi Q'anan is supposedly arriving from Damascus tomorrow to guarantee a safe exit for all the Fatah fighters, then all the Palestinian parties will function disarmed (including the Munshaqine? We query this.).

In the pandemonium of today, ending at around 19.30 from 10 am, we found a site for a hospital/clinic in Slieme building, with three storeys for protection. It needs to be thoroughly cleaned out and water, electricity and sandbags installed. We'll start tomorrow.

23.55 Another bomb. They are shelling us with 160mm mortars now again, so no sleep expected. Little kitten Ghassaney takes fright and runs away. The sweat pours off our faces as we work all day. There are too many injured, with big lumps of shrapnel. Ahmad's father has come frequently all morning, crying and imploring him to leave. Tha'ir wants to go, Ahmad not so much. Tha'ir is really getting to an edgy useless stage so that he gets everything muddled. He should really go out. Ahmad's father left this afternoon, his mother and others pleading with him to leave the camp freely, while it is still possible. Abu Riyad leads a retaking of positions near the hospital in a two-pronged attack. Fighting now up at the hospital. They say the bodies are beginning to bloat in the heat and smell bad. Oh Ghassan – every morning I wake up wondering if the tears I cried the night before for you have dried up? And each day I find they haven't. That there are still more.

The shelling sends lumps of shrapnel and rubble against the door. We are being cornered as piece by piece of the camp is destroyed. Many people including little Abed went out today, forced by his mother. Tomorrow at 5.30 Ghassan will have been dead four days. The damned auriscope still hasn't worked since we used it for him. And his little cat is adorable.

A message comes from Kristine asking when we will leave. We say when there is a valid ceasefire and a hospital functioning normally again.

Now rumours of refusals of Saida and Algiers, so perhaps a plane to Tunis.

8.7.88 Thursday

I have lost track of days and time and have to count the days since Ghassan's death to calculate which it is.

The bombing starts in earnest at 6.30 and continues for half an hour solid from the batteries in the mountains to everywhere in the camp. All the people are so tired and drained, so tired of waiting for death, resisting, defending their houses, families, lives. I've never seen such weariness before. Huge circles rim the eyes of all the boys and men left, at the impossibility of staving off constant bombardment. I saw it in Shatila and now it's happening to us. Tha'ir's mother appeared shortly before the beginning of the bombardment and again begged him to leave. Ahmad goes to find out if his mother is safe or not. Listening to the *phuck* of bombs being launched and women running to shelter in flip-flop shoes. My head aches and my stomach does too. Boys are running past with bullet clips swaying.

8.15 Tha'ir and Ahmad leave the camp.

11.40 All have gone. Hurriedly dressing in uniforms in the clinic and in the street. I give Safwan one of Fatah's discarded shirts to make him properly *askeri* (dressed in military uniform), and he looks terrible, poor darling. We are changing dressings fast before they leave. The Munshaqine are shooting at them before they try to leave.

Women and children first.

Now they enter from the bottom of the camp in a sweep operation. The Munshaqine are in the camp, Fatah too. They came in from our area and searched the houses for guns. First I saw Said Nasser, the uncle of Ibrahim from the war, limping through the emptied, now deserted square. He said, 'Hello, Suzy – *keyfick*? (How are you?)' I ignored him at first, then replied, '*Al hamdo'lillah – mubsut hec*?' ('Thanks be to God – are you happy?') Then I went to see if the boys had all left and found they were still there. I took cigarettes up to Saiqa but as it happened they are not leaving until 5 am. The Munshaqine want them out at 4.00 but Sultan refused and will await the *Jesh al watani* (National Army).

I went to see Ghassan's mother for her kidney pain and gave her an injection, and went on up to the hospital for diabetic tablets for Fatima whose supply had run out yesterday. The road is completely bombed out, especially this morning. The hospital now has Munshaqine in it and I went into the emergency room, blown to pieces, now dark and dusty, having fallen all the way up the road to get there over rubble as high as your shoulders. There was nothing there, everything damaged and glass everywhere from broken ampoules.

Then with one of the Munshaqine following me I went to visit the *shehide* (martyrs). The smell is bad now and they are a little puffy but still as they were a few days ago. The room is still darkened and stuffy with flies buzzing around the windows. I placed a blown kiss on Ghassan's shoulder and left. On the way out someone demanded to know who I was and was told by Ringo's mother I was a Norwegian doctor from the clinic. He said, 'What clinic?' To be told again, 'The one down.' Then I went to the bend and met Salah Hammad. He called me over and one of them was stupid enough to ask me if I like the camp like this. I replied, 'The camp is bombed, people are injured, people dead and no hospital.' 'Yes, we have a problem here,' says Salah.

'Is this how you resolve it – with 240mms and 160mms and no hospital?'

Says Salah, 'You sound like the Arafatists.'

Me: 'Is it Arafatist to speak like this about the Palestinian people?'

Someone said, 'They are all Arafat here.'

Me: 'No, they are not.'

Salah: 'They are all Arafat. Why are you here in the war?'

Me: 'Because we heard of no hospital, no doctors, the people sick and dying and injured.'

Salah: 'Who told you to come?'

Me: 'No one.'

Salah: 'So you came alone to this war?'

Me: 'Yes, I'm not Palestinian, I don't talk politics but it is the people here who have this done to them – that's not politics.'

Salah: 'You sound Arafati.'

Me: 'There is the PNC, use that.'

Salah: 'We talked before and I think you are nervous now – we'll talk later. Are you going to stay?'

Me: 'Maybe.'

Salah: 'We will talk later.'

Me: 'Maybe.'

Salah even beat his mother-in-law, Um al Abed, claiming she too is Arafatist.

Mummy cat is hunting today as there are no bombs. She's brought three mice in for the kittens, who all instantly wake up squeaking as they have learnt to eat mice recently. No rats yet although there are so many we fall over them in the sewers, dry sewers, with torn-up letters floating away in them.

Then I spent time with the Lebanese journalist friend of Brent's who came in and joined up with the journalists and the two women from Reuters.

9.7.88 Friday

The Munshaqine were deployed around here at 20.30 exactly: six in the clinic, five armed upstairs and one downstairs at the door with a gun. I went to protest to Fatah and camp leaders who said they would ask them to leave tomorrow (originally tonight, but none of us really had the courage). But they have to go tomorrow or everyone will be too frightened to come for dressings. People are genuinely terrified. When the Munshaqine came and asked me if there were any weapons I sarcastically said, 'Yes, too many.' They wanted to see upstairs and again asked 'Are there any weapons?' I said 'No – this is a clinic for all the camp – there are no weapons here.'

One man ran out into the street so frightened that he handed over single bullets to the first boy in the street he saw from PFLP. The boy brought them all back to the dormitory separately, spilling them over the table and floor. Rumours of them beating an old man's arm and telling him they will take the weapons by force.

Two of the Munshaqine stationed upstairs speak English well; we are sleeping with our brothers' murderers. I cancel the appointment for Hanni, saying I will go to him tomorrow instead.

Am I as obsessed with Ghassan's burial as I was about that carnation I had saved for him? I don't know. So many tears today. So many people sick with emotion and overwrought; so many mothers, wives and sisters, crying, crying, crying. All of us, all of us. Film shown on TV of Um Tariq and Johina with B-7s, me and Najib talking about yesterday and

Muammer, of Abu Darwish and the damage. All of us crying, crying, crying. Still alive, we can't believe we are still alive. Alive – not dead. Crying and changing into uniforms and bullets everywhere. *Allahu'Akbar.*

Tea with little Ahmad's family, and a talk with a sheikh on Islam – what a kind man. We dream and plan the Karame clinic with Mohamad Fawzi and Sultan for Ain al-Helweh. The Munshaqine are all up and down the street in all the houses by force. Haj has three too. We are to be hostages for a night. Oh Ghassan, your mother is still too frightened to stay in her house. I arranged with Um Ali to fake a sick call at 4.30 so that I can go to watch the evacuation at 5.00

12.7.88 Tuesday Saida
The war is finished and we are in Sidon. Doing what? We sleep on the floor, four of us, and two on each bed then four on the mattress, and three on the roof. Eleven of us in total.

I came to Sidon two days ago after Dr Ighlas took over our house for Abu Assad's family. They moved in the two-hour period I left the camp that day, taking the teapot, tea and coffee, making it impossible to make tea or coffee in the morning. The next morning I couldn't even give the cats an old tin of sardines as they had taken the can-opener too. Poor Cleo was quite upset and disturbed by us moving things around. I said farewell to her on the roof. The little ones were just getting used to the doors, and Nimr got lost the day before and we found her at the Al Ashwas' shop.

This is difficult. I think I don't realize how shocked I am at the moment. The last two days in the camp were awful; the house went, and Ighlas was appalling: 'You are not Palestinian. You are not a doctor, you do not understand. She tries to be more Palestinian than the Palestinians,' etc. I had two political talking-tos: one by Salah Hammad, who called me an 'Arafatist' three times, and one by Abu Walid, his brother, who informed everyone else that I was an 'Arafatist'.

We waved goodbye at the expulsion of the Fatah members, then they left. We waited from 4.15 until 7.00, thinking they were going to kill them all, as they disarmed them in groups. The women talked of Tal al-Zatar. A hundred or so more people dead makes no difference. The place looked damned again. I felt that Beirut was damned, as the sun came up over the mountain and the ruins of what used to be a camp and a street while we sat on rocks, squatting, awaiting the arrivals of the buses and trucks for the evacuation. Lydia was screaming and screaming. Sobhieh's mother fainted, and the Syrians kept pushing us further and further back from them with their guns. The men sang and chanted for Abu Riyad and Abu Ammar. We clapped, then waved them off, cheering them on to Saida. I was questioned by our 'guards' when I came back, after coffee, jasmine and a rose from Haj Dabdoub's mother-in-law. Misery.

We buried Ghassan with the abuse of the Munshaqine ringing in the ears of the mothers of the martyrs. Five days with no fridges and then into a mass grave. The smell was awful. Ghassan's sister came to ask for masks.

I was stopped on the way by a BBC camera team, but avoided them saying that they were burying my friends. Women screamed and fainted as the bloated bodies were tipped off stretchers into the large grave. We cried, sitting in the shade, with the spades and stretchers left around us in the sand; the new earth mounds bare except for the palm fronds of a recent burial. Another blue-skied day, another day of tears.

24.7.88 Sunday
I woke late after dreaming of friends who, when I asked them what they

were doing here, were silent. Got up after ten. Spent the day sweating as there is no electricity in Beirut. We visited Ahmad's grandparents and family; Tha'ir's grandmother was out in Al Ain, so we went around Bourj al-Brajneh and drove up the front street past the camp. The checkpoints are stiffer now. Tha'ir was held for fifteen minutes yesterday while they looked up his name in their books.

The names of all the medical staff whose wages were subsidized by Fatah were taken by the Munshaqine from the Fatah offices in Shatila – hence the rounding up of the PRCS staff and holding them in Mar Elias, or in Shatila itself.

Everything closed for the Eid religious holiday.

Samir, our old friend from the 6-month war, when he used to guard Abu Suhail, went to Beirut, got caught by the Syrians at his friend's house and has now been held in prison in Syria for the past four weeks. Poor Samir.

1.10.88 Saturday

Last night I dreamt I met Ghassan. It was in the house of an old friend and Dolly was with me. He appeared and started to talk to us, and as he talked I realized that he did not know he was dead. This upset Dolly very much and she turned away with tears in her eyes. I asked him how it was there, and he replied that it was okay, but he didn't seem able to meet us and come with us. He didn't know why.

I knew, but I couldn't bring myself to tell him. I asked him again about things with him, hoping he might understand. He looked well, just as he always had been when alive.

Dolly said, 'Doesn't he realize he's been killed?'

I said that the only thing that might give him any understanding was that his skin looked a little grey around the eyes and mouth.

I woke and started to cry. I wanted to stay asleep and be with my dead friend. I cried for Ghassan, and for Muammer too. Dolly cried in the dream as Ghassan didn't understand that he was dead and forever separated from us. I cried because I didn't understand why.

Functioning as best as you can in this way of life.

Beiruts Big wheel
lit up after dark with
multi coloured lights
against palm-trees &
sea. Orb shaped lights.
against a hewed sky
and a crescent moon
hanging in violet pinks
and fading sands.
The moon – amar hilal –
then changed also to
fading gold in a
blue black sky.
I Miss the solitude
required for thought.
I try to turn inward
but still only collect 1/3 of what I usually
remember or ~~think~~. Forgetting names,
emotions and reasons – lost in constant
distraction of being with others
incessantly. Always noise, radios,
talk, visits, attention, never able to
make a decision alone or control
my environment. Relinquished totally.

Index

All extended references (eg 142–5) should be read as *passim*